Romanian Cinema

Romanian Cinema

Thinking Outside the Screen

Doru Pop

BLOOMSBURY ACADEMIC
NEW YORK • LONDON • OXFORD • NEW DELHI • SYDNEY

BLOOMSBURY ACADEMIC
Bloomsbury Publishing Inc
1385 Broadway, New York, NY 10018, USA
50 Bedford Square, London, WC1B 3DP, UK
29 Earlsfort Terrace, Dublin 2, Ireland

BLOOMSBURY, BLOOMSBURY ACADEMIC and the Diana logo are trademarks
of Bloomsbury Publishing Plc

First published in the United States of America 2022
This paperback edition published 2023

Copyright © Doru Pop, 2022

For legal purposes the Acknowledgments on pp. x–xi constitute an extension
of this copyright page.

Cover design: Eleanor Rose
Cover image: A still from *4 Months, 3 Weeks and 2 Days*, directed by Cristian Mungiu.
Courtesy of Mobra Films

All rights reserved. No part of this publication may be reproduced or transmitted
in any form or by any means, electronic or mechanical, including photocopying,
recording, or any information storage or retrieval system, without prior
permission in writing from the publishers.

Bloomsbury Publishing Inc does not have any control over, or responsibility for,
any third-party websites referred to or in this book. All internet addresses given
in this book were correct at the time of going to press. The author and publisher
regret any inconvenience caused if addresses have changed or sites have ceased
to exist, but can accept no responsibility for any such changes.

Library of Congress Cataloging-in-Publication Data
Names: Pop, Doru, author.
Title: Romanian cinema : thinking outside the screen / Doru Pop.
Description: New York : Bloomsbury Academic, 2021. |
Includes bibliographical references and index.
Identifiers: LCCN 2021018328 (print) | LCCN 2021018329 (ebook) | ISBN
9781501366253 (hardback) | ISBN 9781501366246 (epub) |
ISBN 9781501366239 (pdf) | ISBN 9781501366222
Subjects: LCSH: Motion pictures–Romania–History. | Motion
pictures–Europe–History. | Motion pictures–Philosophy.
Classification: LCC PN1993.5.R6 P669 2021 (print) | LCC PN1993.5.R6
(ebook) | DDC 791.4309498–dc23
LC record available at https://lccn.loc.gov/2021018328
LC ebook record available at https://lccn.loc.gov/2021018329

ISBN:	HB:	978-1-5013-6625-3
	PB:	978-1-5013-7503-3
	ePDF:	978-1-5013-6623-9
	eBook:	978-1-5013-6624-6

Typeset by Integra Software Services Pvt. Ltd.

To find out more about our authors and books visit www.bloomsbury.com
and sign up for our newsletters.

To the loving memory of my mother, Victoria

CONTENTS

List of Illustrations viii
Acknowledgments x

Introduction 1

1 The Eternal Flickering of the Film-philosophies Quarrel 27

2 Offscreen Cinema: The Aesthetics of the Non-cinematic 83

3 This Is Not a Film You Are Watching: A Visceral-Conceptual Response 127

4 A Magical Mystical Tour into the Romanian Cinematic Mind 175

Epilogue: Rear-view Glances into the Post-metaphysical Cinema 235

Bibliography 241
Index 259

ILLUSTRATIONS

Figures

1.1 Schematic overview of the major opposing theories in film and philosophy studies 29

1.2 The polarized electron model, a schematic representation of the contradictory definitions of the relationship between film and thinking 33

1.3 The atomic model, represented as an alternative for the conflictual paradigm in the "universe" of film and philosophy 36

1.4 Explanatory model organizing the major definitions in the cinema and philosophy research 41

1.5 Corresponding binary models: Classical versus Modern in film theory and Continental versus Analytical in philosophy 52

2.1 The ending scene of *4 Months, 3 Weeks and 2 Days*, a story raising questions about abortion, presents the two young women silently sitting at a table after their terrible ordeal. Courtesy Mobra Films 84

2.2 *Beyond the Hills* reconstructs the monastery where the last exorcism in Europe was enacted. Courtesy Mobra Films 98

2.3 The dramatism in *Graduation* is provoked by an enigmatic assault and the moral dilemmas of the victims facing impossible decisions. Courtesy Mobra Films 115

3.1 The three men discussing the Romanian Revolution in a provincial television station are questioning more than the banal reality of their immediate experience. Courtesy 42 Km Film 129

3.2 An obscure soccer match and a conversation between a father and his son are the instruments used by Porumboiu in *The Second Game* to create a non-cinematic film. Courtesy 42 Km Film 143

3.3 *Police, adjective* presents the inner turmoil caused by the indecisions of a policeman who is not able to act according to his conscience. Courtesy 42 Km Film 154

3.4 In *When Evening Falls on Bucharest or Metabolism* Corneliu Porumboiu tells the story of Paul, who is trying to direct a movie while searching for directions in his own life. Photo credit Adi Marineci, courtesy 42 Km Film 162

3.5 Cristi, a corrupt detective, loses his identity and moral compass when trying to learn a new whistled language in *The Whistlers*. Photo credit Vlad Cioplea, courtesy 42 Km Film 168

4.1 The opening scene of *The Death of Mr. Lăzărescu* takes us into the decrepit apartment of a solitary old man facing mortality and the nothingness of human existence. Courtesy Mandragora 184

4.2 New story clipping with the true tragedy of the man abandoned by an ambulance on a sidewalk in Bucharest. Courtesy Mandragora 186

4.3 *Malmkrog* is a non-place where a deterritorialized reality creates the empty backdrop for philosophizing about the nature of humanity 229

4.4 Viorel, the murderous husband from *Aurora*, is trapped in a mental in-betweenness. Courtesy Mandragora 233

Table

4.1 List of the most representative movies of the Romanian contemporary cinema: main topics, issues, storylines, and characters 179–181

ACKNOWLEDGMENTS

I have many people to thank, since the development of my speculations about the modes of thinking in recent Romanian cinema went through a long process of transformation, as rewriting and re-thinking are my congenital disorder. I had the opportunity to discuss many ideas that became the foundations of this book with several friends and colleagues, who have been extremely helpful by providing insights and criticism. First I must express my gratitude to Linda Badley, who offered excellent advice at an early stage of the project, which finally made possible the publishing of this book. Also at the initial stages, the concepts that are now part of this book benefited from feedback generously offered by the members of the Center for Intermedial Studies, headed by Lars Ellestrom at Linnaeus University in Sweden. A special gratitude goes to Liviu Lutas, who was among the first to hear, read, and criticize my propositions about the practices of offscreen cinema. I would also like to thank my colleagues at the Ekphrasis Research Center, at the Babeş-Bolyai University in Cluj, for their support and assistance. Also my gratitude goes to the reviewers of *Ekphrasis*, the academic journal I coordinate at my hometown university in Romania, where some of these ideas were published. I would like to extend my appreciation to Christina Stojanova for inviting me to present a paper at the international symposium organized at the University of Regina in Canada, which gave me the opportunity to discuss and critically evaluate some of these topics. I want to thank Mircea Deaca for initiating a similar dialogue at the Bucharest University, where some materials used in the following chapters were also discussed. This project was partially supported by several research grants provided by the Star-UBB Institute of Babeş-Bolyai University, coordinated by Daniel David.

This book brings together thoughts and theories that I have been working on for the last six years. Some of the concepts and conjectures were previously published as journal articles or presented as conference papers. Selected parts of Chapter 2 were first published as "Offscreen cinema," © 2018 The Criterion Collection, reprinted with permission. An earlier version of this chapter appeared as *The Aesthetics of the Non-Cinematic in Cristian Mungiu's Cinema*, in Ekphrasis. Images, Cinema, Theory, Media, vol. 16/2016. Chapter 3 contains some passages and explanations published as *This Is Not a Film You Are Watching. Corneliu Porumboiu's Non-cinematic*

Stylistics and the Visceral-Conceptual Cinema, Ekphrasis. Images, Cinema, Theory, Media, vol. 20, 2/2018 and from *Disaporic Cinema: Dislocation and Paraphrastic Forms of Expression in Recent Migration Films*, Ekphrasis. Images, Cinema, Theory, Media, vol. 23, 1/2020.

Also various ideas proposed in Chapter 4 were initially developed in *Notes on Fatalism and Melancholia in Romanian Cinema: An Imagological Approach*, Ekphrasis. Images, Cinema, Theory, Media, vol. 21, pp. 123–47, 1/2019.

As the materials of the book were written during a time of great personal turmoil and in the background of an unprecedented global pandemic, which had a tremendous emotional impact on our lives and minds, without the help and generosity of many people this effort would not have been possible. I cannot mention everybody, yet, when at some point it seemed gratuitous and even vulgar to deal with film philosophy in such a contrived time the simple existence of my wife and daughters was a point of stability and purposefulness. Perhaps only the Byzantine philosophers arguing about the sex of the angels while their great wall was crumbling under heavy bombardments felt the same and this is why I want to express my gratitude to Katie Gallof, the generous and understanding editor at Bloomsbury who, together with the entire production staff, accommodated my demurrings.

Introduction

Meditations on Externality: Thinking outside the Screen

The title of this book drops the unexpected reader right in the middle of a brainteaser and a conceptual divide created by the rivaling opinions battling out their preeminence in explaining the relationship between film and philosophy. Several opposing definitions, drawing separation lines with the help of various prepositions that are supposed to connect meanings, have accumulated into a long series of formulas and combinations. Film *and* philosophy, films *about* philosophy, film *as* philosophy, films *illustrating* philosophy, films *with* philosophy, philosophy *at* films, philosophy *through* film, and many other definitions are supposed to clarify the complex relationship between movies and thinking. Some authors (Sinnerbrink 2019) tend to overlap *filmosophy* freely with film *as* philosophy, others couple film-philosophy with film *and* philosophy. Why would the adding of yet another preposition to the already-long list of explanatory conjunctions be necessary? By this I do not expect to make the *about/and/as/at/in/is/on/through/with/without* chain more comprehensive. Recursive definitions which are already complicated enough for the normal spectator and even the astute cinephile will not become more manageable by simply adding to the discussions another instable variable, like "outside." Bringing yet another term to the debate is not going to add clarity to the discussions about the thinking practices in cinema. No concept could bracket the existing arguments and instill a new understanding.

For those familiarized with the film and philosophy controversies, this onset makes an evident reference to Thomas Wartenberg's *Thinking on Screen: Film as Philosophy* (2007). The Mount Holyoke College professor opened his own line of arguments by stating an unquestionable fact—films can address philosophical issues. Self-proclaimed as a "moderate," the respectable philosophy professor argued that his approach was based on the premise that ideas can be "screened" in films. All spectators can be "shown" philosophical thoughts while watching movies; yet, by simply stating such a postulate Wartenberg positioned himself in the camp of immoderate interpreters. Proposing universally valid truths like the fact that films are somehow able not only to infuse current and ancient philosophies with "liveliness," qualities which apparently textual philosophies cannot provide anymore, but also to produce "novel philosophical theories," is immoderate. The speculation that a film is capable of "doing philosophy" in a similar way in which the classical philosophical texts of Plato and Descartes did becomes highly questionable. Yet it is not the purpose of this book to deal with such issues.

As Wartenberg moved the discussions toward the practicalities of interpreting movies, finding particular examples allowing the discovery of similarities between Nietzsche's criticism of Hegel and the classical Westerns directed by John Ford, examples seem to be better than concepts. For example, by identifying the main characters as "personifications" of well-known philosophical ideas, the film-philosopher should acknowledge that ideas discovered in movies are *not* taking place *onscreen*. This does not seem to be a problem, since any connections can be justified with illustrations, by claiming that thinking processes are *implicit*. We assume that a movie director has preconceived philosophical ideas, thus admitting a twofold philosophical thinking—one occurring *outside* the magic rectangle and the other *onscreen*. Some ideas are developed by moviemakers who read philosophy, who are familiarized with the *outside* thought processes. Others are inserted into the cinematic by the critics, who also read philosophical works. Thus Tom Doniphon, John Wayne's character, who was obviously not acquainted with Nietzsche, and the shooting of Liberty Valance, clearly not linked with the moral questions raised by Kant, are illustrations of the "philosophical impositions" on films. The philosophical is *extrinsic*, not *intrinsic*. Wartenberg justified his analysis by claiming that he is practicing an empirical approach, which allows discovering and attributing such implicit intentions to the filmmakers. Of course, there is always the problem of what is going on inside the mind of any filmmaker, since even when we have explicit admissions and statements about this thinking processes, the presumed opinions of the philosophising critics do not coincide with the actual philosophical content.

Contesting the "onscreen" formula I realize that by using the "outside" as a central proposition for my arguments might raise false expectations. First and foremost it could distract the attention from the true purpose of my approach. From the very beginning, and in a happy turn of phrase, the title illustrates the capacity of our brains to induce thoughts into contexts that lack any auctorial intention. We are able to discover meanings that are simply not *inside* the thinking material of anything. This happens all the time in art and the movies. An *outside-in* mechanism, which will be discussed further along, is always at play. It would suffice to state here that humans have a peculiar ability to think about things that are not present. In the case of cinema, we can think what was never premeditated by the moviemakers or screenwriters, we can conceive ideas that are not internalized by the manifest contents of the films, or to picture in our minds things that are not represented. Sometimes we imagine that which is not ever imagined by anybody. There are many cinematic examples in which such *extraneous* meanings become fundamental and sometimes more important than the explicit or the visible contents. We "know things" about certain films without even watching them. We also take such preconceived forms of understanding with us when screening moving pictures in movie theaters or at home.

Once we move past this level of understanding, an entire set of interpretations coming from *outside* the cinematic are made improper for further discussions. Some of the most abrupt forms of "thinking outside the movies" are illustrated by contemporary philosophers who are not even interested in the contents of the productions they infuse with philosophical ideas. We can straightforwardly place here any and all philosophers who never saw the films they comment upon. Such *outside-in* philosophers are flagrantly inserting ideas into films, utterly indifferent to their cinematographic and aesthetic components. Those who claim they do not need to watch entire movies in order to philosophize about them, as blatantly stated by Žižek (2010), perform a type of "thinking outside the cinematic" that might by appealing. Such approaches can undoubtedly be useful, as ideas that exist *outside* the movies can be visualized by cinematic examples. Movies are also used to showcase philosophical concepts. An entire field of film studies is now dedicated to such philosophical observations, and they form a body of thinking developed *outside* the screen. No possible arguments and reasonings can prove their cinematic nature; yet, they are now part of understanding films. In my approach, they are not within any relevant range of interest.

Also, when asserting that some forms of thinking can happen *outside* the screen, this statement could be understood as a trenchant adherence to the claims that philosophical thinking can happen only *outside* the cinematic machine. The title might be interpreted as a support for the theories announcements that movies are incapable of creating high concepts; thus, philosophical ideas remain *external* to film practices. It could also be understood as a concession to the simplicity of another line of arguments, establishing that thought processes take place *outside* the movie theater or, even more disparagingly, that thinking cannot be performed by a machine, that films are not philosophical.

Philosophizing outside the Movie Theater

It does not require much observational effort to realize that philosophy can exist without cinema. A vast portion of human thinking was *extraneous* to the screen. As acknowledged even by die-hard film-philosophers like Richard Gilmore (2005: 8–9), the process of "thinking about movies philosophically" takes place most of the time in non-cinematic environments. A large component of philosophical thinking is obviously *extra-cinematic* due to a simple and factual truth that the entire classical corpus of philosophical texts, starting with those inherited from Antiquity to those belonging to pre-Modernity, is chronologically pre-cinematic. Although some film-philosophers, like Christopher Falzon (2002), argue that old concepts can be linked with contemporary moviemaking, Plato never watched *The Matrix*, neither was Kant a consultant for *Star Trek*. That does not mean that their ideas are *non-cinematic*. Plato's dialogues and settings share many qualities that contemporary moviemakers recognize; yet, although Socrates was turned into a movie character, nobody tried to make a movie out of the "Symposion." Eisenstein's unfulfilled ambition to make a film based on Marx's "Das Kapital" proved to be a failure, even if a considerable proportion of film theories are Marxist. The great books of philosophy exist independently from cinema and there is nothing wrong with that. Undeniably (and sometimes mistakenly) filmmakers read and adapt philosophical texts into their cinematic works. Yet, even when the movie directors or their screenwriters are influenced or include philosophical dialogues or debates into their works, these ideas exist before and without discovering them in a particular film. This *externality* of philosophical ideas can be clearly identified when imported wholesale into the cinematic. The lack of adherence between the two mediums becomes obvious, since reading philosophy and seeing philosophy do not add up to the same experience.

This incorporative process is part and parcel of the development of a subfield in the history of philosophy, constantly growing with a long list of studies entitled the "philosophies of ...." In our contemporary popular culture philosophy was transformed into a good for all term and one inescapable consequence is that cinema can provide easy illustrations for almost anything philosophical. When nearly all human activities have a philosophy of their own, and since we have not only a philosophy of religion or one of politics, but also a philosophy of comic books (Gavaler and Goldberg 2019), the elaboration of a multitude of "philosophies" based on cinema examples seems only natural. In my view this is a primitive form of thinking outside the screen, by now established as an autonomous field. It can be practiced both ways. A film critic needs no internal connection with the movies themselves in order to make philosophical speculations, while many philosophy professors use films as tools to attract the visually driven new generations to a part of human knowledge that was created through writing. When used simply as illustrations for already-existing concepts, movies can remain *extraneous* to philosophy and these cases are also not my concern. I must argue that, although Wartenberg (2007) and others support the more-than-illustration thesis, suggesting that even when using illustrations of preexisting philosophical thinking movies can still contribute to the philosophical field by becoming "screened philosophy" (31), this dimension of cine-philosophy is displacing meanings.

A nuanced variant of the illustration thesis, as proposed by Robert Yanal (2005), provides a schematic solution for the many problems raised by the relationship between film and philosophy. It allows film theorists to use a recalibrating philosophical measurement device, with some films described as "minimally philosophical," when they are "simply" raising moral or metaphysical questions (Yanal 2005: 4), while others become "maximal" in their ability to participate in the existing debates, when generating conceptual understanding. While extremely practical, this relative weighing of the "philosophical" in movies opens up to another practical dilemma. Something that is artificially created, like a movie scene or film character, can form a real thought and a truthful experience. Then, if at their most basic form of expression all films are carriers of ideas, generating some sort of thought processes, manifested through the actions and interactions of movie characters, or within cinematic situations, how can these apparently autonomous filmic realities create thoughts, and do they exist only in our minds, or do they have a materiality of their own?

We can easily identify a starting point of the philosophizing processes residing *outside* the cinematic, as films are often *based on* philosophical ideas, narrations, and storytelling forms previously explored. They are present elsewhere (in literature, theater, or painting), and these forms of thinking are *allogenic* manifestations to the film-world. Other functions are less obviously external, with the example being the *allegorical* interpretations of films. Whether these film thoughts are taking shape in the mind of the spectator or they exist in the mind of the moviemaker, they remain extraneous. In these situations, even if a certain "cinematic mind" exists autonomously, together or separated from the individual mind of the director, movies are part of a collective psyche, a mind of a society.

At first a level of questioning opens when we "go to the movies philosophically" (Gilmore 2005: 11), that is purposefully searching for ideas and concepts during the screening of a film. Watching a film and filmgoing are thus transformed into philosophical practices by the simple presence of a "filmosopher" in the darkened room of the movie theater. A philosopher can induce thoughts and ideas into any fictional world, so obviously there is the possibility that cinematic ideas could be indeed shaped *inside* the mind of the philosopher-as-spectator. Thinking is implicit in the process of screening films. As the moving images flow on the screen, to the trained mind of a scholarly philosopher it could appear that everything is philosophical. Whether these ideas are part of the exhibited experience or not is unimportant. The same is true when historians (Roquemore 1999) or judges (Bergman and Asimow 2006) "go to the movies"—they tend to discover the things that they are interested in. A philosopher who is a movie buff will find the concepts he is familiarized with, but this is no irrefutable proof that the philosophical ideas were *inside* that particular film. Even if they are created during the screening by the filmosopher, that does not mean that they were *onscreen*.

This brings us back to the same paradoxical consequence of the set of explorations announced at first. Whenever a philosopher watches a movie, he performs a search for concepts from *outside-in*, "discovering" many ideas produced before the screening, with the most distant to the cinematic experience being the philosophical concepts developed long before cinema even existed as an art, then integrated into the cinema experience. This is due to the fact that during the process of production, writing, and conceptual evelopment of film-ideas, later traceable by the film critics, thoughts and concepts are inserted into the meaning-making structure of a film. Whether or not they are part of the *outside-in* of the cinematic experience remains a question that cannot be easily resolved. The central issues are connected with the agency of particular philosophical thinking embedded in the contents of a film. At this level of the discussion, as explained by the dozens of collections of extremely intelligent essays, published regularly and showcasing the philosophical prowess of many filmmakers, from J. J. Abrams (Brace and Arp 2014) to Mel Gibson (Gracia 2004), it would seem that film directors can be treated as something like a new species of thinkers, that of *cinematic philosophers*.

The Filmmaker as Philosopher Thesis

The *intentional* authorship thesis (Livingston 2005) contends that all works of art are a result of intended creative acts. Yet, as Deleuze pointed out in the "Preface" to the English version of his first book on cinema, we cannot compare the "great auteurs" with the painters or musicians, who also "think," since they are a different kind of thinkers, operating with movement-images or time-images (Deleuze 1986a: x). Nevertheless, in film theory the *intentionalist* paradigm follows the simplest of assumptions that each movie director can insert philosophical ideas into the film text, either by developing their own thoughts and ideas, or by exploring various facets of existing speculations and presuppositions. This premise leads some film critics to the conclusion that all moviemakers can use cinematographic technologies to "do philosophy." By reading the creativity patterns of any film director we can discover a philosophical "trajectory" of his thinking, often manifested in the narrative structure (Gilmore 2005: 10). In this sense a filmmaker is a philosopher who is permanently located *inside* his movies.

The absurd consequence can be, as Richard McClelland and Brian Clayton (2014) argued in their Clint Eastwood monograph, that the taciturn actor turned director can be treated as a philosopher in his own right. If Eastwood can create "substantial philosophical works," then we can elaborate studies on the "philosophy" of each and every moviemaker. Whatever the man who impersonated Dirty Harry might have contributed to the history of philosophy, the argument of these authors remains that philosophy itself has changed that its practices today are different from those of the classical thinkers. By accepting the transformation of the very essence of philosophy, a thesis we must discuss later on, they are following the path of abandoning the ossified ways of "doing theory" and replacing them with innovative expressions, such as cinema. Therefore the propensity to discover the ideas of Plato, Descartes, Nietzsche, or Marx in movies and to elaborate on their doctrines and thought processes with the support of particular cinematic examples becomes not only acceptable, but truly philosophical.

However, these manifestations do not qualify as innate film philosophies, the use of the works of influential philosophers almost exclusively belongs to the extra-cinematic, and the mechanism of bringing the philosophical into movies comes from *outside-in*. While we can, for example, follow the interpretation of *The Truman Show* as a modern allegory of the Platonic myth of the cave, we cannot establish that Peter Weir is contributing to the philosophical understanding of Plato. With the "film directors as philosophers" remaining an important component in film studies today, if such a philosophical instrument would be correct, then all filmmakers would qualify as "second-hand" philosophers. Even in the examples trying to show that great film directors are performing the functions of philosophers, as Robert Yanal compared Hitchcock with Descartes or Wittgenstein, this philosopher's work presumes the implicit fact that the moviemakers cannot engage in "explicit philosophising" (Yanal 2005: 10). When attributing the qualities of a philosopher to a filmmaker, the common practice is to show how they are addressing philosophical issues, defined very broadly as asking questions, providing knowledge, or allowing the contemplation of ideas. As it becomes explicit in other efforts to show that philosophizing can be done in movies, any tool can have an impact, from the simplest props of cinema like the "pliers and a blowtorch," in the case of Quentin Tarantino (Green and Mohammad 2007), to the most complex contributions to the development of metaphysics, epistemology, ethics, and axiology, as apparently happens with Steven Spielberg (Kowalski 2008). These speculations waver between the ability of moviemakers to include philosophical ideas and influences in their works, to the true capacity of an artist to generate ideas in the minds of viewers, resulting from profound questions about reality and life, to real concepts or engendered philosophical propositions.

Here the need for better theoretical distinctions becomes evident. Between various forms of thinking existing *outside* the movies and the *intrinsic* capacity of films to generate philosophical meanings is a gap which the traditional film-philosophy studies do not bother to crosshatch. Some of the most important philosophical ideas existing in films are generated from the outside, even if the viewers might "screen" them in the cinema theaters for the first time. The morality of Oscar Schindler and the ethical issues raised by the Holocaust are definitely filmic, but they are not cinematic. The academic explanations about the philosophical conceptualizations or ideological meanings (Heath 1985) allowed by the encounter with the impossible shark in *Jaws*, no matter how challenging and suggestive, remain arguments developed *outside* the cinematic.

A First Critique of Binary Models: Film-philosophy versus Cine-philosophy

Trying to establish a distinction between the *inside* and the *outside* of the cinematic thinking easily succumbs to the temptation of following the long tradition of binary explanations, which dominate the field of film studies. From the inception of the new academic disciplines that were studying cinema, these two major qualities were competing. This dialectic between cinematic philosophies (Shamir 2016) and filmosophies (Frampton) continues in different forms, but the earliest example of such a duality is present in one of the first studies dealing with the philosophy of cinema, elaborated by Gilbert Cohen-Séat. The founding father of French filmology introduced a classical distinction (Cohen-Séat 1946: 54–5) between the cinematographic and the filmic, between the filmic facts (*faits filmiques*) and cinematographic facts (*faits cinématographiques*), as he enounced a terminological divide between two major dimensions of cinema—one practical, generally attributed to sociologists, and the other aesthetic. This dichotomy, soon to be picked up by Christian Metz and other film theorists, establishes a separation between the external factors of cinema (audience, sales, technology, production, and so on), generally described as cinematographic and intrinsically filmic. These distinctions resulted in the development of separate fields of research that are relevant for this discussion, since the first is dealing with the external while the other is restricted to the internal manifestations of moviemaking.

Cohen-Séat (1946: 25) legitimately observes that the new ideo-motor mechanisms displayed by cinema have created major metaphysical repercussions, thus establishing a separation line between the practical and the philosophical. The consequence, however, was that cinema as an institution capable of generating common ideas, of spreading thoughts to a large number of viewers, an industry influencing our contemporary civilization, was reduced to its practical functions. In turn the films themselves, as particular manifestations of cinematographic devices, were strictly reserved to the act of watching. What happens *onscreen* are the filmic facts, while the cinematographic facts belong to the *outside* (the position of spectators, screening space). This separation between cinema as a public action and the internal reaction, between the mechanical or the material and the immaterial and impalpable; created a dogmatic metalanguage preventing a profound understanding of what was going on beyond the generalized spectacle and the individual impact on viewers. The internal logic of films affecting the minds and bodies of particular viewers and the practices of cinema influencing billions of human beings everyday were decoupled. The filmic images and the filmic discourse were for Cohen-Séat the seat of transformation into emotions and "suggested ideas" (1946: 141–142), while the dimension of our thinking which is collective was to be dealt with by other instruments.

This exceptional film theorist, who was among the first to use the philosophy of cinema (philosophie du cinéma) as an interpretive notion, established a setting in which the narrative dimension (the filmic) and the discursive components (the cinematographic) were disconnected as cinematic meant group ideas and filmic references to manifestations of the imagination. This carried along several unresolved questions—how films can create ideas in our minds (the inside) and how could the screened ideas be part of a collective psyche? Could the "cinematographic" not be transformed into a filmic idea? Are our minds influenced by external factors, specific to cinema, or the mechanics of these technologies have adapted to our consciousness and are now internalized as part of our own identity? The French film theorist accepted that, at one level, cinema remains a form of visible thinking (Cohen-Séat 1946: 187), explicitly present onscreen. On the other, the filmic manifestations have an invisible component that can be projected into our minds, thus existing outside the screen.

The paradigmatic opposition to the binary model must be nuanced if we want a more accurate understanding of **how** films can generate philosophy. At least two more levels of qualifying explanations are also needed here—**who** is creating the thinking process and, more importantly, **where** is this thinking shaped and activated, with an implicit **what** is the content of these thought processes.

I Watch, Therefore I Think

This paraphrase to the famous Cartesian dictum hides one of the most impenetrable paradoxes of film-philosophy, which is not to determine if the thinking cinematic machine really exists, but how to enter the inscrutable relationship established between the mind of the protagonist, that of the moviemaker and the individual spectators. The intricate question is *who* does the thinking at the movies and *what* is going on in the mind of that thinking entity. As the viewer has direct access to the thinking of the characters either by proxy, discursive or textual (when the hero recounts what he/she thinks), or behavioral clues (the hero acts and reacts in a certain way), does this connection provide him with a pathway into the mind of the author or, more abruptly, into the mind of the film?

At another end of the debate are explanations provided by neuroscientists and cognitive theorists, who argue that the mechanics of cinematic thinking processes are profoundly *internalized*. With several laboratory experiments designed to measure the brain activities during film screening confirming the intersubjective correlation between *onscreen* actions and our brain reactions, the evidence allowed many film theorists to pronounce that movies had the ability to "control" the thinking of viewers and that the ideas and thoughts manifested *onscreen* are integral to the minds of the spectators.

Colin McGinn, preoccupied with the problems raised by the philosophy of mind, finds the necessary proof to underline the power of "mindsight" in cinema, arguing that the minds of the spectators mimic the fictional reality projected onscreen (McGinn 2004: 104). The fictional immersion provides our brains with sufficient information for real cognition and for experiencing authentic emotional states. Although some ideas might be inserted into films, the thinking is taking shape only in our minds, directly connected with what is happening *inside* the filmic experience. McGinn deals with the problems raised previously by suggesting that there are two types of thinking—one linked to entertainment, which is reduced to our perceptual ability to see images, and the other generating beliefs, which is connected with mental imaging (McGinn 2004: 134). Such a paradigmatic separation, presupposing that thinking has two distinct possibilities, one to entertain and one to believe, follows closely the classical segregation between films that "think" (through movement or actions) and those that "think" only when reaching spiritual levels. Between an externalized form of thought and the internalized dimension of thinking, as I will try to argue in the particular interpretation of the contributions of Gilles Deleuze, there is an interim option, which must be dealt with carefully. It would suffice to say that such segregation between "bad movies" and "movies that think," between mind-provoking productions and a mode of thinking that remains unaffected by ideas is contradicted paradoxically by the data provided by the brain scanning performed with the help of functional magnetic resonance imaging (fMRI).

The magnetic resonance imaging (MRI) scanners gave scientists the opportunity to measure brain activity during the viewing of films and indicated something contrary to the general opinion. In fact not all movies generate the same level of brain stimulation and not all scenes and actions in every movie are producing similar brain activities. Yet the measurements demonstrated that it was not what we would expect. A piece of evidence dismissed for a long time by cognitive theorists is that highly "intellectual" films, supposedly requiring an important brain effort from viewers, are displaying low-intensity brain activities, while the highest impact came from thrillers and movies that used conventional cinematographic modalities. What appeared to be common knowledge for film-philosophers, namely that "philosophical cinema" elicited thinking efforts, actually happens in contact with the conventions of the cinematic. Thinking is developing through cinematographic means.

By consequence, we must notice that during the *internalized* process of thinking, which is commonly happening while watching actions and situations onscreen, not every experience leads to the formation of "ideas." More so, not every thought produced when viewing a movie ends up with a conceptual discovery. In fact, most of the time spectators can hardly remember what they saw "screened" in the movie theater. Our brain has a limited recollection of the things we see not only onscreen, but in general. Due to the continuous flow of images and actions, when asked to describe a particular scene and sometimes even the names of the characters, the majority of spectators are unable to recollect. If actions and characters are out of our mind so quickly, then the mode of thinking must be *outside* the filmic, manifested as part of the cinematographic.

Warren Neidich, one of the artists contributing to the ever-growing field of neuroaesthetics, took these issues one step further, considering that a neuroscientific exploration of the cinematic dimensions of our brains is required. Stipulating the existence of the "cinematic brain," what he describes as a new type of human mind with neural networks reconfigured by the new time and space relations established by movies (Neidich 2003: 74), he demonstrates convincingly against the limited effects of films and suggests a wider power of cinema affecting our brains at a network level. Our minds are changing in order to adapt to the new visual environments we live in, which in turn transform our cultural experiences. The adaptation of our brains and minds to the formation of cinematic neuralinks induced by movies and the other cinematic media we use today leads to the reshaping of our auditory and proprioceptive capacities, to the transformation of our nervous system and brains. The claim that cinema is inducing a universal cognitive transformation, made possible by the expansion of cinematic images (including the virtual space of games), which are extremely appealing to our brains, is challenging. Unfortunately, the majority of Neidich's arguments, which open with comments on Antonioni's *Blowup* (1966), are limited to 1960s non-narrative and avant-garde cinema examples.

Nonetheless, there is a leap of deductive thinking when moving from finding triggers in films that can produce intense brain activities in the minds of the audience, to the total confidence in the brainpower of cinema-makers or, even more dubitable, that of all cinemagoers. As noted before, the vast majority of spectators are unable to recall particular elements of the actions screened and sometimes they even do not remember the names of the movie directors. Most empirical investigations (Kuhn 2011: 88) show that even if the typical film audience remembers the most intense scenes, the basic movie plot is lost. In time the majority of the viewers have almost no recollection of what actually happens in a film. This tendency of our brains to forget is accompanied by our ability to recollect particular images or scenes, especially those which are linked to our inner memory. For these internalized experiences Victor Burgin (2004) proposed the notion of "remembered film," as he was observing the contradiction between the inner world of the spectator and outside worlds viewed on the screen. While there are many contradictory and divergent explanations for these phenomena, with the emerging field of cinema and memory still developing, the data about cinema spectatorship (Furman et. al. 2007) show that the recollection of narrative details is not only reduced, but also unstable and erroneous. The general tendency is, as Burgin admitted when recollecting his own memories about moviegoing, to forget even the names of the characters and the actors. This is an experience we all share and, although movies can re-enact forgotten memories or can bring back omitted experiences from our cultural past, we remember only those elements which are internalized, those associated with extremely powerful experiences. The information we have about movies is most often *extraneous*; it comes after the screening; today our knowledge is acquired from Wikipedia articles and aggregated sites. By and large, our understanding of cinematic meanings, what we know about particular films, is created by professional spectators, academics, cinema scholars, and reviewers; their ideas are put inside the movies and never leave.

The lack of data in the field and the reduced number of neuroscience-based experiments did not change the major paradigms of scholarly research in the field of cinema studies. If nothing else, presuppositions that viewers have an *inside* experience with the onscreen situations lead to the creation of entirely new fields of film studies called *neurocinematics*, a term coined by Uri Hasson and his colleagues (2008), *neurofilmology* (D'Aloia and Eugeni 2014), or what Shimamura defined as *psychocinematics*, the art or understanding how "movies move us" (Shimamura 2013: vii). Measuring the effects of films on the brain activity of the viewers can definitely prove that the *onscreen* activities are activating perceptual, cognitive, and emotional reactions. Yet the fact that movies have an impact on the minds of the spectators, that the artificial life projected onscreen generates a natural process in which we are mentally stimulated, that we get involved and are immersed in a fictional world is not dissimilar to those induced by other artistic activities.

Another set of data was provided by cognitive neuroscientists such as Vittorio Gallese and Michele Guerra (2020/2015), who define the relationship between cinema and the brain as based on the activation of *internal* neurophysiological mechanisms. Using the theory of mirror neurons, the two Italian scientists suggested that all cinematographic experiences are able to trigger an understanding of the world which is more than a simple perceptive activity. With the help of "embodied simulation," a concept that Gallese and Guerra proposed, cinema becomes a source of knowledge as one of the many intersubjective tools that we use for "empathic" connections. The screen is an interface allowing all viewers to obtain cognitive results by simply watching the stories unfolding. When we are imagining an action as real, this activates areas in the human brain which are linked to particular experiences. Through the film experience the viewer has the ability to transform the imaginary worlds developed *onscreen* into bodily reactions and, more importantly, into cerebral information. However, this neuroscientific explanation is based on the classical understanding of cinema, which takes for granted the narrative and dramaturgic explanations of linear and causal moviemaking. In order to provide the viewers with such intersubjective experiences, moviemakers must purposefully construct storytelling forms and characters that can activate and amplify the activities of the brain (Gallese and Guerra 2020/2015: 44–5).

Certainly, the fascinating field of neuropsychology has more to offer to film-philosophy and theory; these results only seem to confirm the theoretical hypothesis enounced before by Bordwell and other cognitivists—the spectators have the ability to form ideas through the plots and by simply following explicit and logical narrative cues. Using an old Cartesian hypothesis, these explanations consider that any movie can induce a state in which the *cogito* of the spectator is somehow autonomously activated, thus making the viewer a conscientious being deeply involved in the construction of meanings and ideas.

Some remarkable studies, like the experiments created by the researchers of the Gallant Lab at the University of California, Berkeley, using fMRI scannings of the brain to "read the thoughts" of movie watchers, were able to reconstruct what people see onscreen. The studies made by neuroscience researchers (Nishimoto et. al. 2011) who experimented with recording our dreams, those reconstructing the images of film trailers projected in the brain of the spectators, are showing almost incredible results, with Bilenko and Savage (2016) using fMRI scanners to show a reconstructed movie from brain activity images. For now these "movie-in-the-brain" experiments cannot provide answers to the question of how thinking takes place in films; they confirm only that images take shape in a dimension of our brains.

The cognitive philosopher and linguist George Lakoff (1999), who expanded the speculations of the thesis developed together with Mark Johnson (1980), advanced another persuasive demonstration about the formation of philosophical thought. The ideas and every other structures of our knowledge that appear to be "inside" our minds are created by metaphorical structuring and previous bodily experiences. Morality and even metaphysics, Lakoff claims, are the result of the embodiment of mind. If this hypothesis is correct, if what we apprehend in our daily life can become the source of our philosophical knowledge, then we extrapolate it to the virtual experiences mediated by cinema. If the "cognitive unconscious" and the metaphors of thought influence the understanding of the world and play an important role in our philosophical assumptions, then the questions raised by moviemakers about life, morality, or even the nature of reality are the result of the "hidden hand" that shapes all our cognitive processes.

All these examples show how complex the relationships between *onscreen* and *offscreen* thinking can be, as the problem of whether or not thoughts are generated inside the filmic experience. In cognitive terms, the suggestion is that everything we need to know is *inside* the movie. When meanings are offscreen, they are external to the content, thus irrelevant or unresolved. Do we simply think what the protagonists think, and then we internalize their thought process making the outside (the cinematographic) into a form of *internalized* knowledge? Is that "thinking" a result of spectators' emotions, a form of affective cognition achieved by "screened" actions, characters, and dialogues, or is it a part of the meaning-making activities residing *outside* in the cinematic? Can the *outside* thoughts of the filmmaker be put into film practices that become so vivid, so life-like that they lose their extraneous determination? Are the ideas developed in movies inside the minds of the spectators; do they belong to the mind of the moviemakers or the films have a mind of their own?

The reality is that while some qualified spectators continue to meditate about the contents of films after the screening, for many other viewers moviegoing remains a forgettable social event. How often does a spectator perform a philosophical inquiry while watching a movie and how common is the continuation of the conceptualization process after the screening?

How Can Cinema Thoughts Be Created: *Endoscopic* and *Exoscopic* Thinking

Some authors solve these issues by changing the locus of thought formation, presuming that a new form of thinking was created after the invention of the movie camera, that an innovative thought process resides *inside* the cinema machine, which is now part of the human experience. Cinema offered us a new mode of thinking, one that is set up through images. Visual representations are concrete and fixed in their meanings; onscreen images are sufficient to produce thoughts. Basically what we see is what we think. Dissatisfied with such explanations, others are drastically opposed to this *intrinsic* solution, affirming that philosophical thinking can exist only outside the filmic experience, as ideas cannot be created with the tools of cinema. Both answers deserve attention; however, it is not the technical dimension of filmmaking or the types of thinking made possible by the cinematic devices that generate solutions for our *offscreen–onscreen* dilemma.

The movie camera is an important thinking instrument, but more relevant is **how** the cinema camera does the thinking. In order to deal with this, I propose a pair of explanatory concepts, the intuition of which came to me by reading a hypothesis advanced by Maurizio Ferraris (2019). In contrast with the Italian disciple of Gianni Vattimo, who proposes the notion of "mesoscopic" in order to define the ability of all aesthetic forms, including cinema, to represent the "middle forms," an idea first articulated by J. J. Gibson's ecological approach to visual perception, my suggestion is that cinema can represent meaning by either an *endoscopic* or an *exoscopic* mode.

Each mode is based on a specific technique of recording the represented reality that can generate a separate category of meanings and of thoughts. I add these concepts to the extremely powerful conceptual associations indicated before by Winfried Nöth (2001: 21–4). The German semiotician first coined the dual terms *exophoric* (that which is representing the world in my terminology *exoscopic*) and *endophoric* (having the ability self-representation), when explaining linguistic iconicity. These modes, which are also expandable in cinema, can be joined with other degrees of visual representations. The first category, the *exoscopic*, represents the typical presence of the eye of the camera, capturing the objects and situations as they are in reality. The problem with visual thinking and the mental formation in pictures, especially in the fast-paced contemporary movies, is that there is practically no time for generating ideas. Basically the excess of sensorial excitation in the *exoscopic* dimension leads to distraction and does not allow substantial thinking. Being stimulated to constantly see things from an attractive version of reality, we are deconditioned to picture them in our minds. With the onscreen images succeeding rapidly, there is no adjustment to the internal reality of our own bodies.

The difference between endophoric and endoscopic can be illustrated by the mindscreen theory, proposed by Bruce Kawin (1978). Cinema definitely has the ability to provide access to the subjective existence of the characters and their mind can be "screened" with the help of various techniques, taking the spectators into the consciousness (or the subconscious) of these fictional heroes. Seeing inside the mind of a hero or heroine, exploring the dreams and desires of the protagonists is not an *endoscopic* exploration, but of endophoric nature. With the help of illustrations extracted from selected masterpieces directed by Bergman or Godard, where self-reflexivity is a constant trope, Kawin provides a more systematic categorization of all the instances in which first-person cinema offers access into the mind of the characters. The question remains whether this consciousness exists onscreen or offscreen, as a projection of the mind of the filmmaker—in Kawin's terms the "intelligence offscreen" and the "self-conscious mind." The dilemma is of a similar nature with that enounced at the beginning of my arguments: is the thinking mind *offscreen* or *onscreen*? And, if a movie is the creation of the subjectivity of a film director, can this in turn be transferred to the audiences through characters acting on the screen, can we have access to the inner thoughts developed by the moviemaker or do we activate a type of consciousness belonging to the cinematic mind?

Providing an answer to these issues might be impossible; yet, we can clearly identify another mode of introspection. The *endophoric* experience expands beyond the subjective into the material dimension of the beings; it becomes an *endoscopic* penetration, both into the depths of the mind and most often into the body. Visually this can be illustrated by the scenes in which the movie camera functions like an *endoscope*, exploring the inside of the human internal organs or even the brain, extensively practiced in forensic and medical films. The body-penetrating camera, projecting images otherwise impossible to see, presents an almost alien dimension of our being. This interior body, normally made available for medical intervention, gives the viewers a visceral experience that is more than an apprehension of oneself as a subject. It is a material representation that was previously explored by great painters like Rembrandt in his anatomy lessons series. At one level we have the conscience of our bodies as living beings (as Leib, in the philosophical observations of Merleau-Ponty); at the other it offers us a snapshot of our carnal dimension (as Körper). In the "filmofanic" experience this can lead to physical reactions, or it can go beyond the bodily stimulus and reach deep and hidden emotions. This engages the mind at a whole other level because, when seeing our "insides" from the outside, this creates a contradictory state providing a palpable materiality to our self-consciousness.

The other possible mode of representation is *exoscopic*. Here the visual function of the camera is to construct meanings by projecting outside realities. Exoscopic references are everywhere in movies, from the reconstructed environments to the real mise-en-scène; the movie captures a reality in which we exist as if we were present. These two opposing views and modes of recording have philosophical consequences. The endoscopic gaze involves a bodily thinking, a combination of embodied feelings and material reverberation of affects. The camera enters the body like a foreign object, and due to this physical aggression it exposes our interiority beyond the simple subjectivity performed by the *endophoric* representations. Displaying the body as a material machine not only challenges our perception, but it provokes a metaphysical preoccupation with our identity. The *exoscopic* has a wide variety of expressions, and in the vast majority of films *onscreen* representations, which are the basic form of address and the dominant mode visualization, simulate reality in the minds of the spectators. Just as the endoscopic view is removed from the natural condition of the human eyes, the exoscopic can also project images that are not normal outside the cinematic experience. For instance, the so-called "bird's eye view" shots in which we can see the entire setting of a dramatic event are representations of a perspective unavailable to human physiology. Only the unnatural lenses of the camera can provide such an outlook, which in turn raises questions about our own condition.

Extra-cinematic, Non-cinematic, A-filmic, and A-cinematic

Even when we accept that cinematic thinking can be done *with* the camera, we have to recourse to the multiple practices of filmmaking, as they evolved throughout the history of cinema. Many filmmakers and film instructors managed to elaborate detailed descriptions of the various internal mechanisms of cinematography, such as camera movements or the various stylistic functions of shot framing. However, as the early Surrealist cinema-makers realized, there are several *externalities* of the cinematic art, many opening films to profound explorations of the limits of this form of expression. Showcased by the films made by Man Ray during the 1920s or the film-experiments of Hans Richter with abstract cinema, various forms of cinema-thinking are available outside the confines of traditional camera work. I am using here the notion of *extra-cinematic* to describe all the instruments that generate categories of thought or conceptual manifestations *outside* the movie camera.

The most simple forms of extra-cinematic expression are done by integrating into filmmaking *extraneous* visual tools that are not medium specific which are sometimes placed into the wider category of intermedia representations (Herzogenrath 2012). Films made by deliberately challenging the fundamental principles of cinematography, including photographic stills, video camera captures, various digital image capturing, are not only non-conventional, but they also remove the cinematographic from cinema-thinking. Integrated into the film discourse, such techniques are commonly disclosing an *offscreen* intervention or presence—as illustrated by Weir in *The Truman Show* (1998). Commonly these situations belong to "external" forms of thinking, with the extra-cinematic presence induced by devices other than the cinematographic camera indicating "Otherness" (Fahle 2015).

More relevant for the definition of the extra-cinematic are the instances in which it overlaps with the notion of "uncinematic," a concept used by Adorno (1991) to describe the effect of Antonioni's *La Notte* (1961), where the Italian director creates a relationship between the viewer and the movie with the help of static images. These are extra-cinematic functions that perform a negation of the ontological nature of the cinematic, by refusing movement. Adorno, who deplored the equation between technique and technology in cinema, predicted that this art can overcome its mechanical limitations only when films become critical of their own cinematographic techniques. Cinema-making can reach its creative potential by overcoming the representational conditioning of the photographic device, meaning abandoning the "ludicrous" conventions and techniques imposed by the photographic technology and the liberation of cinema from this dependency. For the critical philosopher the future of this art belonged to the "interaction with other media, themselves merging into film" (Adorno 1991: 180–3).

Another related concept is the notion of *non-cinema*. The term, which was used by William Brown with a completely different meaning, labeling all that hegemonic cinema excludes or occults, traditionally identified as "poor cinema" (cinema povera), has to be linked with the concept of non-philosophy. While Brown includes in the non-cinematic everything that is "unusual, minor, or multitudinous," it is nothing but a digital-era version of what Julio García Espinosa identified as "imperfect cinema" (Brown 2018: 2–3). In my understanding also non-cinematic techniques are designed to make visible elements that are invisible, without connecting the concept with issues related to politics or the hegemonic cinema. As I will argue in the following chapter, the *non-cinematic* is an integral part of the process of contesting cinematographic rules, which in turn creates cinematic thoughts and meanings. In contrast with Brown's focus on the digital aspects of "non-cinema," my contention here is that the non-cinematic covers all the "uncinematic" experiments and should not be linked with the particular development of film technologies.

The use of uncinematic devices to create cinema is by no mean a novelty in the evolution of filmmaking and Romanian cinema does not lack such examples. Introducing *inside* the cinematic other forms of representation that are *external* to cinema production (surveillance cameras, archive television programs, old propaganda films) can provide more than an exploration of the media boundaries; they become instruments of thinking about society, the role of the individual, and human condition in general. A remarkable example is *Videogramme einer Revolution* (Videograms of a Revolution, 1992), directed by Harun Farocki and Andrei Ujică, an account of the Romanian revolution made only through archive footage. Challenging the conventional practices of filmmaking, *Videograms …* represents an extra-cinematic exploration of the social reality from outside the filmic universe. In the chapter dedicated to Corneliu Porumboiu, we are going to take a closer look to these practices; it would suffice to say that the unexpected presence of these devices can induce a conceptual and intellectual shock, coercing the viewer to think about the visible representation.

We also need to define the relationship between the non-cinematic and the category of *a-filmic*, as defined by the classical typology proposed by Étienne Souriau (1953), describing the external reality of movies. These categories advanced by the French philosopher (afilmic, profilmic, filmographic, screenic, diegetic, spectatorial, and creational) allowed him to distinguish between the various levels of representations, from the internal to the external. In this set of conceptualizations the *a-filmic* remains opposed to the filmic and is not related to the extra-cinematic, which is integral to the film reality. Here the discussion about extra-cinematic must be understood as directly linked with the definitions of the cinematic space. The conceptual contradiction is explicit in the approach of the film critic Louis Séguin (1999), who critically evaluated the concepts used by André Bazin to define the cinematographic frame ("le cadre"). Bazin (1967: 166) considered that the cinema screen, unlike the frames of paintings who were centripetal, attracting the eye inside and enclosing the reality depicted, had a centrifugal nature. The cinema screen, in opposition with the pictorial space, functioned as a mask, a "cache." In return, Séguin supported a predominant understanding of what is cinematic, considering that in a movie "everything must be *onscreen*" (sur l'écran) and nowhere else (Bazin 1967: 47). All other meanings that are external to the field of vision (hors-champ) or extraneous to the screen (hors-cadre), everything that is outside the rectangle created by framing is part of the psychological perception and must be treated separately. If everything is closed inside the film frame, as this definition would have it, the extra-cinematic cannot exist.

But the visible/invisible dynamics is not simply a matter of representation, an ontological trait that may or may not be present *onscreen*. As indicated by the French philosopher Jean-François Lyotard in a provocative essay entitled "L'acinéma" (sometimes transcribed as a-cinema), published initially in 1973, the cinematic screen is not only an exclusive space for representations, it is also indicative for cinema-thinking. This chapter provides us with an inciting philosophical interpretation of cinema-thinking. Lyotard associates the cinematographic conventions prescribing how to make a movie, which are visible onscreen, with a particular form of philosophy. The predominant mode of thinking always cultivates unity and coherence, requesting that cinema must follow the representational rules manifested in "classical" cinema. Always "clean and proper," driven by order and logic, cinematic productions and cinema directing are practices in which things are put in order (mise en ordre). Keeping out of the film production any other nefarious forms of expression, maintaining a controlled environment in which cinematographic rules must be followed at all times, films are expressions of the rules of bourgeois and capitalist thinking. The way in which film images are created is indicative of a certain mode of thinking, which Lyotard describes as the "libidinal economy of cinema." In a controlled cinematic environment, the libidinal propagation of energy is limited and constricted.

Lyotard picks here a similar observation advanced by Deleuze, who defined two dimensions of cinema, two forms of "inscribing" meanings on the surface of the screen (based on movement and on time). Lyotard adds here a series of Freudian concepts, intended to better explain how the cinematographic materials are categorized in "good films" and "bad films." The implication of the French philosophers is that "good" movies, those in which a perpetual return of the "same" is enacted, a repetition of what is proper and adequate, are separated from the "bad" through castrating mechanisms. The dominant cinema functions as a disciplinary force, controlling movements and impulses, "cutting" (not only by editing) all the "bad" manifestations. The "good movements" are integrated into the mechanism of capitalization and profit and rewarded, while the badly framed, or the accidental is deleted. These elements, considered to be cinematic waste in the hegemonic representations, the "dirty images" that are improperly shot, the unstable pictures resulting from the shaking camera, everything that is undecided (indecidable) is eliminated. The basic operations of the cinematic are established through various forms of exclusions; the director and the cinematographer are in fact "condemning" the images to be identifiable, accessible for the gaze of the numbed spectator. Any form of derivation, any detour or alteration from the rules of "proper representation" are quickly disqualified. The same thing happens then at the projection stage, with the onscreen presentations on the *specular wall* restricted to the *privileged forms*, the "good" films maintaining unity and coherence. Any projection of those representations of bad libidinal desires becomes marginalized, and we are left with a cinema that has eliminated all aberrations, albeit reduced in intensity. A screen offering the spectators sterile discharge of energy is not able to "think."

Thus we must understand that *a-cinema* functions as a form of contrastive thinking, where the elements considered to be unrepresentable or non-recurrent (Lyotard 1973: 65) are adopted and cultivated. As Lyotard observed elsewhere, this is fundamentally an opposition between avant-garde cinema (including underground and experimental films) and commercial cinema, a type of moviemaking dominated by the "kapital." The notion of "reversal of representation" is fundamental for understanding the contrast between mainstream cinema and a-cinema, because the most suggestive examples come from abstract painting (and more rarely in abstract cinema)—either by blocking the access of the viewer into the artworld (as is with Rotchko and the *immobilized movement*) or with Pollock where the excess of movement creates a shift in understanding. Thus there are at least two modes of contradicting conventions—by immobilizing motion or by an immobilized mobilization. One refuses the mobility and any movement, which is the acinematic as immobilization, and the second returns to an excess of movement (Lyotard 1973: 66). Both functions are two extremes of cinema with similar finalities: the immobilization of motion or the intensity of movements result with paralysis.

Even if Lyotard's concept of *acinema* was connected with the experimental and avant-garde philosophies of films, the French philosopher uses in another work (Lyotard 1984: 75–6) the example of Resnais, who is able to contradict these implicit desires of the spectators who watch movies in order to "forget," to escape reality. In *Je t'aime, je t'aime* (1968) Resnais breaks with the logic of time and uses the fragmentation of space while placing the viewer in a reversed position. Such forms of expression must also be treated as acinematic, in the sense that they provoke our thinking by not allowing us to reach pleasure *through* and *inside* the screen. Ultimately, any negation of norms leads to the same results; it gives rise to the capacity of cinema to think.

The course of my reasoning, as it will be detailed in the following chapter, is neither to defend nor to reject the possibility that philosophical thinking is *intrinsic* or *extrinsic* to cinema. In practice, the two dimensions of moviemaking, the *outside* of the cinema machine as the social environment, containing social reality and the extra-cinematic components, and *inside* of the filmic experience, are never separated. Most often they are constantly reversed and intertwined, together with the empirical and the metaphysical explanations. With the reality represented onscreen getting the qualities of the internalized experience, we need another approach in order to understand the instances in which the "outside" is integral to the "inside," where the material and the banal combine, offering a pathway to access a beyond-the-real understanding that is not separated or disconnected from Reality.

Final Methodological Clarifications

Most of the films discussed here as case studies are part of the Romanian cinema culture, and the investigation is focusing on a selection of works created by three of the most remarkable contemporary Romanian filmmakers. Despite this narrow choice of examples, this book is not a film history of recent Romanian cinema, nor a systematic presentation of the "philosophy of Romanian filmmaking". Neither am I proposing a critical evaluation of the most important Continental philosophical ideas which might show up in the national cinema. The discussions about particular Romanian films are intended as illustrations meant to exemplify conceptual issues. I am using these specific films because I am most familiar with these works, so the main reason for selecting the examples presented in the following chapters comes from my personal closeness with Romanian cinema. Many other productions could have served the same purpose; thus, the Romanian films discussed here are not related to a predetermined category. They are a reference point to a larger dynamic, which can be discovered in numerous other similar cinematic productions, from European or international film cultures.

Some reasonable questions would be why should anybody be interested in another account about the cultural particularities of a space and language at the margins of Central and Eastern Europe, why would these artistic products be relevant for wider audiences and a larger debate on cinema? The first part of the reasoning has to do with external, cultural justifications. These movies, which achieved global acclaim, are the product of a space relevant in and of itself. Like many other nations living in various forms of in-betweenness, Romanians were historically "trapped" between East and West, spiritually belonging to the Christian Orthodox, while linguistically attached to the Latin language cultures. To this, we can add the recent historical and ideological divisions between communism and capitalism. There are several other similar cultures with forms of thinking close to the imagining and narrating structures shared by the Romanian contemporary films, so this should not be treated as an expression of a particular identity, shared by common linguistic traits or ethnic backgrounds. When listing this series of thought-provoking Romanian films I am performing my own meditation about the post-metaphysical nature of film-thinking, not a search for an alleged spiritual substance of the national psyche in the Hegelian sense. The issues of cultural specificity, the hypothesis of a unique "national" way of making movies, or the possible relations to European modernity do not interest me here. Since the academic research focusing on contemporary Romanian cinema went from being completely ignored to a series of academic studies dedicated to the groundbreaking movies created by directors like Cristi Puiu, Cristian Mungiu, or Corneliu Porumboiu, I consider these problems to be largely clarified.

Nevertheless, an important question needs to be made explicit from the very beginning. The difficult issues which remain to be resolved are the problem of the national mindset, its relations with the particularities of the local cinema culture, and the general thought processes specific to cinema as technology. Some critics have searched for the roots of the philosophical thinking of particular authors in the national context. For instance, Tarkovsky's cinematic vision could be placed within the context of Russian philosophical debates, as András Bálint Kovács properly linked it with Berdyaev's Christian Personalism (Kovács 2009: 581). It would be only natural to approach films as having a cultural specificity, manifested not only in their linguistic identity, but also in their contextual affinity. The paradox of these interpretations of the cinematic mind is put to the test by movies like Cristi Puiu's recent production entitled *Malmkrog* (2020). A three-hour long film infused with Vladimir Soloviev's mystical and moral theological thinking, directed by a Romanian filmmaker, using the techniques of modernist cinema, dealing with philosophical questions from a Russian theologian and spoken in a foreign language it might look like a monstrous chimera.

In my previous interpretations of Romanian cinema, developed as a survey of the New Wave stylistics (Pop 2014), I followed Thomas Elsaesser (2005) and his suggestions about the common characteristics of European cinema, based on cinematographic and narrative practices that went beyond the national identity of the directors. Later Elsaesser (2019) published a revised version of his own propositions about European cinema, trying to circumvent the same difficulties raised by the film and philosophy debates confronted here. The regretted film theorist was proposing a "bridging" of the divides between film and philosophy, using a tool for reasoning developed for centuries in science, the practices of thought experimenting. As he considered necessary to close the gap between the "national exceptionalism" and the "post-national" explanations, this was done through the narrow framework of Continental philosophy. In this book, I decided to take a different path and propose another solution to this divide, by taking into account the Cavellian premise that all films think alike.

From here on another "balancing act" must be performed, since we need to avoid the simplest and practical viewpoints which are describing the "filmmaking mindset" (Schwarze 2020) only as a technical aptitude. Other, more nuanced perspectives underline the practical way of thinking specific to individual movie directors, or the ideological dimensions of moviemaking generally. Some movies belong to the global cinema industry, which carries its own philosophy of the apparatus; others are rooted in their own national culture, which determines a local philosophical understanding. In an effort to appease these differences, Elsaesser suggests that cinema can remain a "philosophical machine" by continuously negotiating the complex relationships between self-identity and social identity, between individual representations and the historical contexts (Elsaesser 2000: 201–2). Is there a "Romanian cinematic self" part of a larger cultural identity manifested throughout history? Are all the movies taking place in Romania and spoken in Romanian part of a cinema-brain overarching national imaginary formations? Or is there a creation of a philosophical determination, escaping the scope of such narrow factors?

Without extrapolating any of the observations I make to all the films made by the Romanian film industry since its very beginning, or cinema in general, I am performing an interpretation of the particular traits of the "Romanian cinematic mind," as reflected by the works of Cristian Mungiu, Cristi Puiu, and Corneliu Porumboiu, from a very specific perspective. Are these cinema-makers philosophically relevant and if so, what is their contribution to film-philosophy, and what is the relevance of their productions to understanding the concepts debated in this field? As pointed out in a previous work on this topic (Pop 2016), these three important filmmakers (alphabetically: Mungiu, Porumboiu, Puiu) represent the canon of the Romanian cinema.

There are at least three different approaches to these issues, and thus the individual chapters where I proceed to discuss the Romanian films are connected to one of these major solutions/problems: how can film thoughts exist as *non-cinematic* manifestations, and what are the *intra-cinematic* and *extra-cinematic* instruments generating thinking in movies. This approach advances a set of arguments about the relationship between film and philosophy based on a tripartite nature of philosophical thinking, one that can be surpassed only by a post-metaphysical perspective. This is the reason for contextualizing these individual discussions by an extensive mapping of the philosophical approaches in cinema. The first chapter represents a necessary taxonomic endeavor, designed to place the film interpretations in a terminological and speculative structure. The arguments of this chapter are built as a methodological exercise, a preparatory survey ordering the existing concepts and theories in a manageable form, which allows the explanations to generate their own set of significations.

The three interpretative sections of the book, each dedicated to a basic argument regarding a dominant *mode of thinking* in cinema, represent a counter-argument to the schematic tripartite analysis often proposed in film studies. Illustrated by Cox and Levine (2012) among others, the division of the issues into three categories—the epistemological, the metaphysical, and the ethical—was my initial reflex. The first premise of my approach was that these modes of thinking had their particular expressions which could be illustrated by the works of contemporary Romanian filmmakers. Thus, my earliest structure was built on the speculation that we can identify and describe three different approaches, each corresponding to a mode of creating thoughts. The *epistemological* questions raised by an *intelligent cinema*, a type of filmmaking that stimulates thinking by asking complex questions, illustrated by the works of Cristian Mungiu. The *ontological* dimension is active in Corneliu Porumboiu technique to constantly explore the limits of the medium, resulting in a *visceral cinema* that expands the thought processes. Finally, there is the *axiological* dimension of films that "think with the mind of the film director," illustrated by Cristi Puiu, who purposefully practices a type of *cerebral cinema*. Performing an in-depth scrutiny of the case studies selected from these contemporary Romanian filmmakers, considered to be relevant not only for their cinematic value but also for their larger philosophical pertinence, the investigations of each chapter took me to a different understanding of the nature and conditions of this particular form of knowledge which I defined later as the *non-cinematic* and *post-metaphysical*.

Structurally each chapter is opening with a generic scene, from a memorable movie, then expanding the conclusions to wider "philosophical" consequences. Resorting to these case studies from selected contemporary

Romanian films, considered to be relevant not only for their cinematic value, but for their larger philosophical pertinence, each chapter is investigating the nature and conditions of a particular form of knowledge. Clearly, when focusing on a particular moviemaker the selection is extremely narrow, as many of the traits identified in one case are applicable in many other circumstances. We cannot separate each of these cinema-makers into a disconnected category; they are discussed separately only for technical reasons, as each chapter is designed to engage a set of distinct questions. Their works are inextricable and profoundly knotted together.

Last but not least, I am aware that some philosophical questions are harder than others, so my ultimate interest is not to provide answers for problems such as "What is film philosophy?" I am instead taking aim at the mystery of "Where film thinking is situated?" and if thought processes are *extraneous* to the cinematic, what are the instruments for non-cinematic ideas to be formed, while remaining integral to the filmic experience. Needless to say, all these interpretations reflect my own preoccupations with the philosophical questions raised by movies.

I am sure that the debates about the relationship between philosophical thought and cinematic thinking will continue, as the intertwinings of film and philosophy are far more complex than allowing one single and final explanation. Thus the purpose of this book is not to clarify what is philosophical or not in cinema, but to offer a reframing of the discussions on the ways in which movies can "think," bringing a method to the larger theoretical inquiry of what does it mean to be philosophical within and outside the cinematic. I consider this to be a modest attempt to disclose a component of cinematic thinking which takes place in all forms of moviemaking, without claiming that there is a "Romanian philosophy" or suggesting a limited viewpoint in which contemporary Romanian films are part of some exceptional creation.

1

The Eternal Flickering of the Film-philosophies Quarrel

Films make us think, characters in movies philosophize, their stories are carriers of philosophical questions and problems, and cinema is even considered to be a new form of thinking. These statements appear axiomatic, as they are purported by many film philosophers, film critics, theorists, and filmmakers. An entirely new and autonomous academic field was promptly created around these presuppositions, consecrated with a generous label: "film-philosophy." With innumerable publications, journals, articles, and books coming out at an astonishing rate, it would be impossible to deny that films can "do philosophy," or at least that they can generate various forms of philosophizing. A myriad of titles tagged "The philosophy of …" are constantly published, placed in distinctive categories on library bookshelves. Upgraded versions of the same denomination, such as "Philosophers on film" or the various philosophers that forcibly took "to the movies," become activated as soon as a new film production is in theaters. Once a movie is released, far-reaching explanations of its philosophical contents are already available, in-depth meanings of the special thinking residing within a genre are extracted, and revelations about the particular philosophies created by the moviemaker are uncovered. To the surprise of many moviegoers, who find out only in the bookstores what they were supposed to understand while watching the fascinating images quickly shimmering on the big screen, such books suggest a plethora of ideas, presumably preexisting in those films.

My approach is no different; thinking about how movies are thinking is the underlying premise of this work. As it happens when joining late the discussion in any field, the effort to elaborate a theoretical framework designed to explain features and manifestations previously interpreted, to give a clear interpretation of the thought processes *outside* the cinematic is an endeavor obstructed by the multiple competing paradigms already disputing priority and ascendency. An attempt to propose a set of explanations about the specific mode in which cinematic thinking happens outside the screen was encumbered by numerous assumptions generating more confusion than clarity. The following clarifications must be understood not as a summary of the major debates between film-philosophers, film scholars, and film critics, they are intended as a pretext for my own conceptual framework.

In no way am I assuming the Herculean task of summarizing the history of all the encroaching theoretical disputes proposed in this clogged matter. Although many attempts were made to bring balance between the various irreconcilable perspectives advanced by academics and cinephiles alike, there is no consensus on this subject among the theorists and amateurs of cinema. The sheer amount of works that take interest in the relationship between cinema and philosophy might seem overwhelming, as a constant flow of texts, manuals, and compendiums has already tackled similar issues. Comprehensive philosophy and film companions are available (Livingston and Plantinga 2009); reliable handbooks are making the key concepts intelligible for the use of students and film teachers (Carroll et. al 2019), with many more individual studies constantly printed adding to the overall knowledge. This avalanche of publications, which has created an autonomous field in philosophical studies, has brought conceptual controversies and terminological squabbles. There is no consensus about the jurisdiction of the discipline itself. For some authors (Wartenberg 2015) it has fully developed into a subfield of the philosophy of art, while for others (Shaw 2008) it should be placed within the field of aesthetics, or, in a less pretentious way, it is considered to be a component of film theory.

Disregarding the debate about the boundaries of film studies and the questioning of philosophical interpretations of movies residing outside the borders of cinema research, movies always represented an attractive topic, since even philosophers seem to enjoy "going to the movies" (Falzon 2002). Multiple interdisciplinary approaches to cinema were proposed in order to combine the two seemingly incompatible fields and in many contemporary philosophical debates movies are used as either first-hand illustrations or visual aids that can bring accessibility. In a reversible move, philosophy for film critics is an instrument providing credibility and the appearance of knowledgeability.

To make things worse, the confusing mixture of explanations is amplified by the riddles caused by systematically challenging previously staked explanations, with a constant exposure of contrasting explanations for the same phenomena. Since this is a common practice in the humanities, we should not worry much, but it does not help that any attempt to settle the long-standing debates about the nature of cinema or the philosophical dimensions of movies end up often as goose-egged chases. Such an effort seems doomed to fail from the start; yet, since the guns are out, why not give it a go?

Thus a critical overview of the most important approaches and perspectives involved in the film and philosophy polemic becomes imperative. Numerous approaches and answers to the problematic relationship between film and philosophy represent a conceptual face-off.

A Philosophical Standoff: The Banal, the Bold, and the Moderate

This philosophical standoff can be mapped like a Spaghetti Western scene, similar to the classic confrontation from *The Good, the Bad and the Ugly* (Figure 1.1). I am aware that this might look trivial as a reductionist vision of a complex debate. Using a cinematic cliché could bring menacing frowns

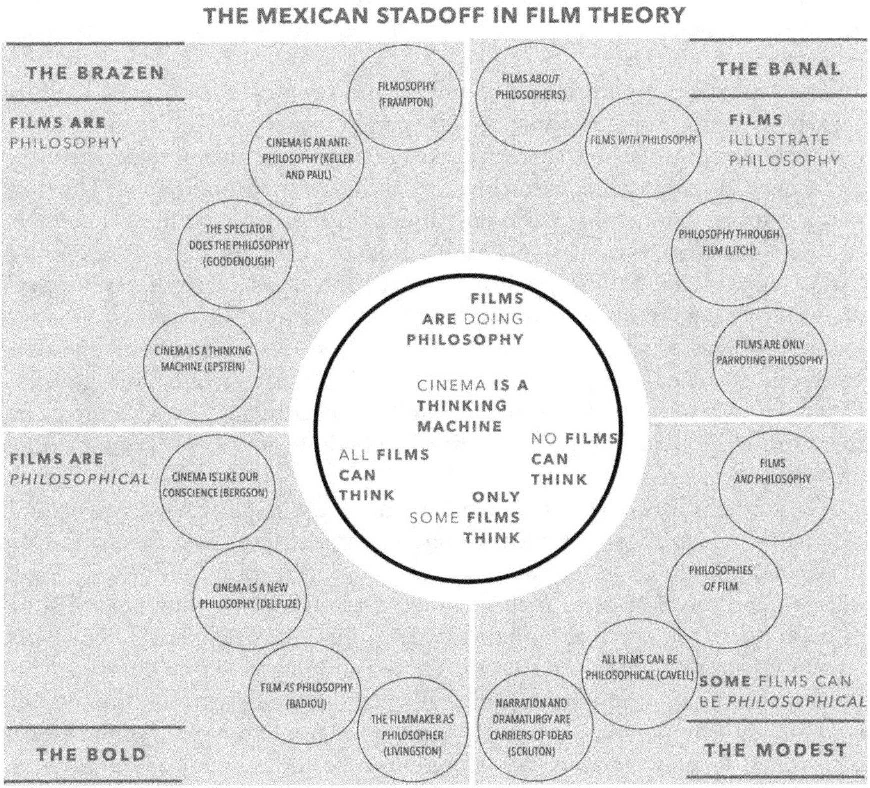

THE MEXICAN STADOFF IN FILM THEORY

THE BRAZEN
FILMS ARE PHILOSOPHY
- FILMOSOPHY (FRAMPTON)
- FILMS *ABOUT* PHILOSOPHERS
- CINEMA IS AN ANTI-PHILOSOPHY (KELLER AND PAUL)
- THE SPECTATOR DOES THE PHILOSOPHY (GOODENOUGH)
- CINEMA IS A THINKING MACHINE (EPSTEIN)

THE BANAL
FILMS ILLUSTRATE PHILOSOPHY
- FILMS *WITH* PHILOSOPHY
- PHILOSOPHY THROUGH FILM (LITCH)
- FILMS ARE ONLY PARROTING PHILOSOPHY

Center:
FILMS ARE DOING PHILOSOPHY
CINEMA IS A THINKING MACHINE
ALL FILMS CAN THINK — NO FILMS CAN THINK
ONLY SOME FILMS THINK

FILMS ARE PHILOSOPHICAL
- CINEMA IS LIKE OUR CONSCIENCE (BERGSON)
- CINEMA IS A NEW PHILOSOPHY (DELEUZE)
- FILM *AS* PHILOSOPHY (BADIOU)
- THE FILMMAKER AS PHILOSOPHER (LIVINGSTON)
- NARRATION AND DRAMATURGY ARE CARRIERS OF IDEAS (SCRUTON)
- ALL FILMS CAN BE PHILOSOPHICAL (CAVELL)

THE MODEST
SOME FILMS CAN BE *PHILOSOPHICAL*
- FILMS AND PHILOSOPHY
- PHILOSOPHIES OF FILM

THE BOLD

FIGURE 1.1 *Schematic overview of the major opposing theories in film and philosophy studies.*

from serious-minded scholars. I am only critically reacting to other film theorists (Livingston 2006) who entered a philosophical duel, reducing the debate to a dichotomy. Two contrasting perspectives are locked in a confrontation, the so-called "bold" versus the "moderate" propositions. My model is obviously a call-out, first and foremost because one must fly in the teeth of the label used by Livingston and the other participants in this "film querelle." Although the Hong Kong-based philosophy professor later revised his own conceptualization, proposing an alternative wording in which he is opposing the "strong" and "modest" philosophical claims—himself supporting the latter—the blanket definition for all theories supporting the ability of films to create innovative philosophical contributions through the cinematic medium (Livingston 2009: 21) has stuck. As I will try to prove in the following explanations, the fact that Livingston and many others are placing authors like Jean Epstein, Gilles Deleuze, or Daniel Frampton in the same category is fallacious and misleading, adding to the confusion of this binary duel of concepts. None of the positions adopted by the participants in this philosophical stalemate can be counterbalanced, as various commentators, critics, and cinephiles simply cross the lines from one stance to another.

The cinematic standoff is not unlike the famous Mexican face-off, as everybody is pointing his philosophical gun in someone's direction. Like in a typical Mexican standoff, there are at least three irreconcilable perspectives, all facing each other and contesting the validity of their opponents. The three major hypotheses dominating contemporary discussions in film-philosophy can be summarized as such: (a) the conception of cinema *as* philosophical and/or capable of "doing" philosophy; (b) the refusal of the assumptions crediting cinema with a structural capacity to think or even to generate viable thoughts; and (c) the effort to identify some aspects in movies that have philosophical meanings, while admitting that not all films have the capacity to generate conceptual thoughts. For each of these approaches there are several subcategories, in turn impeding on the progress of other lines of questioning.

The protagonists of this intellectual combat taking place in the wastelands of cinema and philosophy have different names. The most common form of labeling is done by combining the two terms (film/philosophy) with different prepositions and conjunctions. The result is a complicated series of definitions, organizable alphabetically in the following series: *about/and/as/at/in/is/on/through/with/without*. These combinations are complicated by the fact that, as noted by John Mullarkey (2009), the field of film-philosophy is dominated by partisanships, and the conflictual nature of these positions is disputed fiercely. Various tags and denominations are rejected, criticized, and discharged as defective. A relative consensus in film theory is to settle with three basic modes of cinematic philosophy (Wartenberg 2011: 22): films illustrating philosophy, films conducting philosophical thought experiments, and films performing real experiments. Others (Mullarkey 2009: 13) describe similar forms in which philosophy can manifest: *through* film, *of* film, and *as* film. By using the same formula, Baracco (2017) identified four different approaches to film philosophy: the philosophies *of* film, philosophy *through* film, films *about* philosophy, film *as* philosophy. As previously elaborated by Goodenough (2005: 1–3), these definitions can cover the following basic reasons for a philosopher to "go to cinema": to discover the philosophical dimensions of the movies (philosophy *of* film); to use the films as illustrations of already-existing philosophical topics (philosophy *through* film); to watch philosophical issues displayed in movies (films *about* philosophy); or to see how films are actually "doing" philosophy (film *as* philosophy).

While providing a similar taxonomy of instances in which film and philosophy can "meet" (Vaughan 2013), in fact the spectrum of prepositions which is extremely variegated can often lead to confusions due to their simplistic formulation. These "prepositional explanations," which are designed to set apart different assertions and conceptual disagreements, sometimes accentuate the lack of clarity by producing more semantic misunderstandings. One example of the ways in which these definitions and conceptual divides are perpetuated is illustrated by Philipp Schmerheim, who also catalogued the various theses existing in the scholarly field of film and philosophy. Expressing a disagreement with the group of definitions and configurations belonging to the "through" category, Schmerheim (2017: 21–2) criticized Mullarkey's definition of the philosophy "through" film. The German researcher considers that "through" should include the "philosophicality" of movies, while the Kingston University professor defines with "through" the films that are used as illustrations of philosophical ideas. This important discussion will be reappraised again later in another subchapter.

This is only one example of why I consider that the film about/and/as/at/in/is/on/through/with/without philosophy taxonomy must be reappraised by using proper nouns in definitions, which should take us the apparent handiness of prepositions, conjunctions, or adverbs usually associated in the field. When overlooking the terms coupled in this debate, I also consider it important to offer a couple of new and corrective concepts that are obligatory in order to clarify some of the critical misunderstandings that come from some limitative readings. A strident example is the interpretation of the famous Deleuzian formula: "The screen is the brain." This utterance is quickly translatable with the constituent terms of our debate, where "screen" equals cinema (or film) and "the brain" equals thinking (or philosophy). Nevertheless, this apparently unproblematic definition is misused and its interpretations induce inaccurate understandings of the relationship between film and philosophy—the specific aspects of the discussion will also be clarified in a dedicated subchapter. The lack of agreement between the major theories and theoretical paradigms explaining the relationship between film and philosophy comes with a supplementary divergence from the various paradigms already existing in philosophy studies.

This being said, the taxonomy is unavoidable. We can draw the major divide along two opposing lines of arguments, each offering a basic classification and establishing a large categorical divide alongside two major questions: "Can films do philosophy?" and "What kind of thinking can films generate?" The answers are never easy and are complicated by the remarkable properties of cinema, given by the fact that a *material* reality, with *physical* consistency (actors, settings), is modified in such a way that the experience provided has no physical properties. Unlike painting, where the representation has a material manifestation and a clear intentional determination, the immaterial nature of the cinematic projection, which allowed the creation of a new mode of experiencing the material world for humanity, is highly problematic. The nature of the things that seem to exist only on screen coalesced with the material nature of the cinematic; as the film itself is "real," the actions and emotions that are present in the world created by the movie, which exist autonomously in the minds of the viewer, are factors complicating any answers. Such internal contradictions have led many film theorists and film-philosophers to reach different conclusions about the epistemological, ontological, and metaphysical dimensions of the cinematic.

Positive–Negative Thinking: The Horizontal Models

One of the simplest and most functional representations we can use when dealing with the problems raised by the relationship between film and philosophy is to operate a positive–negative charge of the existing concepts—somewhat similar to the conventional description of polarized electrons. Such a schematic opposition is grouping films according to their philosophical "charge," covering a large spectrum from the profoundly thoughtful to the quickly dismissable as a-philosophical. As illustrated by my rendition of the binary contradictions, the "polarized electrons" model in Figure 1.2 is a simplified drawing of the film-thinking debate. These opposing paradigms are thick-bedded along a *horizontal* divider, with major confrontational lines drawn in a binary fashion. This needs to be discussed more carefully, especially since many other authors who have engaged with the subject found it necessary to clarify these aspects in their own theoretical positioning while maintaining the oppositional line represented by two contradictory prepositions: "and" (philosophy) versus "as" (philosophy/philosophical).

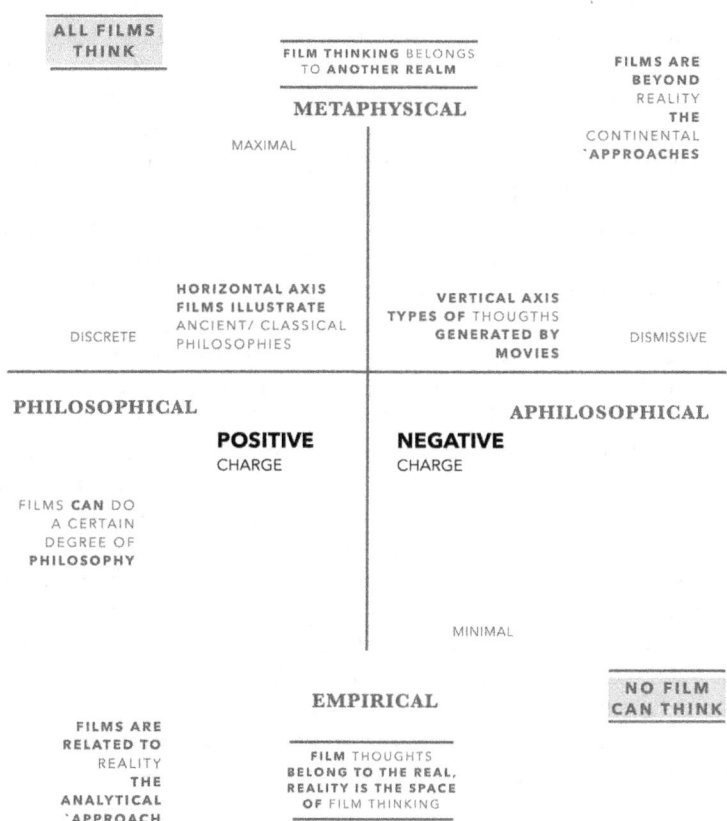

FIGURE 1.2 *The polarized electron model, a schematic representation of the contradictory definitions of the relationship between film and thinking.*

The elementary principle of the *horizontal model* accepts a corresponding tension existing between two major philosophical positions, each occupying one end of the conceptual rift. The negative end of the spectrum is dominated by philosophers and theorists who deny any possible contribution of movies to philosophical knowledge. The negatively charged side of the film-philosophy electron is substantiating the claim that "films cannot think." On the opposing side are positioned those authors and thinkers who submit the arguments based on the premise that cinema has the capacity to be philosophical. Here, in the overcharged or the "radical" versions, those films can even innovate philosophy. Their catchphrase is "all films can think." The *philosophical refuseniks*, opposed by the *film-philosophy zealots*, can concede no possible mollification between their positions. Either films have no contribution to the creation of ideas, or cinema can revolutionize traditional philosophy. In the middle are the *philosophical appeasers*, who try to find a midway in the debate. I would submit later another opinion that a post-metaphysical and a non-philosophical component of cinema thinking must be taken into consideration, exemplified by the Romanian cinema examples analyzed in the following chapters.

The abrupt claim that cinema displays an intrinsic incapacity to provide any philosophical concepts or innovative solutions is based on the idea that the medium itself is incapable of philosophical investigations. Here also we can find a divide, as one line of argument considers the fact that a visual medium cannot provide the same results as a text-based medium, while the other views cinema as a debased form of communication. One side of the horizontal, at the negatively charged end, provides two different types of subsequent explanations, which can be categorized as either *disconnective* or *dismissive*. The *dismissive* view completely disregards any possible contributions of cinema to philosophy, while the *disconnective* approach concedes to some extent that Ideas can be integrated into films, when they are separated from the medium itself. Films are not able to "do philosophy" because cinema simply cannot philosophize; yet, movies can contain debased forms of thinking. When contesting the philosophical properties of cinema, the main assertion is that films lack the necessary language and tools to produce philosophical content. The philosophical refuseniks have an important argument to deny the "film as philosophy" contention—the cinematic apparatus is not designed as a reason-inducing environment or instrument.

At the other end are positioned the supporters of the positive perspective. While the so-called film *as* philosophy paradigm is antithetical to the dismissive attitude of the refuseniks, the domain is also diversified and various divergent opinions collide inside the general scheme of those supporting the idea that films "can do philosophy." One zealot group comprises the *filmolatrical* claims, suggesting that the cinematic machine is profoundly philosophical by its very nature. Corresponding to the film *is* philosophy formula; *filmolatry* offers more than a radical version of the film *as* philosophising assumption. The contention is that the "old" forms of philosophy are obsolete and that cinema is rejuvenating the mode in which humanity is thinking. Other explanations fall into a more nuanced category, similar to the film *and* philosophy model. Films are companions or illustrations of existing ideas; they are ideal carriers of philosophical concepts, providing an environment in which thoughts can be easily cultivated and disseminated.

Because of all the differences in opinions, I considered that a better definition for this group of propositions would be to label them as the *discrete* explanations. As they are not simply opposing counterarguments of the *disconnection* theories, here too we can identify a separate set of arguments. One can be described as the *cogent* interpretations, applicable to all those who consider a partial philosophical relevance in cinema. Only *some* films have the power to generate philosophical ideas. Another is ascribing the entire cinematic medium with the ability to philosophize and to create innovative concepts, which is the *autonomous* perspective. By stating the obvious contradiction, that films *can* think, there are various degrees of philosophical abilities that cinema can display. This set of interpretations is further complicated by its own sort of ineluctable predicaments—to be detailed in a dedicated subchapter. It would suffice to say that the *discrete* category is split between three explanatory functions. One claims that there is an *intrinsic* function of the philosophical, residing *inside* the cinematic; another is searching for meanings in the *interval*, which can be identified as the theories of the *in-between*; and a third placing the thinking at the level of social and ideological functions, the *allogenic* explanation.

We can illustrate how the *film as philosophy* thesis is oscillating between various degrees of realization, by performing a quick survey of the "war of filmolaters." The dispute of those accepting the premise that movies have an epistemic quality, allowing them to function independently as *autonomous* philosophical machines, has created a special type of conceptual conflict. "The bold thesis," as labeled by Livingston (2009: 4–5), and the "null thesis," proposed by Cox and Levine (2012), are opposing versions existing in the same paradigm. When trying to identify the philosophical qualities of films, the assertions about the philosophic dimensions display a profound divergence of opinions. Either films *are* philosophical or they can provide *partial* access to philosophical ideas. Aaron Smuts (2009), who joined this debate by supporting the idea that films *can do* philosophy, organized these variables as they fluctuated from the "super bold" to the "merely bold" versions. When almost every author who enters the debate develops a thesis along these lines, the resulting arguments take confusing turns. The "super bold" position and the supporters of the "simply bold" versions are in the same camp; they all claim that films *are* philosophical. In practical terms, the "super bold" attitude in which Smuts includes anyone supporting the idea that cinema has a unique philosophical property qualifies as a radical view about the philosophical capabilities of movies. I also disagree with Smuts who evaluates Deleuze as a proponent of the "super bold" perspective. The fact of the matter is that the French philosopher proposes a more nuanced approach to the film and philosophy debate; these are nuances that we need to raise concerns.

With the battle for typologies raging at the surface of film theory, more sets of formulaic expressions of the same issues are constantly brought up to claim new territory in these troubled waters. An example is provided by Wartenberg (2011) who developed a new set of binary acronyms in a model dividing the discussions about CPT (which confusingly stands for the "cinematic philosophy thesis"; yet, it includes also the film-philosophy approaches) into opposing categories, the EPCP (for the "extreme pro-cinematic philosophies") and EACP (for "extreme anti-cinematic philosophy"). Finally, the same horizontal is describing the divide between two other basic contraries, the supporters of the MACP position (moderate anti-cinematic philosophy) disagreeing with the MPCP (moderate pro-cinematic philosophy).

The following discussions are dedicated to the same effort of rethinking binary categories. By critically evaluating the existing terminologies and exploring the contradictions within the available explanations of the *binary* explanatory *models*, which I consider unsatisfactory, my purpose here more than simply to overview the current debates. I propose an alternative to the *binary descriptions* by following another intuition advanced by Deleuze in his first "Cinema" book. The French philosopher observed that the moving images are not behaving only in a fixed and predetermined mode; they are in an "interatomic" state defying our efforts to mechanically define them (Deleuze 1986/1983: 58–9). By elaborating an *atomic model* (Figure 1.3)

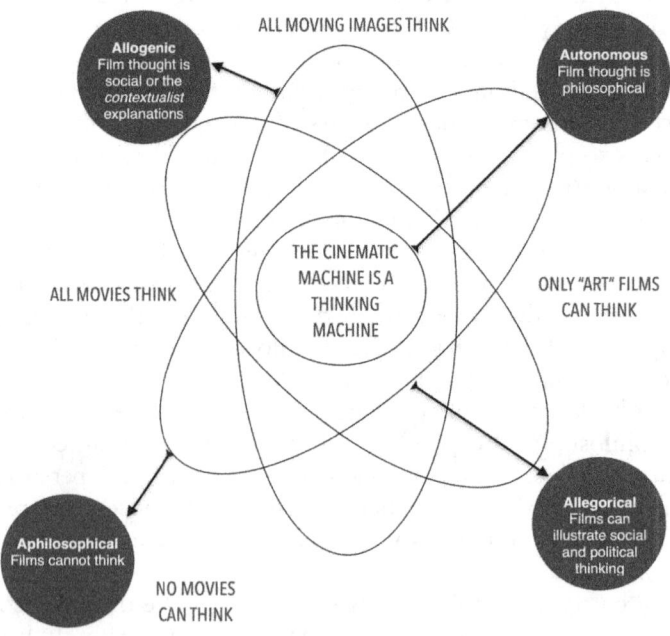

FIGURE 1.3 *The atomic model, represented as an alternative for the conflictual paradigm in the "universe" of film and philosophy.*

I intend to show why we must nullify the separation lines between the negatively or positively charged theories and to replace these oppositions with a general framework in which the particular forms of thinking in cinema are never truly separated. Film-thinking comprises all these components, with the *nucleus* represented by the capacity of cinema to innately create ideas and the *neutrons* manifested as various neutral manifestations. This allows us to elaborate and describe films that disclose a *non*-philosophical thinking, or those that have their contents charged with philosophical meanings extraneous to the cinematic. One of the reasons for proposing a new model, as I will argue further along, is that the thinking processes that coalesce within the cinematic machine, the "screening" of external ideas, and the internalized projection of images that think can coexist. Accepting that more introspective forms of representation, like the metaphysical films, are philosophical must not immediately presuppose that their negative counterparts, the type of cinema I describe as the *post-metaphysical*, must be a-philosophical.

Pro-philosophical Approaches: *Connective* and *Cogent* Definitions

At the positive end of the *horizontal* model are several theories and explanations, ranging from the uncomplicated arguments supporting the capacity of films to contain philosophical ideas (the banal hypothesis) to the more complex propositions considering that thought processes take shape within cinematic narrations or the radical assumptions that films have a philosophical mind. The *connective* approaches can do more than simply link philosophy with cinema or define films as philosophical instruments. A more radical direction is to claim that cinema renews philosophy. This connective perspective is best illustrated by the two major works on film and philosophy elaborated by Gilles Deleuze. The French philosopher considers that cinema has immense philosophical potential. Movies are even thought about as opening new concepts in philosophy. While following his premise that cinema can potentially rejuvenate philosophical thinking, my own approach diverges in the outcome. To emphasize my arguments I must express my divergence with Gregg Lambert's (2002) interpretation of how Deleuze understood the non-philosophical. By overlapping this notion with the non-conceptual an interpretative error is produced. Considering that Deleuze was indeed searching for an alternative to metaphysics, my own reading and understanding of the innovative force of cinema are partially derived from the philosophical propositions advanced by François Laruelle.

Here I diverge from the explanations put forward by the simple model devised by Livingston (2006), one of the most vehiculated models in film theories. We cannot evaluate the film and philosophy hypotheses in a hierarchical range of possibilities, one that is oscillating from the most radical definitions (identified as the "bold thesis"), which consider that films are able to generate philosophical concepts, to the "milder" (also known as the "moderate thesis"), accepting that movies are spaces of thought, stimulants, or carriers of ideas. Since Livingston never gave up his model, constantly "retrying" to define the limits of this design (2019), constantly adapting it to the various degrees of epistemic qualities shifting in cinema, the task of any hierarchical evaluation is to test the conceptual functionality of the "pro philosophical" versus the "moderate" positions.

The simplest connection between films and philosophy appears to be also the "easy" solution (Wartenberg 2016). By observing that movies contain philosophical ideas and by providing examples of films that use philosophy as a meaning-making tool, the "banal hypothesis" allows us to establish links everywhere. Such explanations are scattered over a large area of the film and philosophy domain. This set of pro-philosophy arguments range from the trite observation that cinema is philosophical because films "make us think" to the more presumptuous opinion that cinema is an adequate medium for philosophical discussions and ideas. Nevertheless, the problem with the *connective* explanations is that they muddle the general film-philosophy debate. The confusions are best illustrated by Thomas Wartenberg, who enunciated the aporia that films can *do* philosophy (Wartenberg 2011: 18), later making tremendous efforts to defend the notion that cinematic philosophy exists (Wartenberg 2016). Refuting the objections raised by the a-philosophical theorists, the *cogent* definitions assume that there is a relative degree of connectivity between films and philosophy. From the "mild claims," as Livingston identified them, accepting that movies can contain ideas without contributing to philosophical knowledge, to the "wild claims," stating that cinema has comparable contribution to philosophy like the classical works of Western thinking, similar to the writings of Plato or Kant, the so-called *moderate* position is not providing a unified set of interpretations. Advocating the "pro" arguments of this central axiom, the contradiction in Wartenberg's arguments remains. Movies cannot both be "partially philosophical" and maintain their capacity to "do philosophy." The film as a philosophical medium hypothesis, which is based on the capacity of cinema to generate philosophical concepts, cannot be overlapped with the ability of some films to be philosophically relevant. Wartenberg claims that films are functioning as thought experiments, which qualify them as more than illustrations of a given philosophical text. When moviemakers provide visualizations of ideas otherwise unavailable for the readers of philosophical discourse, they "do philosophy." The problem is that, when following this line of thinking, Wartenberg is forced to expand the notion of film to all forms of "displayed moving images and sounds." Thus video art, television, or any Youtube home movie can qualify as "philosophy."

A more moderate approach to film philosophy was performed by Thomas Elsaesser (2019), who advanced the self-effacing argument that even when films are *not thinking*, they function as *thought experiments*. Following Wartenberg's initial solution, the German film historian uses mind-game films to demonstrate that movies can make the viewers think. His examples, illustrating the preoccupation of European filmmakers for ideas like "freedom, equality, or liberty," serve as evidence for the *cogent* thesis. The regretted German film theorist circumvents the difficulties raised by film and philosophy debates, in an earnest attempt to "bridge" the divides between those who describe films as philosophically relevant and those indicating the limits of cinema to create new ideas. The practices of thought experimenting, which were a tool for reasoning used for centuries in science and philosophy, are traceable back to Plato's dialogues.

Thought experimentation was advanced as another method (Davies 2012: 223) enabling moviemakers to perform activities making them akin to philosophers. Dialogues can open up questions; fictional storytelling situations can provoke flickering thoughts, even expanding into a full spectrum of philosophical ideas. By this logic any film director can become a "thought experimenter," not far from the tradition of classical philosophers. This leads to a perfunctory qualification of any film as a "thought experiment," since any narrative structure in all storytelling formats is based on an inherent cognitive and causal coherence. In consonance with Carroll's (1996) notion of *erotetic* narrative, developed from the answer provided by cognitive theories to the problems of thought formation, any narrative raising questions or providing answers becomes a tool for generating thinking. As Elsaesser compellingly and extensively extracts examples from the European cinema, film narrations are natural environments for thought experiments where moviemakers can explore ethical and political choices, can handle the problems of the body or community issues, and to explore one or more possible or alternative worlds and solutions to our world (Elsaesser 2019: 64).

Agreeing with the respected scholar, as I will be arguing in a dedicated chapter, we need to account also for those situations in which such narrations are not performing explicit thought-provoking functions. Some films are non-philosophical in the sense that the thought experiment does not provide an explanation. It is insufficient to deal with these movies as manifestations of the "crisis of representations." The examples analyzed in the next chapters indicate that a non-cinematic narrative is not only relevant for providing extra-filmic criticism. The "What if?" question, present in several imagined scenarios, stories with "deep" ethical and political meanings, can also have a non-philosophical component, as in Porumboiu's movie where the inverted interrogation is "Was it (or was it not?!"). Based on specific existential experiments of each European nation, some abstract situations that operate properly in experimental philosophy are transformed in other cinemas. Sometimes the differences of cultural perception even prevent the understanding of the philosophical consequences of narratives that refuse "to think normally." Accounting for these *eristetic* forms of storytelling is going to be an important part of this study.

Another divide remains unresolved, since on the one hand we have the "modest" approaches and, on the other, the arguments advanced by Deleuze in his quintessential chapter 7 from *Cinema 2*, entitled "Thought and Cinema." Can the cinematic medium, based on artificially created moving images, change the entire way in which we are thinking? Are movies producing a brain-shock affecting the cortex of the viewers, then leading to the "arousal" of the inner thinker in every spectator (Deleuze 1989: 156). First of all, it would be erroneous to place the "banal" thesis in the same category as the proponents of the "bold" thesis. While the two explanations seem to share several traits, common to the film *and* philosophy paradigm, by contradicting the negative arguments advanced by the *dismissive* approaches, the simplest and the most complex explanations about the ability of films to be philosophical are dissimilar by nature. Some of these theories and propositions, which belong to the large group of positive explanations connecting the philosophical with the cinematic, cannot be simply brought together. Not even the theories arguing that cinema "has a mind of its own" can be grouped in a predefined classification. As I will try to argue in the following subchapters, the radical ideas proposed by Jean Epstein, the misinterpreted arguments of Gilles Deleuze, and the brazen hypothesis put forward by Daniel Frampton are not identical, even if many studies present them as a coherent paradigm. Not every provocative claim about the existence of a "filmind" or a "cinema brain" can be accompanied. As we will see, they provide disjunct and opposing arguments, made evident only when we go back to the most representative directions.

Before explaining the inner defects of such confusions, I propose a redefining of the explanatory model (Figure 1.4) along with a series of concepts that separate the *connective* paradigm into four distinct groups: the *cogent* definitions, including those accepting that cinema can provide access to certain philosophical meanings; the *discrete* definitions, which argue that cinema represents a distinct form of thinking; the *contextualist* and the *immanentist* explanations balance these arguments and nuance the source of any philosophical idea created *at* the movies. Since the *immanentist* dimension of the film as philosophical tools was already discussed, its opposed counterargument must be dealt with. By considering that ideas are *contextual*, it reduces film meanings to simply mirroring the philosophical problems of society. Even though in both of these cases films are *determined* to think, their *cogent* quality either comes from their

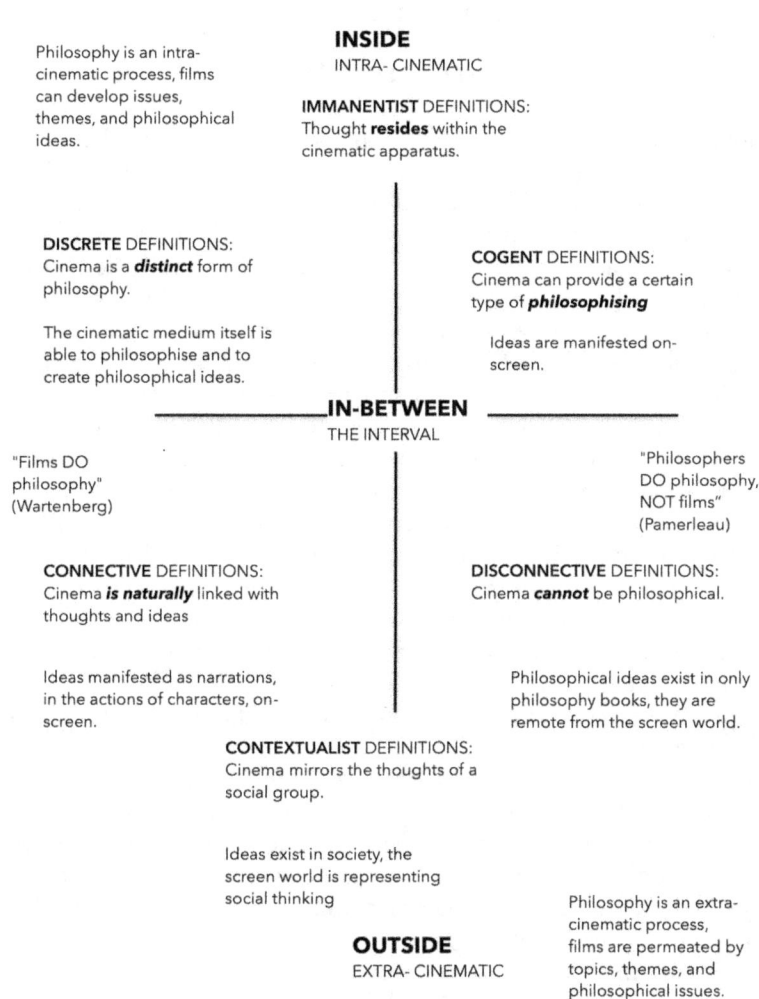

FIGURE 1.4 *Explanatory model organizing the major definitions in the cinema and philosophy research.*

internal driving forces or is induced by external factors. The discrete/cogent/immanentist/contextualist schematic representations allow a description of the philosophical manifestations in movies from the simplest forms, with films that contain narrative illustrations of moral or ethical problems, to films that are engaged in metaphysical questioning and/or are able to create innovative philosophical ideas.

Contextualist Interpretations: The *Allegorical* and the *Allogenic*

Undoubtedly there are innumerable instances in which the ideas we encounter in cinematic representations are mirroring the thought processes of various social groups. The ideas conveyed by film narratives are part of ideological sets that drive society. Ideas are channeled onto the screen world by various means and, as Fredric Jameson (1992) has amply demonstrated, even when the ideological meanings and their social dimension are not explicit, since the representations and the ideas are dialectically fused together, social thinking. All narratives have a socially symbolic function, and movies make no exception. Jameson argues that, when we watch Steven Spielberg's *Jaws* (1975), we are not simply viewing and thinking about the anxieties of movie characters. These fears have a social and historical content; thus, the value of film-thinking comes from the ability of particular movies to make us think *about* society. The philosophical also derives from the preoccupations residing the society, movies are based in the material reality, yet they disclose the political unconscious of our social group. Thus the notion that films are allegorical must be tied with the possibility that cinematic content produces and reproduces social thinking. All movies are cultural forms that "think" beyond the intentions of the film director; they are allegorical representations of political ideas otherwise deeply hidden in the collective unconscious.

When discussing how the sources of our knowledge are socially determined the most important "contextualist" work remains Siegfried Kracauer's endeavor to link Weimar cinema to the "deep layers" of collective mentality in interwar German society, to explore the otherwise inaccessible dimension of the "German mind" (Kracauer 1966: 60). This film and culture theorist get his critical method off the ground by assuming that movies are historically linked to the socially collective; they are a type of cultural product that is both collaboratively produced and popularly consumed. Thus thinking *about* movies and discussing the content *of* films become a pathway to understanding society. In my model, Kracauer presents us with some of the most relevant examples for the *allogenic* nature of film-thinking. Although many other thinkers and philosophers, from Baudrillard to Žižek, have adopted a similar approach and presented many more explanations for the relationship between ideology and cinema, his theorizing about society through moving pictures is by now a well-established method field. It was Kracauer who first observed that the mental processes are not simply unidirectional. The capacity of movies to project thoughts inside the mind of the audience is complicated by the fact that many of these ideas are residing deep below the surface, in the social unconscious, accumulating into collective mentalities which cannot be traced otherwise. Each particular film and each individual spectator are irrelevant; only together they form a collective disposition, disclosing ample attitudes toward social reality, manifested in the aesthetic forms of cinematic representations. As filmmakers use themes, motifs, or ideas that are already circulating in the fantasy of a social group, they become manifest forms of the subconscious thinking of "the masses." As illustrated by the seminal essay "The Ornament of the Mass," published in 1927, the German sociologist establishes an unavoidable correlation between the psyche of the mass audiences and the screen representations (Kracauer 1995: 75–88). In a similar fashion, we can validate a direct connection linking ideas and their aesthetic manifestations. Later this interconnection will be used to argue that the characters dominating the films of the so-called New Objectivity cinema were in fact anticipating the dominant ideological figures of Nazi Germany.

Kracauer's provocative thesis, often misunderstood or criticized, provides us with an important instrument to extract knowledge from the cinematic, offering access to a level of consciousness that resides in the depths of the psyche of the mass audience, otherwise unavailable. In my understanding, this *allogenic* dimension of film-thinking is part of the extra-cinematic and must constitute the foundation of any film interpretation.

Philosophy All-inclusive: Everything Will Be Philosophised

When accepting the allegorical function of movies, this premise has tremendous consequences, expanding the *banal* hypothesis. The field of cine-philosophy, distinguishable from film-philosophy on account of the banality of examples provided, oftentimes takes a philosophical twist to the worst. Cine-philosophy allows the formation of "cobbled up" philosophical explanations, filled with doubtful speculations and questionable conceptual amalgamations. However, Wartenberg (2015) and other supporters of the films-as-illustrations conceptual scheme, which is more or less similar with the banal thesis, consider these contributions to be a sign of the proper development of a distinguished domain. Nevertheless, a book on the philosophy of a popular TV animation which claims to be "Socratic," using sexual innuendos as "philosophical" instruments and by exposing the "bullshit" of contemporary society the contributors claim to be combatting "pussy epistemology," presents the crude outcome that all philosophizing can be "good philosophizing" (Hanley 2007). This approach is symptomatic not only for popular culture studies, where everything becomes philosophical, often cinema is used as universal remedy for all our private and political problems. In order to drive away from any terminological confusions that may appear between these approaches and my own understanding of *non*-philosophy, the utter negations and the radical perspectives are not my concern.

In film theory there are many books illustrating the limits of these approaches. For instance the study published by Paul W. Kahn, which opens with the major assumption that any film playing in any cinema could constitute a good place to "start philosophising," is sufficient evidence that this elementary understanding based on the generalized statement that everything can be philosophical is inconsequential. Following a simple line of reasoning, it illustrates how generalizing interpretations do not bring "new directions in philosophical inquiry"; they are just making complex concepts more accessible. By pretending to offer a more "exciting" perspective on what philosophy should be, they are by no measure generating new philosophical explanations. With Kahn proceeding to identify the arguments for his philosophical renewal in blockbuster movies, the only unintended effect is the vulgarization of philosophical thinking. In a world where everybody has a "philosophy" of their own, where anything generates a form of thinking which is considered philosophical, philosophy "can happen anywhere" (Kahn 2013: viii). More importantly, this form of thinking takes place *after* watching a movie, as the narratives of the films impact our private and public existence. All practical approaches to philosophy lead to the assumption that viewers can find advice about how to lead their lives simply by watching movies. This enables spectators "to know themselves," to examine who they are, with an almost Socratic finality.

The proposition formulated by Tom McClelland (2011) and endorsed by Thomas Elsaesser (2019: 62–3) describes the "Socratic" dimension of meaning-making in cinema. The argument is that movies can function like a "philosophical midwife," providing insights for the spectators, who can later use these ideas in social debates or in pedagogical contexts. I consider that the obvious distortion of Socratic thinking performed by McClelland is unnecessary and unwarranted. While the ancient philosopher was cultivating a constant dialogue with his pupils, illustrating ideas with the help of narrative situations, the film director (and the film itself) is not operating at the same level.

Not only because there is no interaction between the philosophizing moviemakers and their viewers. More problematic is the presumed "discovery of the truth" that can be delivered in all movies, especially since the vast majority are delivering pre-digested versions of a truth created by a cultural–industrial machine. Even though watching a blockbuster film can become a philosophically inspiring moment, the transformation of cine-philosophical knowledge into practical actions is never reaching an intensity that can alter our society.

Richard Gilmore, who previously supported a corresponding claim, concludes with a more restrictive solution. Cinema has the power of a "reconfiguration tool"; it can change the lives and the experience of life only for those moviegoers who discuss the films after watching them. Gilmore advocates that the only way in which we should watch films is "to go philosophically" into the movie theater. Immersing into the thought processes of the protagonists and their actions, films would then present us with "externalized thoughts" (Gilmore 2005: 10–11). By closely observing action heroes like Ethan from *The Searchers* (1956), their decisions can become *meaningful experiences* for how human beings should think and act. Gilmore's assumption was that the American film director is able to put in place a Socratic mechanism, which is compelling the spectators to think about revenge or guilt and thus improving their understanding of society. The deductive argument is that popular movies have more meanings than we are able to see in their immediate contents; their philosophical functions exist beyond appearances. Such meanings are instilled in rediscovered archetypes, or mythic themes, which reside inside every narration. So, when watching a movie we have the chance to go beyond the literal dimensions of the storytelling; thus, we are all able to "do philosophy."

In a more recent publication, Gilmore took this perspective one step further, finding more arguments for this pragmatic understanding of how movies are "ameliorating" the conditions of life (Gilmore 2017: vii). His optimistic perspective on cinema as a thought-liberating form allows him to treat every movie as a "spiritual exercise," a pathway to practices that change our behavior, transform the way in which we are involved in our daily activities. To believe that individual spectators can go through a "sublime conversation" by seeing a film, which in turn provokes a spiritual sense of existence (Gilmore 2017: 149) and then transforms them into better citizens is an enticing presupposition. It remains to be confirmed by empirical data if popular cinema can be more than simple entertainment, but associating movies with such philosophical depths remains attractive. A philosophical way of watching films, based on a process of reflective thinking, of searching for things that are more than they appear (Gimore 2005: 21), would certainly be desirable.

The undisputed fact is that the storytelling forms in popular films are containing democratized versions of philosophical thinking—and by stating this Gilmore is a good disciple of Cavell. When we are engaged with the fictional worlds projected in our minds by a movie, the plot and the characters can raise problems and questions which have transformative power. Whether or not they can "prepare" the viewers for future rational decisions is still debatable, especially since this philosophy professor builds his arguments with examples from a couple of hand-picked movies, where their inherent "strangeness" presents a good start for "doing philosophy" (Gilmore 2017: 7).

The fallacies of this line of reasoning, together with the erroneous results of the all-encompassing approaches to philosophy, are made more visible in the books published by Mark Rowlands, who followed this generalizing principle to its bitter end. The Welsh professor and philosopher not only takes for granted the premise that *all films* are philosophical, but also supports the possibility that anyone can understand philosophical ideas by simply watching a movie. In the book ostentatiously entitled "The Philosopher at the End of the Universe," retitled and republished as "Sci-Phi: Philosophy from Socrates to Schwarzenegger," Rowlands (2005/2012) argues in an amused tone that philosophy is everywhere and all around us. This makes popular cinema a perfect candidate for philosophical speculation; thus, the author has Tom Cruise congregating with Plato, while Keanu Reeves becomes a mentor for anyone studying René Descartes. Rowlands, who is also a widely published practical philosopher, defines philosophy as "doing," and by this "doing philosophy" means to make direct use of the ideas received from the fictional universe of cinema. While using a similar conceptual background with the idea of a future film-philosophy, the "sci-phi" or science fiction as philosophy advanced by Gregory Flaxman (2008), my book does not take the path of the hypothesis advanced by this American disciple of Deleuze—more in the discussions about Deleuzian thinking. The entire argument is that philosophy can be embodied in several contemporary science-fiction blockbusters, a "new genre" of films capable of transmitting knowledge. Unfortunately when using the exhaustively mentioned examples from *The Matrix* or the presumed capacity of *Blade Runner* to make us think about the meanings of life there is nothing of a future philosophy here.

Finally, we must address the transformations induced by the digitalization of cinema and pertaining to philosophy. One possible answer is provided by William Brown, an artist who considers that a version of "supercinematic thinking" was made possible by the development of contemporary digital technologies. From this perspective digital cinema presents the opportunity of a new way of doing *cine-philosophy*, one that can lead to the exhilarating and exciting "love of all films." With individuals having unlimited access to digital movies today, it could seem that we are now able to freely "do philosophy" in front of our laptop screens, even reaching "beyond the human condition" (Brown 2013: 5). No matter how attractive the idea of millions of philosophizing spectators watching digital movies on their laptop screens or on-demand, the philosophical inquiry happening "in the cave" of our digital movie theaters is most probably a loss of the philosophical, since it happens mostly in the absence of other human beings.

At the other end of this spectrum of thinking is positioned Berys Gaut (2010), who took these arguments to their ultimate conclusion and asserted that all media related to cinema, such as video games, can be philosophical. Gaut's answer for the complex philosophical question raised before is to separate "traditional" cinema from "digital cinema," thus considering that cinema was nothing more than a large form of expressivity and artistry that now can take us into another realm. Thus, the philosophy of cinema is no longer limited to traditional films; it has expanded into other "cinematic" forms, including the visual media which are functioning like "interactive cinema." While this interpretation deserves more discussions, in the context of its philosophical relevance and the impact of moving images on thinking it does not bring any new solutions.

A-philosophical Approaches: The *Disconnective* and the *Dismissive* Theories

A large corpus of critical approaches to cinema has coalesced around the assumption that there is no connection between films and thinking, that cinema has no philosophical relevance. Supporting the key contention that cinema is fundamentally *a-philosophical* are some of the radical *refuseniks*, labeled by Noël Carroll (2017) as the "skeptics" (like Murray Smith or Bruce Russell). They could have been labeled as films *without* philosophy, a term that was never elaborated by any of the film-philosophy approaches. The category of *disconnective* definitions can delineate the set of explanations claiming that the cinematic medium is functioning separately from any philosophical abilities. Due to its lack of specific instruments philosophical, as pointed out by Russell (2008) in his rebuking of Carroll and Wartenberg, cinema has no access to the tools developed by classical thinkers. It is relevant that Carroll, who is an astute supporter of the assumption that films are *partially philosophical*, concedes that films like *Sunset Boulevard* can foster philosophy, described as a particular form of the philosophical, the "popular philosophy" (Carroll 2011: 65). In fact, such definitions place cinema at the periphery of philosophical thought, isolating films in a domain already disregareded by "high" philosophy.

Returning to some of the entangled arguments previously advanced by Carroll (1996), once we deny that there is an "essence of cinema" and we disconnect the film medium from any specificity, then the non-essentialist definitions provide an interpretative framework for rejecting the distinct possibility of film thought. We can understand why some most obstinate skeptics reach the ineluctable conclusion that thinking is not cinematic, as philosophy is linked to a particular medium and a specific language. A visual medium is unable to create philosophical concepts that are distinctively connected to written words. Films are not philosophical because of an ontological incapacity of the "moving objects" to create conceptual thought; movies lack the necessary conditions required by any systematic thinking. Carroll famously tried to resolve this issue by proposing his own conceptualization, replacing "movies" with "moving image." Yet the articulation of this "ontology of the moving image" by the American art philosopher is a counter-proof of the same problem. By simply reformulating the assumption that "films" cannot think, with the argument that "moving images" can philosophize, we are not escaping the paradoxes of the ontological specificity.

Maurizio Ferraris and Enrico Terrone (2019) raised some important issues regarding cinema and ontology, and their arguments can be best summarized by the idea that while cinema can generate concepts and ideas, they are the result of a technological art. The question is whether these ideas (and by this any philosophical idea created in movies) are the product of the technological medium or a side effect. For the Italian media philosophers the answer is that all artworks are "automatic sweethearts," that is, they are physical objects capable of inducing spiritual and emotional reactions. This component of the discussion will be explored further in the examination of the metaphysical dimension of cinema; yet, we can state that films provide a *disconnected* experience which is then transformed into an internalized effect.

A special group of anti-philosophical theorists is formed around a more radical set of arguments, advancing hard to refute observations against the *discrete* paradigm. Elaborated by Roger Scruton in a provocative paper published in 1981, these polemic assertions illustrate the basic reasonings of media *disconnectedness*. Scruton, who was analyzing the relationship between photography and representation, denounced the capacity of any photographic media to provide the viewers with access to an intentional expression of thought about the properties of the depicted objects. This conservative political philosopher argued that cinema together with all the photographic media are "thoughtless" tools of communication. By blatantly dismissing the possibility that photographic (and by extension film, television, and any other visual medium) thinking can exist the inference is radical. Since the products of any photographic medium are always indexial artifacts, all such representations are devoid of intentional thoughts. In the case of cinema, this ontological defect of all photographic media coerces authors to create manifestations of thoughtless reproduction or, to better put it, empty displays of visual resemblances. Unlike painting, where the representations of reality contain the signs of the presence of a subjective mind, an artist "doing" the thinking about reality, the cinematic camera cannot offer "knowledge" about anything, since it only captures the real, producing a superficial copy. The philosophical dimension of films can be generated by the "dramatic" reenactments, induced by the film directors, but such interventions are fundamentally non-cinematic.

We shall return to the intentionalist problem, but for now this epistemic rejection of the qualities of the cinema as media is not without value. My own conceptual propositions regarding the *extra-cinematic* are developed considering the validity of Scrutton's criticism. A foundational problem remains if the elements providing philosophical meanings are filmic or extra-cinematic, since they function outside the boundaries of the photographic medium. Following Scruton's observations about how meanings are created by dramatic means (narration, dialogues, acting)—with the remarkable examples provided from Bergman's *Wild Strawberries*—any presence of intelligent thought activities in movies is a result of the director's mind inducing thinking by means other than those of the photographic camera. While the inner mechanics of cinematic production are incompatible with thinking, as the apparatus only creates the illusion of thinking, nevertheless thoughts are created by other means, which are perfectly integrated in the cinema machine.

We can group a separate category of authors who do not recognize cinema as a possible source of philosophical knowledge from another line of appraisals. The approach, which is following a culturally *dismissive* attitude, considers that films are only a form of facile amusement. Even when manifested as a form of philosophizing, movies are vulgarized versions of philosophies, designed for mass consumption, nothing more than primitive and superficial versions of profound thoughts. Their total rejection of the very possibility that films could think is also based on the assumption that the nature of the cinematic medium prevents the creation of autonomous thoughts. Here films are incapable of producing thinking not because cinema is *disconnected* from the philosophical, but because the thoughts created by cinema are *a-philosophical*.

This contemptuous attitude, which Mullarkey (2009) defines as philosophical "chauvinism," comprises all cultural critics who consider that mass culture, cinema included, undermines our deep thinking abilities. The main argument, as presented by Horkheimer and Adorno (1947/2002) in their seminal study on the *Dialectic of Enlightenment*, establishes an opposition between high arts (like painting) and lower arts (like photography), which places cinema into the discredited category of "light arts," based on distraction and gratuitous pastime. Integral to the cultural industries of capitalism, designed for the amusement of the multitudes, cinema never allows the expansion of the minds of the viewers and does not provide the intellectual space for subjective thought formation. Because films are mere reproductions of other mind's films, simply legitimizing "trash thoughts," "predigested ideas," we cannot acknowledge their contribution to the development of human thinking.

The a-philosophical set of assumptions, which range from the radical rejection to the utter disregard, presume that cinema is not simply incapable of profound thinking, but also that it makes us stupid. As popular entertainment uses multiple mechanisms of suppressing thinking, cinema is an integral part of this intellectual debasement. Instead of creating an environment for thought development, films are dumbing down our abilities to think; they block profound ideas from entering our minds or replace them with idiotic stereotypes. As the two critical theorists profess in their classical interpretation of the cultural industries mechanisms, films are crippling our ability to think (Horkheimer and Adorno 1947/2002: 100); they do not allow imagination and reflection to take shape. Fascinated by the moving images we are in fact distracted from thinking; the spectators are victims of absolute delusions and prone to imbecility.

A Nuanced Hypothesis. Not All Films Think Alike (Philosophically Speaking)!

An attempt to correct the negative effects of the binary model proposes a separation between "bad movies" (products of a cinema industry without the ability to generate thoughts) and "movies that think" (generally described as "good" movies, narrowly identified as "art films"). This setting apart of the "mind provoking" productions and those that lack any traces of thinking is deepening an already-wide fracture and raises another problematic set of definitions induced by the "hierarchical" ordering of films. When in one category we have art films and smart films, sharing the common qualities of thought-provoking activities, it is easy to identify "good movies" as the philosophical, with "the bad movies" placed at the bottom of the heap of cinematic creations.

This leads to an artificial differentiation between movie genres and moviemakers, while it eludes the real question, that of the thinking processes in cinema. When we separate the films which have philosophical meanings, from those that are unable to attain a higher level of conceptual relevance, we are in fact rejecting the possibility that the cinematic machine can think. By limiting what can qualify a film as "philosophical" these theorists are in fact creating a negative category, formed by the majority of cinematic productions, identified implicitly as *a-philosophical*. These issues are raised by the series of arguments developed by Noël Carroll, who proposed the restrictive definition, by establishing a high standard for films that can "do philosophy." The American philosopher of art suggested that a movie must provide an "original philosophical idea" in order to be philosophical. Thus, according to such constraining definitions, by which the film itself must provide an original contribution to the general exchange of ideas, opens a limited category of productions in which the cinematic content indicates a direct ability to produce innovative thoughts. Carroll, in an effort to prove his hypothesis that movies can do more than just "illustrate" philosophical ideas and concepts created outside the filmic universe, performed a partial evaluation. With the help of a minimalist artwork, Ernie Gehr's *Serene Velocity* (1970), we are encouraged to think that philosophy can be created only through those films that have an experimental approach to the means of "the art of the moving image" (Carroll 2006: 174). Carroll is in fact reducing the philosophical potential to the avant-garde and experimental films, which is not the case as I will attempt to demonstrate with the analysis of Porumboiu's films. A "philosophical thought experiment" is possible in any other cinematic form that explores the essences of the medium, without being limited to the avant-garde, by maintaining strong conceptual roots in this kind of experimentalism.

Nevertheless, we should establish whether films are philosophical works to the extent of the entire art form, created by the contribution of the ensemble of cinematic productions, or are not philosophical at all. This line of reasoning which takes us to the conclusion that *only some films* can be declared to be philosophical, while others are simply "parroting" philosophy or simply ineligible for this high status is not presenting a real solution to the question of film-thinking. With the help of the contemporary Romanian films discussed later, my argument is that a film can produce original ideas not only when the limits of the medium itself are questioned, but also when the interplay of other media is used as a thinking mechanism. And not only experimental films become credible sources of philosophical innovation, as they are "philosophzsing" about the nature of the art, but conventional productions can also give way to similar concepts, albeit under certain conditions.

A similar premise was advanced by Nitzan Ben Shaul, who places his own approach among other followers of the binary delineation separating a majority of films, which are simply cultivating a form of "close mindedness," and a few outstanding examples of movies in which our cognitive biases are contrasted and provoked. His reasoning involves a special category of films that "open the mind" and provide the spectators with "optional thinking." Ben Shaul's perspective is based on a cognitive theory foundation, and moves the center of attention to the viewers, rather than the ability of the cinematic machine or the moviemaker to generate innovative forms of thinking. The basic assumption is still within the *dismissive* approach, as it states that most films do not encourage thinking. Ben Shaul generally describes the cinema of "close mindedness" as a disparaging category, the one that encounters with films that lead to cognitive deficiency, where there is no efficiency or knowledge (Ben Shaul 2012: 113). At the other end are the distinguished films that naturally sway viewers to develop an "optional thinking," inducing a thought trajectory leading to unexpected results. Once again, the majority of the examples come from the same tradition of "modernist cinema," with Godard's *La Chinoise* (1967) providing the example for "loopy thinking" films that take the viewer into a mental maze, opening the mind to "optionality." While the Tel Aviv University professor critically re-evaluates the existing theories about classical cinema narration, definitions such as "incomprehensible films" presume that "optional thinking" is rare and that traditionally movies are underdeveloped when it comes to their ability to think.

This brings us to the other component of the binary model, which can be best described as the vertical separation dimension. This secondary axis divides again two major categories of films, those that exist outside the "industrial" and "amusement" complex versus a "profound" type of cinema, driven by ideas and providing a deep understanding.

The Vertical Model: Classical versus Modern Cinema

The positive–negative charging of the ability of movies to generate thoughts brings us to another problematic set of explanations, which are also perpetuating the limitations of the binary model. By separating two types of film-making practices, the result is the further division between two modes of thinking (Figure 1.5). The early example of this model was proposed by Gilles Deleuze, then was later assumed by many other film theorists. It

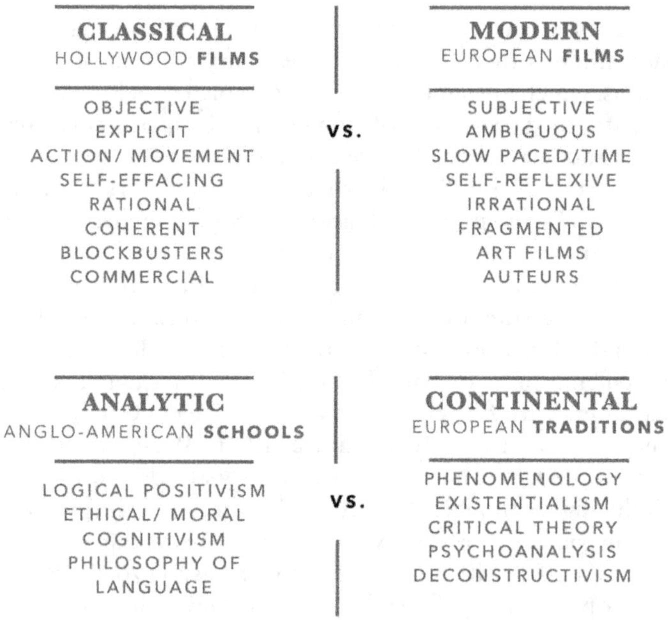

CLASSICAL HOLLYWOOD **FILMS**		MODERN EUROPEAN **FILMS**
OBJECTIVE EXPLICIT ACTION/ MOVEMENT SELF-EFFACING RATIONAL COHERENT BLOCKBUSTERS COMMERCIAL	**vs.**	SUBJECTIVE AMBIGUOUS SLOW PACED/TIME SELF-REFLEXIVE IRRATIONAL FRAGMENTED ART FILMS AUTEURS
ANALYTIC ANGLO-AMERICAN **SCHOOLS**		CONTINENTAL EUROPEAN **TRADITIONS**
LOGICAL POSITIVISM ETHICAL/ MORAL COGNITIVISM PHILOSOPHY OF LANGUAGE	**vs.**	PHENOMENOLOGY EXISTENTIALISM CRITICAL THEORY PSYCHOANALYSIS DECONSTRUCTIVISM

FIGURE 1.5 *Corresponding binary models: Classical versus Modern in film theory and Continental versus Analytical in philosophy.*

establishes a counterproductive distinction between the "classical" cinema and the "modern" cinema. Its prejudicial nature is based on a bias, already existing in the typologies advanced by the French philosopher. Convinced that there was a "Hollywood mode" of creating moving images, one based on linkages and using only rational cuts, he differentiated them from the presumed "modernist" films, a category of productions dominated by interstices and irrational cuts.

The same binary thinking was swiftly integrated in the studies of David Bordwell (1985) and his colleagues, who famously delineated the "classical" paradigm, or the so-called Hollywood style, from the "modern" stylistics. The classical was defined by an "excessively obvious" mode, based on "centered framing," while the "modern" ways of making movies were characterized by a different "mental set." The first paradigm presumably allows the viewers to think only by following logic and consistency, while the other is discontinuous and purposefully fragmented. Even if many contemporary movies made in Hollywood do not contradict such premises, authors like Quentin Tarantino or Christopher Nolan indicate that the regimes of cinematic representations are never following the binary model. Such dual modes of *cinematic thinking* are never unchangeable.

While another conceptual error is to use the "classical/modern" opposition for a medium that has nothing to do the with classicism, some practices are indeed an attribute of modernism. Many cinematic productions, in which various dis-narrative forms prevail, were developed by filmmakers like Antonioni or Godard who contested the "classicised" practices of mainstream cinema. Their use of the techniques of *décadrage* (dis-framing, see Bonitzer 1985) remains a basic tool for any modernist director; yet, these cannot be attributed to a single cinematic approach. While these instances seem proof enough to certify the binary thinking practiced by Deleuze, who distinguished between the presumed different modes of thinking in cinema (the movement-image and the time-image), such a vertical divide separating art cinema (often understood as modern cinema) and classic cinema (limited to Hollywood production) offers a set of typologies that are inoperable when trying to define how cinema really thinks. This set of distinctions only amplifies an already-existing dichotomy between two categories of films: those that *cannot think*, mostly because they "act" and are based on physical action and a basic narrative structure, and those that "think" because they have an inherent metaphysical predisposition, often confused with narrative complexity and ambiguity. Some films are naturally profound, reaching metaphysical depths, while others are providing access to an empirical understanding of reality.

I am not following this negative opposition for reasons to be detailed later, suffice it to say that by pursuing this train of thought we reach some extreme conclusions, as indicated by yet another preconception often vehiculated. Gilles Deleuze established that modernist cinema began with Visconti's *Obsession* (1943), thus imposing a perspective not only segregating "commercial cinema" from "art cinema," but also bringing about an additional complication resulting from the assimilation of "art films" with "modernist films" (Deleuze 1985/1989: 3–4). The idea was supported among others by András Bálint Kovács (2007) and Hamish Ford (2012), and traces a direct connection between subjectivity and modernity. Some of the important studies published by the Hungarian film critic are based on the presupposition that any film in which one can identify the stylistic features of modernism (minimalism, naturalism, ornamentalism, and theatricality) can be labeled as "art film"—with a special quality attributed to the "European art cinema" which are specially centered on subjectivity and reflexivity. By extension, all movies using cinematographic techniques that are unconventional become "deeply" philosophical.

A discrepant consequence, made possible by developing such premises, is illustrated by Daniel Frampton (2006). In his elaborated series of *filmosophical* arguments, mixing the "cinematic thought" of the avant-garde with various readings from Epstein and Deleuze, Frampton expands on the basic and relatively fatigued argument adopted by Carroll (2006). The narrow perspective identifies in all avant-garde films the intrinsic ability to "do philosophy," which has restrictive side effects. By extension, any incomprehensible and unintelligible film, any "moving images" based on any sorts of narrative incoherence or a slight stylistic ambiguity, assuming dissonant "artistic" principles and contradicting rules and conventions, becomes a source of film-philosophical thoughts. While the American art theorist equates avant-garde with the ability of filmmakers to articulate philosophical ideas and acquiesces to the implicit speculation that a limited number of art films (sometimes overlapping with European films) are "philosophical," Frampton jumps to the conclusion that almost all movies have a high degree of conceptualization. Later Carroll (2013: 207–8) also rejected parts of his own arguments, adhering to the possibility that "Europeanized" films can provide similar results. Using Christopher Nolan's *Memento* as an illustration, although Nolan is a British filmmaker, Carroll continues to search for arguments supporting his perspective, arguing that a "movie made philosophy" is possible only in the confines of the philosophy of art and only when commercial cinema opens to "deep" thinking, specific to experimental moviemaking. It must be pointed out that this horizontal separation between the nonlinear and enigmatic films, which might seem to be opposing the continuous and explicit productions, can lead to discriminative answers about the very nature of film-philosophy.

This divide is complicating any coherent account of the film-thinking processes and it derives from the competition between the wide range of philosophical sub-disciplines involved in the general debate. Since film-philosophy studies are marred by the separation lines created through the evolution of contemporary schools of philosophy, they engage movies following the sets of assumptions already developed in their respective field. Philosophers, as a result of their education and personal inclinations, tend to represent particular approaches. Coupled with the previously discussed predisposition to separate "European" and "Hollywood" film-making, this coincides with the expansion of another artificial demarcation. John Ó Maoilearca (2019), who elaborates a thorough overview of the divide between Analytic and Continental approaches in film-philosophy, the great conflict between the two is more a "conversation" than a philosophical confrontation. However, the consequence of this decade long philosophical clash spilled into the field of film theory, with David Bordwell and his followers radically rejecting any contributions of the "Grand Theory" to understanding films, considering that the ideas of European philosophers are irrelevant, and drawing their resources from the analytical thinking traditions. Maoilearca, formerly signing as John Mullarkey (2009), identified another set of opposing paradigms—"the Cavellian approach," defined as *pedagogical*, and the "Deleuzian perspective," understood as the "creative" method. No matter how we establish the relations between the "Continental schools of philosophy" (including Deleuze and other "Euro-culturalists") and the Analytical philosophies (generally involving the American philosophical schools), these are further deepened by the cognitivist and the culturalist conflicts mutating into film theory. The boundaries set by philosophers within their domain are influencing the critical discourses about cinema.

One preconception on this matter becomes explicit when overviewing the examples of "film-thinking" provided by various film theorists, with one particular illustration put forward in Bruce Kawin's (1978) seminal work on cinematic subjectivity. Trying to illustrate the instances in which the "intelligence" of movies is manifested, the film critic tends to base his arguments almost exclusively with excerpts from the movies of Bergman or Godard. The hidden problem here is not only how we establish the categories of films analyzed, but the implicit divide with the philosophical categories used.

Figure 1.5 organizes the fault lines going along the imaginary separation between two "grand philosophies," identified by Mullarkey (2009) as Anglo-Cognitivism and Euro-Culturalism, and establishes the links between the "culturalists" and the "cognitivists" in terms of the respective film theory approaches. Clashing on battlefields of concepts and ideas, they are blinded by the fact that they do not see eye to eye. When philosophical positionings are mutually exclusive they create predetermined choices and interpretations, thwarting the history and criticism of cinema. When showing preference for either the pragmatic approaches or the interpretative traditions, the range of movies discussed becomes limited by this philosophical theory bias. Since my own examples are extracted from recent Romanian cinema, the simplest and most aversive categorical segregation would be to dismiss these films as part of the European, modernist, art cinema traditions, which makes any discussion about their content reducible to the (multiple) perspectives of Continental philosophy. As I have put forth the reasoning elsewhere (Pop 2014), there are compelling arguments for positioning the Romanian New Wave films within the aesthetic currents of modernist cinema, mostly those of Neorealist extraction. I consequently realize that, by constantly using references to Deleuze or other European thinkers, my approach could be condescendingly linked to the "European" tradition of philosophising. Discussing movies in which self-reflexive representations are preponderant, presenting examples of filmmakers that easily fall into the paradigm identified by Elsaesser (2019: 13) as the European tendency for the "biopolitical," my approach might be mistaken for something else than I intend it to be.

As a matter of fact, I consider these positionings as restrictive and subsequently limiting any pertinent discussions. For the analytical philosophers, who are claiming ownership on the traditions of empiricism, positivism, or formalism, the Continental philosophy is an appalling betrayal of science, as it includes approaches close to psychoanalysis, Marxism, critical theory, poststructuralism, and phenomenology, as well as other hybrid forms of all these schools of thought. As Allen and Smith (1997: 1–36) perniciously simplified the discussions, the existing discord between what is called Continental philosophy (European thinkers from Nietzche to Deleuze) and the analytic philosophers (Anglo-American positivists and political thinkers) appears to be the cause of several intellectual biases. The Continental tradition has been attributed the traits of ambiguity and obscurity, while the analytic approach has occupied the territory of explicit and technical (Allen and Smith 1997: 2). As we can clearly observe, the pro-Continental versus pro-analytical divide is overlapping the "modernist" versus "classical" cinema segregation. Several contributions published in the volume edited by Allen and Smith indicate how post-structuralist theories and authors like Lacan or Derrida can be quickly discarded, while analytic philosophers are raised to an important status. The analytical philosophy claims empirical ascendancy and pretends to be the only one to provide "hard" scientific proofs in film studies, while the continental philosopher approaches seem to be heterogeneous and subjective. In contrast to the analytical philosophical perspectives, which are more politically motivated and oriented toward cultural history, the critical discussions or those focusing on film discourses are labeled as "metaphysical" considerations.

My perspective is based on the observations advanced by Jaques Rancière (2006), who convincingly argued that the theoretical separation lines segregating Hollywood cinema and modernist or art cinema are conceptually flawed. The cinematic medium itself was created within the paradigm of the modern aesthetic regime, and it remains part and parcel of this "aesthetic age." The mechanical reproduction of images allowed every form of representation to be elevated to the dignity of art, even the most banal objects and situations are prone to meaning-making. As the oppositions between "entertainment" and "artistic" were abolished by this French philosopher, who criticizes both Bazin's approximations and Deleuze's theorizations (Rancière 2006: 107), he annuls also the cogent explanations provided by the Deleuzian dichotomy between time-image and movement-image. Cinema is in fact a dream come true of this new regime of art created by modern thinking and we should never forget that moviemaking is quintessentially a modern technology, born out of the revolution induced by modern art and especially by Dadaist thinking. As the importance of Dadaism will be further analyzed, another philosophical paradigm needs to be addressed at this point.

The Radical Posture: Cinema as an Anti-philosophical Machine

The truly radical definitions about the role played by cinema in the transformation of human thinking were formulated in a series of essays published by French avant-garde filmmaker Jean Epstein, in the first decades of the twentieth century. While he is better known for coining another important notion, that of "photogénie," the genius of the movie camera, this remarkable poet and philosopher also elaborated a thought-inspiring theory about cinema, which we cannot simply label as a "bold" thesis. The definitions proposed by Livingston (2006) and others are inapplicable since the arguments advanced by this remarkable film theorist and moviemaker elude the classifications of such trite categories.

The influential opinions published by Epstein during the early 1920s in a book of poetic essays entitled "Bonjour Cinema," anticipated the idea that the philosophy of cinema will be to be created (Epstein 1921: 35). At that time he was pondering the possibility that the cinematic screen was a psychic device that, together with the celluloid, was transforming the way in which ideas were created and understood by humanity. The new technology taking over the world was displaying a particular form of thinking, which was just another manifestation of ideas that permitted a special thought process. In cinema, claimed Epstein, the ideas were substantiated without a conscience of their own. Once recorded as a material form, the film itself, they are projected on-screen, and by this ideas shifted their consistency, becoming "ideas of an idea" (Epstein 1921: 38).

This intuition, that ideas resided on the material surface of the celluloid, was later revised in a more revolutionary outlook, which in turn influenced authors like Deleuze and the entire group of foundational explanations based on the underlying conviction that cinema was a true *thinking machine*. Epstein (1946: 46–7) observed that cinema functioned like a *mechanical brain* and that a form of intelligence was displayed in films, generating a *robot-brain* philosophy ("philosophie d'un cerveau-robot"). As this cinematic *machine to think* ("machine à penser") was developing, it was slowly creating a philosophy of its own (Epstein 1946: 71), one that Epstein predicted two decades before the development of the field of studies we are discussing here.

Another extreme claim made by Epstein was that this brain was completely different from that of the human organ. It is here that the superficial readings of his conceptualizations created the biggest confusions between the capacity of cinema to generate philosophical thinking and the real nature of the ideas produced by the "mechanical brain." The cinematic form of thought was not similar to anything that was previously available to human philosophers. Epstein trenchantly describes the intelligence of the cinema machine as a *new form* of understanding the world, one completely opposed to the "old" ways of thinking. As he concludes the highly original subchapter from "The Intelligence of a Machine," dedicated to the philosophy of cinema, even if the cinematographic thought has some recognizable manifestation similar to traditional philosophy, it would always be an *anti-philosophy*.

This is why we cannot simply place Epstein as a proponent of a "bold" thesis; he is forthright antagonistic to philosophical thinking as understood by human culture before the arrival of cinema. In another work, more provocatively called "The Cinema of the Devil" (1947), the French theorist and artist took further these controversial explanations, stating that cinema was a *diabolical* art. Here too we must understand such assertions as diametrically opposed to the "traditional" philosophical processes. By consequence, the Cartesian or Kantian traditions of philosophy were now obliterated and replaced by a revolutionary new philosophy, having destabilizing effects since the real intelligence of cinema was instinctual, poetic, and not reasonable. Any philosophical effects of cinema are thus a result of the liberation it provides from the captivity of "primitive" thinking and this is why for Epstein this "diabolical" philosophy was sharing the traits of anti-dogmatic, revolutionary, and libertarian thinking. Films are "diabolical" in the sense that they are liberating us from the "despotic expansion of logic" (Epstein 1947: 325) belonging to "the first reasoning," derived from Cartesian thinking.

The arguments from "Le Cinéma du diable" place the philosophy of the cinema in a novel and unfamiliar ground. Any form of thinking produced by this machine is based on a revolutionary type of reasoning, one which he calls "a second reason," contrasting with the common sense of rationality, and contrary to the causality-based reasoning. Cinema functions like a "super-organ," one which is receptive to fluidity and inconsistency, not stability and certitude. As traditional thinking, based on continuity and consistency, is replaced by a new sensorial mode, films are creating a completely new experience, producing a change of knowledge, transforming the ideas that we form in our minds. Even our relationship with time is changed and a new dimension of space is created, which is profoundly *unnatural*. This makes any philosophy residing inside the cinematic machine, to be anti-philosophical in the sense that we normally understand Western philosophizing. Even if Epstein's conclusion was that the cinematographic universe was closer to Sartrean thinking, characterized by an existentialist fluidity, basically this philosophy of the fluid experience offers a radical as provocative perspective. By altering the mental state of the viewers, their memories, and their dreams, cinema reshapes our personalities and is providing access to our "irrational ego."

Thus the claims that the cinematic machine has its own intelligence must concede to the fact that cinema functions as a new "thinking machine" allowed by modernity, one that is creating its own philosophical mode that is not based on reason, rather a result of "a multi-sensorial" experience. Because they provide a completely different form of thinking, movies are opening a pathway to what Epstein called the fourth dimension (la quatrième dimension), one making any cinema an "anti-logical" machine.

As an avant-garde filmmaker, Epstein created some of the most challenging cinematic works of his time, and it is relevant to point out that movies, such as *Cœur fidèle* (*Faithful Heart*, 1923), *La Chute de la maison Usher* (*The Fall of the House of Usher*, 1928), or *Finis Terrae* (*The End of the Earth*, 1929), are explorations of the limits of moviemaking, using reality and even narration as a pathway to break the boundaries of understanding to bring about that which is beyond the represented world, an experience transcending the appearances. He called this practice the cine-mystical (Epstein 1921: 115–16) illustrating his view that films should not adhere to rational logic, that cinema should function as an antidote against the existing literary culture, providing a sort of irrational and intuitive experience.

Malcolm Turvey (2008) described this vision about a cinematic art capable not simply to show reality, but to disclose those dimensions of human existence that are invisible, as "revelationist cinema." This remarkable property, which can be traced in many movies, is extremely important for my exploration. While Turvey limits the "revelationist" dimension to the practical and technical abilities of cinema (close-ups, slow motion, time-lapses, irrational editing) and explains his conceptualizations as part of a "visual skepticism," the French essayist and filmmaker defined the "intelligence of the machine" as an autonomous system of conscience, capable of developing a "rich philosophy full of surprises" (Epstein 1946: 71) and having a "revelatory" function.

Epstein, clearly inspired by the philosophical thinking of Henri Bergson, developed his own understanding of cinema as a "machine to think." Defined as an "intellectual robot," cinema re-thinks the main categories used by the human mind, such as time and space. The argument that the machine mind of cinema and the human mind were completely different manifestations was a truly radical conception about movies and thinking. Consequently, this definition leads to the inference that a new form of thinking is produced by films. This is a mechanical philosophy inherent to the nature of cinema, one that is changing the human mind. This is why Epstein is inappropriately presented as a precursor of filmosophy and other similar approaches. His understanding of cinema is radically different from those of Frampton and the supporters of cinema as philosophical mind theories. Actually, the French filmmaker and writer considered cinema to be a form of *anti-philosophy*. Any philosophy created in and by cinema was the result of a revolutionary transformation of reality into a second reality, which was fluid and gaseous, producing a new type of reasoning, identified as a "second reason" (Epstein 1947).

Anti-philosophising: In the Spirit of Dada

Boris Groys (2012) traces the roots of "anti-philosophy" in the works of Lacan and Badiou and observes a direct connection between "anti-art," in the sense proposed by Hans Richter's "Dada: Art and Anti-Art" (1964) and "anti-philosophy." The foundational element of this association is represented by the "Da-da" attitude, which can be linked with cinematic anti-philosophy. The analogy between anti-philosophy and the aesthetics of Dadaism and Duchamp's "Fountain" used by Groys is relevant also for our understanding of how cinematic anti-philosophy works. When a character in a film acts in an apparently ordinary situation, for example, in Antonioni's *L'Avventura* (1960), which seems to be emptied of any profound meaning besides its realistic depiction of a life lacking complexity, the moviemaker in fact approaches the life situation as a readymade object. By placing the drama in contexts such as a banal kitchen or a public park, a cinematic situation becomes a form of producing philosophical meanings by simply transferring usages—from an original purpose lacking any depth to another dimension with aesthetic and philosophical potential.

Since the most important characteristic of any anti-art is the reuse of a readymade object, also manifested in the ability of Dadaism to take existing texts or contents and repurpose them in another form, cinema can be anti-cinematic in the most profound sense. I follow here the line of reasoning proposed by Rancière (2011/2014) when developing the notion of *deviation*—for a better understanding of the translation problems for the French *écart* see Bowman (2013). Cinema was a new artistic machine capable of producing art without leaving any trace of its artistic mechanisms. This *écart* means a "deviant" ability activated whenever a filmmaker takes objects from reality and transforms them into a new form and content, without leaving any perceptual sign to trace this transformation. The French philosopher argued that cinema did fulfill its anti-representational promises, although commercial films might induce the sensation that it did not. In fact, the cinema machine, even in popular movies, provides access to an impalpable reality; its meanings are created in the gaps, deficiencies, and the apparent defects (Rancière 2011/2014: 11–12). Cinema truly achieves the perfect solution to the problems raised by futurists like Marinetti or constructivists like Mayakovsky; it hides any signs of its production mechanisms (Rancière 2011/2014: 32).

In this sense, a filmmaker acts like an *antiphilosopher*. Using pre-existing forms of thinking, then placed in un-philosophical contexts, such as the cinematic mise-en-scène, the thoughts and ideas are transformed by the re-enactment within the new medium. When cinema-makers take readymade philosophical ideas and refurbish them in a different context, it might appear as a banal endeavor. When done in a simplistic manner, this is a form of film *with* philosophy. Yet it does not mean that all moviemakers are simply parroting philosophical concepts. The proof relies upon the fact that the cinematic machine itself can be a creative environment generating a type of anti-philosophical transformation.

As observed by Groys (2012: xiv), anti-philosophy is not by any measure a form of philosophical destruction. In point of fact, it provides the necessary context for the survival of philosophy and philosophical thinking. When philosophical discourses available only outside the cinema are integrated into the multiple layers of the film production, from the simplest form, as aggregated pieces of dialogue, where the characters exchange ideas that can be linked to great thinkers, to the structural integration into the narratives of moral problems and thought-provoking situations, the moviemaking machine is transforming them into anti-philosophical instruments. Since I will return to the importance of Dada thinking in cinema, a partial conclusion here is that film-making provides a type of philosophical experience even when it seems to be *non-philosophical*.

The *Discrete* Paradigm—Cinema with an *Intrinsic* Capacity to Think

The possibility that film-thinking can happen *inside* the cinematic machine was approached from two different directions. One is more controversial, while the other is based on the generalizing assumption that all movies can create meanings that cinema naturally "meets" philosophy (Vaughan 2013). Both expound on the principle of *connectivity* which, as pointed out before, allows us to reconceptualize the previously advanced hypotheses. These divergent positions, usually grouped together, constitute a general category describing films as being "able to think," together with the idea that philosophy is inherent to cinema. They can range from the material speculations about the presence of the philosophical ideas inside narratives to the narrower considerations that cinema is somehow an autonomous philosophical machine or that films have an intrinsic capacity to generate philosophical concepts.

Since these theoretical propositions are addressing the same claim that films somehow are able to function independently from extraneous (or allogenic) influences, we can briefly describe these explanations as the *discrete* paradigm. Any theory proposing that cinema has "a mind of its own," either material or spiritual belongs to the *discrete* assumption. The authors supporting it consider that cinema thinking happens autonomously and separated from any other form of thought process, both the radical presuppositions and the "banal" thesis, are following the *discrete* hypothesis. Either by attributing cinema the qualities of an autonomous mind, or by interpreting philosophical ideas that reside inside movies, we accept this paradigmatic presupposition—the ability of films to think or to elaborate thoughts within the apparatus.

The *discrete* theories, presented usually in the film and philosophy textbooks, take for granted the fact that philosophical thinking is individualized in cinema. While the practical definitions understand the ability to "do philosophy" as a matter of finding external explanations or to identify discernible solutions to various problems (social, personal, aesthetic) in cinematic examples, the discrete approaches are always searching for internalized manifestations. One relevant example is provided by the various philosophies of particular cinematic genres, such as the philosophy of horror, as it was developed by Noël Carroll (1990) in his influential study, or the multiple philosophies of films noir. By identifying the repetitive conventions in a particular genre, which accumulate into a specific form of thinking, the philosophical analysis reaches the conclusion that certain films can raise questions internally linked to their particular mode of expression.

Probably the most comprehensive definition for the *discrete* perspective was articulated by the French filmmaker Jean-Luc Godard in the fifth episode of his video essay entitled *Histoire(s) du cinéma*. Tracing back to modern painting, and specifically to Manet, the ability of cinema to behave like a "form that thinks" (*une forme qui pense*), Godard considers this art a form *made especially for thinking*. In the following discussions, the focus moves toward this predisposition, one that Godard did not develop any further.

The *Autonomous* Hypothesis. Films Are Naturally Philosophical

A group of philosophers and media critics propose the idea that all contemporary technologies, including cinema, are "philosophical machines."

Our technologies are special because they allow us to think in a different way, and the movement of images on the screen is considered to be the most influential, by inducing various movements in our minds and bodies. The "thinking-with-images" hypothesis must be placed in a larger perspective, consistently addressed by Ron Burnett, who extensively discusses what happens in the minds of contemporary humans under the effect of technologically generated images. The Canadian professor supports the premise the all visual media are able to think, with the implicit suggestion that all our "intelligent instruments," the media that are creating images (photography, cinema, video), are also implicating our minds in a process of thought creation. They serve more than a cultural role and have more than just a psychological impact or an aesthetic effect. Visual technologies not only create thinking, they even represent new ways of thinking (Burnett 2004: 102). The claim that all the images available in the global visual media dominating the contemporary world are no longer simple representations, they reached a level when they express the technological intelligence that created them, that they are tools by which we are making sense of our world is provocative but impossible to substantiate. There is no conclusive evidence to suggest that we are thinking with images more than our ancestors did before us. The presupposition could be that we are "wired for images" (Burnett 2004: 9) at a much more primitive level needs to be taken with a grain of salt until conclusive evidence can be provided.

While Bernard Stiegler described this process as "technogenesis," a continuous influence of technologies on humanity, where our machines have reorganized the human mind, his hypothesis also claims that the invention of modern mnemotechnical apparats (phonograph, photograph, cinematograph) allowed the rise to a new kind of memory, functioning besides the genetic and somatic memories. Stiegler (2011: 6–7) identifies this as "epi-phylogenetic memory," the direct result of the transformations happening during the nineteenth century, when the structure of modern human consciousness was subjected to a cinematographic alteration. In contemporary globalized capitalism, where technological images are omnipresent, thinking is ingrained in these visual media.

A similar assumption was also developed by the media philosopher Vilém Flusser. Arguing that the photographic medium is profoundly philosophical and, more importantly, that it represents the starting point for any form of philosophy (Flusser 2018: 68), this media theorist is rejecting the long-standing arguments that there is a metaphysical dimension of the apparatus. Clearly opposing the thesis advanced by Scrutton and other media disconnection theorists, Flusser's perspective nevertheless accepts that the invention of photography was a major turning point in human history. This ushered humanity into post-history, with "textolatry" replaced by photography (Flusser 2018: 16). This new magical ritual of technical images is not based on "objectivity." All images generated by optical, chemical, or mechanical devices are expressions of subjectivity, since the camera is always operated by a human being modeling the subsequent experience with that reality (Flusser 2018: 14–15). Flusser (38) criticizes the opinion which claims that we see the real world *through* the photographic device, that somehow the universe depicted by photographic machines can be identifiable with the world outside. The philosophy of photography (68) is created by the inherent dialectical tension between man and machine, between the apparatus and appearance. The simplest example, used by the Brazilian philosopher to illustrate his arguments, is black and white images. When we see them in contemporary movies, like *The Artist* (r. Hazanavicius 2011), we perceive them as authentic; yet, they never exist in normal reality. So the film meanings, albeit realistic, are never created at the immediate surface of the photographic representation. When we look at any images created by any photographic machine (photo camera, video camera), we do not see reality itself. In the opposing opinions about the nature of photographic images, they are either *transparent* or *opaque*, with an ontologically realistic dimension (as it is for Bazin 1967) or capable to produce or reproduce thoughts as translucent (Walton 2008) manifestations.

If the thought processes are not simply intermediated by the photographic machines and philosophy is inherent to the functioning of the apparatus, which is the basis for defining film-thinking as autonomous, we need to explain how our experience with these mechanical machines is transformed into thoughts. Some critics of the philosophical capacities of cinema are presumptuously denouncing the lack of discrete qualities, since there are no independent conditions in which philosophical ideas can be expressed only by film means. Cinematic thinking cannot be autonomous because the *transparency* of the medium presents us with a direct experience of reality. There is nothing more than what the photographic camera records; the photographic medium has no possibility to penetrate the surface of the represented reality.

As we already discussed, the central argument of these theories remains similar to the disqualification of cinema as philosophical since it lacks access to the traditional philosophical instruments. Cinema, as a visual medium, is fundamentally a-philosophical; its access to textual forms of communication, which are necessary conditions in order to become "philosophy-like," is limited and primitive. One possible counter-argument against such inadequacies is related to the allogenic explanations. The rationalization, as formulated by Felicity Colman (2009), is that all "screen-based" arts are in a dynamic relationship with their users; they can "question and destroy" philosophical beliefs, thus have the power to reconfigure knowledge. In practice, all forms of communication sharing "cinematic" traits (video games, other mobile screens included) have the ability to convey thoughts and opinions. Colman (2009: 1–2) considers that meanings are created by the overall "screen form" and not by each individual film. Philosophical thoughts take shape in our engagement with the screen representations, since films inherently have an impact on our thought processes.

The second type of answers expand some of the theories elaborated by Soviet filmmaker and theorist Sergei Eisenstein. The assumption is that, because it can create ideas in the minds of the viewers, cinema is a *conceptual* and *mental medium*. Eisenstein extensively problematized the ability of films to "form thoughts" in our minds (Eisenstein 1976: 12) and realized that this is done within the mechanics of this art. Attempting, for political reasons, to understand how films can convey ideas (or rather ideology) Eisenstein identified editing as the fundamental means through which cinema induces thoughts. In the tradition of revolutionary cinema, this was a new art that could provide the working class with an instrument of social consciousness. Movies could make people think, and the problem was how to make them think in a "proper" way.

The solution of the soviet moviemaker was practical, expressed in the theory of the "intellectual montage." The modality through which cinema was able to change the world resided in its inner mechanisms. While the Eisensteinian theories about montage are complex and manifold, for the purpose of this discussion it would be relevant to point out only that his famous theory about "intellectual cinema" identifies several processes which materialized ideas and thoughts on screen. Through montage and from the collision of opposing shots (Eisenstein 1949: 28–44) a moviemaker was able to create ideas. A derived idea functions as an ideogram, the famous metaphor used by Eisenstein in which cinematic images have a correspondence in Japanese hieroglyphs. Two distinct images, linked together in the cinematic machine, had profound conceptual aptitudes and they could change the minds of human beings.

Eisenstein reached the limits of this mechanism and faced the impossible transformation of cinema into a purely ideological machine when he tried to make a film based on *Das Kapital*. As explained by Annette Michelson (1976), one of the translators of his essays, his intention was to make progress toward the "films of the future" which he believed will be philosophical. However, as it transpires from the diaries kept by Eisenstein, he was forced to abandon this ambitious project.

The only palpable result was the film *October: Ten Days That Shook the World* (1927) which was rebuked by Party officials as "unintelligible for the millions." The difficulties of such a project, while not directly linked to the possibility to illustrate Marx's ideas, were reworked by the author of montage theory in other films, but the problem remained the same. How can the cinematic experience created by the collision of visual elements, which obviously can lead to cognitive transformations, be more than "a tractor plowing over the audience's psyche"? (1925/1988: 62). Through montage the moviemaker can generate ideas and symbols, controlled meanings instilled by the director into the film experience. Himself influenced by the material and cultural constraints of society, the director is unable to transmit the subtleties of his ideas beyond the limitations of the cinematic medium.

Eisenstein realized that the relationship between the "material-technical" dimension of film making, its social significance, and the ideological relevance is by no means resolved. Some of the following discussions will move along this line of questioning, as the contention that films have a philosophical dimension that supersedes the attributes of the cinematic mechanisms will be central to my arguments. The *discrete* qualities of movies, their technical power to generate ideas, are also their limitations. Only by breaking these constraints cinema is able to be more than a philosophical "machine."

Can Films Do Everything That the Philosophers Do?

Films can provide a stimulus for philosophical reflection and they can certainly be thought-provoking. As extensively argued in a recent work published by Robert Pippin, who follows closely the tradition of Stanley Cavell, films are forms of philosophical reflection whether or not we consider them as philosophical. This American philosopher maintains that, since films already function as vehicles of thought, allowing us to think about ourselves, about others, and about our world (Pippin 2020: 6), their function is uncontestable.

But the question here is not if we can consider films as "modes of reflective thought," as argued by Pippin, who is disinterested in debating if the results are philosophical. When accepting the hypothesis that *all films* are philosophical, as initially supported by the American philosopher Stanley Cavell, followed by others like Stephen Mulhall (2002), the extension of these arguments is not unproblematic. If there is a *cinematic mode of thinking*, then all films are able to think alike and all films are making a contribution to the intellectual debate of humanity which can ripple back to Descartes and even Plato. This is an assumption that leads to incredible efforts of persuading us that even contemporary blockbusters are carriers of philosophical meanings.

So what is the "philosophical mode" of cinema, one that we can identify in every and all films, even in those that are apparently designed for sheer entertainment that grants them with this ability? For Mulhall (2002: 2) films are "thinking in action," philosophical exercises capable of enacting philosophical themes. As argued by Cavell (1971) films are natural recipients for thinking. By providing viewers with the ability to learn from their cinematic experiences, they automatically generate philosophical solutions. Another philosophically buoyant answer is that the cinema machine can handle the same philosophical issues like any other medium invented by humanity, that the ideas generated on the screens all over the world can form a particular continuum of thoughts that is not inferior to the total output of classical authors. We can hear the "philosophical voice" of cinema (Mulhall 2005: 67) because films have a "distinct register" in which they are emitting philosophy. This allows many authors, as is the case with William G. Smith (2004), to identify philosophical ideas in almost every genre possible, from Holocaust movies to romantic comedies.

We can question the accuracy of this premise with a brief but relevant discussion about another truism formulated by the French film critic and filmmaker, Alexandre Astruc (1948). In his theory about the "caméra-stylo" (the camera as a pen), he proclaimed that Descartes today would choose cinema as his expressive instrument. This apparently groundbreaking observation is only a paraphrase to Maurice Nadeau, who claimed that Descartes would write novels if he were alive. But Astruc presses this idea forward and claims that the philosophers would "shut himself up in his bedroom with a 16mm camera and some film, and would be writing his philosophy on film" (Astruc 1948: 159). Notwithstanding the incongruous nature of this observation, since one can only wonder what kind of films could Descartes create alone in his bedroom, the proposition that movies have the capacity to be a new philosophical instrument is exposed. With Astruc claiming that contemporary ideas and the present-day philosophies of life are represented properly only by cinema, he also distinguished between the "cinema of thought" and the cinema of entertainment.

Returning to the assumptions that films can contribute to philosophy, we need to question if there is a technical dimension to this "reflective" mode of thinking, which is produced by the camera, or we can describe a more profound transformation of the reasonable mind (the Cartesian "cogito"), induced by cinema.

The Brazen Hypothesis: The *Intrinsic* Thinking Capacity of the *Filmind*

Daniel Frampton's provocative book entitled *Filmosophy* (2006) is advancing a self-proclaimed "revolutionary" theory, one that could provide a completely new way of understanding how "film thinks." Often described as the most important exponents of the "bold" thesis, Frampton's manifesto takes the philosophical potential of films to the extreme. Although the arguments presented are not necessarily innovative, the insinuation that there can be a "film-being" capable of thinking is inciting. Frampton attempts to redefine the cinematic thinking processes with the help of a couple of newly coined concepts—such as filmind or film-thinking. Even more ambitiously, the filmosopher stakes the creation of a new science; "filmosophy" is centered around the possible "conceptualizing" of all film as an "organic intelligence" (Frampton 2006: 7).

While this theory might be placed in the *autonomous* paradigm, as the author presupposes an intrinsic capacity of the cinematic machine to think, Frampton acknowledges that his approach is in fact a return to older arguments. The premise was already put forward by French cinema Impressionists, like Dulac or Epstein, and was combined with readings from Deleuze and some contemporary phenomenological propositions. By picking bits and pieces of his exposition from Epstein, who, as we have seen before, was in fact speculating about a different form of "cinematic thinking," Frampton advances the notion that all movies, from the very beginning of this new art form to the digital cinema of today, are producing a "filmic kind of thought." This "a new mind" identified in films, however, is clearly separated from the notion of film-thinking in Epstein's view. Instead, the creator of filmosophy redefines the "filmind" as having more than its own particular film-phenomenology, it has its own "new kind of thinking" (Frampton 2006: 48); it is not a mechanical or a robotic brain, but an organic manifestation. Here the confused and unclear dialectics between the organic and the mechanical nature of film philosophy and also the relationship between the metaphorical and the technological rearranging of reality made possible by cinema become counterproductive. With the author professing the elaboration of an "ur-method" of understanding film philosophy, his work is a little less than a follow-up of the thesis that films are philosophical. This completely "new science," one that Frampton inspiredly labeled and conceptualized, is nothing more than another portmanteau misnomer for an older paradigm, speculating that the films themselves are somehow coalescing into a distinct film-thinking mode.

Unfortunately, the presumed existence of a "filmind," a practical and simultaneously idealistic mode specific to cinema, unique kind of thinking specific only to this technology, is not supported with any innovative examples. The few practical examples that are supposedly indicating how "filmosophical cinema" works are extracted from authors like Béla Tarr, Michael Haneke or the Dardenne brothers, who were already used as exemplary for philosophical filmmaking. Suggestive as they may be, the inconsistent cinematic evidence do not provide enough illustrations for how all films are able to think. The "filmosophical" lingo of the book fails to provide plausible explanations for the divide between the "film being" (basically the creator of the movie) and the "film mind" (the thinking of the film itself). The readers are presented with a very sketchy account, even when it comes to the in-depth analysis of the few movies selected. The most convincing arguments, based on interpreting a new generation of canonical movies, which are developing unreliable narrations, together with the easily recognizable transformation of the narrative strategies in contemporary cinema, are not enough. While the foundations of the innovative concept of filmosophy are similar to those of all authors linking film-thinking and the human mind, when we are simply claiming that films have a mind of their own produced by a "para-narrational" manifestation, which is both poetic and affective, this is not much different from that of the already-existing narrative interpretations. And, however attractive the idea of a general filmosophy might be, the fact is that classical Hollywood films do no "think" in the same way as those created by the New American Cinema, and the spectacular 3D cinema extravaganzas do not share the same "filmind" with the avant-garde experiments.

The debates around Frampton's concept of *filmind* reveal in fact the limitations of all explanatory models based on the *connectivity* between films and the human mind, especially when coupled with the notion of *autonomy* in film-thinking. Frampton pushes the presuppositions about the cinematic machine as radically different from the human mind in a completely contradictory direction. On the one hand, he reuses the concept of "film-thinking" as if completely different from "human thinking," then adds the presumed possibility of "film-thinking" to manifest as "a combination of idea, feeling and emotion." Many problematic issues remain unresolved by Frampton. Films are non-human, yet organic; they "think," but need a filmgoer to be present and watch them; there is no external force driving the filmind; however, the mechanisms that show the thinking, the characters, and actions doing the "thinking" cannot be ignored. Despite the criticism, this filmosopher's argument that the filmind produces a different kind of philosophy, as a manifestation at the "end of philosophy," remains meaningful.

For a New Philosophical Machine

Frampton's arguments are basically a re-reading of a fundamental premise developed previously by Gilles Deleuze, who claimed that films not only think in a specific mode, but also advanced the idea that cinema can provide philosophy with an unprecedented access to a dimension previously unattainable. For this reason, we must take a closer look at the arguments of the French philosopher, who is considered by many theorists as the most important representative of the "super bold thesis" (Smuts 2009). At a first look, it seems that the argument that films *are* thinking sounds like a "provocative" suggestion. Nevertheless, Deleuze's philosophical writings on cinema are unjustly identified only with the "films *as* philosophy" paradigm. We should also ignore the deformed readings of his cinema works, since the author of two of the most philosophical books about cinema ever written was not simply proposing a new philosophy *of* cinema. While Deleuze offers the perfect example of a philosopher who simultaneously functions as a film theorist, his interpretations and typologies describing what is happening *inside* the cinematic are not preoccupied with film practices or techniques.

The analysis is opened to a larger understanding, that of the cinematic modes of thinking. It is not the object of this book to go deeper into the taxonomies proposed by Deleuze, nor to explain the method of "cineosis" practiced by the French philosopher; the studies of Marrati (2008) or Deamer (2016) amply explain these aspects. Instead, the second major proposition of his system of thinking, that movies can "wake philosophy from its catatonic sleep," is more relevant.

As observed by D. N. Rodowick, the foundation of the philosophical reversal attempted by Deleuze stems from the idea that cinema has become a "philosophical machine" (Rodowick 2010: xiii), one generating ideas that reside *outside* the individual films we are watching. The announced "marriage" between philosophy and cinema has engendered a true *cinema of philosophy*, illustrated for Deleuze by the innovative film of Alain Resnais. The Deleuzian method cannot be apprehended without a clear comprehension of his effort to re-negotiate the nature of philosophy. His intuition was that the essence of the cinematographic apparatus contained the necessary illustrations for the wholesale renewal of the philosophical. In fact this is one of the most important contributions Deleuze has made to the field of film and philosophy, albeit not in the conventional sense attributed to him. There are two aspects important for our current discussion. The first is, following the conclusions from *Cinema 2*, that "cinema's concepts are not given in cinema" (Deleuze 1985/1989: 280). The "cinema of thought," which basically represented the main stimulus for Deleuze to be interested in cinema generally, brought about some of the most remarkable works in the field, providing the necessary illustrations through which the French theorist was able to rethink the relationship between the philosophical ideas and "thought-images." Considering that film images work as concepts and sometimes as pure philosophical thoughts, Deleuze discovered a new set of philosophical concepts *within* cinema. His works would later inspire many other film-philosophers, some ignoring the Deleuzian caveats that not every philosophical conversation is "Philosophy" and that not every concept becomes relevant philosophically.

With cinema becoming a preferred site of philosophy, a new mode of thinking was made evident by the intervention of the philosopher, who extracted thoughts from film examples. For Deleuze the philosophical concepts are *inside* cinema, they reside in the cinematic medium itself. The premise is no longer to try and discover the philosophical references within movies; it is the other way around, with the cinematic generating concepts for philosophy.

This change of perspective is made more explicit in another study, dealing with a more complex question, what is philosophy? As a result of the collaborative work of Deleuze and Guattari, this book opens with defining philosophy as a discipline that *"creates* concepts" (Deleuze and Guattari 1991/1994: 5). This is why, when Deleuze lines up examples from cinema, he makes an effort to salvage philosophy in an age that has replaced philosophical thinking with other forms of vehiculating ideas—sociology or mass communication are just two of the surrogates that conquered the space of traditional philosophy (Deleuze and Guattari 1991/1994: 15). Only when philosophy is combined with the novelty machine that is cinema, the potential of this "marriage" brings about an innovative way of discovering new philosophical concepts. The fact that the cinematic machine exists outside the traditional philosophical discourses can provide the necessary rejuvenation of an "old" mode of conceptualization.

A better explanation of this effort is clearly stated in *Difference and Repetition*, where the French philosopher considers that "doing philosophy" in the modern world represents a combination of a detective novel and science-fiction (Deleuze 1968: 3), both mechanisms perfectly integrated into cinematic productions. Since philosophical books can no longer be written in the "old style," the philosopher must search for new forms of expression. Since the proper medium for philosophy is no longer provided by traditional books, with other media like cinema offering a new platform, the objective clearly stated by Deleuze was to rediscover the true source of philosophical ideas. From the apparition of philosophy in ancient Greece, to the announced death of philosophy (Thomas-Fogiel 2011) or the apparition of "post-philosophies" which consider Western and European philosophical conceptualizations as obsolete disciplines, the apparition of cinema represented the most innovative force of "fabricating concepts." This does not mean a new and vulgarizing form to problematize philosophical ideas, as illustrated by the *banal* approaches. By expanding its reach in cinema, Deleuze believed that by creating a "pop'philosophie" (Deleuze 1996: 10) a new philosophical "mode" (or style) can be uncovered to human thinking. It is a term misleadingly translated in English as "Pop philosophy," since Deleuze was looking for answers in modern cinema, not in blockbusters or popular movies. Once again, it must be underlined that by using cinematic examples we are not explicating existing theories, nor can we indicate what philosophy means. We are simply extracting the philosophical from the cinematic.

As noted by Gregory Flaxman (2008: 10), one of the specialists in Deleuzian thinking and cinema, cinema breathes a "new air" into philosophy; it becomes a pathway to stimulate a practice as old as human civilization, one leading to the creation of a "future philosophy." Flaxman (2008: 324) concludes that where philosophy ends, cinema begins. This future development of philosophy and the new form of thinking will be able to "express the inexpressible," a capacity now available in cinema. More importantly, Deleuze and Guattari (1991/1994: 205) conclude their mapping of the philosophical mind with the observation that philosophy needs a non-philosophy in order to be understood. And what better non-philosophical instrument than the cinematic?

Cinema Thinking from a Non-philosophical Perspective

In the early 1990s, the French philosopher François Laruelle (1989/2013) advanced an important set of explanations leading to the creation of an autonomous discipline, named *non-philosophy*. Proposing a non-philosophical method, which must be understood as a critical discipline contesting the higher Authority of philosophy as the unique or superior form of thinking, this theoretical and practical approach does not mean a denial of the philosophical, nor a nihilistic destruction or a radical negation of philosophy (Laruelle 1989/2013: 2). The argument is that the non-philosophical is not *a-philosophical*, quite the opposite since it practices philosophy *within* the philosophical. The non-philosophy represents a mutation in the syntax of philosophy and its relation with the real (Laruelle 1989/2013: 22). After all, it is not my purpose here to discuss the problematic nature of philosophy today; Laruelle systematically scrutinized these issues.

Nevertheless, there are two important aspects of the non-philosophical method that are relevant to my own approach. The first has to do with the definition of the non-philosophical, since often in the debates about cinema and philosophy the term "non-philosophical" is commonly used as negative and pejorative—as it happened also in the general field of philosophy. For example, when contesting the claims that cinema as a medium is able to generate conceptual thinking, most authors use "non-philosophical" as synonymous with "unable to think." The second aspect, which derives from this negative charge, is that non-philosophy as a concept can deal better with the methodological discords created inside film studies. One possible illustration is the Carroll–Scruton debate. The entire battle around the formula "no thinker—no thinking" (Carroll 2006b: 9), which tries to deal with the possibility or impossibility of the photographic apparatus to contain ideas, can be bracketed when the medium of cinema is described as *non-philosophical* (not a-philosophical or anti-philosophical).

Used as an instrument to decenter the ample divide between "thinking media" (representational arts, like painting), where intentionality marks the presence of a thinking entity, and the so-called "non-thinking media" (non-representational arts, like photography), the *non-philosophical*, which I link with the notions of extra-cinematic and non-cinematic, presents multiple solutions to some of the intricate conceptual problems in film theory. I would argue that it is not relevant if the cinematographic medium does any "thinking," a more pertinent consequence for the matter at hand is that cinema thinks as a *non-entity*, as it has the ability to escape its own boundaries established by the "malefic parallelogram" of the screen. Basically it can operate with extra-cinematographic means. Just as non-philosophy presupposes a "change in vision," in which the trivial and the otherwise banal are now central to the "democratization" of philosophical discourses, the non-cinematic can bring about the idea of transformative powers coalesced by the discourses of cinema. While the new "non-philosophical" language of philosophy, induced by the "transcendental cloning" of the Real, makes possible the de-philosophizing of philosophy, the non-cinematic leads to the challenging of the philosophical thinking previously developed by respecting the rules of cinematography. More importantly, by this definition cinema is fundamentally a non-philosophical instrument, as it can provide another form of thought, one different from the traditional set of conceptualizations. A non-philosophical mode that moves the thinking processes outside the domination of the institutionalized philosophical currents, ideas, and principles is paralleled by a non-cinematic cinema.

Others had similar intuitions, with John Mullarkey (2011) among the authors who previously indicated how we can use the non-philosophy framework proposed by Laruelle in cinematic contexts. Observing that movies continue to "resist" the "textualist" dimension of philosophy, Mullarkey argued that films cannot become philosophical because we have not redefined philosophy itself. Only by getting rid of all the previous definitions about what thinking and even philosophy are about, we could reach a point in which we can truly understand what film philosophy was. In another contribution, Mullarkey (2009) reversed the established perspectives defining cinema as a reflective form, and reinstated its function as a "refractive" instrument in a close relationship with philosophical thinking. The editor of the *Film-Philosophy* journal states that non-philosophical cinema can "think" in a "non-philosophical way" (Mullarkey 2009: 12–13). Since some films can exhibit the ability to develop a form of *metathinking*, the productions that *refract* philosophy and not simply *reflect* philosophical ideas can have an "unphilosophical" quality, which Mullarkey (2009: 215) advocates it allows us to reach a form of non-philosophical thinking, in turn leading to understanding philosophy. As cinema "unphilosophizes" what philosophy previously presented as a form of thinking, films can continue to generate thoughts.

The Brain as *Interstitial* Device

A couple of final aspects need to be clarified at this juncture. During a round table published by the 1986 edition of "Cahiers du Cinéma" Deleuze famously established a connection between the screen and the brain. His formula was soon to become one of the most famous philosophical assertions about cinema, but also one of the most misunderstood. "The brain is the screen" (le cerveau, c'est l'écran) is a statement simultaneously simple and cryptical—as many Deleuzian propositions. The expression is often interpreted as a tangential reference to Bergson, who was in fact the first philosopher to argue that the human brain functioned *as* the cinematographic apparatus. This is true, but there is an added ambiguity embedded in the French language, a confusion read by some authors (Colebrook 2006: 9) at its face value, translated as "the brain is *a* screen." The difference between the cinema machine functioning *like* the human brain and the brain understood as a projection screen is important. As it was also highlighted by Gregory Flaxman (2000), this is a problematic formula because it associates cinema with an external projective surface. In the mechanical sense, since our psychic displays the ability to project images that appear to be cinematic by nature, the screen–brain connection might be justified.

In my opinion, Deleuze was suggesting something completely different. The screen is functioning like a brain because it creates linkages; it allows the formation of new circuits of meanings, which are not present in the images. The canvas as a material membrane is not the brain of cinema; the metaphor directs us to another membrane, manifested when thoughts appear that are not even thought. The human brain is reconfigured in the presence of the cinema screen, allowing the viewers to think beyond the cinematic. The screen which is not *seen* is more similar to the human brain than the perceivable surface in the movie theater.

These problems have an added complexity when the relationship between brain and body, which represents a preoccupation for Deleuze in many other works, is linked with the dynamic of thoughts and the cinema machine. The brain and body interplay, together with the tension between thinking and films, do not open easily to explanations. Deleuze (1989: 189) stressed the fact that we need to perform a philosophical reversal in order to overcome the restrictions of our understanding. Extracting the idea from Antonioni and his method of transforming the "unthought" into thought, where the incommunicable is invested with meaning, he asserts the possibility that the interval can bring these together. It is here in the relationship between the "intellectual cinema" and the "cinema of the body" that Deleuze (1985/1989: 204) identifies a connection. Linking the cinematic brain capable of thinking, illustrated by Resnais" movies, where the main character is "Thought" (Deleuze 1985/1989: 122), and the cinema of Godard, he further associates the cerebral (Resnais) and the "physical" cinema (Godard), with Antonioni's ability to provide a reunion of both brain and body, since these are just two poles of the same intention (204). When the French philosopher observes that everything can be "cinema," since cinema functions as "a flickering brain" designed to create links, a "new brain" (un nouveau cerveau) which stands like a membrane between the exterior and the interior, simultaneously the screen, the celluloid, and the camera, he also acknowledges that not every cinematic experience is producing a thought experience (Deleuze 1985/1989: 215).

Not all the images projected onto the material screen of the movie theater room become part of a mind screen. This line of thinking, a separation followed by the French thinker, distinguishes two manifestations of the cinematic—one that can be labeled as "idiotic," manifested as "bad cinema" and the "real cinema," where thoughts are created.

We must move away from the immediate signification contained by the allegorical connection between the screen and the brain. The cinematic machine is nothing like the physical brain, its billions of neural connections and the vast memory can be neither displayed by the screen as a material surface, nor contained by the camera. The screen is a "cerebral membrane" (Deleuze 1985/1989: 185) where the inside and the outside are colliding. The brain is not "*the* screen" in the material sense as the white surface, and it is not related to the mechanical cinematic apparatus. When Deleuze compares the brain with *a* screen, this assertion must be understood in connection with the notion of the "crack," the fissure or the fold, other memorable concepts from his theory (Deleuze 1988). This "fold" (*le pli*), manifested as the interval specific to the Baroque, or the Bergsonian distancing (*écart*), is converted by contemporary society into the film strip (*pellicule*), operating as a membrane similar to the mechanism used by our brains to connect the exterior with the interior.

Deleuze (1985/1989: 211) acknowledged that the source of his meditations was represented by Bergson's understanding of the brain as an interval (*écart*), basically a distantiating void or a gap, that is "*a* screen" placed between the representation and the represented. Henri Bergson (1896/1939) was among the first philosophers to define the brain as a different entity than what anatomopathologist can describe. He considered the possibility that our brain was not an organ of memory or a place of representation, but an "indetermination zone" (Bergson: 1896/1939: 22) between the perceived and the real. The mind screen was similar with the surface of the photographic apparatus. Bergson noticed the resemblances between the perceptual mechanisms and the new photographic machines, and he established that we are also preserving in a material container the "phantoms" of objects. Our memories are part of the physical but are never only mechanical; our brains are not simply recollecting immaterial objects, rather the actions of that object. It is in this gap and in the interval between the action and the representation of the physical object, between memory and gestures that our minds operate. For Bergson, the brain was not a container, nor a machine of linkages and connections as described by contemporary cognitive neuroscientific models.

This influential French philosopher, who is writing at the very moment of the birth of cinema, compared the human brain activities with various modern machines, like the telephone or photography. More importantly, just a decade after the invention of the new technology of capturing moving images, Bergson established a connection between the inner cinematograph of the mind and the cinematic mechanism. In a chapter dedicated to these associations, between the cinematographic mechanism (le mécanisme cinématographique) of thinking and the mechanistic reproduction of objects, Bergson observed that the ability of cinema to transform immobility into motion was an "artifice" similar to our conscience. The apparatus of conscience was also recording movements which were then transformed, as in the cinematographic mechanism, into records. His conclusion was that the mechanisms of knowledge were "of cinematographical kind" (Bergson 1907/1911: 322–3); our minds operated like an "inner cinema room" (espèce de cinématographe intérieur). By defining our conscience as a cinematographic device we are not simply describing the *interior cinema*, the device which is perceptual and intellectual, that helps us to "take images" from reality, then to transform them into abstract contents and finally to project them in our mind.

Later, in his 1911 Huxley Lecture, entitled "Life and Consciousness," the French philosopher amply discusses the mechanisms of thinking and clearly describes consciousness as a "hyphen." Consciousness is the human capacity to remember what is not present (the past) and to anticipate that which is not manifested (the future); it is a bridge between these two absences (Bergson 1975: 9). This notion of absence becomes fundamental for our understanding of the cinema thoughts, since cinema works like an absence machine, a mechanism of consciousness that allows us to experience the past and the future as manifestations of the present. All movies are past constructs since we can never watch any action when it happened. When we are in the movie theater or in front of a screen we see recorded images, traces of a time that does not exist; yet, it appears as if being present. This follows Bergson's definition of consciousness as the intersection between the horizontal, the spatial perception, and the vertical, the time recollection.

It is also important to observe the Bergsonian inspiration in the Deleuzian system. By closely reading Bergson's observations, these are integrated with his own understanding of cinematic thinking. For instance, Deleuze uses Bergson's definitions of the brain (Deleuze 1983/1986: 62–3) when describing it as an *interval* between action and reaction, a "center of indetermination in the acentered universe of images." The solution to the problematic metaphor "the brain is the screen" is disclosed by the deep paradox of both the cinematographic machine and the functions of our mind. It is this paradoxical operation of the brain that Deleuze observed at work in the new "intellectual" cinema, where the outside and the inside are simultaneously present as two sides of the same membrane (Deleuze 1985/1989: 213).

Once again, Deleuze negatively opposes classical cinema to modern cinema, convinced that the Hollywood mode of thinking was rational (generated by logical cutting and narrating), while only the modernist films are able to think in the interstice. Cine-thoughts could be produced by the cinematic "nooshock," the forceful inducing of ideas by exposure to images, in different ways. These two different answers to the question of "how cinema thinks" provided by Deleuze are a direct result of his dialectical-semiotic model, the "cineosis." First there are the image-movements (with their subsequent classifications—perception images, affect images, action images, and so on), where the thought of cinema is generated by movement. Here the shock takes a material form and is manifested either as violence or as a reaction to physical actions. In the "good cinema," where a "good brain" is formed, the shock of understanding happens in the *interval*. Thoughts are induced by a state of disconnection, which is touching the brain directly, and not by actions or movements happening on screen (Deleuze 1985/1989: 156). Deleuze would also indicate that the possible formation of thoughts which takes place in the "fissure" between images, not *from* the images themselves (1985/1989: 180), or what he identified as Godard's "intersticial method" (1985/1989: 214).

The same intuition was further developed by Jacques Rancière, who suggested that in order to truly grasp cinema's aesthetic and political importance we should explore the continuities, but more importantly the ruptures, the crevices, what he calls the *gaps* or *intervals* (*écarts*) of cinema. The French philosopher refers particularly to his own recollections about the place of cinema in the lives of cinephiles during the late 1950s and early 1960s, as during those eventful decades the "seventh art" induced multiple "gaps," political, social, and aesthetic. Rancière (2011/2014: 12) observed a paradoxical nature of cinema, the ability to be hidden in plain sight, which is based on its internal dialectical contradiction. Movies are fundamentally part of the visual arts; they are constructed of and with images; yet, this perceptual art is driven by another artistic dimension, that of narration. This is where another interval takes shape, at the frontier between cinema and literature. Many other intervals exist, between films and theater, films and music, with cinema-makers compelled to overcome these pre-existing modalities. For the French thinker this is where the only true cinematic thinking can take place. By reconsidering the relationship between interior and exterior, between the "thinking" and the "acting," never separated and never distinguishable, Rancière (2006: 3) determines their intimate connection in the cinematic. Because the implicit and the explicit are inseparable, we must search their manifestation within the interval.

Bergson's understanding of the film camera is deeply anti-cinematographic. He practices a critique of the effects that movies have on modern society and by this he is wrongly presented as a forefather of film-thinking. As explained by Stephen Crocker, the initial reaction of Bergson was to discuss the cinematographic in a negative context, which must be placed in the wider context of his opinions about any mechanical forms of thinking. In fact, the French thinker was describing as inauthentic and caricatural any forms of thought made possible by the new technologies (Crocker 2013: 20).

This misunderstanding was perpetuated by Deleuze himself, who ignored the criticism and used Bergson as a springboard for his own positive considerations about cinematic philosophy.

Yet by following the Bergsonian model and further exploring its resources, Deleuze was able to provide us with a different understanding of what our thinking organ was able to do. Contradicting the dominant opinions about our own apparatus of thought, the French philosopher was not simplistically equating the brain with its capacity of knowledge or the ability to compute information. It did not refer to the natural instrument we have to find solutions, nor to the powerful instrument that creates connections. His view of the brain was radically different, considering that the functions of the brain evolved in such a way that it was able to function better when "turned towards the invisible" (Deleuze 1985/1989: 212). Our mind is not just using mechanisms designed to explain the immediate material reality, it operates in a fold, a juncture where reality and its representations coalesce.

This was the only thing that attracted Deleuze to cinema as he recognized in a later interview (Deleuze 1990: 204). His main interest for studying movies was the inherent possibility that the screen could work like a brain, with the implicit consequence of describing the brain-like operations of cinema. The result is two major cinema books meandering in a multitude of connections, exploring several "lobes" of the cinema-brain. Deleuze tried to link these innumerable circuits, as he searched for the new capacity of films to create ideas. And it was here that philosophy connected with cinema, because philosophical thinking is created by similar "synaptic fissures" happening in the brain (Deleuze and Guattari 1991/1994: 206). As philosophical thoughts are generated by these intervals, so cinema thoughts are activated in the gaps connections within the films.

Ultimately the famous syllogism must be extended to explain the philosophical dimensions of cinema: if the screen is the brain, and the brain creates philosophical concepts in its folds, then cinema is an *interstice* for thoughts.

Cinema as a Post-metaphysical Machine

My own arguments begin and end here at the roots of Bergsonian philosophy. Based only on the observation that the process of *thinking is cinematic* by nature, and the unassailable evidence that "cinema thoughts" are created in our minds, we cannot solve the problem of *how* and *where* this thinking takes place. Before we proceed to the analytical chapters, let us return to the main arguments supporting the ability of films to "think" described in the final part of this extended summary as they are based on two contrasting explanations. In the first approach, the cinema apparatus is identified with a *non-human* capacity, functioning either as a robot brain or as a machinic mind. The second perspective places *human-like* qualities in films; just as the nature of the mind is cinematographic, cinema has an organic brain. This last thesis was supported by Henri Bergson, who stated the following basic explanandum: if the cinematograph works in a similar way to our minds, then our knowledge is cinematographic. From here derives the claim that "conceptual thinking," as practiced by philosophy, is possible in films. Cinema has the necessary qualities allowing a modern machine to accomplish thinking processes equal to those of the human brain. Of course, the opposing opinion is that cinema thinks exactly because it is nothing like the human mind; its thinking is nothing more than the result of non-human mechanics.

The return to the foundations of Bergsonism is legitimated by another insight provided by the French thinker. As Bergson himself described his approach to philosophy as a rejection of the mechanical reasoning, linked in the domain of philosophical studies with his anti-Cartesianism, we must understand cinematic thinking *outside* the confines of the photographic machine. By removing thinking from the scientific positivism and material explanations, he intended a recentering of the mind in subjectivity, with intuition returning as an instrument of consciousness and knowledge. Bergson's (1907/1911) arguments in favor of this metaphysical turnabout, developed in the study on the evolution of the creative mind, were built on an appeal to interiority. The metaphysical understanding allowed the human mind to open toward an internal reality, one that was blocked by our interest in the external and material meanings. Bergson (1907/1911: 135) considered that a profound error vitiated philosophical thinking, separating intelligence and instinct. The intellect and the scientific knowledge were not able to fully understand life; only the metaphysical approach, understood as a critical denunciation of positive science, allows access to the true nature of living.

It is in this context that Bergson introduces the idea of the "cinematographical mechanisms" of thought, as it is in this sense that cinema must be understood as a technology making possible the metaphysical thinking offering humanity access to a subjective encounter with a reality that has no material manifestation. The cinematographic allows the thinking about the uncertain through the means of the material, as it brings together the moving and the immobility (Bergson 1907/1911: 273). The flickering images on the screen, which appear coherent and unified, have no palpable consistency, not even the celluloid can count as a natural manifestation. Only the pure artifice of the cinematic, which is paradoxically both material and immaterial, can produce a "new metaphysics," one that Crocker (2013: 9) properly located in the "intervals" of the medium. Of course, this does not mean that I am following authors like Martha Blassnigg (2006) who connected Bergson (and Deleuze) with a spiritual dimension that was supernatural. While comparing the cinematographic experience with that of clairvoyants, where the minds of the spectators enter a relationship with that another dimension (Blassnigg 2006: 115–16), is relevant, it is not my intention to search for cinematic ghosts and other supernatural manifestations.

In order to avoid such confusions, I am using a concept proposed by Jürgen Habermas (1992), who suggests that *postmetaphysical* thinking could liberate philosophy from all the constraints developed during the entire history of philosophy, eliminating the two fallacies of metaphysics, the *idealistic* separation between brain and body and the *naturalistic* distinction between self-referentiality and objectivity. Post-metaphysical thinking no longer addresses the "grand" philosophical topics; instead, it is recentered on human interactions, made explicit by communicative practices that are centered in the everyday (Alltägliches). Post-metaphysical thinking is capable of articulating and disclosing the true nature of the world by annihilating the difference between the outside world and the inner world.

I consider cinema as a natural *post-metaphysical* instrument, by following the reasoning exposed by Habermas (1992) about the impossible return to metaphysics. The announced liberation from the confines of philosophical traditions cannot come from a film-philosophy depending on naturalism or realism. The only option is to follow the path of a cinematic thinking which is offering an alternative. Cinema works as a metaphysical machine, in the framework described by Habermas (1992: 30–1), who identified three major characteristics of metaphysical thinking (identity thinking, idealism, and a preoccupation for the consciousness). All the examples from modern cinema qualify this definition. The metaphysical thinking, evolving in a continuous movement from Plato to Kant and Hegel, together with its opposed currents from the anti-metaphysics of Ancient materialism to modern empiricism, has reached its ultimate resources. Philosophy was trapped in the separations between the natural sciences and the humanities, between the outside and the inside, and the disjunction between essence and appearance (Habermas 1992: 35). Only a new understanding of lifeworld can solve these conflicts between metaphysical and anti-metaphysical thinking, and cinema can offer the platform in which, the extension of life beyond the natural, we can obtain an understanding of reality.

In order to deal with cinema as a *post-metaphysical* machine, parallel with the envisioned post-metaphysical moment in philosophy, that could overcome the devaluation of thought (Habermas 1992: 29), we must prove not only that movies bring together both the metaphysical thinking, simplified as a subjective integration, and the material and mechanical impulses generated by everyday existence, but that films can be simultaneously realist and concrete, while maintaining their spiritual dimension. Films always had a subjective dimension, which exists even in the most vulgar forms of the cinematic, and a material dimension. But the redefinition of the metaphysical into the post-metaphysical is closing the gap between the two opposing views, sealing the differences separating art cinema and mainstream cinema. This rupture is no longer applicable, because even the most grotesque and primitive productions can stimulate the creation of an Idea in the minds of the viewers. This does not mean that the mechanical thinking of the modern machine is somehow nullified, or that those who support the premise that all movies are philosophical are not mistaken.

Just as the philosophy of consciousness created the translational mechanisms leading to post-metaphysics, the ability to be self-conscious, most often manifested in art cinema, or the movies using metacinematic techniques, which are a major indicator of the metaphysical dimension of cinema, are followed by new manifestations of the cinematic. The possibility that movies can do philosophy, the fact that they instigate thinking through images that function as "nooshocks" (stimulants of thinking), is not the only ways in which thinking images exist. In order to understand the idea of a post-metaphysical cinema we move into the uncertain zone of interruptions and disconnections, where thinking can be an indeterminate state, a spatial intermediary, a cultural or a psychological interval.

This was the central premise when selecting the case studies from contemporary Romanian films, that is, to search for the instances in which cinema creates thinking as a post-metaphysical manifestation. Close to a similar observation made by Alain Badiou, who pointed out the phantomatic nature of ideas in cinema (Badiou 2004: 77), the following interpretations are efforts to position the philosophy of cinema in disparate parts of life and reality that are not separating the inner existence or the impalpable from the material and the tangible. Ultimately that which cannot be arrested in the constant movement of images onscreen can be discovered in the offscreen, in the passage between mind and reality, the interstice of everyday life and transcendental meanings.

2

Offscreen Cinema: The Aesthetics of the Non-cinematic

The ending sequence of Cristian Mungiu's outstanding *4 Months, 3 Weeks and 2 Days* (4 luni, 3 săptămâni și 2 zile, 2007) contains in essence the core of my arguments. Developed throughout my line of reasoning and used on the cover of this book, the scene provides a material illustration for how film thoughts are created. *4 Months ...* remains the most acclaimed Romanian production of the last decades. Awarded with a Palme d'Or at the Cannes film festival in 2007 and placed by a group of international film critics at the top of the best 100 films of the twenty-first century (BBC Culture 2018), this movie was interpreted in a multitude of ways—a typical story for the former Soviet bloc moviemakers (Ebert 2008), an allegory about abortion and about authority, an emancipatory political statement about womanhood (Andreescu and Quinn 2016), or a puzzling exploration of ethical dilemmas (Teays 2012).

With all the complex meanings that can be discovered, this final scene is built with the simplest tools of cinema. This is an unremarkable setting, with a darkened table outside the restaurant of a hotel in communist Romania of the 1980s. The cinematography is also austere; everything is shot with a handheld camera that records the scene from outside the window of a cheap brasserie. The screenwriting is based on a banal conversation between two female protagonists, placed face to face in a mise-en-scène resembling a sketch of a Post-Impressionist painting (Cézanne's "Card players" comes to mind). The interaction lacks any action and the soft-voiced dialogue is contrasted only by an undistiguishable background noise; a wedding takes place in the hotel. The exchange of words between Găbița and Otilia, who just went through a terrible ordeal, one having an illegal abortion, the other helping discard the fetus, both sexually abused and traumatized, does not appear to be very much philosophical. The lack of complexity in terms of cinematography, screenwriting, and even philosophical meanings is deceitful.

This very unremarkable setting (Figure 2.1) contains in fact some of the most germane cinematic instruments, which explain why this director remains the go-to choice of international film critics as one of the best moviemakers of this millennium. In this emotional closure moment, when everything that happened during the ill-fated day comes to an end, the protagonists and the spectators as eyewitnesses are about to draw conclusions. This is not framed as an explicit meditation about the human condition; it is not a contemplative or a melodramatic moment, nor a moral deliberation and an ethical pronouncement. The ending was painstakingly anticipated by various movie buildups. In a typical mode specific to suspense cinema, with Otilia as the driving force of the story running the streets of the darkened Bucharest with a fetus in her purse, the director brings her back to the relative safety of the hotel. Now she is searching for her friend Găbița, the other female protagonist, a young woman who just had an illegal abortion. In the logical evolution of the story, she is now afraid that something wrong happened, that they were discovered by state authorities, maybe even that her friend has died. Nobody opens the door as she knocks frantically, while a neon light on the hallways is blinking menacingly. As she goes downstairs, in a twist of events, she finds Găbița standing silently at an empty table, smoking and looking for something outside the visible field. In an anticlimactic development, Găbița tells her worried friend that she was "very hungry"; thus she left the room. As tension dissipates, Otilia sits in front of her simply states: "We will never talk about this."

FIGURE 2.1 *The ending scene of* 4 Months, 3 Weeks and 2 Days, *a story raising questions about abortion, presents the two young women silently sitting at a table after their terrible ordeal. Courtesy Mobra Films.*

By so doing a *narrative interval* (a subject matter explored in more details later) is generated. The spectators are deeply involved in this extremely emotional story, immersed for one and a half hours in the troubled film world, then Otilia tells her friend that "this" will never be discussed, which creates a reasoning gap. Obviously "this" will become the main topic for the spectators as they exist the theater. The event of that day will never cease to exist, because cinephiles and film critics are never going to stop processing this filmic experience. The two of them will continue to be thought about and their tragedy will continue to influence our thinking. The very absence of talking and the refusal of language determination become inferential for the presence of meanings production. The unspeakable ordeal they endured (the Outside), now prohibited and transformed into the unspoken (the Inside), is suspended in the thought processes of the cinema machine (the in-between, the interstitial).

We cannot avoid noticing the direct link between Wittgenstein's (1922) concept of the unspeakable, as it was set forth in the "Tractatus," and this dialogue line. "What we cannot speak about, we must pass over in silence," the famous number 7 dictum stated, raising the problem of reality transformed into language and then transferred into thought. This is a question ontologically inherent to cinema, as Szabados and Stojanova (2011: xv) properly argued, because all films are subjected to the tension between dialogue and action, between saying and showing. While the absence of language is natural to pictures and moving images, the refusal of dialogues is considered in mainstream cinema a defect. Some infantile interpretations of *4 Months ...*, which use risible concepts such as "the mute frame," consider the silence is politically justified. The two women performed an action that was not sanctioned by the Party; thus, any record must be suppressed, end of story.

The movie and this special scene are more complex than that, as my contention is that we are exposed to the inner functions of the *non-cinematic cinema*. This is a mode of creating significations that takes shape not only *on-*screen, it is more than a reaction of the *outside* during post-filmic reception; it takes place in the *intervals* between the sequences. In the silences of the frames—not the silence in the interactions—and in the operations of the camera which is refusing to act like a "proper" moving image apparatus the *non-cinema* contradicts the rules of the cinematic. As indicated before, if we want to understand what is going on in this type of moviemaking we must repurpose Rancière's concept of the gap (as *écart*). Together with the corresponding explanations provided by Deleuze, who tried to account for the mechanical dimensions of the gaps, as the intervals between frames, we can have an understanding of the forces which in cinema can bring "the Outside" into the visible while coalescing the invisible. The undisclosed, when placed in the interval, activates meanings that are in-between; they are *outside* while *within*, here a representative case for how filmmakers are extracting thoughts from the clash between cinematographic and non-cinematographic. It is in this interstice, in the refusal of Otilia and Găbița to talk, the cinema-thinking is generated. Ultimately, the meanings do not have to be manifest in the explicit or the viewable; the jolt-provoking thinking is produced by the *unthinkable* and the *unspeakable*. As previously noted by Manohla Dargis (2008) in *The New York Times* review of the film, the camera is not only presenting us with actions and interactions, it provides access to consciousness itself.

Another instance in which the unexpected can happen in the banality of human interactions is provided by narrative counterpoints. Here a dark humorous intervention inside the storytelling happens when the waiter arrives at the table, bringing Găbița a plate filled with various meats. Describing the menu in an amusing jargon, audible only for those familiar with the Romanian language, the presence of this male figure dressed like a caricatural manservant takes us once again in the interval. While he enumerates mechanically the contents, the beef and pork tendons, the stewed liver, the fried brains, and, horrifically, cooked bone marrows from the Ceaușescu era cuisine, this reality brings about another reality absent from the physical screen, but atrociously present on the screen of our brains—the aborted and discarded fetus. Gradually the music in the background becomes more audible, as the song goes on, the lyrics of the love ballad extremely popular in Socialist Romania create dissonance. The music, interpreted by Adrian Daminescu and composed by Vasile Veselovschi, was entitled "And I fell in love with you" and was part of the popular hits (*șlagăr*) of the time. Mungiu's irony is evident, and the allegorical reference to the contradictions of the Communist society is explicit. At the same time this musical contrast gives way to a thinking gap. The technique was also used by Cristi Puiu and other contemporary Romanian filmmakers. The end of *The Death of Mr. Lăzărescu* (2005) is punctuated by the voice of another Socialist pop singer, Margareta Pîslaru, who evokes the night falling over the sea. The song about the happy life on the Romanian Litoral running for seconds over a dark screen before the credits, immediately after we saw the old man prepared to undergo the operation, is more than a sarcastic conclusion. Two non-cinematic devices (the archive music and the black screen) create a gap of significations where the thinking of the spectator is invited to become manifest. Unlike the abstract experiments of Walter Ruttman in *Weekend* (1930), a film in which for eleven minutes we see only the black screen and disjointed sounds, these non-cinematic functions are integrated into the overall logic and coherence of the storytelling.

Another non-cinematic nooshock, intermediating our access to meanings, is created by the alterations of filmic movements. When the "moving pictures" are deprived of their mobility, the lack of motion on-screen becomes a non-cinematographic decision. Once more the interval is created, which stimulates the internal movement of our mind. As the two female protagonists stay almost immobilized at the table enclosed in the interstice created by the actionless screen, we discover another practical example of how cinema can think in non-cinematic terms. The type of cinematography used by Mungiu in this film, and by many of the filmmakers of this generation, was described by some film critics as a "triumph of the minimalist model" (Nasta 2013: 181) or as adhering to the "slow-movie norms" (Jaffe 2014). Both evaluations are correct; the abstinence of movements and the deliberate lentor of the apparatus are motivated in terms of cinematic stylistics.

Here we must uncover another mode of filming, similar but not identical with the long take. As time is slowed down (or accelerated) with the help of the "unmoving camera," the long take not only alters time, it also affects space. The screen which appears to offer access to us into the real space of these young women, to the "inside" of their actions taking place in the visible field, is nothing more than a glass cage, a remarkable metaphor the director is using as a meta-cinematic reference. Bert Cardullo (2012), in a genealogical depiction of European film directors, identified as a recurrent characteristic of recent Romanian films their capacity to transform into an *intrinsic* experience of the stories, the characters, and the settings (Cardullo 2012: 327). However, when Cardullo proceeds to a close reading of *4 Months* ..., he is unable to notice more than the "strange effect" of how time is made present into the environment. More relevant is the way in which the mise-en-scène, in which the movie camera apparently functions as a substitute for our presence, generating the impression of an observational position for the spectators, opens another perspective into the outside space of the story. At the very end of the sequence, during the long silence instated between the two friends, there are the imperceptible lights of cars passing by. At the last moment, the sound of the car engine and the headlights attract Otilia's gaze, as she is breaking the fourth wall for a fleeting moment. The "breaking the fourth wall" must be understood, as Tom Brown (2012) demonstrated, more than just the ability of the characters or the author to address the audience directly. It is an expression of counter-cinema, another manifestation of the extra-cinematic, or at least a form of rejecting the norms of conventional moviemaking. When an "on-screen" character speaks or looks at the camera, as this device was revolutionized by Godard in *Breathless* (1960), it radically rejects the separation between the fictional world and the real world.

The ending of *4 Months* ... allows Mungiu to profoundly alter the notion of "screen" and the entire functioning of the "on-screen" space. Only when taking a closer look at the structure of this particular setting, we observe that there are at least three "screens" at work, each intermediating our relationship with the cinematic actions and meanings. The first is explicit and easily understood; it is the screen of the movie theater, the projection surface intermediating our participation in the tragedy of these two young women. Their story is unfolding clearly and visibly in a naturalistic and realistic fashion. The second surface resides *inside* the movie, the material screen creating a spatial indetermination, the glass window that we do not notice, through which Otilia looks. Her gaze is "outside" her field of vision as she appears to be looking at us, while remaining inside her storyworld. But this is not a classical boundary-breaking of the fourth wall, since Otilia is both looking and not addressing the spectators. With this, a third and most important transparent skin of the movie is formed, the invisible screen connecting and simultaneously separating these realities. It is precisely what Deleuze intended with the notion of the brain of cinema. Looking through the several screens, the screen of the real space, the screen of the camera, the movie screen, and the imaginary screen separating fiction and reality, the young woman is providing us access to the surface of our thought processes. As noted by the French philosopher of cinema, in this *interval* films make possible the generation of thinking and even the formation of concepts. Together with the lack of movement, it brings into being a different kind of thoughts than those produced by the movement-images (Deleuze 1985/1989: 34). The lack of action and the relative immobility of the scenography, which Ira Jaffe (2014: 99) properly observed when discussing the instruments of slow cinema, are favoring distance and detachment. Also helped by the reduced chromatics, with colors dominated by tones of green and brown, the screen is changing our perception and by this our understanding.

The entire setting is purposefully misleading, by placing us in a spectatorial position when we are in fact prevented from realizing its *refractive* dimension. When Otilia is "looking at us" we can quickly describe her action as a form of self-reflection, or, as it was commonly interpreted, as a form of artificial crossing into the realm of contemporary society. By reading the scene at these levels, the real signification can easily evade us. Her gaze is in fact blocked inside the action. The car lights which are briefly appearing in the window indicate that Otilia was attracted by an external movement and what might appear to be a meditative regard, a reflexive and pensive look at the audience, is simultaneously a display of the opaque membrane preventing contemplation and the possibility of knowing what is happening. In reality the screen is not intermediating any relationship with her tragedy; it prevents access to the intimate nature of that filmic experience. This is the *non-philosophical* dimension of refraction, as indicated by Mullarkey (2009: 46–7), an action that moves the significations from the reality of the life experience to another dimension of the Real. Between the film and the audience there is a physical screen (the projection surface) and a material screen (the glass) that forces our mind to think precisely because it has refused thinking, activating the profound screen (the membrane of the brain). In the simplest of settings, with two female characters sitting mostly silently and face to face at a neutral restaurant table, the undetermined and undisclosed collides with the explicit and meaningful. Cinema-thinking takes form in such perfect interstices, like the one in which Otilia and Găbița are enclosed.

They are beyond the confines of their storyworld, at the borders of the film space, staring into the screen, trapped *inside* while already *outside*.

Take Me to the Limits of the Screen

When scrutinizing in-depth the cinematic mechanisms used by Cristian Mungiu, we need to expand the focus of analysis. *Beyond the Hills* (2014) and *Graduation* (2016) are two other feature films in which the structure of the narrative, the camera techniques provide insights into the exploration of the "outside" of the cinematic (not only of the offscreen space). The direct observation is that these two movies are similar in their inner mechanisms with *4 Months, 3 Weeks and 2 Days*—they are based on validated visual and storytelling modalities. Additionally, they contain further refinements of the most important cinematic instruments recurrent in many contemporary Romanian films. Last but not least, these masterpieces directed by Mungiu illustrate his preoccupation with the relationship between the Outside (as the extra-cinematic) and the Inside (the on-screen storyworld). This being the central concern of this book, I must underline again that this manner of constructing significations with meanings that are residing *inside* the frame, yet fused with the *outside* of the screen, can be found in *The Death of Mr. Lăzărescu* (2005), directed by Cristi Puiu, or in *Police, adjective* (2005), the influential work of Corneliu Porumboiu, and in many other recent Romanian films.

Before advancing any more interpretations, we must clarify the possible confusion between the outside of the screen and the offscreen. The offscreen (sometimes transliterated as *off-screen*) is a dual meaning concept—and this is one of the reasons why I prefer to use the "outside" for the non-cinematic manifestations. The many-sided nature of the offscreen was defined by the set of explanations proposed by Pascal Bonitzer in 1978, in a classical article entitled "Décadrages." Bonitzer's (1985) premise was that "deframing" (decadrage) is a technique inherited by cinema (together with several other mechanisms) from modernist painting. The framing of the subjects practiced by authors like Degas and Monet, who were using the unusual and interrupted dimensions of the margins of their paintings in order, provided access to "unseen" dimensions of the visible field. Here the offscreen is simply the extended field of representation. As previously indicated, "deframing" was also used by André Bazin to point out the differences between the frame as a window and the frame as "cache", as a mask. The ability to de-center the visual field and the interplay between the on-screen reality and the off-screen space is inherent to the modernist explorations and strictly technically speaking the practice of using unseen parts of a movie is not a novelty, nor an exclusive property of "art cinema."

Actually, as shown by Patrick Keating (2019), Hollywood moviemakers used the interplay between onscreen and offscreen space in the earliest stages of the development of the film industry. This basic method of activating the spectator's imagination by keeping crucial details offscreen is only one component, and it is limited to the spatial dimension of cinematic thinking.

Eyal Peretz (2017), who explored the history of the cinematic offscreen and the questioning of the limits and the visual boundaries of representational space, also supports the idea that the technique did not start with modern movies. Artists and writers have always searched for modes of transmitting hidden ideas and meanings, contents that were not explicitly present. Cinema obviously inherited this concern from modern art, where painters were thinking about extending the significations outside the limits of the frame. I disagree with Peretz when he identifies Bruegel or Shakespeare as illustrative for modern thinking. Instead, I prefer the explanation that modernist painters were following Manet's style of painting, where subjects such as Olympia are looking offscreen, outside the space contained by the representation, exploring the process of *un*-framing (which is not similar to the cinematographic terms deframing or décadrage). My reading is, in the light of the arguments presented by Lyotard, that the offscreen is not a spatial dimension. By this I consider that there is no point in returning to the very relevant set of definitions provided by Noël Burch (1969/1981) and his fundamental explanations about the six "segments" of the "off" space.

Another problem, perpetuated by Peretz, who uses the examples from literature and painting as if these media were indicative for the inner mechanics of cinematic image, is that not every relationship between what we see in the frame and what is outside its boundaries corresponds to what we can identify as the "principle of the off." The "off-screen" in cinema is not simply an improvement on the limitations of painting or theater. The dialectics between the "on" (of the screen) and the "off" is not restricted to the "off" space as the invisible part of an image or a story. I consider even more debatable the explanations provided by the Indiana University professor who considers that the "invisible outside" belongs to the fictional world. The "offness" is more indeterminate than claimed by Perez, who uses Tarkovsky's *Solaris* (1972) as exemplary for the cinematic manifestations of the off-screen. After suggestively comparing the Soviet filmmaker to Shakespeare or Bruegel, the author jumps to the conclusion that these external manifestations must be connected to various forms of "haunting." The arguments that "off" can be characterized as the fundamental condition of film as a medium, while the absent image in films can be compared to the apparition and disappearance of Hamlet's father, are not convincing. Even if with Tarkovsky the absences have ghostly characteristics and the scenes are always made somber through a menacing presence that cannot be identified, the logic of the "off" is multifaceted, and not contingent on the material determination of the "off" space. Last but not least, Peretz is searching for the political and historical dimensions of the "off," with examples ranging from Griffith and Chaplin to Tarantino.

Only when he identifies the "off-screen" with invisibility, as a manifestation of the absence that can become present, Peretz touches upon the most important component of the offscreen. The "off" functions like a "metaphysical frame" because the offscreen contains more than the hidden; it is the non-represented as the un-representable. While indicative for the invisible dimensions of meanings, which can be disclosed with the help of cinematographic means (the camera moves and discloses the previously "off" space), the metaphysical can be accessed only through extra-cinematic tools.

Many other film critics explored exhaustively the functions of the remarkable stylistic possibilities presented by these cinema-making practices. My own speculations were prompted by Badiou (2004: 87), who used a hardly translatable French play upon words by asking where does an idea take shape in a film, is it in the shot (*prise*), or does it come to life outside the shot, extra-cinematically as a *sur-prise*. I consider that this type of surprise is integral to the extra-cinematic formation of thought, since any meaning revealed from the margins and the ends of the onscreen representation gives way to "unthinkable" thoughts. More important is that, as indicated by Badiou, the real offscreen operates as on "out of the cinematic" (*hors image*), manifested when the actions represented on-screen do not coincide with the idea conveyed by the film world. Here the extra-cinematic functions are derived from the offscreen, but they initiate an ontological mutation of the medium itself.

I keep arguing that, even if at the most basic level the *non-cinematic* can overlap with the extra-cinematic and the off-screen techniques, since they are an unavoidable component of any moviemaking processes, the "outside" is never restricted to the machinations of the camera. Following this logic, whenever the cinematic apparatus is not involved in the meaning-making, we are experiencing the non-cinematic dimensions of a movie.

Other issues are related to the social framework in cinema production and reception. In the strictest technical sense, the social is external the aesthetic, the *inside* is the filmic and the outside in the cinematic, as Cohen-Séat (1946) observed. More so, since cinema can have a role of a "moral art," which is supposed to generate and to influence our social conscience, then the *inside* (the aesthetic relevance) is limiting our access to the outside (the political or social functions). This tension is explicit in the story of the two young students living in Communist Romania. Although carefully reconstructing the settings and the props of the past, a film director is always leaving most parts of the space *outside* the reach of the filmic experience. The camerawork is coerced by the artificial constraints of moviemaking; everything else that is not staged for the screen is an a-cinematic *outside*. Then, at the level of narration, there are multiple layers of meanings purposefully or inadvertently left "out." In *4 Months ...* Găbiţa is waiting for her father to come; yet, he never arrives and we never find out what was the point of his announced coming to town. And, finally, there are the offscreen meanings which belong neither to the cinematographic nor to the narrative. The simplified argument is that the social drama developing in front of us on-screen, constructed with cinematographic instruments, is only an apparent canvas for another projection, one that is essentially non-cinematic. This can generate a profound impact on the filmic experience, without ever happening on-screen and without being constructed as an off-screen component of this experience. Contrary to the commonly held opinion, sometimes shared by the film critics discussing these films, the "controversial issues" are not simply those which are handled on-screen.

In the following interpretations, I intend to use Mungiu's works in an effort to find more examples and possible strategies to access the same non-cinematic dimensions, considered to be integral parts of his moviemaking instruments, and indicative of a philosophy of cinema that is not limited to this director.

Non-cinematic, *Extra*-cinematic, and *Post*-cinema

The nature of the "art of cinema" has been exhaustively discussed by many authors, in innumerable works and from multiple perspectives. Since this is one of the most problematic issues when it comes to understanding cinema as a "new art form," the debate remains open. As André Bazin famously asked *Qu'est-ce que le cinéma?*, the question "what is cinema" remains a puzzle and a maze. Bazin's classical answer is double folded and has dual consequences. First and foremost cinema is "objectivity in time"; the fact that the cinematic image has a duration allows us to understand its meanings. The second presupposition is that cinema represents a language in itself (Bazin 1967: 14). Another problem is that, when trying to describe how cinema functions, we are compelled to compare it with other similar arts. As cinema was developed it naturally acquired elements from painting, theater, and photography. So Bazin was justified to search and describe the particular elements that make cinema a specific mode of visual and narrative expression. He considered that the cinematic was produced by the specialized tools of the medium, inherently through camera works and montage (Bazin 1967: 63).

These early definitions equated the cinematic with the technical components of moviemaking. It was at this level that most definitions of the *non-cinematic* as a *non-philosophical* identified the rejection of any and all practices that allowed the material determinations of filmmaking as a craft to be philosophical. To simply put it, whenever a filmmaker contradicted the elementary functions of cinematography, he performed a *non-cinematic* action leading to philosophical results. Yet, when trying to elaborate a working definition of the *non-cinematic*, we must also take into consideration the elements that remain present and active during the making of a movie, the inner workings of cinema that cannot be eliminated, always being part of the cinematographic machine.

The basic forms of non-cinematic expressions, easily recognizable as non-visual ingredients used to make films, present without being on-screen are the audio-visual components. As Michel Chion (1994) indicated, we can separate the *offscreen* sounds and the *on-screen* elements by describing those physically present in the movie as cinematic, with all the other components being *extra-cinematic*. Whenever constitutive elements are external, that is when they are not created through the cinematographic technologies, they become *non*-cinematic.

The closing scene from *4 Months* ... provides a complete set of illustrations for these simple distinctions. The story that unfolds on-screen, the characters present *inside* the visual field, and the camera movements or the editing interventions generating *cinematic* meanings provide a direct access to the thinking of the film director. Meanwhile, the narrative loopholes, the absent characters and actions, and, more relevantly, the visual absences are constructing a *non-cinematic* level of meanings. Many film critics have already noted (Barrow 2015) that there are many commonalities Mungiu shares with other moviemakers of the twenty-first century. Besides the commonly observed ability to show life in real time, he also explores the elliptical functions of cinema and the relationships between the explicit (on-screen narratives) and the implicit (offscreen) significations.

We also need to consider the fact that the viewers, even of those movies that are realistic in the extreme, are always placed in the extra-cinematic dimension. The predominant way in which films integrate the spectators in the filmic experience is by creating the necessary environment in which externality is internalized through identification. My predilection for using the concept of *non-cinematic* comes from the need to account for those instances in which the transfer of responses is impeded, thus refusing the classic modes of cinematic involvement. The psychological and cognitive connections in this innovative way of moviemaking are severed and these atypical interruptions make possible the formation of cinema-thoughts.

While at a conceptual level, the *non-cinematic* is easily defined when opposing the preconceived practices of cinematography and the experimental approaches, another distinction must be made between *post-cinema* and *non-cinematic*. Recent studies have described *post-cinema* in synonymous terms with the *non-cinematic*—they deal with the transformations of filmmaking practices in the digital media and, more importantly, with the fact that films are no longer "consumed" in theatrical environments, as a form of disbanding the classical techniques. My understanding of the *non-cinematic* proposed here is not simply technical. It does not refer to the abandonment of photographic film with the distribution of movies using hard drives or the projection of 3D images. The distinction that I am trying to establish has nothing to do with the war for the "holy of holies" in cinema, the film strip. The *non-cinematic* does not entail an attack on the "sacred celluloid," as many film directors, like Quentin Tarantino or Christopher Nolan, perceive as an attack on the purity of cinema.

The definition of the *non-cinematic* derives from the very fact that even under the pressure of many new media (like video gaming) the cinema-making techniques remained relatively intact. Several changes can be described, and film theory should address the aesthetic components and the narrative dimensions of digital cinema. But in practical terms even if a movie is not made on celluloid, this does not automatically make it a *post-cinematic* production. We need to move beyond the simplistic opposition "film versus non-film" when establishing the differences between cinema and non-cinema. It leads to oversimplified explanations when reducing everything to the digital transformations of the medium. The best example is provided by blockbuster movies such as those directed by Peter Jackson. While *The Hobbit* trilogy is completely recorded on digital formats, are these films post-cinematic in their essence, or they are simply cinematographic products made possible by another type of support, nevertheless remaining similar to the "film-based" productions predating them. Are there any differences between the "classic" Lord of the Rings trilogy and *The Hobbit* trilogy?

Holly Willis (2016), who reviewed some of the most important definitions of "post-cinema," which include the idea that we are at the end of the domination of cinema, together with the end of realist narratives, argued that we should consider the post-cinematic as a cultural mutation. It was removing filmmaking from the paradigms of control and linearity, transferring it to the category of de-centered networks (Willis 2016: 26). Although I concur with the broad conclusions of this research, we need to add another level of understanding, that of the transformations happening in the regimes of representation.

With post-cinema, and more importantly, in the non-cinematic dimension of moviemaking, the celluloid versus digital wars, and the conflicts about the changes happening in the industry, we sometimes ignore the aesthetic transformations. As Jacques Rancière (2013) has put it, there is an aesthetic transformation that gradually brings ambiguity at the center of meaning formation. Rancière keenly observed that we need to deal with the relationship between three different regimes of art: the ethical component of representations, the poetic dimension, and the aesthetic mode (Rancière 2013: 21–2). For the French philosopher, in all artworks (and we need to include cinema here) the political (or ethical) regime is first to be observed and is the first to be configured. Nevertheless, as is the case with all arts, the nature of the cinematic cannot be understood simply at its external dimensions, or through the formal manifestations or in its stylistic modes. This is why Rancière proposes the concept of the separation of the sensible (*le partage du sensible*), one where the visible can be reconciled with the invisible (the non-seeable), the audible with the inaudible (that which is not explicitly heard), and the presence is reconnected with non-presence.

In watching movies, we are often following only the external subject of the story and the first level of representation, generating political or social significations. This can become misleading and often prevents the spectators (and every so often the film critics) to understand the "sensible" effect of cinema as a whole. At the same time, without the political and ethical dimensions, we cannot establish firm significations. It is only through the abolition of the separation between that which is ethically present and the mode of representation of the aesthetic regime, we can arrive at the fundamental understanding of the *non-cinematic*. While looking only at the indexical level of the movies (the social activities, the movement of actors, the realism of the settings) we are constrained to access only what is factual and clearly represented—that is the *mimetic* dimension of the images. On the other hand, the aesthetic search for meanings disconnects the viewer from the specific political context. A third option, one that I follow to the entire extent of this book, is based on the idea that another regime of representation is needed to explain what happens with the significations that are simultaneously onscreen, absent from the screen, yet remain an integral part of the moviemaking mechanisms.

Crossing beyond the Visible Membrane of Reality

Beyond the Hills (*După dealuri*, 2012), which also tells the story of a real-life event, the tragic death of a young woman after being submitted to shockingly medieval practices uncovers more than the social backwardness of the Romanian society. It also discloses several important *non-cinematic* practices allowing the generation of film-thinking.

This terrible event, bringing again Romania into the attention of many international news media, reached global audiences, raised attention, and created controversy. Even the French philosopher Pascal Bruckner, who came to Romania with the intent to document the atrocity, was intellectually stimulated by the situation. Soon after the events, a couple of nonfiction novels were published by a former Romanian BBC reporter, Tatiana Niculescu Bran, who further investigated the case. The first book then became the main source for Mungiu's cinematic version, telling the events that took place within the confines of a small monastery from the backwaters of Moldova, close to the home town of Cristian Mungiu himself.

This was the last known exorcism in Europe and, before becoming the subject of the third feature film of one of the most important moviemakers in contemporary European cinema, was a real-life Romanian tragedy and a source of public debate.

No wonder that, when the film was released, many Romanian and international critics ostensibly described it as a "social drama" or even a "social tragedy." The way *Beyond the Hills* tells the story of these brutal religious practices and describes the deplorable social conditions in Eastern Romania cannot be taken at its face value. The film represents more than a simple adaptation of a nonfiction novel, a real-time reproduction of actual events. These can be easily followed at the superficial level of the narration, with the film director laying out chronologically the chain of misunderstandings that lead to the exorcism and death of Alina (the real name of the young woman exorcised was Maricica Irina Cornici). Alina (played by Cristina Flutur) and Voichița (played by Cosmina Stratan) grew up together in an orphanage, where they apparently had had an intimate relationship. Later they took different paths in life. Voichița went on to become a novice nun within the small and austere Orthodox community near the city, headed by a stark but charismatic priest. Alina went on to work in Germany, filling the ranks of the millions of Romanians emigrating for poverty reasons.

The surprise that leads to the unthinkable happens when Alina arrives at the monastery, trying to convince Voichița to leave with her, which starts to unravel an emotional turmoil, setting in motion the misguided interventions that ultimately ended her life. We must notice that the story shares many similarities with *4 Months ....* Alina and Voichița, like Otilia and Găbița in *4 Months ...,* are functioning like an animus–anima pair and their tragic destiny is mirroring the same hubris. Alina is trying to "save" Voichița, but fails terribly. The two young women are facing impossible choices, with the metaphor of the "sailing ship" being extremely relevant for the motif of the impossible salvation. Just as is the case with his masterpiece about abortion in communist Romania, the director explores the intricate moral consequences of human decisions. Yet to see these characters as victims of their social conditions would be too narrow. Brilliantly choosing his two main actresses—both Cosmina Stratan and Cristina Flutur were awarded the best actor prize for their remarkable roles—Mungiu is showcasing an austere approach to cinema that is specific to his technique. Their inner struggle and the complex psychological dynamics are built upon minimalistic nonverbal cues, fugitive smiles, and frowns, gestures like Voichița making the sign of the cross as she passes a church in the bus or Alina always asking "but why?" without getting answers. This is why Mungiu must be praised—he is one of the movie directors who explored in depth the problems of women and who brought into the Romanian cinema some of the most complex women characters.

Nevertheless, the director is not making a political movie; he is not motivated by the desire to criticize post-Communist institutions, which are clearly dysfunctional, nor does he take on the patriarchal structures of society. Instead, he creates a complex tapestry of life as it is lived in contemporary Romania. This plunges the viewers into the world of the disenfranchised, the marginalized, and those who are helpless when confronted with the power of institutions (the monastery, hospitals, the police, social services), without performing a critical-political intervention. The main plot of the film only apparently deals with the religious practices of the Orthodox Church. Describing objectively the series of events leading to the famous "chasing of demons," which resulted with the death of a young woman, Mungiu does not intend to "criticize anybody"—as he stated publicly at the Romanian premiere of the film.

This did not prevent the local representatives of the church to be offended by what they perceived as the negative representations of Romanian society and the purposeful darkened depictions of the monastic communities. The most abrasive attacks against the film labeled the director as anticlerical and even denounced *Beyond the Hills* as a denigratory film, considered by some officials of the dominant religious denomination in Romanian as a "slap on the face" of their religiousness. The director was charged with ideological "deformation" of reality and with promoting Western values by bringing gay–lesbian themes into the public attention. Some even accused him of falsifying the events. Nevertheless, the fact is that many of the negative opinions expressed by the priest in the movie about "the West," the blunt denouncing of sexual liberties and the abandoning of the "rightful faith" are ideas promoted by the Church media. More importantly, the characters depicted by the director are never caricatural; they are never treated with prejudice; they are in fact humanized and contextualized.

The director is not simply making an anticlerical work; while performing a parabolic criticism, *Beyond the Hills* is replete with religious references. Compared with other works, such as Pasolini's masterpiece, *The Gospel according to St. Matthew* (1964), there is no revisiting of Christianity. Nor does he follow the blasphemous vision of Buñuel, who mockingly uses the rituals of the church in *Viridiana* (1961). *Beyond the Hills* is both visually and socially consistent with the dogmatic imaginary of Orthodox iconography and the on-ground reality. As noted by some film critics, most often the visual references to this religious imagination are basic and even excessively courteous. Transparently using Byzantine icons and images, as projected by the omnipresent visuality of the Eastern Church tradition, the Romanian director explores their aesthetic value without derision or malice. The three basic iconic representations of the traditional Orthodox churches (The Crucifixion, the Holy Family, and the Last Supper) are recurrently used by Mungiu. The background of the Orthodox monastery provides not only the social reality, but also the possibility to reconstruct a deeper dimension of this reality. Some references are easy to grasp, as the exorcised Alina, physically chained to a wooden cross, is a direct symbolic reference to the Crucifixion of Christ. Others are more subtle—displayed on the wall of the church we can see an atypical painting, representing not only the Mother and the Child (the Theotokos), but also including Joseph beside them. Here the dark clothes of Mary and Joseph are atypical and non-canonical, and they allegorically refer to the psychotic component of the main characters of the movie.

We realize these intentions only when the two young women arrive to the gates of the "Holy Trinity" monastery, a reconstruction of the real Tanacu community, where a group of nuns and an Orthodox priest lived at the fringes of a small and impoverished town. The scene showing the girls looking "beyond the hills," towards the city life left behind, must be seen more than a directorial effort to focus on social awareness. Mungiu is purposefully avoiding the dramatic elements of the real story—we are not exposed to the sexual abuse endured by the orphan girls during their institutionalization, the slavery and exploitation of child workers are missing, and the backward nature of other social interactions is reduced in intensity. While the absence of direct social criticism does not mean the absence of social relevance or social conscience, in order to understand Mungiu's films we need to remain aware of another important trait of the Romanian New Wave cinema. In order to maintain cinematic objectivity, the moviemaker cannot be judgmental about any of the social dysfunctions represented. These films treat social reality without intervening in the process of understanding the given reality (Figure 2.2).

FIGURE 2.2 Beyond the Hills *reconstructs the monastery where the last exorcism in Europe was enacted. Courtesy Mobra Films.*

At the *allogenic* level the look "beyond" the hills is a look toward people leaving behind modernity to lead an existence without electricity, using oil lamps and having no running water, the profound social reality of this country. By taking the viewers into the harsh life of his countrymen he generates more than social conscience; he explores a very specific type of cinematic thinking, one almost impossible in other forms of cinema. We should also look beyond the external dimensions of this movie to avoid quickly and simplistically identify its outside problems.

With this film Mungiu displays many qualities, some of which can be considered as the foundations of important contemporary European film schools. The production, also awarded with some major prizes at the Cannes Film Festival in 2012, winning the best screenplay and the best actress awards, is the work of a mature *auteur*. Mungiu has developed a particular approach to cinema, while exploring his own themes and motifs; he is further elaborating on filmmaking tools that are not limited to a national or regional approach.

Among these tools, one is used by all the moviemakers belonging to the Romanian New Wave stylistics. Practicing a multilayered intertextuality, their most common trait is the revisiting of the canonic genres of classical cinema. This is obvious in a movie about exorcism, which cannot be understood without its indirect mirroring of the typical genre films—*The Exorcist* is its immediate reference. Like the French Nouvelle Vague directors, who were constantly referring to American productions, these films are always operating at a *sub-textual* level. *Beyond the Hills*, for instance, deals with the demonic presence by removing the supernatural dimension. Thus the Romanian moviemaker is able to explore the more profound narrative and stylistic possibilities, mirroring his own cinema in the already-existing practices. Mungiu, more than most of his fellow moviemakers, uses the mainframe of his storytelling as an extraneous support for more subtle and hidden meaning-making pathway. Although all his movies are basically films within films, this one in particular is extremely important for describing the logic of the cinema practiced by Mungiu. It is never only about what we immediately understand from the visual field. The cinematic storytelling takes place most of the time outside of the frame itself. Looking at each sequence, they are developed as distinct storyworlds, developing within the frame of the main story. One of the best illustrations of this mode of cinematic narration is the development of the main plot. The background history of the two girls growing at the Bârlad orphanage is never discussed directly; it remains out of the screen. This deviation is one of the most important qualities of Mungiu's approach to storytelling. Through brief references, like the discussion taking place at the police station, where the policeman is interrogating Voichița about the German citizen who was taking photos of the orphan children, we are exposed to bits and pieces of a larger puzzle. The spectator must mentally reconstruct what is never explicit. The same goes for the homosexual relationship between the two young women. Unlike in the novels of Niculescu Bran, where their sexuality is out in the open, the movie never exposes the viewer to any explicit gestures. This is not done out prudishness; it is a narrative mechanism used almost in every scene. There are several stories here: the young girl who jumped to death because she was pregnant; the people who believe in the miraculous healings of cancer; the drama of mother Pahonia, a wife abused who ran away from her aggressive husband; or the backstory of the woman doctor who uses witchcraft to keep her husband from abandoning her for a much younger woman.

Such a complex narrative style cannot be depicted only as a framework for social drama. It would be unfair to describe Mungiu's work only as political, since he is one of the most complex psychologists of the recent generation of Romanian cinema-makers. The finesse of his observations about human nature generates remarkable introspections into the unknown dimensions of the human soul. There is always a psychoanalytical dimension in all of Mungiu's cinematic explorations. In this particular film the obvious Freudian scene is created by the priest who controls the monastery and who is called "Tati" (Daddy), with the help of the head nun called "Mami" (Mommy). They both function as manifestations of the super-ego and while the director is clearly exposing realities of the monastic life in Moldova, he is exploring the inner drama of the main characters. As Alina wants to take Vochița with her to Germany, where apparently she has found work for both of them, she soon finds out that her object of desire is no longer available. First, she is not allowed to sleep in the same bed with Voichița; then, as their previous intimacy is no longer available, she finally realizes that her girlfriend is not going to follow her. It is only now that Alina becomes a disruptive force, and her violent "Id" is unleashed against "Tati" and against what she perceives as depriving her of the object of desire. While this turns into a spiral of violence, which begins with Alina physically attacking "Tati" (whom she believes has a sexual relationship with her girlfriend) and ends with the exorcism, the dramatic evolution has psychological dimensions. Devoured by jealousy, suspicion, and helplessness in her efforts to bring back her relationship with Voichița, Alina falls into darkness.

Another important dimension of this movie, which has to do with the collective psyche and not simply with an overt social criticism, is illustrated by the scene in which Alina looks back toward the town while climbing uphill toward the monastery. There are multiple significations here, from the social uncertainty to the biblical references or the semiotic suggestions present in the title. While these meanings are functional and their lives are indeed taking place in the *beyond*, the title must be understood as a direct reference not only to social connotations, those of a backward society, but also to mythological meanings. This is "the eternal Romania," an atemporal civilization based on myths such as those suggesting that the country was the "garden of the Mother of God" (*grădina Maicii Domnului*). At this level Mungiu sharply reconstructs "the land where time has stopped," a chronotope where people exist in the backyards of history and backwaters of time.

Even more relevant than this spatial "beyond" is what can be described as the emotional and psychological "in between." Illustrated by another remarkable scene, in which Voichița stands between the monastery and the mundane lure of the city, as she is unable to be part of either world, all the characters in this film are living "in-between." The tragedy is that this "in-between-ness" is unavoidable, as the director depicts a no-man's land of moral incertitude and of emotional imbalance. Alina is the most powerful expression of this impossible return; she is trapped in-between. She never manages to find her own place, and because she dwells in-between her only escape is death. In each scene of the movie there is a person captive a dilemmatic destiny, a manifestation of their existence "in-between" worlds. Even at the convent, the discussions never only about spiritual things, the petty material problems of firewood or eating are expressions of this simultaneous existence in two incompatible realities. All the characters are caught in a constant back-and-forth movement—Alina comes from Germany to Romania, Voichița moves from the monastery to the city, the nuns take Alina to the hospital, only to have the doctors release her back. Such movements are followed by the same back-and-forth shifts of the mise-en-scenes. Structurally the entire movie is built on displacement, taking us from the outside world (the train station), to the spiritual world (the monastery), the city (the orphanage), then various institutions (the police), only to bring us back at the convent, then return to the hospital. This existence in between is ultimately the source of tragedy. The priest and the nuns believe they are helping Alina, but tragically fail. The doctors, the policemen, the surrogate family, all are driven by the best of intentions, yet are unable to change anything. The failure of authorities, the failure of social solidarity, and the personal failures result from this overarching and inescapable uncertainty.

The camera works illustrate the same functions. While in the first part of the movie the focus is on Voichița, the camera later is re-centered on Alina. This technique practiced brilliantly in *4 Months ...* exhibits the strength and durability of the observational style in cinema. Avoiding any editing interventions within the scenes, using exclusively the intra-diegetic sound, the absence of interventions from outside the cinematic reality provides an aesthetic experience that has become the trademark of the New Wave Romanian cinema. Constructed in series of long shots, remarkably handled by Oleg Mutu, the DOP of several important movies of this generation (including *The Death of Mr. Lăzărescu* and *4 Months ...*), Mungiu paints a cinematic fresco with the help of the participatory camera. From the opening sequence, in which Voichița goes through a crowd of travelers, followed by the camera placing the viewers in her immediate perspective, to the final scene where the metaphorical sullying of the screen suggests the intervention of Real invading the Imagination, Mungiu uses the camera as a form of syntactic instrument. This sensation is amplified by the desaturated colors which are naturally selected, with people, places, and objects wearing cold or neutral colors, marking visually the emptied nature of their reality.

While the aesthetic and narrative structure of this film has many common elements with other contemporary Romanian productions, Cristian Mungiu always explores the limits of the cinematic art and its potential innovative capacities. With this film Mungiu becomes a complete *auteur*, in the sense that he has a fully developed cinematic stylistics and a narrative style that further enhances the tropes and tools that made his productions easily recognizable. His approach to moviemaking, based on the devices previously developed by the multiple European New Waves, is now manifested as personal trademarks.

The Temptation of Controversial Topics

It has become a usual practice in recent Romanian filmmaking, and Mungiu's movies display the same strategy to take a controversial subject, which deals with a reality explicitly connected to the Romanian society (abortion, the retrograde religious beliefs, the educational system). The questions placed in a given social background are then transformed into deeper interrogations about human nature, morality, or identity. When performing a superficial analysis, interested only in the social dimensions, these can be easily identified as "what cinema thinks about." A thematic classification could show the predilection for the life of certain marginal social groups, the appetite for traumatic experiences or for troubled protagonists. By questioning the functioning of the most important Romanian public institutions, the directors are able to use these social shortcomings as a pathway to investigate psychological and philosophical issues. This is a narrative driving force of all the stories told by Mungiu so far. Either by dealing with the medical system (albeit during Communism) in *4 Months ...*, the Church, in *Beyond the Hills*, or exposing the weaknesses of the public education system in *Graduation*, the logic behind these memorable works is to transform the controversial topic, which is reverberating from the social into the personal, so that it generates multifaceted responses. This is a larger trend in contemporary Romanian cinema; yet, it is not confined to the national film industry. For example, another director belonging to this generation, Tudor Giurgiu, made a film about the problems of the Romanian justice system (*Why Me?* 2015) in which he addressed a heavily charged subject from the politics of the day, transparently dealing with a case related to the prime minister at that time. This pushes many young directors, who are searching for meaningful topics, to choose ideologically charged stories, as Romanian cinema seems to grow more and more political.

Mungiu managed to refuse these "external" temptations by placing his characters in social contexts that are both contentious and open to interpretations, with characters placed in moral and behavioral difficulties, in situations where human relations and intimate dynamics are perturbed by doubt and insecurity. The problems related to the baccalaureate exams represent the potential of such a topic. Yet, even if this is the central problem of the latest movie directed by Mungiu, it is also the canvas for exploring multiple other layers of meaning. In Romania "to take your baccalaureat" does not mean simply to "graduate," it is also proof of maturity, a modern version of a rite of passage. And, by expanding the signification, we are "graduating" every day the various exams of the "school of life" when faced with decisions that impact our existence and our destiny.

Graduation (*Bacalaureat*, 2016) confirmed once again the reputation and the status of Cristian Mungiu in recent Romanian cinema, also proved his standing as one of the most important directors in international filmmaking. This production got not only the financial support of the Romanian National Center for Cinematography, receiving the highest amount of money in the 2015 competition (almost 1.9 million lei), it was also supported by Eurimages, Cine+, Wild Bunch, Why Not, Les films du Fleuve, and France 3, making it a widely international co-production. In 2016, Mungiu was awarded the "Best Director" prize at Cannes, while his movie was nominated for the prestigious Palme d'Or. Soon after, *Graduation* became one of the most distributed movies produced by the Romanian film industry, screened almost all over the world, from Japan to Australia, from the United States to most of the European Union countries.

Translated for the global market as "Graduation," *Bacalaureat* is a play upon words that could have been better suggested by "baccalaureate," as the Latin term describes the laurel crown placed on the head of the graduates, not only the final examination at the end of high school. We must underline that the title is closely connected with a social reality specific to Romania, where these graduation exams, also called "maturity" tests, have become a subject of extreme actuality. When the legislation was changed and new policies of zero-tolerance against fraud were imposed in the educational system, wide public attention was drawn by these policies. This remains a very delicate issue, since the government, in an effort to eliminate any suspicions about the examining process, has decided to install video cameras in all classrooms, and an atmosphere of police control was instated all over the country. In some cases entire examining commissions were arrested, some professors who were heading these commissions were condemned to jail time, and in many cases students and teachers were prosecuted.

The Social Criticism and the Non-cinematic

This is why, together with our explorations of the manifestations of the non-cinematic at the narrative of the visual levels, we need to address the problems that emerge from this intricate relationship between cinema and socio-political thinking. Needless to say, the straightforward social and political dimensions of Mungiu's film were immediately noted by many critics and, regrettably, almost all receptions of his remarkable cinema works were confined to the external connections. Most of the observations were centered around the social criticism present in the content of the films; local and international critics discussed either the ability or inability of the director to describe accurately a politically charged reality (from Communism or the present-day institutions), with the social and moral issues considered to be more important than the cinematic.

Perceived as a movie about the corruption in the Romanian society, an ethical and politically important piece of our realities, exposing the wrongs of "the system" films like *Beyond the Hills* or *Graduation*, was easily circumscribed in the "portraits of society" category. Seen either as well reconstructed mirrors of communism/post-communism, exposing the diseases "devouring" our institutions and our social interactions, these stories have either a national or a regional relevance. For instance Peter Bradshaw (2012), described *Beyond the Hills* as an exotic "tragi-comedy" about irrationality in Eastern Europe, then later identified in *Graduation* the "bleak picture of a state of national depression in Romania" (Bradshaw 2016). To the point of understanding the cultural intricacies of compromise and poverty in Romania, such interpretations of the actions as the source of "cronyism" of bureaucracy, nepotism, and epidemic moral debasement are valid observations.

Seen only at this level, these movies might even seem to be teleplays depicting various components of the "small corruption" in the institutions in undeveloped democracies (this is a politically charged word widely used in contemporary Romania). *Graduation* exposes us to patients who bribe honest surgeons in local hospitals and to a father who decides to break his code of ethics for the sake of the wellbeing of his child. In *Beyond the Hills* we can witness the indolence of policemen and medics, for whom justice or health does not matter. Such situations can all come out as if the main interest is to expose the flaws of this society. Alina Mungiu-Pippidi, one of the most vocal opinion leaders in Romania and supporters of a "clean society"—relevantly enough also the sister of this movie director—used the movie of her brother as an ultimate argument for local political debates. Mungiu-Pippidi claimed that, since *Graduation* was about "corruption," all Romanians must see the film in order to understand the profound need to "save Romania" from its guilty past and from the people who prevent the society from changing to the better (Mungiu-Pippidi 2016).

On the other hand, others critics more radical in their refusal of the political role, claimed that the movie is presenting only a "soft" version of the more brutal corruption in Romania, and that the storytelling itself is limited to "didactic and pedagogical fairy tales" (Popescu 2016). As noted by some Romanian critics, this generated a huge wave of antipathy toward Mungiu's approach (Bogdan 2016), with many comments biased by the limited reading of his film as ideologically relevant.

I doubt that such crude perspectives provide a true appreciation of Cristian Mungiu's works. A more relevant intuition is the medical metaphor used by French journalist Thierry Chèze, who noticed the "surgical" like clarity of *Graduation*. The camera functions as a "stethoscope," "listening into the Romanian society" (Chèze 2016). This idea will be further detailed in the chapter about *endoscopic cinema*, with a special attention to Corneliu Porumboiu's mode of applying the technique. It would suffice to note that when the Romanian director approaches social reality, he does that because these *external* events are creating a slash into the fabric of reality; they open a deep cut in the flesh of society and humanity, permitting access to the substance of *internal* thoughts.

Obviously, at the simplest narrative level, Mungiu builds a story easily relatable. Any parent in any country can identify with this plot inspired by the immediate reality. The extraneous background, which the Romanian society, does not undermine the fact that *Graduation* is about a father, an appreciated and honest doctor working in a local hospital, who has to do the unthinkable for his child. When an accident brings him to face a moral dilemma, this could ruin his own dreams about the future of his daughter and his self-image. Romeo Aldea (played by Adrian Titieni) loses his bearings.

The "surgical" cut incised by the camera in the Romanian reality opens wide a view into the flesh of a middle-aged man, who is in a difficult relationship with his wife and an uncertain extramarital affair, who has to deal with the consequences of an awful abuse perpetrated against his daughter, while trying to remain honest in a society in which moral corruption is the norm. Eliza, his daughter, grew up in a bourgeois family, is an eminent pupil at school, and has a great future, since she was accepted as a student at two British universities. Now all needed to do was to pass her "baccalaureate." But the order of things is sliced by a terrible event, which puts her high-school graduation exams in danger. She was assaulted by a stranger and now she is physically unable to properly pass these so-called "maturity exams."

We can observe the same tension between the explicit and the implicit, explored by Mungiu in *4 Months ...* and in *Beyond the Hills*. The background of Communist Romania or the monastery were only pretexts for accessing human relations and the human mind. In *Graduation* reality is present and unavoidable; however, the main purpose is not social criticism. Mungiu's works, like those of his fellow moviemakers from the same generation, illustrate a concept proposed in the nineteenth century by one of the most astute critics of Romanian society, Ion Luca Caragiale. This important satirist identified the typical behavior of his countrymen as "the chain of weak links" (lanțul slăbiciunilor). It governed the society of his time and that of today, where the various interactions between human beings are determined by small favors and rewards. In Mungiu's movies the causal links within the narratives are always produced by such chains of decisions, most often bad reactions, which seem to be perfectly integrated into the Romanian psyche. In a culture where interactions are built upon small unethical gestures, one thing leads to other. Simple unethical decisions produce more noxious immoral consequences.

As we discussed, in the case of Otilia and Găbița the implacable pathway which led to their ordeal was generated by several small lies and minor compromises. Găbița lied about her pregnancy, knowing all too well that she was in a later stage of the development of the fetus; Otilia lied to Mr. Bebe, pretending to be Găbița's sister; she never disclosed to her boyfriend the trouble she was having, although his parents were doctors and they were more than able to help her; the two girls lied to Mr. Bebe about them having the amount of money necessary to perform the intervention, which leads to his abuse. The same happens with the story of Alina and Voichița, both victims of a chain of bad choices, ending with a terrible tragedy. In *Graduation* Mungiu performs a more complex interconnectedness as the story accumulates into a thin web of small compromises made by several characters how all owe something to somebody else: The head of the local police asks Romeo to intervene for the vice-mayor, who intervenes on behalf of the school master's wife, who in turn helps Romeo with his daughter's graduation paper. This is a constant reality of everyday life, with Romeo's mistress helping him to fraudulently enter the school during the "baccalaureate" exams, while he helps her with her son's speech problems. Romeo, together with him and everybody else, is trapped in several Dantesque *bolgias* of petty forms of corruption.

Once again, as pointed out before, the narration is suddenly cut with a cinematographic scalpel and an interval opens up, where everything is rethought, refracted by the gap in reality. Father and daughter relationships, which represent one of the most important tropes in the New Wave Romanian cinema, together with the theme of the rape or abuse, are broken by the immoral behavior of Romeo. In this generational gap, Mungiu introduces a secondary level of significations, more important than the political or social messages developed at the most obvious layers of the film. Eliza, the young daughter of the provincial doctor, refuses to take part in the corrupt practices of her society and she shuns her father for trying to help her in an unethical way.

Ekphrastic and *Ekstatic* Cinema

It would seem that the philosophical treatment is not Mungiu's immediate concern, as his movies explore real situations. Yet, as it becomes explicit in *Graduation*, reality in cinema is never one dimensional. The more the story is unfolding on-the-screen, the more we realize that a dual dynamic of representation is put into action. This double quality, one profoundly *ekphrastic* and another *ekstatic*, is not restricted to realistic films, nor to the contemplative cinema. All moviemakers construct their film worlds (as a holistic experience, in the sense used by David Yacavone 2015) either by using images or through words. Thus, by *ekphrastic cinema*, we can describe the type of movies based predominantly on discursive representations, in which the dialogues drive the actions as interpretative or philosophical tools of the film director. Also, the productions that are the visual narrations are conspicuously created so that we understand everything, where the cinematographic techniques are designed to be explicit and are also identifiable as *ekphrastic*. On the other hand, when what we see and hear is *not* what it appears to be, then the *ekstatic* function of cinema is activated.

We can illustrate this dialectic between the *ekphrastic* and the *ekstatic* dimensions of cinema with some relevant examples from Mungiu's works. A most evocative scene from *4 Months* ... is taking place immediately after the rape of the two young women. After a suggestive ellipse in the narrative, the two women are alone in the room. The rapist-abortionist is in the bathroom, while Găbița prepares the bed for the intervention. No words are spoken, and silence dominates the scene. Then Otilia starts rummaging through Mr. Bebe's briefcase only to find a knife, which she takes out and then hurriedly walks away with it in the offscreen space of the room. As Mr. Bebe enters the bedroom, the expectation is that everything will evolve toward a revenge episode. But none of this happens. The camera remains inert for minutes, in a non-cinematographic frame, where we see only the hands of the man getting ready to perform the abortion with the help of a plastic tube. In this *interval* of silence, with the total absence of the main protagonists, with no explanatory instruments devices, the *ekstatic* cinema-thinking is activated. What are the two women about to do, is Otilia going to act, should they exert violence on the man that abused them? None of this is happening. Otilia becomes the assistant of Mr. Bebe, an accomplice to the abortion, as the pretense doctor gives them advice in a mild voice, totally transformed into a helpful and benign character. The atrocity was transformed into banality.

In *Graduation* there are several scenes in which the characters explain reality in an ekphrastic mode. For instance, Romeo repeatedly tells his daughter about the inability of his generation to change society ("let others try, since we have tried, nothing can be changed here, we have failed");

other characters connected with corruption (the vice-mayor, the school manager, the policeman) also verbally declare that there is nothing to be done with society. Here the mode of representation, in Rancière's terms, is clearly political. When the characters are muted and the interpretation of reality ceases to happen directly, the *ekphrastic* ends, and Mungiu's film becomes thoughtful and relevant. The director is gradually abandoning the social dimension and the political messages, creating scenes and images that are *not* about anything in the story. The topics of corruption, the political hypocrisy, or the generational conflicts (part of the *ekphrastic* cinema) are abandoned, replaced with the manifestations of the non-cinematic.

Once more, in order to better explain the apparently paradoxical idea of a "cinema which is not," I have to return to a concept put forward by Jacques Rancière in his interpretation of the relationship between cinema and the other arts. For Rancière cinema is "a multitude of things," manifested as "a set of inducible gaps" (Rancière 2011/2014: 5). Rancière's original concept of *écart* means the interval as distancing and can be used to explain the external gaps between different media—the space between writing and images, between theatrical and cinematographic, and so on. Translated into English as "the gap," *écart* suggests that the "interval" functions whenever a displacement is present. When the images or the protagonists recede to a less important role, when dialogues are replaced by visuals to deflect attention, they are creating an *écartement* (distancing) within the medium.

As an impure art cinema is divided between multiple components, my contention here is that moviemakers that explore the *non-cinematic* are accessing meaning through the interval provided by non-represented reality. This process can take place in a large variety of forms, most commonly in the organic *in-betweenness* of cinematic sequences, with the help of editing. "The cinema which is not" can take place only a fraction of a second, in a fade to black or an ellipsis of narration. A more complex negation can happen when on the actual screen the actions and representations are disconnected by illogical expressions, as is the case with the experimental films.

In the scenes discussed here, the *non-cinematic* is represented by what happens offscreen. These are not in the traditional "off"; these are actions which are never to be seen; no physical manifestation or explicit description, no reference is made to their existence. Yet our brain operates within this interval; it is here that the dimension between action and our own reactions allows us to see what we do not see "on-the-screen." Even when these operations happen in a split of a second, without any conscious intervention, or in the long intervals of silence, it is this transition from *ekphrasis* (the explanatory) to the *ekstasis* (the revelatory), or the other way around, that meanings begin to transform into thinking.

In cinema, when the images on the screen are not integral, they are not fully available to the viewer; the very lack of integrality allows the formation of the meaningful *interval*. The best example is the already-analyzed rape scene in *4 Months* .... The Romanian director proves how the non-cinematic refusal of visual access to the most important scene of the film becomes an interval for thinking. With viewers purposefully blocked from viewing the actual violent act, its importance is amplified and its force is intensified. A similar technique is used in *Graduation*, possibly in an improved manner. Not only that the brutal act which slices reality is not within the visual field, as was the case with the raping of Otilia and Găbița, but it is also placed in the split between two sequences. In this interval, when the intervention of the editing takes place, the *non-cinematic* is manufacturing thoughts. Romeo, himself living in an (inter)space, he never had a place of his own, is making love to his "secret" mistress, who is a former patient. It is during the same time that his daughter goes through an ordeal that would change all their lives.

Following Bordwell's dichotomy, while "ostentatious" cinema-makers usually try to show the viewers as much as possible, prompting them to understand the meanings, the "cinema of ambiguity" relies on the relative nature of truth (Bordwell 1985: 212). While classical cinema places all the important cinematic elements "on the screen," the purpose being to make people understand what is going on, art films are following the strategies developed by modernist literature and refuse explanations and continuity. As I indicated before, this binary division is unsuitable and improper. In *Graduation* Romeo's story is developing in a classical format, with the protagonist in the center of the actions. However, the *non-cinematic* mode can divert the causal structure, without transforming the production into an "art film." Throughout the movie we are constantly prevented from accessing the whole story; we are presented with fractured information, without losing coherence or logic.

Clearly, ambiguity is a device that can be found in many other works of fiction—since it was practiced in works as old as Plato's dialogues it can provide innumerable examples. However, cinematic ambiguity and the narrative de-framing in movies are accentuated by the natural polysemy of visual representations. As Romeo begins to reconstruct what actually happened, he takes the spectators along in this process of discovery. Even when the father takes his daughter to the police station, we are refused access to the details about the assault. As Eliza becomes more confused about what happened and begins writing her statement, the camera moves away to the discussion between the doctor and his friend, the head of the local police. The same ambiguity is later completed by half-true reactions from the mother, who tells the father that the assailant performed an oral act on his daughter, only to later let him know for the first time that Eliza was not a virgin.

More important for the arguments in this chapter is the fact that the main event of the movie, the attack and the abuse suffered by Eliza, is kept outside the filmic experience; we never have access to the act. This is a purely *non-cinematic* mode of dealing with visual narration. Throughout the entire story the father is investigating the conditions of the attack and his reactions are induced by what he finds out, which proves to be the partial truth and these findings are constantly changing, together with his understanding. Initially Romeo believes that Eliza was not raped, then he realizes that she was threatened with a knife, that the assailant took her phone, credit cards, and house keys. First Romeo is going through the work-site where everything happened, not knowing what to do, and then we hear that the assailant could be a convict that just escaped from the local prison. At some point, the grieving father has doubts about why his daughter did not protest, as he is unable to elucidate if the rape actually took place his uncertainty takes him to tedious action.

Naturally, when he finds out that a public camera was recording the intersection in front of the school, he wants to watch these images. This is the best pretext for a film director to use the video recording as a narrative tool, which usually functions as a post-cinematic intervention. Mungiu instead makes recourse to a non-cinematic function, with the video camera showing only what we already knew, making visible things that were described narratively by the characters. With the visual aid deprived from its supposed access to truth, Romeo is drawn into a mind game. Believing that he spotted Eliza's boyfriend in the pictures, he starts questioning the young man. The spectators are also deceived, and initially Romeo's suspicions toward Marius are justified, as the boyfriend seems to be guilty of something. Once again, as the father tries to reconstruct the absent assault, he invites Marius to the work-site and the two men end up fighting. Instead of confirming an expected result, the middle-aged doctor quickly is thrown to the ground by the younger man, exposing his physical weakness. In one of the final sequences the molestation is once again reproduced. During a police line-up four men, stereotypically selected, swear and yell over and over toward the police screen, threatening to kill the people behind the opaque shield. When one of them snaps, we are again led astray; we are encouraged to think that there is going to be a definitive answer. It is another instance of falsifying narration, as Eliza refuses to recognize any of these men as her assailant. At the end of the cinematic narration we are left without any explanation about who did the crime or what really happened that afternoon. It is here in this out-of-the-visible space that the true movie in our heads takes shape. With the camera following around a troubled father, after all his strife and troubles, the difficult decisions made and turned down were a subterfuge for another movie to coalesce outside the filmic experience.

And, just as the story reaches its final stage, Eliza does not accept her father's machinations. It would appear that it was all for nothing. Basically, this counter-narrative device points to the fact the entire movie was just an interlude, an *interval* apparently with no purpose. In fact, the ultimate cinematic experience was fundamentally non-cinematic. It takes place outside the screen that is in the *ekstatic* state of mind of the spectator, in the interval made possible by the screening room which extends beyond the confines of the movie theater, without ever being disconnected from it.

The Invisible and the Ineffable

Another important *non-cinematic* mechanism that must be discussed here has to do with the refusal of the traditional "cinematic beauty." In classical terms, movies always had to be aesthetically pleasing, with popular movies especially treated as forms of pictorial art. When movies refuse to provide visual pleasure, sometimes even building purposefully unclear pictures, they belong to the non-cinematic paradigm. The technique, present in almost all of Mungiu's films, is not about making ugly movies; it is a conscientious refusal of the visual gratuity.

With actions taking place in darkened alleys, with night shots making everything unclear or with natural elements (rain, snowing) blurring the visual field, the cinematic quality is reduced, not to zero as in abstract cinema, but still reaching a confusing dimension. Relevantly enough, such visual obstructions are placed in extremely important moments of the narrative. In *Graduation* these scenes are placed at the end of each day, while in *Beyond the Hills* they punctuate the moments of inflection that lead to tragedy. Such apparent lack of aesthetic clarity and the cinematic imperfection work at the same time as a mechanism allowing the formation of the *ineffable*.

In art theory, the ineffable was described as an "unexplainable quality" of representations, the intrinsic ability of visual objects to express more than their manifested meanings. Since the ineffable is integral to any type of media, with openings toward levels of meaning-making beyond the direct manifestation, we need to address the issues of *cinematic ineffable*. One possible definition of the ineffable is to describe it as the level of artistic expression beyond words, in fact any manifestation for which we have "no suitable words" (Kennick 1967). When it comes to cinema, the nature of the ineffable becomes more complex, as meanings can be immediately conveyed to the viewers. The perceptual specificity of the moving images prevents the ranges of *cinematic ineffability*. At the immediate perceptual level, the viewers participate in the story-building efforts of the director; they are directly and constantly addressed by the narrative, both visual and dramatic. Also, we cannot link the ineffable to the reactions of the spectators toward what is depicted on-screen, since the ontological posture of spectatorship is muteness. The collective expressions of feelings through bodily reactions (viewers crying or laughing together) cannot overlap with reaching for the ineffable, as affects are not uncertain.

We must go back to the key questions raised in the "Introduction" of this book. If more or less all the members of a cinema audience are living the same filmic experience, why do we have different ideas about what is going on, why do we think differently, why film-thinking is disconnected from images and narrations? At a personal level, each individual viewer in a movie theater audience can build his or her own impressions and private interpretations. In this sense, the part of the ineffable resides in the ability of the work of art to generate an *impression*, to leave a trace in our consciousness, that is untraceable otherwise.

Another component of this process was described by Rancière as *the aesthetic Unconscious*. The French philosopher contends the idea that significations are generated by thinking and instead proposes the possibility that they are created by a "thought that does not think" (Rancière 2009: 45), one that is located in the obscure places of the heart (52). When the invisible meets this kind of ineffable, as it happens in *4 Months ...* when Otilia walks through the dark alleys menaced by dog barks and indistinct loud noises, her breathing is the only cue for what is going on. There is nothing visible on-screen, no aesthetic beauty in these shots, which are even defocused in the handheld camera movements. Nevertheless, this absence of visible information only intensifies cinematic thinking.

The same happens in the first dark scene at the end of the first day of tribulations in *Graduation*—here we cannot avoid the same symbolism, which is going through the entire movie, linking Romeo with the myth of resurrection. And it is not by chance that Romeo (and his wife) is always listening to Händel, and more importantly the arias from *Messiah*. In this night scene, Romeo and his daughter are returning from the police station, the Händel's oratorio creating an eerie atmosphere inside the car. The frame is dark and cold, with almost no action and no elements of representation. This monotonous state is broken by a sudden appearance, as Romeo hits something with his car. He steps out of and, in the pitch darkness, he checks the damage of his front bumper. Later, at the end of the second day, Romeo returns to the same spot and he is now just a shadow, an unclear figure walking through the bushes. Suddenly he starts sobbing uncontrollably with the darkened screen not allowing the viewers to see anything, with the camera treatment accentuating the opaque manifestation. Not understanding anything that is going on on-screen, in a typical *non-cinematic* manner, makes these incomprehensible and external movements into transformed unconscious realizations of the doctor's thoughts.

The more the ambiguity is building up and the less we are given clear explanations or perceptual clues, our understanding is enhanced. The final night scene, when Romeo follows the presumed assailant, is even more complex, as a long shot following him around a seemingly abandoned urban space. This sensorial dimension of cinema-making is not necessarily innovative, and it was previously explored by Mungiu, in the brilliant example previously discussed. In the similar sequence from *4 Months ...* Otilia is carrying a dead fetus in her peregrinations in a dark Bucharest, provoking an emotional and even kinesthetic reaction that is beyond the direct experience. This experience is enhanced by the participative camera, following the main character who often drops outside the perceptual field. In the darkness of the cinema theater Mungiu is creating a sensation that is neither complete, nor easily understandable, amplified by the distress of the powerless father running around covered by darkness. Moving beyond the transparency of the visible, and through the fabric of social significations and realities, the director puts the spectators and the film on a path of searching for the ineffable nature of the thoughts.

Sometimes the ineffable is built up in a darkly comedic way. We have a remarkable illustration in the scene where several policemen are searching for a presumed escaped prisoner. Developed in an amusingly non-cinematic way, where two dozen of law enforcement representatives are sitting on top of a hill, in marionette poses, without doing anything. Mache, the police chief, is looking pointlessly through his binoculars, and the entire episode is turned into an absurd silent theater. The same mechanism is activated in the scene in which Romeo is supposed to take care of Matei, and is witnessing a confrontation in the playground. The over-the-shoulder camera is focused on Romeo's back, while in the unclear foreground a fight between a mother and a father takes place. Mungiu is ironically dealing with the idea of social justice—Matei throws a rock at the boy who does not respect the rules, leaving a bitter sensation about the lawless nature of human beings.

The Silence of the Frames

Ludwig Wittgenstein, the great philosopher of human language, was famously quoted with the following memorable dictum: "What can be said at all can be said clearly" and "whereof one cannot speak, thereof must be silent" (Wittgenstein 1922: 27). In these apparently brief remarks from the Preface of *Tractatus Logico-Philosophicus*, Wittgenstein actually places silence at the center of the philosophical ineffable. Silence should not be understood simply as a form of laconic thinking, but rather as a path to discovering truth and allowing thoughts to be better manifested.

In all his movies, Mungiu has proven to be a master of silences, a true (albeit undisclosed) disciple of Wittgenstein. Once more we must return to *4 Months ...* and its remarkable ending scene. The two young women, after going through their ordeal, sit silently in front of a restaurant window, and the movie is concluded with Otilia asking Găbița to "never speak again about this." As the young woman abruptly turns toward the camera and breaks the "fourth wall" by and gazing directly toward the viewers her eyes are not simply diverting our attention *outside* the frame; they become instrumental for pointing to the ineffable nature of the *intrinsic* meanings. The same procedure is used at the end of *Graduation*; here the story concludes with a collective photoshoot, as the end of the movie and at the end of the high school have a similar punctuation role. This illustrative moment indicates what the non-cinematic can bring into any film production. While the father takes a snapshot of his daughter, surrounded by her colleagues, the music in the school backyard echoes a song from a popular movie about high-school life, made during Communism. As the popular vocalist Stela Enache chirrups about the happiness of being a student, the silent and sad smiles on the faces of the real students, frozen in a freeze-frame, bring about a final non-cinematic meaning.

Just like the spoken language becomes more relevant when silenced, the cinematographic language becomes more profound when it does not depend on the camera anymore, when meanings are not produced by the lenses, but rather by the incapacity of the photographic objective to capture the entire reality. The Real is never disclosed, never spoken fully, and by this it is made more significant. At this level the meaningless becomes an integral part of the meaning-making mechanism. This has been one of the traits of Mungiu's narrative style and a proof of this we find again in his masterpiece *4 Months* .... The entire setup of the movie and the main story is told by a filmic *mise en abyme*—the viewers are suddenly in the middle of an already-existing situation, through a typical *in medias res* device. The two girls have already planned the abortion and there is a tacit understanding that there has been history behind everything, a history that would never be revealed. How did Găbiţa get pregnant? What is her relationship with the man that got her pregnant? And, more importantly, what is happening with the father that they expect to come and bring cookies from home? Why does he never show up?

The narrative that always remains unspoken, with story threads that are not fully connected and the development of a world in which absent narratives become more important than the explicit ones, is one of Mungiu's trademarks. Obscured storylines and incompletely solved plots become an integral part of the narrative non-cinematic in *Graduation*. The movie begins with Romeo having a terrible secret of his own, a secret which may account for the mysterious attacks on his house. Yet we never find out why stones are thrown through the window of his flat and the windscreen of his car. The same is true when it comes to Romeo's estranged relationship with his wife, who calls him "Tică" (also a diminutive for father in Romanian), yet refuses to have any intimate relationship with him. In fact all the relationships in this apparently clear story are ambiguous. Romeo's mistress tells him she has missed her period; yet, this stringent issue is never solved; Magda, his wife, keeps away from her husband the fact that Eliza has begun her sex life; Eliza's boyfriend, Marius, is never contextualized; we are never provided much information about him; also, very late during the evolution of the story we find out that Romeo sleeps on the living-room couch, and we never find out why; at first it appears that nobody knows about his secret relationship; yet when the grandmother gets sick, we find out that Eliza knew all along where the lover of his father lived, and many more.

The development of the secondary characters also maintains several things unspoken, with subtextual references made, innuendos and allusions uttered, but we are never provided with more details. This is the case with Romeo's Hungarian assistant, Csilla, who has no background story, but is always helping the doctor beyond a normal and professional relationship. She takes the doctor's car to the repair shop; she makes calls and arrangements on behalf of the absent surgeon; she appears to be in control of a part of his life. Another strange character is Matei, the young son of Romeo's mistress (who is also puzzling and uncertain). He appears in the middle of the conversation between his mother and the doctor with a wolf mask on his face, and during this brief encounter we realize that the young boy has never met his mother's lover. Then he disappears from the screen only to reappear at the end.

But perhaps the most intensely non-cinematic instrument remains the mystery about the identity of the attacker. This assailant is not simply enigmatic, as it happens in the classical mystery stories. His non-objectified nature becomes an integral part of the complex mechanisms put in place by Mungiu. He becomes part of the incomprehensible nature of the non-cinematic. This is extremely problematic in art representations because, as Adorno has famously put it, in the work of art apparently nothing counts if it is not there; yet, this paradoxical nature of meanings as "chimeras" remains its most profound form of interpretation (Adorno 2013: 374). It is in this sense that Mungiu constantly explores the need of going beyond appearances, and in *Graduation* this is where the absent meanings become more important than the apparent manifestations and their objectification in reality (Figure 2.3).

FIGURE 2.3 *The dramatism in* Graduation *is provoked by an enigmatic assault and the moral dilemmas of the victims facing impossible decisions. Courtesy Mobra Films.*

Non-cinematic Narratives: *Erotetic* and *Euphoric* Storytelling versus *Eidetic* and *Eristetic*

A premise set forth by Noël Carroll (2013), that motion pictures are fundamentally narrative forms of expression, remains a major reference point for determining how non-cinematic narrations can be distinguished from the traditional ones. Carroll (2013: 133–4), while operating within the cognitive paradigm imposed by Bordwell and others (1985), accepts that the limits of filmmaking narrations can provide an opportunity for the philosophy of "the moving image." His explanation was that the "power of movies" resided in the dominant form of narration developed by cinema, one based on the "question and answer model." To describe this formula, the film philosopher created a new concept explaining the functioning of standard narration forms, repeatedly activated in motion pictures oriented toward closure. This inclination for resolution opposed for example to the never-ending recycling of plot lines in soap operas, the *erotetic* narration (another name for the so-called problem—solution model). Carroll (1996: 89–91) extensively argues that filmmaking is predominantly using a "question and answer" schematic formula. Most of the film opens with fundamental questions (of moral or political value) and then is "wrapped" when the director, through his characters and situations, has "answered" all the questions. This *interrogatory* form is creating an environment in which thinking is not autonomous, and is always directed and organized by external inputs.

The *erotetic* principle is undeniably contradicted by modernist cinema, especially those carrying the explicit traits of avant-garde film thinking, but also by several examples of metacinema addressing. Carroll (2008) later admitted that the completion principle is not universal, yet still deals with movies like Antonioni's *L'Avventura* (1960), which refuse to offer answers, as marginal or as manifestations of structural reflexivity (Carroll 2008: 142–3). Here the thought processes are limited to the philosophy *of* cinema.

Deleuze, at the other end of this spectrum, proposed the formula *eidetic* cinema, which is used to describe the films that perform narrative operations reduced almost to zero. This reduction, sending us back to Husserl's phenomenological principle, covers abstract and experimental cinema. What ensues from here is a conflict observed by Ted Nannicelli (2013), when attempting to develop an ontological explanation for how screenplays can function philosophically. Between the stories we read and the story we see, more broadly between "thinking with words" and "thinking with visual images," there is a clear separation line. Nannicelli, who supports the hypothesis that the screenplay of a film cannot provide cinematic information to the reader, follows Carroll and other cognitive theorists.

Another mechanism, one of the most important features of the French New Wave cinema storytelling, must be addressed. These filmmakers, who are simultaneously screenwriters and directors, are contesting and dismantling the classical mode of narration (the *erotetic*), while creating movies that are not abstract or meta-narrative representations (*eidetic*). These stories with an internal logic that are not remote from the external are heavily influenced by the Italian Neorealist mode of storytelling. The experimenting with plots and story structures, as put in place by Truffaut and Godard, continues in contemporary Romanian moviemaking. Their way of telling stories is not as radical as the Impressionist or the Surrealist attempts to find other narrative modes. Accepting and cultivating ruptures, discontinuities, and ambiguity, these storytellers are not refusing narration. Their preferred technique is, in fact, the *open-ended* narration, perhaps best illustrated by *400 Blows* (1959). Truffaut closes the series of events centered around the young Antoine Doinel without a resolution. The French director continued the story of Antoine, since the hero was obviously his alter-ego. Several films (Stolen Kisses, 1968; Bed and Board, 1970; Love on the Run, 1979), can be put together as "The Adventures of Antoine Doinel," yet the overarching mechanism remains the narrative irresolution.

A film historian who is specialized in the French New Wave Cinema, Richard Neupert, identified at least four categories of endings (closed, open story, open text, open discourse), all belonging to an "aesthetic of openness," initiated by the Italian Neorealists and illustrated by Rossellini's *Rome Open City* (1045) or DeSica's *The Bicycle Thieves* (1948). Neupert's (1995: 76–7) explanations remain inside the interpretative framework of the continuing opposition between art cinema (based on open storytelling) and classical Hollywood films (driven by closed texts). As Françis Vanoye (1989) observed, these are forms of narration radically different from the *euphoric* mode of storytelling dominating the Hollywood cinema screenwriting. Deleuze (1985/1989: 126) also described this as a *falsifying* power ("falsifiant"), integral to the crystal images (recollections, dreams), and opposed to "organic narrations." At the other end, as the French film philosopher observed, are the slowed-down movements specific for the New Wave cinema, which he categorizes as "crystalline narrations," creating an anomalous experience of time and space. This is the common thinking style of Ozu or Antonioni, also shared by the Neorealists, the French New Wave directors, and the New York avant-garde (Deleuze 1985/1989: 129). By freezing motion in the space–time continuum, cinema reaches a point where the mise-en-scènes and their storyworlds are completely immobilized. When the inside and the outside are fused, they create a cinematographic mutation, where the undecidable and the forgery allow the discovery of truth.

Examining similar non-erotetic examples of unresolved storytelling in Romanian cinema, I propose another concept, opposed directly to the terminology advanced by Carroll. These stories that are cultivating gaps in their resolution are not only contradicting the simple narrative structures of hegemonic cinema, but they activate another form of thinking altogether. These can be described as *eristetic* narrations, from the Greek goddess of discord and strife (*Éris*). They can perform questions; yet, most of the time these problems remain unanswered or partially unresolved. This undecidable component is then carried out of the movie theater by the spectators, who continue the thinking *outside* the filmic universe. What will happen to the leading characters? What is the future of their moral conflict? How the events will unfold in the future, after the film is over and how are they going to impact the protagonists and the involved moviegoers? These are transformed into *extra-cinematic* problems, behaving like *eristetic* questions affecting the mind and the souls beyond the immediate cinema experience.

An important and necessary discussion when trying to identify how the *eristetic* operates is stimulated by the inner levels of Mungiu's dealing with the narrative problems and solutions. Although most often the central storyline of his movies can be easily summarized, everything follows a chronological and linear progression—there is more than meets the eye in these narrations. Mungiu develops an inconspicuous narrative mode that is structurally *non-cinematic*. We can understand the way in which he is contradicting the rules of classical cinema narratives by contrasting it with the elaborated puzzles in Quentin Tarantino's movies or Christopher Nolan's efforts to cheat the natural order of time and space. His technique is close to what Vanoye (1989) has identified as the "deceptive" procedure of *dysnarration*. Vanoye used some of the movies directed by French novelist and film producer Alain Robbe-Grillet. Best known for writing the screenplay of the outstanding *L'Année dernière à Marienbad* (1961), directed by Resnais, he directed his own films. *The Man Who Lies* (*L'Homme qui ment*, 1968) can be used as a suitable example of how dysnarration works as a narrative disjunction between the story and its own narrative practices. This is a technique previously used by literary works and, when exported into cinema, takes on unusual traits. Robbe-Grillet's protagonist Boris, who dies and then returns to life, is entangled in multivariate storylines, never explained and confusingly contradicting each other. As we discover more information about the character he modifies his traits, thus constantly disorienting not only the unexpecting viewers, but the protagonist himself.

Such narrations which go against their own premises can be divided, as Vanoye pointed out, into two different categories. It is important to separate the typical avant-garde narrations, which are completely refusing narrativity and all the traditional structures of narration, with the practices of *dysnarration*, which are based on a rupture between fiction and narration (Vanoye 1989: 199), that is not destroying the storytelling procedures. An important modality, also illustrated by Robbe-Grillet and his ambiguous characters, is by building the main protagonist of a movie from several inexplicable and uncertain elements, while this shifting identity and the changes that happen throughout the story are not breaking the logical chain of events. A suggestive example is Mr. Lăzărescu, from Cristi Puiu's homonymous movie. From the very beginning, the title creates several false expectations; we anticipate another story within the typical pattern of a "chronicle of a death foretold." This is joined by many more elements functioning as contradictory building blocks. Not only that the film never ends with an actual death, but Lăzărescu's diagnostic is constantly changing and his final surgery will have nothing to do with his initial reason for calling the ambulance. Suffering from cancer, he is operated for a brain hematoma, caused by his falling in the bathroom while surrounded by people. The entire character development arc is in fact pieced together from such small ambiguities. We gradually discover various aspects of the life of this decrepit pensioner and we realize that he is more than we first thought. Even if we never find out what he did in life, we get bits and pieces indicating that he is not what he appears to be. Ultimately the title could have been "The Life of Mr. Lăzărescu," since the viewers reconstruct, from pieces and scraps of information, a convoluted life. While watching an old man gradually degrading, we are provided with enough narrative detritus to build a new identity.

This *falsifying* form of narration is a typical device for many Romanian moviemakers, who act like storytellers telling apparently simple histories, yet playing with complex and oblique references hidden in plain sight. Geneviève Sellier (2008 129), who previously linked the "New Wave" plots to the "ideology of ambiguity," indicates Jacques Rivette's film, *Paris nous appartient* (*Paris Belongs to Us*, 1961), as exemplary for these strategies of obscuring the meanings as the story unfolds. A similar mechanism is used by Mungiu in *4 Months ...*, where we never know the backstories of Otilia or Găbița, or in *Graduation*, where the real identity of the protagonist changes constantly, as we find out more about his personal history. In fact, *Graduation* takes the technique to a whole new level, through a series of minor ambiguities that are linked in multiple loops, which only grow wider until we don't even know what is the main point of the story. What appears to be important for the movie, the moral questions of a father trying to help his daughter, is transformed into the disassembling of his own identity. The opening scene is also indicative of this altering direction. The beginning *in medias res*, as we are placed in the middle of an ongoing action, is turned into an unimportant situation. Under the false pretense of the enunciation mode of the typical realist cinema, Mungiu brings us to a derelict suburban space, with somebody digging a hole in the ground in front of a block of flats. The camera then moves into an apartment, where there is nobody. The content of the story and the substantial meanings are falsified from the beginning, and the construction of this *eristetic* effect continues until the end.

Thinking in the Interval, Showing Stories That Cannot be Seen

To simplify the arguments, we must briefly observe that even the *eristetic* narrations constructed by Mungiu respect some of the rules and conventions of screenwriting. In the dominant mode forms of cinema narration, as developed by Hollywood storytelling, grounded in the classical paradigm of Aristotle, the basic principle is that all interactions between characters and the overall story development must be linked through causal connections. Historically, the American screenwriters were always compelled to follow such classical canons, which resulted in what Bordwell described as the "Hollywood way" of storytelling. The mechanics of screenwriting follows rules such as the "arrangement of incidents," the story elements buildup in a continuous enhancement of causalities, based on the "three act template" (Bordwell 1985: 29). Paul Gulino (2004) labeled this "the sequence approach," with many "practical storytellers" in contemporary film industry, like Syd Field or Robert McKee, further elaborating on its benefits in various instructional books and manuals. The prescribed mode of developing stories "the cinema way" is expanded even in the "post-classical" cinema or the "New Hollywood" as Kristin Thompson (1999) defined it. Maintaining a strict adherence to the "guidelines" of storytelling continuity, connected with the principle of cinematographic continuity, remains predominant. All these screenwriting practices are considered to constitute today a specific mode of *cinematic narration*, a universal modality of telling stories in movies, distinct from literary fiction or theater plays.

While such normative devices are formally accepted and applied in most of the Romanian contemporary films, the conventions in and by themselves do not necessarily lead to the same philosophical results. *4 Months ...* provides us with another relevant example, in another emblematic scene, placed at the center of Mungiu's widely acclaimed and awarded movie. Disclosing one of the instruments of the non-cinematic, at the climactic and most tense moment there is a puncturing of the story structure. The director and screenwriter presents this dramatic account of the practices of abortion during Communism by respecting the overall rules of logic and continuity. Within the limited time available, since the story started only a few hours ago, there is an outward simplicity and the basic coherence is maintained. We clearly understand the premise; two young women are preparing to pay an abortionist, Mr. Bebe, and things get more complicated as they progress; the students do not have the necessary amount of money; thus, they cannot make a proper hotel reservation in town and are submitted to the abuse of the fake doctor. This easily understandable plot, the clear-cut storyline, and the inner drives of the main characters are suddenly punctuated with a disjunction.

Some film theorists describe this as a manifestation of an "epistemological uncertainty" (Strausz 2017: 127). These intervals, the gaps and cracks in time, space and signification can be considered inflection points not only for cinematic thinking, but for larger, social instabilities. As László Strausz claims it, they are forms of "hesitation," stimulating not only the thoughts of the spectators, but a form of expression with social-historical interface. In order to understand this mechanism I propose to follow a suggestion advanced by Alain Badiou, who observed that the intra-philosophical ability of cinema, its ways of thinking (ethical or philosophical), must be connected with the fact that films can "make the Other exist" (Badiou 2013: 221). In an essay entitled suggestively "Cinema as Philosophical Experimentation," this French philosopher indicates that when we are watching a film in a "philosophical way," we are about to think about what we usually do not do in everyday life.

Now back to the mechanisms at work in Mungiu's cinema. In a shocking turn of events, a total incision in the mind of the film happens. Mr. Bebe demands that both Ottilia and Găbița, who we know by now is very advanced with her pregnancy, have sexual intercourse with him. Găbița, desperate to get rid of her baby, quickly accepts, while Otilia tries to find a way out by telling him she has her period. As the tension escalates, Mr. Bebe wants to leave, which prompts suddenly Otilia to accept the crudely indecent proposal. She begins to take off her clothes mechanically with Găbița stepping out of the hotel room. Then scene in which her friend is subjected to the brutal act is never depicted directly, Mungiu choosing a profoundly *non-cinematic* mode of expression. The fixed camera focuses on Găbița, by now standing barefoot outside the hotel room, breathing heavily, while knowing that her friend is sexually abused inside. The relationship off-screen/on-screen is no longer "political" or "social"; it serves the purest function of cinema-thinking. Suddenly another breaking of the rhythm takes place. A door is slammed shut and the camera gets moving again, as if waking up from a slumber, with Găbița approaching this stranger and ... asking him for a cigarette. For the entire scene the visual field is totally removed from the room and, as the young woman returns with the cigarette she steps into the bathroom. Meanwhile the atrocious sexual act keeps going on behind the closed door of their room. Now she turns on the water to block any noises. After a cut suggesting the passing of time, Otilia comes into the bathroom half-naked and starts frantically washing her genitals. Her friend steps out only to be raped in turn, with the viewers refused once more access to the sexual assault. This takes place again in the interval, during long minutes of silence, with the water splashing with an intercut on Otilia, seen from behind, only a shape on a wall, accentuating the visual punctuation.

Dudley Andrew interprets the unseen nature of the sexual act as an expression of "a moral black hole" (Andrew 2016: 146) of the movie, with the missing visual elements functioning as a black spot in the gaze of the viewers. Relevantly enough, Andrew uses the same scene from *4 Months ...* as an illustration for the philosophical possibilities of the movie camera, and he properly reads the Sartrean dimension of this cinematic point of view. The film "auteur" allows us to philosophize about life with an existentialist turn. Cinema functions as a tool for subjectivity—we as spectators experience the reality of the protagonists; thus, the limitation of the perception becomes a vision of the lived world. I would argue the contrary that here the camera does function as an instrument of knowledge not because it is situated in the position of the character. In fact, as the camera is dis-placed, its *non-situatedness* provides the opportunity for the thinking processes to develop. Not having a subjective access to the atrocity, it generates synaptic connections.

It would be another line of investigation to discuss the existentialist dimension of Mungiu's film. For now one short explanation is necessary, following the existentialist approach used by Daniel Shaw (2017), who is correct to refuse the immanentist and the intuitionist explanations about the meanings of films. Their basic narrative function of all cinematic stories is to provide access to existential situations and questions. The Romanian cinema, as will be discussed at length in the final chapter, has a profound affinity with the absurd and tragic conditions of human existence, which is extremely vivid in the case of Găbița. The story of this silent victim of abuse can be connected with the myth of Sisyphus, in the version of Camus. While many interpreters focus on Otilia, the friend helping her to overcome the life-threatening situation she is exposed to, it is her experience that functions as a real "non-philosophical" act. We do not get her vision about life as she goes through the absurd events; she is not saying anything, nor showing affects or emotions. The true gap is produced in her existence, as Mungiu purposefully refuses to explain what is the nature of the relationship between the two young women; we never understand why would Otilia go through with this horrible deal, who is the father of this unborn child and many other questions. If there is a philosophical result of this non-cinematic buildup, it has more meanings than in the typical existentialist cinema (Pamerleau 2009: 41). The problems of the human condition are not central to the story; it does not provide insights into "the meaning of life" through narratives, characters, or events. The lived experience of the main characters is not available to the spectators, and the personal and intimate sufferings are not depicted. The viewer is abandoned in the interval, without answers and without a guideline, which allows us to label the story as post-metaphysical.

The impact of these gaps and intervals is even more explicit at the narrative level. Critics have interpreted differently the fact that Mr. Bebe raped the two women. The episode is problematic for various reasons, especially since it appears to have uncertain motivations as his behavior is clearly non-sexual. One explanation is symbolic—the illegal abortionist is an allegorical reference to the Communist regime and its authoritarian leader. The historical context provides another extra-cinematic meaning, most probably the rape was perpetrated as a form of protection and control for Mr. Bebe's personally. His illegal interaction with the girls, in the case he will be charged or prosecuted for performing the illegal abortion, could be justified as a private matter.

The entire scene is an illustration of the "cinema which is not a cinema," a type of moviemaking and film storytelling not created to take place exclusively on-screen, that of the theater room or in the screen of reality, but outside the movie itself. It also stands outside the social and political and it does not belong only to the minds of viewers. Through accumulated silences, absences, and non-cinematic representations, by using indeterminate storytelling techniques and constantly pushing farther the resources of the extra-cinematic space, the director creates intervals where meanings are formed without the intervention of the camera, the editing, or the storytelling.

Mungiu explores the qualities of what can be defined as a *non-cinematic cinema* in all his films. Another example comes from *Graduation*, where the sexual abuse that Eliza goes through is built in a similar manner. A continuing accumulation of unexplainable acts leads to a powerful scene, which illustrates the inner mechanisms of this technique. When Romeo comes to the police station, as he enters the interrogation room we overhear the head of the police talking to Eliza, trying to convince her of something, attempting to persuade her to make a certain decision. When the father enters the frame, he notices Eliza asks what is going on. His policeman "friend" tells him that they were "just talking," even though Eliza clearly looks scared, fixating her father with a reproachful gaze. Once more, the absent and suggested narrative, the gap of information, and signification provide the main source of meaning-making. The non-cinematic mode refuses the typical representations of cinema as our attention is diverted in other directions. In the final scene in which Romeo is alone riding the night bus, as he sits silently he spots one of the men from the police line-up. Getting out of the bus, Romeo follows this man through the dark streets of Victoria (the industrial city where the movie was shot), just like Otilia was moving in the darkness of Bucharest. As darkness takes over the visual field, abstraction and non-representation substitute the meaningful space of cinematic narration. There is no finality to this action, as we will never know who was breaking the windows of Romeo's apartment or the windscreen of his car, and we will never find out who was the attacker who raped his daughter. Romeo, the provincial doctor troubled by moral dilemmas, proves to be the person who never passes the "maturity exam," whose existence is a series of accumulated failures.

These stories are never offering the spectators determinate solutions, and by this they allow an *ekstatic* understanding of human existence. The structural integrity of the narrative, as is the case with *Graduation*, is always maintained externally. The drama of the high-school graduate who is raped and her father's attempts to find solutions take place in a well-defined arrangement, during three and a half days. Each day is contoured to fit in a coherent sequence of its own, with everything made intelligible and seemingly continuous. The three-act formula seems to be respected; each act opens in the morning and ends the following evening, with the fourth morning bringing everything to a symbolic conclusion. To all appearances this shares the traits of a "classical" plot. Yet each scene, and in fact each new sequence, is based on gaps of signification, which are then connected as broken and falsifying narratives. Each morning an unexplained incident opens the storyline. The entire chain of events begins with an unexplainable breaking of the window to the apartment where Romeo and his family lead their apparently calm and bourgeois existence. The following day after the assault, Romeo steps out of his apartment, only to find that his windshield wipers were lifted by an unknown person. The third day starts with the cracking of the lateral right windshield of Romeo's car, this time amplified by a direct hit toward the camera (which is placed inside the vehicle). Just as we perceive reality through the shattered pieces of glass for a couple of minutes, adding to the general unease, the broken windows function as metaphorical representation for the overall sundered narrative. Each episode of the story is based on an accumulation of absences and multiple indeterminate relationships between the characters. The entire plot is punctured by small secrets which amount to an overarching series of equivocal situations.

Unlike the experimental narration forms, where digression or fragmentation are used in order to generate signification, in the non-cinematic approach the story amounts to a coherently un-articulated narrative, with the chain of explanations repeatedly broken, yet apparently kept intact. Like in *4 Months ...* and *Beyond the Hills*, in *Graduation* the most important things are left unspoken and untold. Meanings have to be reconstructed from small reactions—such as the wife telling Romeo "this has not been your home for a long time"—or from repetitive gestures—as is the fact that Romeo honks each time when he is passing by a certain spot on the road. Pieces of information are hidden, then uncovered constantly, only to add more secret and unseen spots. The mother is keeping away from her husband the fact that Eliza already began her sex life, or the father who does not tell his daughter about her grandmother's fatal illness, or Eliza who does not know that her mother is aware of her husband's infidelity. These bits of the story accumulate into large narrative absences, missing elements that are never told by the director. From the very beginning we realize that a background story has been in place before, as Romeo later tells his daughter that he remained with his wife in order to give the impression of normality and so that she could lead a balanced life. In one of the most remarkable and ambiguous scenes of the movie, Magda finally breaks up with Romeo, and the husband asks: "Why do we hate each other so much, do you remember?" Immediately after Magda enters into a self-defensive posture, and with both characters sitting with their backs to the camera, in the narrow corridor between the rows of books in the library, we wait for an answer that never comes.

Unlike in puzzle films or other strategies specific to contemporary post-cinema, we are not expected (nor helped) to reconstruct meanings. The point is, as illustrated with the several examples selected from these three remarkable movies, that the space *between* these absences becomes relevant. In non-cinematic filmmaking the interval is the golden pathway to thinking and philosophizing.

3

This Is Not a Film You Are Watching: A Visceral-Conceptual Response

The curtain-raiser point of this chapter is the pivotal sequence from 12:08 East of Bucharest (2006), a dark humor masterpiece directed by Corneliu Porumboiu. Before discussing the content and meaning of this particular setting, some brief considerations about the original title (A fost sau n-a fost) are necessary. While the English version of the movie carries an extremely specific description, linked to a very particular political context, international audiences cannot understand this reference by simply watching the story. In order to fully grasp the meanings and the social connotations of the title, viewers need internal cues for contextualization. The importance of "12:08" for understanding the movie and the transformation of the Romanian collective psyche is that at precisely 12:08 the Romanian Revolution has begun (or maybe not?!). There is a second suggestion in this story that takes place in a small town in the Eastern part of Romania, a premeditated premise since this is also Porumboiu's hometown. "12:08" was the exact time when, on December 21, 1989, the television discourse of Nicolae Ceaușescu, the authoritarian rule of socialist Romania, was interrupted. In this brief interlude, when the broadcasting broke off for only seconds, when millions of TV sets went dark, a rupture in the collective mind of a population held captive by a semi-literate dictator happened. The only "bloody Revolution" in Eastern Europe began, a popular uprising started and with it a new social and political age was inaugurated as a televised event. It was as if an entire community went for a couple of seconds in an interval of thinking, then returned to another reality. As we will discuss in this chapter, the fact that the Romanian Revolution was a televised revolution that most of the traumatic events of those days (including the execution of the dictatorial family) were broadcasted live by television is fundamental for understanding the non-cinematic practices of contemporary filmmakers.

The Romanian title, on the other hand, has a completely different meaning and a more subtle connotation. "A fost sau n-a fost" is a philosophical question, a paraphrase to the famous Shakespearean interrogation from Hamlet, which can be literally translated into English as: "Was it or was it not? (a Revolution)." As the main subject discussed by the protagonists, this has an *internal* function, that of an onscreen narrative device. Simultaneously it also refers to an *external* issue, the unresolved problems of Romanian society. This is a question for the Romanian society for more than thirty years now. What happened during the days and weeks of the Romanian Revolution remains a mystery and a controversy. It is a crack in our public conscience, a fold in which many secrets of our recent past are hidden. When the same question is raised by the three men discussing the events of the Revolution in their provincial town, sitting in a television studio sixteen years later, the cinematic setting creates a multi-layered dramatic representation that only partially happens *onscreen*.

With this first feature film Porumboiu, today one of the most important Romanian filmmakers, got the attention of international festival juries and impressed global audiences, but never got much popularity at home. The worldwide sales of this movie made with a budget of a little over 200,000 Euros reached more than 520,000 USD. However, according to the official data of the Romanian National Center for Cinematography, only 13,355 Romanians bought tickets to watch this film. Perhaps to ironically expose the defects of a society is never the best way to attract appreciation at home. This is another possible reason why his approach to cinema evolved slightly different than the direction taken by his fellow filmmakers.

12:08 East of Bucharest is directed in the typical style of the Romanian New Wave cinema, respecting a kind of realism connected with the philosophies of the Italian Neorealists and the traditions of the French Nouvelle Vague. The first half of the story introduces the everyday life of three banal protagonists, with the handheld camera entering their apartments, scrutinizing each detail of their irrelevant existence. As this chapter will indicate, Porumboiu, who was constantly growing as an artist from one production to the next, constantly explores unconventional modes of expression. This attitude toward filmmaking, always looking for innovative ways and for alternative cinematic modalities, which could take his movies beyond the appetite for meaningful stories, accumulates into a distinct philosophy *of* cinema. Identifiable in many other Romanian contemporary films, the movement from an *intelligent cinema*, practiced by Porumboiu in his early movies, toward more *conceptualized* forms of expression, is indicative of the transformation in film-thinking discussed here. This evolution will be illustrated with examples from other important films of this Romanian director—*Police, Adjective* (*Polițist, adjectiv*, 2009), *When Evening Falls on Bucharest or Metabolism* (*Când se lasă seara peste București sau Metabolism*, 2013), *The Second Game* (*Al doilea joc*, 2014), *The Treasure* (*Comoara*, 2015), and *The Whistlers* (*La Gomera*, 2019).

What Plato Has to Do with Porumboiu?

The emblematic scene created by Porumboiu (Figure 3.1) is revealing for the multiple possibilities moviemakers have to generate film-thoughts. As pointed out by Lester Hunt (2006: 401) films can "elicit knowledge just by asking questions," and the simplest modality is to have the characters ask those questions, which can become either philosophical meditations or moral judgments. When we consider philosophy as "questioning," the easiest way in which films can engage audiences in philosophical thinking is through reflective conversations between the protagonists. The technique of the "philosophizing characters," extensively used by Cristi Puiu and other Romanian directors, is also illustrated in this scene. In a very long and static debate taking place in the television studio of a provincial town, we are confronted not only with the staleness and unsophisticated daily existence in the backwaters of Eastern Europe, but also with some of the main problems of film-philosophy and human knowledge.

FIGURE 3.1 *The three men discussing the Romanian Revolution in a provincial television station are questioning more than the banal reality of their immediate experience. Courtesy 42 Km Film.*

Like in other Romanian films discussed before, the setting is deceivingly simple, which allowed some critics to describe this stylistic as minimalistic or, even worse, as an "entirely static film." This sensation is given by the fact that all we see in this second part are three men sitting in front of a fixed and frontal camera, which is recording their conversation for more than forty-five minutes. The onscreen framing is mechanical, capturing a standard medium close-up, with intercutting to close-up shots. Sometimes even defocused, the faces of the protagonists are contrasted with a backdrop showing the main square of the town. This totally uninteresting format of broadcasting, a rudimentary talking heads television program, interrupted by phone conversations and a brief advertising pause, is surreptitiously creating the framework for more serious issues. In a parodic reference to Christian iconology, which is one of Porumboiu's visual motifs (Pop 2014: 147–50), we see the moderator, Jderescu, sitting at the center, asking questions and making conjectures surrounded by two other characters, a sympathetic and somewhat senile old man named Pișcoci and an alcoholic local teacher, named Mănescu. They debate for almost an hour the problem of truth, the limits of human perception and reality. As they are questioning the petty events happening in their insignificant town, a probing of human understanding and knowledge is performed.

The Romanian filmmaker uses here for the first time his trademark technique, basically an intermedia stratagem, a diversion of perspective. While the spectators are sitting in the movie theater, instead of watching a proper film, the second half of this production is nothing more than a low-quality TV program. This *intermedial* practice, where the film is no longer filmic (an issue discussed in detail later on), becomes one of the most important mechanisms of the *non-cinematic*. With undertones from the absurdist theater, Porumboiu builds up the dialogue between the alcoholic teacher, the disconcerted pensioner, and the narcissistic TV producer with the typical bitter–sweet irony of Romanian storytellers which I discussed extensively in another study (Pop 2014: 153–80). At this level, the interaction between the three men is nothing more than a parody of philosophical dramaturgy. For example, just before the beginning of the debate one of the guests leaves the set, the other begins drinking and they all have a conversation about not swearing during the show while cursing and exchanging obscenities.

The station manager and self-appointed anchor opens the debate by making a reference to the "great Plato" and the even more famous "myth of the cave." The director and screenwriter carefully prepared this moment; when he introduced Jderescu in the first part of the movie, we could observe that on his home bookshelf he had the busts of Plato and Aristotle. When Jderescu asks in his live program "What if, when we exited a cave, we entered another one?" (here, in a funny counterpoint, Mr. Pișcoci knocks on wood superstitiously), the filmmaker plunges the viewers into some of the deepest philosophical questions (albeit sarcastically).

The reference to Plato is clearly ironic, but it also carries a non-philosophical component. Coupled with the cinematographic decision to shoot half of the film like a TV program, it discloses a level of meanings that goes beyond the visible and the explicit onscreen projection. The way in which the question is asked by the character is humoristic; yet, as Jean-Louis Baudry (1975) argued when raising the problems related to Plato's famous myth of the cave and the cinema apparatus, we cannot avoid understanding here that the allegory from the "Republic" is about the limits of moviemaking. All spectators sitting in a movie theater are in a Platonic cave, where the narratives, the dialogues, the characters, and the visual elements projected on the wall are illusions, fake experiences induced by an unnatural source of light.

Obviously, Jderescu is just a fake philosopher, thinking in platitudes such as "there is no present without a future, nor a future without a present." Next, he takes a leap of reasoning quoting Heraclitus and the central statement of the doctrine of the universal flux: "No man can dip in the waters of the same river twice" (which he most probably looked up previously in a dictionary back home). Then he invites his guests and spectators to "dive into the Ocean" and discuss what happened sixteen years ago. This is when he addresses a direct question to Mănescu: "What do you say, was it or was it not a Revolution in our town?" What is the philosophical relevance of such trivial questions, what can we learn besides the transparent references to the political dilemmas of post-communist Romania? By interrogating if there was or there wasn't a real Revolution in Vaslui, Porumboiu is simultaneously opening a wide expanse of philosophical questionings. It is in this purposefully simplistic mise-en-scène, in the banality of the debates about the local "revolution" led by an alcoholic teacher, we begin questioning our own ability to really grasp the reality of our everyday existence.

This remarkable debut feature film is practicing a type of philosophical doubt with profound consequences. In fact, the key issue is not *onscreen* at any time. As the director probes and questions the very nature of cinema, the debate about reality and history being nothing more than fiction, induced by our representations, becomes an indirect question of the moviemaker. This goes beyond the problems raised by the characters and their dialogue; it is invisible in the immediate representation. The unassuming retiree, Mr. Pişcoci, raises an apparently unimportant issue: "Do you know how they turn the streetlights on?" Like his conversation partners, who fail to see what is the connection between street electricity and the Revolution, the viewers are not aware of how cinema generates thinking. It is only at the end of the movie, when we see the final shots with the streetlights in

Vaslui turning on and off, and as we hear the interior monologue of the TV station cameraman, we begin processing the meanings. The light bulbs that a movie turns on in our heads, the thinking processes stimulated by the film experience are never immediate, but extra-cinematic.

While asking what are the limits of the philosophy *of* cinema (intermediated by the tension between the medium of film and that of television) or how movies can provide philosophical arguments (with the help of the philosophical questioning in the dialogues), Porumboiu is concurrently performing a *non-philosophical* examination. Unlike the great "philosophical blockbusters," such as *The Matrix*, fusing together kung-fu and Plato's cave, which brings together Hollywood cinematics and ancient philosophy (Irwin 2002: 10), Porumboiu's *anti-philosophical* approach creates the conditions of uncovering the truth by negating any intention and possibility to find meanings. Just as Socrates tells this strange story, recounted by the seventh book of "The Republic," in a parabolic reference to himself, since he was the "liberated" cave-dweller who returned to his fellow countrymen trapped by the darkness of ignorance, only to be killed by their blindness, the non-philosopher moviemaker is concealing the any real meanings. When the philosopher claims that this is the human condition, to contemplate shadows on a wall, unwilling to liberate ourselves from the captivity of artificial projections, the same "knowledge gap" happens with us while watching a movie. We are limited by the sensorial imperfections to reach a profound understanding. The allegory of the cave provides extremely tempting associations with cinema, with the enticing possibility that the movie theater is a "cavern of ideas." This explanatory effort, already made in film theory by Nathan Andersen (2014) who overviewed the possible connections between Plato and filmmaking, brings us to the important philosophical meditations about the meanings residing *outside* the film frame, beyond the confines of the "moving images." The argument, explored by many other authors, is that cinema becomes a space for "real philosophy" since films confront the viewers with philosophical questions that naturally induce philosophical thinking. More recently, Andersen (2019) amplified this assumption, by performing another close reading on Godard's *Breathless*. For this professor of philosophy, films can perform "the art of asking questions" by raising issues linked with aesthetics (the classical philosophies *of* film), by provoking moral and ethical issues or epistemological interrogations showing the limits and the nature of our knowledge.

These are proper forms of film-philosophy; yet, my assumption is that the Romanian cinema-makers are practicing a "film non-philosophy," where the lack of cinematic qualities and the negation of the traditional means of expression used in motion pictures lead to philosophical discoveries. Thinking takes place outside of the cavern, never within.

Eristetic Cinema and Mindfucking

Another trend in contemporary moviemaking, which some authors identified as the "mindfuck genre," or "mindfuck cinema" (Eig 2003), can be easily confused with modernist film practices. Several contemporary film directors, who are purposefully manipulating the thoughts and emotions of their spectators, by constantly contradicting the understanding of reality and by systematically using deception, have created a special category of film-thinking. Productions such as *Fight Club* (1999), *Memento* (2000), *Donnie Darko* (2001), or *Shutter Island* (2010) are considered representative for the "thought-provoking" filmmaking. The somewhat uncertain premise is that spectators enjoy being "mindfucked." Through deliberate confusion, these films are able somehow to provide an intellectual pleasure that stems from a state of mental discomfort. Filmgoers reach a form of cerebral stimulation intermediated by the mind-games played by the filmmakers. As it was first proposed in Harry Frankfurt's essay "On Bullshit" (2005), the notion of "mindfuck" is one of the most recent additions to the debates about how thoughts are generated in movies.

Identified as puzzle films with complex plots (Buckland 2009) or as mind-game films (Elsaesser 2009), these productions are supposed to stimulate philosophical inquiry by distorting the classical narrative mechanisms, through story misdirections and uncertainty. What makes this discussion relevant for our current investigation is that we can trace, together with McGinn (2008: 14), the resources of "mindfucking" back to Plato, where it was a negative reaction against the Sophists and their rhetorical tricks. While I do not agree with the reputable philosophy professor's comparing of the Socratic questioning with mindfucking, which was clearly not resulting in "doubt, confusion and mental soreness" (McGinn 2008: 64), in my examination the problem of cinema as a vehicle of altering reality through cinematic devices represents a focal point.

As I attempted to show in the chapter dedicated to Mungiu, *eristetic* questioning is a peculiar form of interrogation, practiced extensively by Romanian filmmakers, which brings them closer to modernist ambiguity and can create similarities with mind-game cinema. Yet, when compared to "mindfuck" films, which end up providing disclosures and solutions to the problems of the protagonists, *eristetic* narrations leave out various parts of the story, many questions remain undisclosed and unanswered. Although both modes of narration alter the viewers experience and cause a similar state of confusion, the difference is that *eristetic* narration is not simply preoccupied with generating an intelligent cinema, nor do they belong to the paradigm of the "smart cinema," as described by Perkins (2012).

The major dissimilarity with the notion of puzzle film, or mind-twisting narratives, is that these films are genuinely results of effort to *un-fuck* the minds of the viewers. Porumboiu practices this type of "un-fucking" in *12:08 ...* and in all his following movies. Elements that appear to create "uncertainty" or "hesitation" within the storytelling are truly instruments opening to the possibility of a better knowledge. By negating the direct access to meanings they expose the false assumptions we have about reality. Non-philosophical cinema is about un-thinking false truths and biased ideas.

The interest in re-creating the events of history or the immediate reality represents a constant narrative incentive for many Romanian cinema makers. Starting with Lucian Pintilie's *Reconstruction* (*Reconstituirea*, 1968), where the re-enactment of a minor incident leads to a terrible tragedy, to the particular interest for reconstructing the events of the Romanian revolution, moviemakers like Cătălin Mitulescu, Radu Muntean, Radu Gabrea, or Andrei Ujică worked on this premise. Perhaps the most relevant example is the documentary film made by Ujică, *The Autobiography of Nicolae Ceaușescu* (*Autobiografia lui Nicolae Ceaușescu,* 2010). In this remarkable reconstruction of history the filmmaker pieces together the identity of the dictator by using only official propaganda television footage. While it is not actually a fiction film, this cinematographic reassembling of the past and of the hidden meanings of history by non-cinematographic instruments is illustrative for the approach specific for the contemporary Romanian directors discussed here.

It is not the reality of a socialist society that is re-constructed with the help of a convoluted cinema technique. Porumboiu is not only performing a form of remembrance of the past, as suggested by some critics, but he is also addressing the very ability of cinema to write and rewrite historical facts and history itself. Just as propaganda films were a falsification of history, the *non-cinematic* practices are creating narratives that are not concerned with the events, nor do they alter the meanings as completely fictional stories. They are questioning the role of cinema in altering our perception and understanding by fully incorporating this alteration into their discourse.

Thus a second premise I want to introduce here is that the Romanian contemporary filmmakers are creating a type of cinema exploring forms of expressions that are not targeting only the brains of the viewers. Through more personal forms of representation, belonging to a *visceral* cinematic modality, they create filmworlds not projected only "onto" the material screen of the movie theater. A displacement is enacted opening to meanings beyond the immediate perception. The analysis of the following films takes into consideration this transformation of the artistic forms of expression, based on processes that can be described as *de-cinematization* and *de-dramatization*.

As it will become explicit from the analysis of the experimental movie *The Second Game* or the more conceptual *Metabolism,* we are exposed to a purposeful de-dramatization of cinema, part of a larger effort of emptying creating meanings outside the cinematic. The apparent emptiness of these films becomes an important element only when understood as part of a search for an enigmatic sensation, for the palpable and the sensorial in a medium that is predominantly visual. As Roland Barthes (1957/1972) used the term, we can identify in Porumboiu's movies a quest for "visceral signs" for a hidden dimension of significations which are still residing within cinematic representations, yet absent from the visible field. This term describes a type of cinema that supersedes the sensorial and the emotional (inherent to the cinematic) and circumscribes a profound search for the invisible nature of representations in filmmaking.

That Cinema Which Is Not a Cinema

By paraphrasing the title of a famous Magritte painting, "Ceci n'est pas une pipe," I propose to explore first the conceptual intent in Porumboiu's approach to cinematic art. Understanding the philosophical treatment of these movies with the help of Magritte's expression does not mean that the Romanian director has anything to do with surreal cinema (although sometimes the real is displaced toward a surreal sensation). While the narratives remain deeply rooted in the logic of cinematic realism and the social dimensions are kept intact, we can ascribe the following explanation to many of these movies: "Ceci n'est pas un film" (This is not a movie).

As noted before, Corneliu Porumboiu did not start his career as the most innovative contemporary Romanian filmmaker. His first films, dominated by an acute realism combined with a touch of dark humor, were adhering fully to the New Wave stylistics. Yet, unlike other authors of this generation who kept repeating in a mannerist fashion the same practices and modes of expression, Porumboiu constantly explored the boundaries of cinematographic and narrative norms. By this, he was gradually transforming his entire philosophy of moviemaking. Particularly after 2013, as he engaged in various experiments with cinema-making techniques, the remarkable transformation took his art toward a fundamentally *non-cinematic* dimension. This shift from conventional storytelling to a more conceptualized cinema must be understood as part of a widespread tendency in recent Romanian films, followed by many others—including Cristian Mungiu, Cristi Puiu, Radu Muntean, or Radu Jude.

We can undoubtedly identify two distinctive movements in the development of Porumboiu's cinema-making matrix, with differences noticeable at the level of content and well as in the modalities of expression dominating each production. The first group of films is limited to earlier attempts, like *On the Wings of the Wine* (*Pe aripile vinului*, 2002) and *A Trip to the City* (*Călătorie la oraș*, 2003). Two of the masterpieces of this director, *12:08 East of Bucharest* (*A fost sau n-a fost*, 2006) and *Police, Adjective* (*Polițist*, *adjectiv*, 2009), are also based on narrative coherence and strong social references. They continue to follow a basic, linear construction, while also respecting the logic of realistic representation. Preoccupied with presenting an unembellished image of Romanian society, the director uses mostly an *exoscopic* mode of representation. These films are critical commentaries about Romania's past and present, depicting contemporary society from an ironic point of view and offering a bitter–sweet perspective on the nature of human relationships in post-communist societies. However, Porumboiu moves toward a more radical option, in dissonance with some of his fellow cinema-makers, as he abandons the compelling realist representations of life and starts pursuing more *conceptualized* forms of expression.

This shift taking place in Romanian cinema-thinking, defined by my reformulation of the Magritte formula, is not presupposing that a moviemaker creates a cinema which is *not* cinematic, as in the "no film" experiments; rather, it means that a *non*-cinema is made possible. Following in the footsteps of avant-garde filmmakers, without going as far as to reject the celluloid support, the experiments with narratives and cinematographic practices, with stylistic and thematic approaches, are predominant in this second stage of evolution in Porumboiu's cinematic art. This alteration begins when, after four years of cinematic "silence," the Romanian moviemaker was finally able to direct his third feature film. Without establishing any psychoanalytical connections, it becomes explicit why after a long period of "artistic silence" he ended up finishing a self-reflexive movie, relevantly subtitled *Metabolism*—full title *When Evening Falls on Bucharest or Metabolism (Când se lasă seara peste București sau Metabolism*, 2013)). This marked a radical transformation in his vision about cinema and the artistic role of a filmmaker, marked by a breakthrough that I identify as the *endoscopic* properties of cinema. The following two movies—*The Second Game* (*Al doilea joc*, 2014) and *The Treasure* (*Comoara*, 2015)— were continuations of this transformative direction, deepening his constant conceptual and philosophical inclinations. Finally, with *La Gomera* (2019) he accomplished the transformation of the modes of expression, by exploring the *a-lingual* dimensions of moviemaking.

In all these productions the Romanian director addresses one of the most profound questions about his craft, investigating the ontological nature of the cinematic, and exploring the most problematic components of the substance of cinema in the new millennium. By conceptualizing meaning-making practices in film and, more importantly, by internalizing the relationship between the medium itself and the effects on the author and the viewers, Porumboiu offers us some of the most acute insights on what it means to be a movie director and about the internal mechanisms of cinema-making. For the following interpretations I am using examples extracted from the works of the Romanian director as case studies, representative for alternative cinema-making practices that are not specific to Romanian cinema. They are indicative of many other explorations of the *non-cinematic* in the seventh art today.

Discrepant Cinema and the Non-cinematic

At a certain level, there is a predicament of contemporary cinema that seems to be irresolvable, caused by a practical transformation. Filmmaking is confronted today with profound changes induced by digital technologies. New movie cameras and innovative practices are pushing the limits of the cinematic; thus, many media theorists and film critics consider that cinema is reconfigured by the new technologies. We are now in a *post-cinematic* moment (Willis 2005), the new practices producing new cultural paradigms. Before moving forward with my own arguments, I must underline that my line of interpretations is not based here on the distinction between the "analog" and the "digital," as suggested by Holly Willis or Anne Friedberg (2006). I don't consider that there is any difference between the films made "traditionally" and those that are not created on celluloid. The fact that recent movies are made and screened on "digital" or "analogous" support does not make them more cinematic, nor automatically *non*-cinematic. The numerous examples of digital films created by European auteurs or Hollywood blockbuster directors do not indicate that the changing of the medium itself results in a revision of film practices. In order to avoid any confusions I need to stress that my definitions of the *non*-cinematic are not connected with these transformations.

Also, the truth of the matter is that these problems are not new; multiple experiments were taking place in European art cinema, with the avant-garde films of Buñuel and the cross-media experimental films today showing that moviemaking is never impervious to the presence of other media capable of visual representation. Neither photography, nor television, nor the democratization of video productions was able to disrupt the practices of moviemaking. Even as multiple screens are integrated into moviemaking practices, they are not mutating the foundational practices of cinema. Instead, as it is explicit in the works of many contemporary Romanian filmmakers, the clash between these competing media has become a source of thinking, a media critical perspective, a form of philosophizing about the nature of the cinematic.

Film critics have observed an uncontestable and similar trend in recent Romanian films, as many productions seem to be "contaminated" with different media, like home videos (in *Adalbert's Dream* (*Visul lui Adalbert*), 2011, directed by Gabriel Achim) or found footage (in *A Film for Friends* (*Film pentru prieteni*), directed by Radu Jude)—suggestively both are casting the same actor, Gabriel Spahiu, as the main protagonist. The argument advanced by Mircea Deaca, one of the most important cognitivist theoreticians in Romanian film criticism, who applied the concept of post-filmic when interpreting Cristi Puiu's movie *Aurora* (2010), deserves more attention. Deaca, by using the suggestions of Garrett Stewart (2007), attempts to explain this trend as part of a *postfilmic* cinema. The compelling conclusions presented by this local cognitivist are that some Romanian movies convey the feeling that they were shot by a "psychotic camera" (Deaca 2013: 275), more importantly that the camera has another objective than the reality we see immediately. This is a level where the *profilmic* is close to the non-cinematic. In his thoroughly documented book searching for relevant examples in the films of other investigative European directors, the Romanian critic also discusses the issues of the camera that hides reality, while seemingly disclosing it. More relevant for this current discussion is the point that the philosophy of cinema as a representational art and not the ability of particular films to integrate other forms of visualization must be considered a true transformation.

Here I am also discussing the component of the *non-cinematic* which can be manifested at another level than in Cristian Mungiu's *4 Months* .... By briefly returning to the classical distinctions presented by Bordwell (1985: 5) separating "classical cinema" (often identified with Hollywood cinema) and avant-garde modes of filmmaking (also described as "art films" or "European cinema"), the simple separation between the conventional and the non-conventional approaches to the cinematic practices does not account for all situations. The "classical paradigm," today one of the major conventions in global cinema, remains intact. It is not the practical use of cinema tools that changes; what makes a movie cinematic or *non*-cinematic is the attitude of the moviemaker. At the opposite end of the "excessively *obvious cinema*" (Bordwell 1985: 1) are not only the avant-garde experiments. The *explicit* mode of filmmaking is particularly designed for a viewing experience keeping the spectator relatively safe emotionally. It does not provoke any complex thought functions and it provides all the necessary information *on*screen. The narration, together with the cinematography, is constantly "orienting" the spectators and provides quick cues for understanding. This makes cinema a logical and stable visual environment (Bordwell 1985: 50–6), a "classical" mode of expression (albeit, as discussed before, "classical" is an improper term).

In contrast with this taxonomy and diverging from the *explicit* cinema, there are several moviemaking practices contesting the assumption that meanings must be created immediately, or in a direct relationship between the images *onscreen* and their intended impact on the mind and the soul of the spectators. We can radically contrast this type of moviemaking with what the French artist Isidore Isou (born in Botoșani, Romania as Ioan-Isidor Goldstein) described as *discrepant* cinema. Isou provocatively encouraged his fellow artists to cultivate a type of spectator who was able to "eliminate the photo from cinema" (Cabañas 2015: 14), to create a form of film without photography. His definition of "cinema as insolent art" is a radical expansion of the Dadaist vision about art, as he claimed the need for constructing a cinema where the meanings were never expected nor easily anticipated. Besides this *non*-cinematic definition of cinema, Isou advanced the idea that the medium itself must be used against its own technical limitations. So, instead of a type of cinema where everything must be explicit, simple, and direct, a new form can be created.

As Kaira Cabañas demonstrates in the analysis of the works of Isidore Isou and the Lettrist films (which included other authors, like Lemaître), these avant-garde artists dismissively refused the rules of "bourgeois" cinema, taking further the important battle of contesting the "obsolete" ways of making art in movies. In this exploration for new expression forms of expression, one of the solutions explicitly showcased by the infamous "Chapter III" of the *Traité de bave et d'éternité* (*Venom and Eternity*, 1951) was the re-definition of cinema as a type of creation that "does what it should not do." For the Lettrists this was the only way in which the medium could reinvent itself, by becoming its total negation, a *non-cinema*.

Obviously, Porumboiu's approach to filmmaking is neither Lettrist nor radical. Yet it belongs to the same attitude; his experimentations extract their resources from the vanguard thinking. The modes of expression he uses are going against the conventions of the medium, as Porumboiu is exploring not only how meanings can be generated "on the screen," but also how the significations emerge when emptying the cinematic space and style of their intrinsic characteristics. Porumboiu opens the way for a "mysterious" dimension of cinema, one that cannot be discovered by following the canons of classical cinema. By refusing the rules of a prescribed cinema, by reaching toward the very limits of the medium itself, he discovers the resources of the *non-cinematic*.

In order to proceed with these arguments, I consider it important to take the idea back to some of the most radical forms of contesting the conventional cinematic strategies, as elaborated by many of the representatives of Surrealism and Dadaism, and to find the inner motivations of these reactions.

The Dada Attitude, the Dada Thinking

We cannot understand the practices of *cinema discrepant* without connecting Isidore Isou and his guttural cries to Tristan Tzara's Dada sound poetry, and their refusals of language will reverberate in Porumboiu's film, *The Whistlers*. This is more than a superficial connection, since the Dada movement has deep Romanian roots. As documented by Tom Sandqvist (2006), it is not by chance that three of the founders of the famous "Cabinet

Voltaire" in Zürich, the official birthplace of Dadaism, were born and raised in Romania: Tristan Tzara, Arthur Segal, and Marcel Iancu. These young men grew up in the literary avant-garde environment that fermented in Bucharest at the beginning of the twentieth century. Tzara (born in Moinești, Romania, as Samuel Rosenstock) together with Iancu, a close friend, and illustrator of many Dada works, or Gherasim Luca, later one of the most important surrealist French poets, also born in Romania, were part of the many avant-garde movements in Bucharest.

It is not my purpose here to provide an understanding of this complex avant-garde group and its many facets. There is a Berlin Dada, a Zürich Dada, a Paris Dada, or New York Dada, and the paternity of this movement was claimed controversially by Marcel Duchamp, Francis Picabia, and many others. Whether or not Tzara invented the name of the movement (as an ironic reference to the Romanian use of "yes/yes" as a form of "no") is less relevant, since the Dada spirit is more important than the word itself. While some attributed the term "Dada" to Hugo Ball, it is certain that Tzara most (in)coherently defined the "dadaist attitude" in his 1916 "Dada manifesto." Dada is a type of negativity that embraces contradictions, a refusal of canons based on vagueness and an attack against all forms of cultural seriousness, rejecting (and even despising) stability and formalism.

Tzara, who was a self-proclaimed anti-philosopher, stated in his 1916 manifesto that Dada "means nothing"; it "represents nothing definite," yet is always "growing, constantly changing and developing." Later, in a 1922 lecture, Tzara defined Dada as "a state of mind" which is based on simplicity. It is simultaneously a manifestation of the new and the celebration of the already used; it is subversive and destructive; it goes against art and yet it remains a form of renovation of the artistic forms of expression. The predisposition for experimentation in Dadaist thinking is easily mistaken with a destructive compulsion. Yet, as Malcom Turvey (2013: 20–1) keenly observed, it would be wrong to understand Dada only as nihilistic, nor as Noël Carroll defined the Dadaist cinema, as being dominated by a "spirit of negation." Dada is constructive and, while being critical of modernity, it represents an attempt to find alternatives to conventional thinking and making art. While treated sometimes simplistically as "experimental," the Dada attitude is not solely about experimentalism. As Tzara acknowledged when explaining his "techniques of destruction," these are not simply actions of cutting and randomly rearranging pieces of newspaper. The Dada mode of thinking art is not simply limited to the techniques of collage or photomontage, nor to the aleatory coupling of disparate significations.

More commonly known for its language experiments, its typography, and photography collages, Dada had an important cinematic component and the principles of Dadaism very profoundly influenced Tzara's American friend, Man Ray. The famous rayograms and his a-photographic renunciation and rejection of the photographic machine have common roots with the idea of a *non-cinematic* cinema. Just as the rules of grammar were subverted by the a-grammaticality of Dada poetry, the a-cinematographic experiments of Man Ray are close to the anti-poetic and anti-literary efforts to find the lost purity of these forms of expression. Like Dada poetry, the non-cinema is a negative affirmation, a rejection intended as an assertion, not a total annihilation. Non-cinema must also be connected with Dadaism through its rejection of traditional narrative "reasoning." Non-artistic art and non-cinematic cinema are linked with the Dada movement since, as noted by Richardson (2006), Dadaist cinema is a form of anti-film, an expression of the radical negation of cinematic conventions and rules. While such a generalizing definitions might allow us to include here any non-conventional film, it is clearly too broad and it opens to an improper taxonomy which incorporates all "unconventional" films.

While there are many examples of films influenced by Dadaism, we cannot label them as "Dadaist" simply because they mix elements of avant-garde experimentation with surrealist tropes or by claiming a radical anti-art attitude. In fact, we do not have a specific film style which can be undoubtedly identified as Dadaist cinema, not even Man Ray's experiments can qualify as such. Some authors have included in this potential category Fernand Léger's *The Mechanical Ballet* [*Ballet Mechanique*, 1924], or the short film directed by René Clair, *Entr'acte* (1924), which violates all the principles of the cinematic narrative. These productions, containing many Dadaist elements, can be classified within the purist paradigm, a cinema with Dadaist traits. Relevantly enough, among the interpreters of *Entr'acte* were the composer Erik Satie, the painters Marcel Duchamp and Francis Picabia, together with Man Ray. Presented as an "intermezzo" for a Dada event it was actually ignored by the spectators, who later admitted they never knew it was "a movie."

The mixture of absurd, grotesque, abstract, and randomness, all specific elements for the Dada thinking, are surpassed by the extraordinary *The Return to Reason* (*Le retour à la raison*, 1923), really pushing the boundaries of the cinematic beyond its filmic limits. This three-minute long film created by Man Ray for the final "Dada Soirée" organized by Tzara in Paris under the sarcastic name "Evening of the Bearded Heart," which ended up with a fight between the public and the organizers, was a contradiction of terms starting with its own title (as we will discuss, a practice recurrent in Romanian contemporary cinema). Making an appeal to reason in a film exploring the irrational, this is the quintessential Dada gesture.

Ray, who provocatively signed his letters to Tzara as "directeur du mauvais movies" ("bad movies director"), remains our best guide for understanding how the Dadaists envisioned their new type of "bad" moviemaking. Exploring the possibility to make a movie without the movie camera, the experiments designed by Man Ray, who was among the first to suggest that films do not have to go through the movie camera in order to capture reality, are some of the purest forms of representation. Ultimately the camera is nothing more than an intermediary that falsifies reality. Ray expanded his rayographic technique, already experimented in various photographic works, and applied it to moving pictures. The American artist exposed various objects directly on the surface of the celluloid and made a film that was not a film at all. Instead, he generated a negation of all cinematic rules, with random movements, light games, body projections inducing meanings directly on the material of the film itself. Called by Ray "obscenema," it was supposed to be the cinema of the future, one that could allow more than the juxtaposing of visual elements or various ludic practices, otherwise considered incompatible with cinema. Unfortunately, Ray made only two more films, *Emak Bakia* (1926), a cine-poetry (cinépoème) experiment, and *The Starfish* (*L'étoile de mer*, 1928), both starring Kiki "de Montparnasse," his muse at the time. No further developments of these capabilities of the Dada style were ever made, as Ray never returned to cinema-making anymore.

Nevertheless, Ray himself remains an embodiment of the Dada spirit. His desire to free cinema from all the rules and his courage to explore the irrational and to use irony as forms of meaning-making are all manifestations of the Dada attitude. This avant-garde artist has shown how the technological foundations of the cinematic can be contested, that the photographic camera, in fact the very nature of cinematic representation, is not the only means of making movies. By extension, we can consider all provocative and innovative forms of cinema, any ironic mockery of the existing cinematic norms, as part of the "Dada attitude."

Without contesting the important scholarship about this current, my understanding of Dada thinking and the Dada postures expands beyond the specific manifestations of the art movement. While Dadaism remains one of the most important European artistic and cultural phenomena of early modernity, the multitude of Dada manifestos never coalesced into a single art philosophy. Since there is no single definition as to what Dada is supposed to be, we can identify the Dada attitude as any form of challenging the limits and restrictions of traditional forms of expression. Dada approaches to art are more than simplistic words games or the enactment of shocking events, designed to impress the bourgeois public. Although it was often described as an anti-art movement, the Dada attitude in literature or painting can be expanded into cinema and subsume any rejection of rules. To indirectly respond to Katherine Dreier's lecture entitled "Do You Want to Know What a Dada Is?," Dada is any form of repudiation or denunciation of the mechanisms of any art form.

Finally the greatest mystery of all, as Tristan Tzara (1975: 384) proclaimed, was that anybody knowing the secrets of Dada could never tell what Dada is. Let us ignore Tzara for a little while and expose some of these overt secrets.

The Non-cinema as a Negation of the Cinematic

Without trying to argue that Porumboiu is a Dadaist moviemaker, I consider that this kind of film-thinking is deeply rooted in a conceptual approach to cinematic art and, for that matter, to a particular philosophical understanding of the world. Porumboiu's films indicate several functions specific to conceptualism. The most famous conceptual representations, such as the widely known Magritte pipe or Duchamp urinal, are real objects contradicting intellectually and textually the very nature of the representable. When a film director approaches cinema with the same negation of the purpose of the materials and representation practices of movies, when the cinematic object is substituted completely and the movie camera is no longer part of the cinematic process, this refusal of norms and conventions produces a complete conceptual turn (Figure 3.2).

The Second Game is such an "everyday film," in which a conversation between the moviemaker and his father, taking place while watching an old football match on a video-recorder, is transformed into an artistic object. And by doing so, during the projection of a cinematic production, the director is announcing his spectators: "This is not a movie." A similar mechanism will be put into action in other films, such as *Metabolism*, as the cinematic nature is subverted during the very process of watching the movie. We see a film projected onscreen and, at the same time, we are witnessing another movie being made. While watching this secondary level unfolding, the metacinematic is used as a reference for the absence of that very film. In

FIGURE 3.2 *An obscure soccer match and a conversation between a father and his son are the instruments used by Porumboiu in* The Second Game *to create a non-cinematic film. Courtesy 42 Km Film.*

Metabolism a remarkable scene shows the main protagonists, a film director and his actress, rehearsing for a scene of the movie they make, that we will never see. What we are actually presented onscreen becomes an expression of a representation intended to remain *outside* the cinematic. This disruption of our understanding of the nature of representations makes us part of a film that is only a substitute of an absence. The film director is disclosing his intentions again: *this is not a film you are looking at,* but *keep watching!*

With *The Second Game* Porumboiu challenges the rules of cinematic representation in a typical Dada attitude, by practicing a multi-layered negation of what a film means. Contesting all our expectations about the epistemology of moviemaking, he creates an almost unwatchable film. With the visible field blurred, centered around a story that is nothing more than a banal conversation, and with no apparent meanings, is there anything left of the cinematic? By using only archival material, viewing a soccer match recorded by television cameras in Communist Romania, reproduced on a video recorder, only to be then projected in a movie theater, the entire ontology of cinema is subverted.

At this level, *The Second Game* must be understood as an *intermedial experiment*, in the sense attributed by Lars Elleström (2010), who compellingly argued in his book about media borders that the relationship between intermediality and multimodality is fundamental when trying to understand the interplay between arts. The combination of any recent media, like mobile phone pictures or other digital screen recordings, with old media (as analog cinema is today), becomes relevant when discussing their interval created between them as a meaning-making tool. The function of each particular medium of expression is negated by the intermedial fusion, and by this each media can access new possibilities previously prohibited.

Exposed to the absolute contempt for the rules of cinema-making, some critics doubted that there were any profound meanings in *The Second Game*. Failing to recognize its complexity, the projection seemed to be just another "boring Romanian movie." Seemingly filled with "senseless pictures," monotonous to exhaustion, it was evaluated as a trivial and simplistic mode of making films (Totok 2014). Indeed, one can ask what is the point of creating a movie which exposes the viewer for an hour and a half to an old soccer game, almost impossible to watch and taking place in December 1988—not even the year of the Romanian Revolution. A blurred television image, commented by a father and a son who, from time to time, even speak on the mobile phone, can qualify as cinema-making. How can home video or cell phone technology coalesce with an obscured screen and, more importantly, how can such an approach be relevant for the way in which the cinematic meanings are generated?

The immediate level of significations is generated with the help of another non-cinematic instrument, as the projection begins with an explicitly personal intertitle. The textual narration is recounting how, when the director was seven to eight years old, somebody called him on the phone and told him that, if he did not persuade his father to give up being a football referee, his father will "return home in a coffin." The director creates a self-reflexive framework for his story, generating an extra-cinematic context enclosing the 100 minutes remaining in which the spectators are presented only with "bad images" captured by an old videotape of an old football match. These unclear images are overlapped with the voices of two men, and it soon becomes apparent that they are re-watching this game at home, while discussing other apparently unimportant things. As we receive more cues from their interaction, we realize that the two are father and son—Adrian Porumboiu, Corneliu Porumboiu's father, and the director himself. Porumboiu the elder was one of the most famous football referees during Communism, and later he owned his own soccer team in their hometown of Vaslui. His attitude is somehow detached as he appears to be unaware of the fact that the son is recording this discussion.

More importantly, the two teams playing are Dinamo and Steaua, at that time the most important teams in Romanian soccer league. Once this external context is established, it allows father and son to talk about the past, while making small-talk observations about the present. The match, which took place late December 1988, was refereed by Adrian Porumboiu himself, and was important not only for the Romanian sports but also for understanding how individuals perceived reality. Another important ontological issue is related to the politics of the recorded reality we see onscreen. As the cameramen at that time were under heavy political surveillance, the Communist regime prohibited them to show the viewers what actually happened on the field. In fact the television operators were instructed to move the camera "over" to the spectators, in order to cover any negative attitudes of the players during the matches. At some point an important player appears on the field with a head bandage; yet, the spectators never saw the actual incident, as the physical conflict between the two teams on the field was hidden by the technical intervention of the cameramen during the "live" shooting of the event. By re-framing the picture in a neutral portion of the visual field, the offscreen becomes a negation of reality. By this, the director is pointing to the hidden and edited nature of "the Real," thus revealing the most relevant part of the discussions between the two men.

Found Footage Philosophy, or How to Make a "Bad Film"?

Porumboiu operates like a "bad movies" director, in the sense used by Man Ray. In order to understand this approach, we must start by questioning the nature of this production and describe the strategies used to transform a video into a film which is considered worthy to be projected in movie theaters. The first level of intervention, always activated whenever filmmakers use found footage, is the implicit exploration of authenticity. To reacquire "found footage" materials as original and unaltered representations means that the film director expresses a distrust in the cinematic medium. Cinema might be "fake," but the archival material is corresponding to reality.

The practice of integrating home video footages in movies is not a novelty in filmmaking. "Classical" found footage techniques were used before in order to present fictional stories as if they were real recordings—the most famous example remains the opening sequence in *Citizen Kane*. More importantly, after Soderbergh's *Sex, Lies, and Videotape* (1989), the technique itself has become an integral part of mainstream Hollywood practices. The success of films such as *The Blair Witch Project* (1999) leads to the integration of fake television footage or live recordings into the cinematic discourses (as is in *Cloverfield*, 2008). Yet as the "real" becomes a staged real-time, such reconstructed live recordings are the ultimate fake and simulacra of reality.

In Porumboiu's experiment the exploration of television footage and its projection onto the movie theater screen is not practiced as a validation of reality. In fact we are not simply exposed to a television program; the televised mode never takes over the cinematic. We are not seeing "live" images in a real context, as in found footage cinema. Instead an intermedial environment is recreated allowing the film director to insert a secondary screen, functioning as an in-between. The video-recording is altering an already-altered material; thus, it soon becomes clear that we are seeing a transformed version of reality. The live presentation, the match that took place in Communist Romania, is no longer the "real" game, once it is trapped in the media no-man's land between cinema, video, and television.

At first glance, watching this null match appears to be gratuitous. It has no clear purpose and no apparent consequences; we know the outcome; there is no dramaturgy or action. However, this is precisely what makes it a *non*-cinematically relevant production. Only by paying attention we realize that it reveals the murky nature of society during Communism, providing a setting for a further exploration of the intimate relationships between human beings during a time of total social control. The anguish of a young boy and his perspective on reality, completely different from that of his father, exposes the multifaceted nature of the Real. When the director tells his parent that, when he saw the game for the first time he was filled with fear, his father asks him in a detached manner: "How old were you?" "I was 13," the director replies, and father simply gasps. It is in these interstices between their two "realities" and their different reading of that reality that our insights as spectators are generated. While watching the game the son observes that the players were fighting, while the father ignores it; then the son claims that the match is beautiful, and the father declares that is irrelevant. Not only their "realities" are completely different—with the son reminiscing about his fears and emotional discomfort, and the father considering the entire game to be unimportant—but their usage of reality is altered. "Nobody watches things from the past," Porumboiu Sr. dismissively tells his son, and this inference contradicts the very nature of what they are doing. An old football match is just like cinema or any other art form. It has its moment in time, only to then disappear into immateriality.

This discussion about the irrelevant nature of the soccer match, and by consequence, of any content production, has to be connected with the deeper questioning of the qualities of cinema as art. Using a term proposed by Bernard and Rabin (2009: 23) to describe the role of archival materials, the *ephemeral* nature of the initial footage comes with a predetermined function, many recorded representations have a limited purpose. From the very moment that they were created, many images and materials from the past (televised or photographed) served the purpose of being shown only once. They were never intended to be re-watched ever again.

The soccer game footage, no matter how relevant at the moment of its original broadcast, is now a degraded signifier. Almost all the emotional and personal meanings are lost; the event itself has been blurred and its relevance lost. Most probably during the real-time broadcasting of this particular program it influenced the real lives of the people watching it, and the players involved in the game were affected. But in the present this is a non-event. The father observes this paradox when he suggests that his moviemaker son should have picked up a more "memorable" television broadcast, like the Cup Finals in 1988, when the entire Steaua team left the stadium, considering that their goals were unfairly annulled by the official referees. By internally contesting the relevance of the material, the subject/object positions the viewers into a frame of understanding denouncing the very nature of the representable. This question makes even more problematic the relevance of this visual representation. Why should we watch unclear and washed away images when even the participants of these events discard their importance? Why expose ourselves to a "bad film," with indiscernible moving images and discussing trivial matters. Once more, it is the interval that becomes relevant. Adrian Porumboiu is simultaneously an "actor," as the father of the moviemaker, a real person, as the referee of the real match, a commentator, and a viewer of the archival footage. This is a state of absolute in-betweenness that provides the ideal context for cinematic-thinking.

As suggestively indicated by Jihoon Kim (2016) when discussing Hito Steyerl's films, another relevant mechanism is the usage of unclear pictures. This must be connected with the "politics of poor image," a cinematic strategy compelling the viewers to re-configure the qualities of the medium and its ability to carry messages. This is a common element in Porumboiu's productions created during the second stage of his career. *Metabolism, The Second Game,* or *Comoara* are all movies that deal, albeit in a different manner, with the limits of the medium and explore the possibilities provided by the presence of non-cinematic media, conveying meanings otherwise inaccessible. When Porumboiu uses different non-cinematic media inside the medium of film, this intervention allows the questioning of the ontological and epistemological limits of cinema as a representational tool. Using antiquated television footage in *The Second Game*, including an endoscopic recording in *Metabolism*, or displaying ultrasound recordings as an integral part of the visual field of the spectators in *The Treasure*, the film director is interrogating the nature of his own craft. During the crossover from one medium to another, through the constant intervention and overlapping of media, from television to digital screens, from endoscopic recordings to ultrasound scans, the "transmedial" encounters expose the limitations of the cinematic.

In order to process these media intervals we need another set of definitions, allowing us to interpret the explorations of the non-cinematic resources in moviemaking. The televised archival images in *The Second Game* are *outside* the medium of cinema; yet, their presence within a film cannot be described as a form of intermediality, nor as a manifestation of transmediality. The significations traverse the boundaries of both media, and this particular filmic experience is not a "combination" of cinema and television, nor a "dialogue" between home videos and movies. Such meaning-making does not belong to any medium; thus, a new concept needs to be put in place, which can be described as *extramediality*.

Extramediality and the Borders of the Cinematic

My understanding of *extramedial representations* derives from the Derridean concept of *parergon* and the notion of *parergonal logic*, elaborated with reference to the nature of truth in painting (Derrida 1987). To simplify the arguments, I suggest we define *extramediality* as a mental, visual, and conceptual plane, generated wherever an invisible dimension of representation is projected within the medium. As discussed previously, the exteriority of the visible, the hidden nature of the representable in cinema remains a problematic issue in film theory. The dialectic relationship between the visible and invisible, or, as Noël Burch puts it, the complex dialectics of an art which exists in-between the *presence and absence* onscreen (Burch 1969/1981: 17) cannot be dealt with easily. Cinema needs practices of showing which activate a direct visual experience. Yet it can also deal with the unseen, as masterfully illustrated by Hitchcock. Any movie is constructed through a dialectical tension between the elements that are present within the visual field, and those that are only suggested or even absent. This dynamic is also the central premise to my discussion about how *non-cinema* functions. When making a movie the director does more than just to decide what to show. As Jacques Rivette (1961) pointed out in his seminal article about abjection in filmmaking, it is more important what is *not* presented to the viewers, what the director leaves *outside* the screen.

Cinema, and for that matter any art form based on visual representations, is nothing more than a flat image, limited spatially by a predetermined frame. It is a form of expression clearly limited by its own technical restrictions (Aumont et al. 1983: 11–12). As the French film aesthetician suggests, the material nature of the visible provides the specificity of any medium. Limited by the borders of the tableau, restricted by the ends of the projection canvas and the camera format, any representation needs to take place within a visible field. This is even more important in the canonic cinema, where cinematic meanings are always coerced to take place *inside* the visible, that is, *onscreen*.

To concisely review these possibilities, already identified by cinema theory (Gauthier 1982), we can describe four basic visual spaces where narratives can take place: the frame, the extra-frame, the field, and the extra-field—using the French terminology advanced by Gauthier as *cadre, hors-cadre, champ, hors-champ*. The represented space in cinema is ultimately conditioned by the relationship between screen (frame and/or cadre), which delineates the perceptual field of vision, and the field of imagination. The cinematic frame, which contains the cinematic image, is the rectangular shape with fixed boundaries manifested within the movie theater whenever a projection takes place. When used as a positive space, the frame keeps the actions and actors *onscreen*, thus maintaining the "proper" order of meanings. This restricted nature of the cinematic space is considered by classical film theorists as an integral part of what makes moviemaking a "real art," where the composition and aesthetic arrangements of space are essential (Arnheim 1957: 17).

Yet the essence of cinema, as noted early on by cinema-makers like Sergei Eisenstein (1937/1991: 16), is also generated beyond screen limits; it exists in the mysterious space not contained by the frame. As a matter of fact, we never perceive the cinematic visual space as closed. Any spectator when watching a movie has a perceptual experience that is never enclosed by the artificial boundaries of the screen. Eisenstein referred to the differences between these two spatial realities as "kadr," which is different from "frame" as the *inside* of the photographic. The *kadr* (*cadre* in French) contains more than the images made available onto the screen. The particular strips of film (the frames) contain more than what was cut by in camera framing or determined by set construction. As the Soviet director and film theoretician explained, through the process of mise-en-cadre (the putting into a frame) the filmmaker makes reasoned decisions about what is kept *inside* and what is left *outside* the visible representation. In the same time, spectatorship involves an inverse process, sometimes unconscious, by which a reconstructing reality takes place, one that always resides *outside* the frame (as the shot).

The main problem produced by the screen delineating the "outside" of the film is related to the *invisible cinematic content*, often becoming more important than what is actually seen during the screening. Sometimes the directors are using camera movements to show the spectators such previously unseen spaces. Even so, it can never be fully revelatory, with each disclosure we are left with *outsides*, many other parts of the space remain unseen. While Noël Burch (1969/1981) systematically described the possibilities of the "off" space in his seminal work about film practices, identifying the *outside* as the four edges of the frame (left-right, and up-down), there are spaces behind the scene or behind the camera making reality never fully accessible through cinematic means. The *offscreen*, which is a constant and important part of cinematic narration, cannot be predetermined or fully explored.

Many European directors have systematically investigated the spatial aesthetic and the resources of the *outside* of the frame. Most commonly this is done through the techniques of de-framing (decadrage), which in classical films allows the outside of the frame, the "off" space (imaginary or real) to remain a negative dimension. When a character is stepping out of the frame this is either going result in death, or some monstrous action will take place outside the reach of our gaze. In European cinema this is a common practice, with the Romanian New Wave directors transforming it into their trademark technique. As discussed before, some of the best illustrations are provided by *4 Months ...*, as Cristian Mungiu brilliantly uses the interplay between the offscreen (the atrocity of the rape), while keeping the narrative intact (the inside). Both the *outside* (the visible) and the *inside* (the film-world) of a real-life situation are amplified by the interval between the two.

A similar technique is illustrated by Porumboiu in *Metabolism*. By creating the premises of a sex scene between the metacinematic movie director and his actress, he then refuses his viewers the direct access to this intimate interaction. Placed within the possible field of vision, yet separated by the boundaries between what is *inside* the frame and *outside* the visible, the setting is signaling the presence of film-thoughts. The refusal of perceptual experience, as it will be explained in a following section, leaves a bodily trace that generates an immaterial stimulus for the mind.

Once again, by proposing the notion of *extra*-mediality I am taking into account these manifestations that are usually limited in classical film theories to the descriptions of the *offscreen*. My understanding is leaning toward an understanding of non-canonical means of expression, many belonging to the category of "paraerga." When using *extra*-mediality linked with the concept of *extra*-cinematic the system of reference is to those elements that are not intrinsically cinematic (like dialogues), without ever being completely "outside" the functions of the medium. As Derrida argued, no artwork can be understood by simply "showing" or "referring" to something else; the meanings are not only "inside" or "outside." Any external surplus is linked with an interior absence; the excess and the lack thereof are sites of signification (Derrida 1987: 59–60). Such extra-medial expressions can range from the simplest absences or rejections of the ontological properties of cinema as a medium, to the intermedial presence of other forms of representation that are technologically non-cinematic (such as television screens, surveillance cameras, and so on).

In *Metabolism* we have several examples of how the extra-mediatic experience can be created. One of the most intriguing methods is the use of the offscreen as an extra-media space—the scene in which Alina, the actress/lover of the director in the metacinema narration, receives a phone call and quickly exits the visible and audible fields, creating an extra-medial experience. The character is part of the offscreen; she is engaged in a discussion with another person through another medium, one totally inaccessible to the cinema viewer. This cinematic lack, caused by the remote reality of the protagonist, opens the possibility to reconstruct that reality through a second intermediary. When the movie director appears on scene, he opens the door and returns to his own room, which makes the actress visible for a while onscreen only through an opaque window. She is now present and absent simultaneously; the shadow of her body is transmitting messages beyond the access of the camera to her reality. The final extra-media intervention, which induces confusion and makes this reality unattainable, becomes an instrument of knowledge. When the movie camera is recentered between the two rooms, this produces a transfer of ontological dimensions, and it affects the very nature of the cinematic. Just as in *The Second Game*, where the almost opaque television program makes explicit the inapparent meanings, the deformed images of a medium, in this case a wall and the glass of a door, offer more information than the film as a material representation of reality.

The exploration of the offscreen experiences and their extra-cinematic functions are augmented by the use of *multimodal non-cinematic* tools. In *The Second Game* the limits of cinematic representations are signaled by the use of the videotape replaying a television program punctuated by phone conversations. The screen of one medium, although blocking our access to the representational field of another, intermediates the development of significations. When meanings are exported from one medium to another, the absence in one of them is transformed into meanings in the other. As the recording of television cameras loses quality, this facilitates our access "behind" the visible. And when the recorded television show is synchronized with another medium, the sound generated by the microphone in the room that we never see, the sensation of presence created by the sound is not broken by the visual representation; it is an absence creating extra-cinematic ideas. We never see the father and the son who have this conversation, and we only see the ghostlike presence of the father as a young referee in the televised game. Once more, that which is not visible becomes more important than what is presented onscreen.

The apparent banality of the dialogues between father and son *hides* the profound and complex realities uncovered about Communist Romania and about their intimate relationship. While the two are discussing the Communist Secret Police (Securitate), or the connections between the team of the Romanian army (Steaua) and the team of the Miliția (Dinamo), we are presented with a reality that is actually cloaked, not disclosed. The meanings are constructed in the *extra*-cinematic, where we get information that we cannot attain through the medium itself. The political schemings and interpersonal dealings that were taking place "behind the scene" during Ceaușescu's regime are only one part of the *unseen* nature of reality. In fact both the media (the television and the cinema) are acting as instruments of hiding the truth. The "live" television transmission broadcasted at that time was "doctored"; the film we are watching is deceitful; the only access is provided via extra-cinematic mechanisms.

The ontological negation constitutes the principle of extra-cinematic; its functions are instated when the conventional role of a medium is contradicted. Although tele-vision means viewing from a distance, the Romanian director uses the "distance" of the medium to generate intimacy, both domestic and psychological. The same goes for the cinematic, which is supposed to be generated through moving images visible on the screen. Nevertheless, by placing his discussions with his father behind the "curtain" of the soccer match, Porumboiu is able to generate a significant contradiction of the medium. The final negation relies on the long minutes of silence, when we only hear the sound of cigarette lighters, the breathing, coughing, or smoking noises emitted by the two men that we never see.

Porumboiu makes an extra-cinematic film because he simultaneously refuses the conventions of both cinematic *offscreen* and *on* the *screen*. Unlike the classical *offscreen storytelling*, where the all-knowing "Voice" of the narrator creates the coherence of the plot, here the father–son dialogue provides no cues for who is conducting the discussion. The narration is taking place in an intermedial space of indeterminacy. There are no gaze directions, no visible movements; even the offscreen gaze is absent. There is nothing that allows the spectator in classical films to orientate within the visual field. A similar misdirection is happening in the "real-time" of the televised program, which disorientingly overlapped with the real dialogue. The simultaneous projection of two separate timelines generates a confusion of timeframes, the ultimate result of extramediality. Actually the cinematic time ceases to exist in these experimental productions. Here the father and son are constantly moving from one timeframe to another; their past and present are overalapping with the present time of the viewer (who is in the future, from the standpoint of the moviemaker). The "live television" broadcast, which is broken internally, with the nature of visibility contested, is transformed into a present time experience, in turn lacking transparency. The broadcast we see deprives television as a medium of its specific traits—notwithstanding the indirect exposure of the role played by the Communist propaganda machine in the altering of reality. This in turn deprives the cinematic representation of its inner characteristics.

"Doesn't this game look like one of my movies?," Corneliu Porumboiu asks his father bemusedly, observing in a self-ironic way that "it is long and nothing happens." "You are not going to make a film out of this," his father warns him, and clearly the son did not listen to his father since *The Second Game* was projected in cinemas all over the world, winning in 2014 the Best Romanian Feature Film award. It is here that this movie becomes essentially a masterclass for how to practice the techniques of showing the unshown, of hiding the visible in order to make things more explicit, and how contradicting the rules of cinema creates more profound cinematic experiences.

The Meaningless Meaning and the De-dramatization of Cinema

A major point in this line of arguments is that Corneliu Porumboiu's moviemaking practices evolved toward cinematic *de-dramatization*, which is part of a more important development, that of *de-cinematization*. The trend was obvious already in *Police, adjective*—the non-dramatic nature of the story was reasserted by the apparent absence of mobility of the main character, coupled with the relative immobility of the camera. The protagonist, a policeman confronted with moral dilemmas, appears for extended periods of time in a solitary pose. His movements seem to lack direction; his actions are impaired by his own incapacity to react. This process is part of what I previously described as the "abstinent Romanian cinema," a term used to describe the New Wave stylistics adapted in the national film industry (Pop 2014: 65–6). While an *abstinent* cinema is purposefully reduced in intensity and refuses any overtones—opposed to the unclear and pejorative definition of "minimalist"—the *non-*dramatic adds to this type of moviemaking some auxiliary functions. One attribute can be best described as *dramaturgical negation*, a mode of storytelling that is reducing the tension building of the conventionally "active" genres. In *Police, adjective* the instruments of *abstinent* moviemaking allow the de-dramatization of classical police and crime genres. A movie about a policeman which is totally contradicting the tropes of criminal investigation, a typical detective story told in a format that becomes an anti-police movie, centered about a policeman who does almost no policing, leads to the negation of all the tropes the genre. In fact all the prerequisites of "action films" are reverted into a series of in-actions, an accumulation of absences, and non-activities (Figure 3.3). Even the most important element of the genre, the final arrest, takes place in an extra-cinematic space; the entire action is represented with a chalked-out drawing on a blackboard.

While in *The Second Game* Porumboiu practices a total refusal of any theatrical interventions—there are no actors, no entering or exiting the scene and basically there is no scene—other more conventional movies, like *Metabolism*, tone down the negation, but follow a similar logic. More than half of *Metabolism* movie is built around two characters, and even these two protagonists are most of the time unclear, their presence in the visible field is limited. This is a movie where there are no camera movements during the first six scenes, with the first movement happening only when a third person enters the visual field, disrupting the relationship between the director and his actress-lover. Through immobility and de-dramatization Porumboiu creates new dimensions where cinematic expressivity is made possible.

The device of storytelling de-genreification is further conceptualized in Porumboiu's 2015 movie entitled *The Treasure*. Like Godard before him, who enjoyed rescripting the stereotypes and conventions of American popular cinema, the Romanian filmmaker uses the trope of "treasure hunting" and dismantles its inner mechanisms. Treasure hunting is today one of the most popular genres; a movie like *The Pirates of the Caribbean: On Stranger Tides* (2011) reached sales of more than 2.3 million USD in Romania, with

FIGURE 3.3 Police, adjective *presents the inner turmoil caused by the indecisions of a policeman who is not able to act according to his conscience. Courtesy 42 Km Film.*

over 346,000 viewers. The conceptualized version of the genre had a total of 7,045 spectators—not a personal low for this movie director, since *The Second Game* sold only 497 tickets overall in Romania! In financial terms this makes *The Treasure* a failed treasure hunt; thus, we should ask why such revisited versions of one of the most widely used narrative devices in literature (in the prose of Robert Louis Stevenson or H. Rider Haggard) or cinema (from the *Indiana Jones* series to *National Treasure*) did not stimulate the common moviegoers. Why should we bother with failed attempts to create meanings; who do they generate film-thoughts?

There is nothing new about this story; there are no remarkable cinematographic innovations; the inspiring event is utterly banal. Apparently this was a private family memory of Adrian Purcărescu, one of the actors who had a grandfather who buried all his economies in the backyard of his home and forgot about it. Porumboiu even reuses some of his own "buried" visual stereotypes, identifiable in almost all his feature film, such as the three main characters structure—like the professor, the pensioner, and the producer in *12:08 ...*, the three policemen in *Police, adjective*, now we are following around yet another team of three protagonists. This limited number of protagonists, three men searching for a treasure in the backyard of an old, abandoned house, the stylistics of long takes, dominated by slow-paced sequences, is not simply a return to the New Wave practices. This purposefully minimalist setting creates the conditions for a non-cinematic experiment, the result being a multi-layered movie, with multiple intra- and intertextual references.

At the first level some of these references are directly linking *The Treasure* with the classical tropes, then connects the movie with cinematic works only to finally question of the inner mechanisms of cinema.

Porumboiu evacuates the basic dramaturgical elements of storytelling; in this narrative gap a thinking space is created, for exploring and understanding the challenges of cinematic ideas, through non-cinematic devices. The de-dramatization does not need to reach the same radical levels as those proposed by supporters of the "pure cinema," who reject any narrative structure. By simply contesting the classical mode of making movies and the narrative conventions rooted in preexisting melodramatic forms, that dominated the early nineteenth century, the moviemaker is able to raise questions about the very nature of the cinematic art. The most important part of this movie is built as a series of repetitive searches taking place in the backyard of an abandoned house. The two amateur treasure hunters and their hired scanning specialist move purposelessly from one side to the other of the garden. After spending all daylight in unsuccessful efforts to find the hidden treasure, the three men are ready to give up, as the treasure is visible on the screen of the scanner, which makes it present, but never reachable. In an unexpected twist, their void efforts turn into materiality, as they find a metal box, filled with old bonds for the Mercedes company.

In an ironic and final reversal of outcomes the main protagonist, Costi, makes an unexpected decision. Because he promised his son a "real treasure," not wanting to disappoint and intending to stay true to his word, he sells his share of the bonds and buys a treasure chest, which he then fills with gold and diamonds. In Lacanian terms the Real (the extremely valuable papers) are transformed into the Imaginary (the glittering fictions), because their symbolic content was empty. Seen from the perspective of this transformation, *The Treasure* is not only a slow-paced story about treasure hunting. Porumboiu brilliantly builds up to two distinct philosophical movements in the gaps of meanings, both dealing with the ambivalent nature of our existence and the nature of artistic representations.

On the one hand, there is the utter platitude of reality, as depicted in the first part of the movie. The camera follows the main hero leading an unremarkable life, going to work, reading his son during the evenings from a Robin Hood booklet. The major function of de-dramatization intervenes and, by removing the dramaturgical elements (character arc, conflicts, plots), it creates a conjuncture of circumstances leading to film-thoughts. Costi's decision to transform a real treasure into a fictional one becomes a metaphor for all content creation, in language, in culture, in movies, and in art. This is the inner working of any art process, to take the dullness of the ordinary and to turn it into the illusory and more pleasurable manifestation of representation.

Ultimately this is also a movie about the nature of cinema. It is a search for something that is not present, for meanings that are only partially visible on a screen, that force us to a difficult exploration of an imagined reality. The search for the treasure is a substitute for our search for true understanding, for something that is *not* in the visual field, something requiring many efforts, a material manifestation that does not always present itself in the way we expect it. It is only after exhaustive searches and digging for the "treasure" in the wrong places we can, like the three unwise men, find something rewarding. When there are no more significations, we find meaning. By directing this movie, Porumboiu takes the same pathway; he extracts meanings from his own cinematic works after exhausting all the possible resources. After going back and forth through the same paths, over and over again the dullness is transformed into meaningfulness.

Another Cerebral Attack Provoked by Conceptual Filmmaking

Corneliu Porumboiu began his moviemaking career by following the social criticism route. This model was predominant during the first decade of post-communist cinema, when the directors were constantly exposing the shortcomings of society. The denunciation of alcoholism, the criticism of authority abuse, or social hypocrisy characterizes his early short films. Based on simple stories reporting the institutional failure in Romanian society, with a clear political purpose, Porumboiu seemed to join the ranks of other movie directors of that generation, who kept dealing with politically charged subjects.

By a fortunate decision he took a more conceptual approach, as his techniques evolved from the blatantly dark humor and the caricature-like depictions of society, toward a conceptualist aesthetic. His interest for the internal mechanisms of the human mind and soul, together with his artistic experiments, was gradually evolving toward clearly distinguishable filmmaking practices.

Before overviewing these transformations, a couple of clarifications need to be made, as is the case when describing cinema with the help of terms adopted from art theory. While broadly we can understand *conceptual cinema* as a particular ability of moviemakers to use cinematic representations beyond their immediate reality, an effort to produce ideas and not emotional effects, the "conceptual" is often confused with art conceptualism, traced back to Marcel Duchamp.

Cinematic conceptualism, while following a similar rejection of the conventions of art, has to deal with the specific issues of this particular medium, handling the technological dimensions of the art of making movies. Unlike essay films or the purely experimental forms of cinema, a *conceptual* cinema uses the camera as an inquisitive tool, without radical abstract reductions. Also, while allowing complex visual experiments to explore the limits of the cinematic, the cinematic conceptualism does not create the same ambiguity, since it would hinder the natural filmic experience. Luca Barattoni (2012) used the notion of "conceptual realism" in order to describe the Italian post-neorealists. Since we can identify similar traits in Porumboiu's recent works, with the predisposition for an auctorial subjectivity always searching for the "invisible" dimensions of images and stories, without making this approach to filmmaking overwhelmed by the presence of the voice of the artist, the "conceptual" label is suitable for the Romanian director.

As noted before, my precise proposition is that Porumboiu evolved from a *social* cinema, to a more *cerebral* form of cinema-making, which many critics have noted, to a *conceptual-visceral* mode of expression. Jay Weissberg (2013), who properly identified the "cerebral" trend in Porumboiu's films, argued that *Metabolism* marked a turning point in this direction. Using my own examples from this unusual movie, I will argue that this approach is no longer purely cerebral, as it has strong *visceral* dimension. Many other examples could be provided in order to illustrate how this type of cinema functions; yet for the central argument it would be best to focus on this particular movie. Here the director clearly moves toward a stylistics based on *conceptualized* interpretations of the ontology of filmmaking, while adding a *visceral* dimension to the meaning-making processes.

The contention here is that, after *Metabolism*, Porumboiu can no longer be considered a "realist" or a "naturalist" filmmaker. Not only because he abandons the conventions of representing reality, but because he chooses a conceptual path in which the description of reality is driven by ideas, not by realism. The "Real" is now a by-product of ideas and concepts and not the other way around. The following interpretations are based on the conceptualist principle stating that our brain is making the matter of the real, and our conceptions about the objective world always intermediate our relationship with the given reality. By consequence, one major manifestation of the conceptual approach to cinema is the constant return to questioning the nature of cinematic representations. We can find a memorable example in Jean-Luc Godard's decade-long project *Historie(s) du cinéma*, which represents one of the most relevant and exhaustive cinematic efforts to conceptualize filmmaking within a filmic framework.

Undertaking a critical view of the craft while making a movie is also central to *Metabolism,* one of our closest examples of how conceptualization operates in the development of cinematic significations. The film title itself provides a multi-layered metaphor for moviegoing practices—"When Evening Falls on Bucharest" is simultaneously indicative for the "twilight" of cinema, a purposeful reference for how watching movies takes place in the dark, and an implicit hint to the shadow-casting nature of moviemaking, to the illusory character of any film. Just as conceptual artists are pushing the limits of the representable beyond the canons, Porumboiu is testing the limits of the cinematic beyond the conventions we consider intrinsic to the medium.

Any form of conceptual cinema is implicitly philosophical, in the sense that entails a constant meditation about the condition of the artist in the world and about the human condition overall. It is not only a reflection about the mechanics of cinema as an art, or a bemusement about the characteristics of the medium in strict technical terms. Conceptual cinema produces a type of practice no longer preoccupied exclusively with the typical modernist metacinematic problems, nor with the tensions between representation and the realism of the represented. Oriented toward understanding the intricate texture of reality and questioning the attributes of the real, the conceptual cinema also reduces its social and political meanings. The characters and their personal stories provide almost no external references; they provide a limited contextualization and, more importantly, no explicit ideological meaning is attached to their identity.

Last, but not least, by asking what is the essence of the cinematic at the *conceptual* level, Porumboiu's cinema takes the path of an introverted view, preferring to look into the presence of humanity and inside the representable and non-representable. As I will argue in the following, this takes us to a *visceral* dimension of cinematic signs. In order to understand this process I use the terminology introduced by the French semiologist Roland Barthes, who first created the notion when dealing with the analysis of what he identified as difficult signs, or duplicitous signs (Barthes 1972: 29). Looking into the structures of conceptual cinema, *visceral* forms of meaning production are unequivocally activated.

Inside the Metabolic System of Cinema

Metabolism was considered early on by many critics as a "self-reflexive" movie, a metacinematic rumination about the condition of any filmmaker. Obviously, as Porumboiu himself acknowledged in many interviews about this movie, it is intended as a meditation about his own evolution as a film director (Porumboiu 2013). This purpose is transparent from the main plot of the story, taking the viewers into the inner machinations of cinema as art. It presents the difficulties of moviemaking and, particularly, it becomes a meditation on the condition of the artists involved in the creation of this art. Self-representation is easily perceivable, as we can link the film with an autobiographical dimension. A moviemaker named Paul, played by Bogdan Dumitrache, who shares many of the dilemmas that Porumboiu faces in other productions, is an obvious alter ego. As Paul is pondering about the nature of cinema, as he meditates about what it means to be a filmmaker and discusses nostalgically about the importance of celluloid in an age of digital cinema, we are exposed to the first level of meanings in this film.

Following a day in the life of a movie director, who first appears to be loquacious and inquisitive, determined in his efforts to tell "his" story, the story uncovers the deficiencies of a man dominated by his actress and controlled by his woman producer. Juggling with production problems, having an illicit love affair with one of his actresses and suffering from acute stomach pains, Paul is trapped in an emotional and relational *interval*. This psychological state of interlude is paralleled by the visual structure of the entire movie. Once more, in the typical fashion of the Romanian New Wave stylistics, the apparently simplistic visual setting allows the uncomplicated narrative construction to unfold. In a chain of seventeen sequences, with a brief intervention, the director is alternating long shots and short ones, putting in motion an cinematographic rhythm easy to resonate with. The camera dynamic is also revelatory, with the first part dominated by immobility, and the second part using excessive camera movements. A major role is played by the color transformations, with a clear shift from warm to cold tones, designed to mimic the internal evolution of the storyline and of the character. Everything is arranged so that it can provide access into the unconscious of the protagonist. By performing a dissective account of the film we can observe a technical structure based on seventeen sequences, each briefly described and easily understood. By identifying the length of each scene, its subject, and cinematographic techniques, the immediate result is an adroit anatomy of the movie. Nevertheless, the true meanings of cinema are not instantiated at this level; the narrative and cinematographic structures are not the movie. Meanings reside in the space–time *intervals* between these constructed shots, in the silences and gaps of each well prepared scene.

I. Car-drive at night, with two characters surrounded by darkness. Topics discussed: the nature of cinema. Length: six minutes. II. Paul alone in the white kitchen has a cell phone discussion with Magda, the producer. Topics: Paul is in pain he cannot go to filming, references to film production. Length: four minutes. III. The rehearsal of a scene with his actress and mistress, Alina. Topics: dialogues and cinematic spaces, what is expressive in filmmaking, bodies, mise-en-scène. Length: eight minutes. IV. A closed door covers a sex scene. Topics: the relationship between sound and image, silence in films. Length: two minutes. V. Chinese restaurant dinner, built as a two shot. Topic: becoming an actor, the nature of content production and mediation, form and content in art. Length: nine minutes. VI. Reverse shot in the car during the day, with Paul and Alina. Topics: international cinema, ethnicity, identity. Length: six minutes. VII. Paul and Alina meet with the producer, Magda. Topics: practical dimensions of cinema-making, contracts, bills. Length: 6 minutes. VIII. Paul is alone in the car. Topic: silence and simple setup. Length: two minutes. IX. Back to rehearsals. Topics: rehearsing and performing, acting in real time, the nature of reality. Length: eight minutes. X. Postcoitum scene, with the camera following the actress, then the director. Topic: the film within film. Length: eleven minutes. XI. Dinner, starting with a two shot, then a three shot. Topics: screenwriting, budgeting, other perspectives on cinema, director's competition, cinema history. Length: eight minutes. XII. Exterior scene, Paul and Alina are smoking while waiting for a cab. Topics: the uncertainty of playing and directing, the difference between theater and cinema. Length: four minutes. XIII. The director starts watching parts of his movie on a projector, a single camera pan with him. Topic: the solitude of the creator. Length: two minutes. XIV. Opens in a hotel lobby scene, with the camera panning almost 360 degrees. Topic: real time interaction. Length: one minute. XV. Meeting with the actress at the bar, camera is fixed. Topics: the social dimension of a movie. Length: two minutes. An intermediate sequence with the endoscopic evaluation, overhearing the comments of the doctor and the producer. Length: two minutes. XVI. Final discussions about the endoscopy. Topics: the doubtable nature of representation, the importance of focusing on the subject of filming. Length: four minutes. XVII. Taking place within the same scene, but with the changing of characters. The make-up artist and the actress enter the trailer. Topics: the role of make-up, understanding the purpose of cinema. Length: four minutes.

By overviewing the formal construction of *Metabolism* we can immediately observe how Porumboiu develops a simple story elaborately establishing links between the narration and the limitations of cinematic art. Moving from ontological problems related to the medium (the celluloid vs. digital debate), to the intellectual strife of the film director, from the narrative structure development to the relationship between actors and other fellow directors, the movie evolves from an *extrinsic* inquiry to an *internal* interrogation on the nature of cinema. By discussing film practices, human interactions, or narrative structures, each shot functions as an illustration of a particular cinematic concept. Thus ultimately the entire movie can be understood as a *conceptual* challenge, where cinematic ideas are transformed into film representations.

Metabolism provides an illustrative case of how an apparently unremarkable story, de-dramatized actions and situations, pictures dominated by over-the-shoulder shots, and redundant framings in fixed two shots, with dialogues taking place in austere mise-en-scènes, can be more than it meets the eye. Such a *non-cinematic* specimen might give the impression of a movie emptied of complex cinematographic elements. Time and space are reduced to a minimum, interactions are devoid of tension, and narration is schematic. Yet, at a closer look, the "minimalistic" effort discloses once again the *conceptual* dimension of Porumboiu's vision about cinematic art. Once the explicit self-reflexive contemplation or the minimalist references are overpassed, we can observe that the entire movie becomes a glossing on the nature of cinema, a meditation on the specific elements that make any movie to be cinematic. Ultimately, this is an extreme exploration of the *metabolism of filmmaking*.

Inconspicuously every scene of this movie revolves around the nature of cinema. As indicated by the brief overview of the sequence buildup in *Metabolism*, the scenes are contexts for questioning how directing affects understanding, how location scouting is problematic, how acting and creating dialogues affect the viewers, and how to decide camera movements. This accumulation of cinema issues provides the *conceptualized* dimension of this film, as the meditations on the ontology of filmmaking substitute actions. Moviemaking is no longer centered on situations; it becomes an environment in which concepts and ideas ferment and grow.

Some of the most remarkable scenes are those in which the trope of the movie within a movie handles the nature of filmic representation. Paul is casually discussing with his actress the limits imposed by the length of the film strip, trying to figure out the root of a major problem in filmmaking. As he ruminates about the fact a film cannot be shot in more than eleven minutes sequences, the indirect consequence is that none of the scenes in the actual film are longer than that. Also, when the fictional director in *Metabolism* muses about the fact that films are going to be different in a couple of decades, making witty commentaries on how the ontology of cinema is going to change, he describes *a mode of thinking through cinema* that is mirroring the efforts of the real director. Through the words of Paul Porumboiu tells his viewers: "This is how I think." Last but not least, in a final reversal of roles, the fictional movie director is watching his own unedited film and, as he sits in the darkness of his living-room, a movie within the movie is projected. Nevertheless, the spectators are not given access to this projection. We were provided enough information to run this film which exists without being made; it is running in our minds. This is where the utmost form of *non-cinematic cinema* can be created, in *a film that is not a film*.

Visceral Signs, Visceral Cinema

Some of the most important meanings in *Metabolism* are created in intermedial settings. Paul, the fictional movie director, is having difficulties with the process of production. Troubled by the reality around him, which is a fictional universe, he has abdominal pains, reverberating into the reality of the screened experience. In this narrative setting the necessary context is created to build another non-cinematic device. As the director of the unmade film is viewing an endoscopic footage of the entrails of a human being, we overhear the offscreen discussions between the doctor and Paul's producer (Figure 3.4). With this maneuver Porumboiu explores several inner mechanisms of moviemaking. The scene, which is an obvious metaphoric reference to the "metabolism of cinema," allows the probing of movie-meanings. The meditation about the functions of cinema is paralleled

FIGURE 3.4 *In* When Evening Falls on Bucharest or Metabolism *Corneliu Porumboiu tells the story of Paul, who is trying to direct a movie while searching for directions in his own life. Photo credit Adi Marineci, courtesy 42 Km Film.*

by the endoscopic probe, searching *inside* a human body. With the help of an utterly a-cinematic technology a complex exploration of the *visceral* dimension of filmmaking is made possible. It would be noteworthy here to point to the fact that Porumboiu also makes an intertextual reference when naming his main character Paul. Using the same name as the screenwriter in Godard's *Le Mépris*, the Romanian filmmaker uses another thinking pathways of the non-cinematic. Intertextuality makes the two movies, based on similar premises, think together. With Godard also contemplating autobiographically the nature of his craft, the thinking is transferred into the Romanian film.

In order to understand properly the mechanics of this transference, we need to elaborate a parenthetical discussion about the functioning of cinematic signs. The majority of film critics follow the traditional, structuralist view which describes the nature of cinematic signs within the classical paradigm supported by Christian Metz (1974). The central assumption is that cinema has no process of signification outside its predetermined values, that the objects that we see onscreen are already coded with significations. This apparent technological transparency was contested by Roland Barthes (1957/1972) among others, who observed that the visible signs are actually an indirect source of hiding meanings. The screen is not simply providing us with an observable reality that is leaving nothing implied. What seems to be obvious and explicit in cinema, as is the case with other visual arts, the direct access to the visible world often lacks the explanations necessary to understand the significations as they were intended. In the words of the French semiologist, viscerality represents that dimension of the visual signs in which "an internal, hidden facet" is revealed (Barthes 1972: 26).

At this point, we need to clarify that the use of *visceral signs* must be understood as different from the competing concept, that of "carnal cinema," as proposed by Bordwell (2000). The visceral does not mean the bodily stimulation, nor the corporeal excitation. The distinction is important, since visceral cinema is not synonymous with carnal movies, although in some contexts it might be perceived as a manifestation of the corporeal film. This distinction is valid in the case of *Metabolism*, where the movie begins with the director stating forcefully: "Tomorrow I will shoot a nude scene." This is a misdirection, as it offers the pretext to plunge into the middle of a very intense discussion between Paul and his actress/lover about the beauty of a woman's body, the ugliness of the male body or the fact that the penis is an organ that "ruins the harmony." These considerations are followed by the refusal of the actress to "act naked in a sequence that is not justified," albeit this does not prevent her from engaging in a sexual affair with the director, while having conversations with her partner at home. The visceral is created by the refusal of the corporeal, as the stimulation is created by the absence of bodily disclosure, not by the sheer physical display.

Robert Furze comprehensively explains the other uses of cinematic visceral signs, manifested as a way of hiding the intentional presence of the film director (Furze 2015: 12–13), by covering the filmmaking strategies with emotional intensity. In this definition, the visceral is not opposing the intellectual; it functions as a tool diminishing the presence of the artist/creator, thus making possible the immersion of viewers into a subjective experience allowed by the screening. This level of viscerality is active in Porumboiu's subjective representation of the inner world of the fictional film director, which hides his own cinematic presence. Thus visceral meanings are manifested a way that, even when created by the mind of the director, they exist beyond the control of the conscious mind. As the visceral is taking over reason and intelligence, the viewers get alternative access keys to the secret dimension of film-meanings.

It is relevant that Porumboiu always tells stories that are explorations of his personal life. Thinking happens when things become intense and intimate. Many of his feature films take place in his hometown of Vaslui and all have an autobiographical dimension. For example, when asked about the motivation for directing *The Second Game*, the filmmaker confessed in an interview that it was "something extremely visceral"; he could not make any sense of the soccer match he first saw on TV, as the snow blocked access to the event. So he made the movie because he wanted "to understand" (Porumboiu 2014). Any visceral exploration of the cinematic kind is motivated by an internal drive for using films to understand things that are otherwise inaccessible to the mind.

There are many ways in which the visceral dimensions are made available in movies. There are several *visceral genres*, with many movies creating an empathic relationship between the visible (the onscreen) and our bodily reactions (the affective response). Like the ulcer of the director in *Metabolism*, we are subjected to direct reactions induced by the external stimuli projected on the screen. Our bodies naturally react to images and actions we experience by proxy. Slasher films and other violent sub-genres can be described as part of a larger "visceral trend" in global filmmaking. Often exploring the emotional properties provided by the offscreen, they provide and elicit direct reactions from the viewers or, as Bordwell (2000: 153) argues, these techniques of arousal are designed to "seize our senses." In opposition to this external and mechanical function, there is the visceral thinking exemplified by Porumboiu's works. They are closer to the experimental films of Stan Brakhage, best illustrated by *Window Water Baby Moving* (1959), where the American artist is documenting the birth of his daughter. As he provides an intimate and carnal entry point into reality, otherwise inaccessible in the fictional representations of carnality, no matter how gruesome they might be, the viewers are compelled to think differently.

Metabolism provides another relevant illustration for the coagulation of significations between the conceptual and the visceral. For several scenes the intense discussions between the director and his actress revolve around the strategies to shoot the sequence. After all this trouble, in the movie within the movie, they fail to properly accomplish the task. The rehearsed part of the fictional movie becomes a true and accomplished scene only when the absence substitutes the real presence. Once again, this allows Porumboiu to create a visceral experience, one that is simultaneously non-cinematic, because the film is never finished, and a personal experience, a mediated, secondary expression of reality. The movie within the movie transforms the conceptual into the visceral.

As some critics previously observed (Deaca 2017), a recurrent mechanism is used by many Romanian movies, with the eating scene becoming the best context for generating viscerality. In *Metabolism* we have two of these examples—one in which the film director and his actress are eating at a Chinese restaurant and the another episode taking place in the presence of another fictional movie director (played by Alexandru Papadopol). The dinner discussions (which belong to the conceptual level) are transformed into visceral meanings (which belong to the non-cinematic). In the first example, Paul gives a long monologue about Oriental cooking and cuisine—one extremely similar to the arguments provided by Barthes in his comments about Japan (Barthes 1983: 3–4). As the fictional moviemaker argues that the external tools we use to eat are actually creating cultural habits, the entire discussion, which seems tedious and even erroneous (since fried chicken is part of the Oriental cuisine), he punctuates the nature of reality and by this he provides visceral access into the deepest layer of the relationship between men and women.

In film theory viscerality and corporality have long been controversial subjects, with many philosophical and practical evaluations attempting to establish the impact of cinema on our brains. The viewer reactions have been extensively researched in film studies; following Münsterberg and Arnheim many specialists claimed that the experience we have with the moving images is fundamentally psychological. Our minds tend to react when the actions onscreen are intense. By seeing others suffer or experience happiness, we generate similar reactions in our minds, which are transformed into bodily sensations. As many cognitive psychologists have pointed out, the direct perception of reality is not the only way in which we understand the world and our place in it.

A relevant concept for our discussion is the notion of "visceral perception" (Ádám 1998). The argument is that visual stimuli are transformed into bodily activities not only at the level of our perceptive system or as immediate psychological reactions, but in a profoundly carnal way. This allows us to take into account what happens within the body when a sensorial experience takes place onscreen. When exposed to images our brain does not receive only cerebral information; a set of visceral data is transmitted at levels that we are not aware of most of the time. In fact the external movements of the actors on set, the images of bodies projected on the screen, or even the words we hear are transformed into internal movements of our bodies. Thus the idea of visceral cinema integrates the fact that there is *a visceral understanding* generated by the situations we view on the screen, and the material experience is transformed into *meanings beyond the visible*.

An important dimension of our cinematic experiences is placed within visceral processes. The disgust, sympathy, or attachment we experience toward the actions or actors are processed beyond the screen, even beyond our conscious minds. This allows the activation of another *non-cinematic* mechanism, the creation of a movie that is not only *on the screen*. The fact that actions and interactions in movies can have a direct impact on our guts is not a novelty. Spectators have cried at the movies, books readers were moved by fictional stories, and lovers of the ancient theater were emotionally affected by the on-stage tragedies. What makes watching a film different in terms of affecting our bodies beyond the emotional and sentimental reactions? "Movies" are just that, visual machines that "move us"—they can make us sad, happy, nervous, or fearful. Many of the visceral capacities of cinema as a visual medium are explored (and exploited) by the practical *visceral genres*. The erotic or pornographic, the violent movies or the revenge films, all provide a path to "carnal knowledge." Some controversial filmmakers, like Catherine Breillat, are purposefully using violence and sexual exploitation as a form of self-knowledge (Keesey 2015: 132). There is no space here for a larger discussion on the topic of visceral manifestations in cinema, but clearly any onscreen manifestation of physical interaction (aggressive or pleasurable) can be turned into a visceral experience. More importantly, such movies can "move us" without the help of images, the best example being the manipulation of sound design and of other non-visual special effects.

The process described in neurosciences as "interoception" (Cameron 2002) allows us to understand how the overall activities taking place in our bodies are the result of a complex sensory-perceptual system. In fact, our entire body processes and transmits signals and creates awareness, not only our brains. Jeffrey Zacks, who was among the first scientists to use fMRI equipment in order to provide explanations for how movies impact our brains, persuasively argues that our brain was not "made for movies." If nothing, the movies are taking advantage of our preexisted ideomotor reactions (Zacks 2015: 4), with a large part of our brains designed to react to such external stimulations. Accepting the premise that our brains have evolved in non-cinematic environments, where the ability to mimic the actions of other humans was fundamental for survival, leads to extremely important conclusions. Our brains have built-in somatosensory mechanisms that allow us to decode what "we see with our own eyes" and then turn these into bodily reactions. What we see is overlapping with what we experience as our own existence. The scientific foundation for the visceral cinema is that we constantly incorporate what we experience at the perceptual level into our body reactions. This "mechanism of translation" allows the brains to transform emotions into reactions, or, as Greg Smith clearly explains it, movies can put us into specific moods (Smith 2003: 41).

Finally, we need to circumscribe the phenomenological functions of visceral cinema. Merleau-Ponty gives evidence of the phenomenological connection between the flesh and the act of seeing in his influential book on the visible and the invisible (Merleau-Ponty 1968: 151–155). This French philosopher observed that the phenomenological dimension of cinema was explicit in the capacity of movies to create a mind–body connection in which the visible world and our brains are mutually expressing each other (Merleau-Ponty 1964: 48–59). According to Merleau-Ponty, this bond between the subjective experience and the cinematic experience of other bodies represented the profound innovation made possible by the new visual medium. When watching a film we know that this is only "a film" and we maintain a superficial level of contact with the story, the figures of actors or the changing actions. The barriers of consciousness are not broken at the level of visual representations; instead, the ability of movies to bring forward the invisible, that which is absent, which takes place outside the perceptible, has a stronger impact.

The undeniable fact is that the apparent and constant visibility of the medium is actually preventing our immersive predispositions. There is nothing "organic" or "natural" in cinema; its material manifestation (the celluloid) is never in contact with us; we are not provided with any direct tactile or carnal experience. How is this deep visceral effect created? My argument is that the interval created in Porumboiu's movies, where large parts of the movie take place outside our reach, is activating an impalpable manifestation, one that I described as non-cinematic.

How Can the *Alingual* Cinema Speak?

The most recent film directed by Porumboiu, entitled *The Whistlers*, deals with another series of extremely problematic issues in cinema. The action is suggestively placed by the Romanian director on the island of La Gomera, part of the Canary Islands. In a typical police genre plot, Cristi is an undercover detective who tries to infiltrate a gang of international money laundering criminals. This external and misleading narrative structure led some film critics, like Leslie Felperin from *The Hollywood Reporter* (2019), to describe the production as a "noirish crime thriller." Once more, the Romanian moviemaker operates against the conventional narrative mechanisms of the criminal investigation and its suspenseful twists. Porumboiu manages to reach beyond the typical questions of moral ambiguity or the characteristic good versus bad dilemmas. On the island of La Gomera, Cristi learns a new method of communication, which confronts him and the viewers with some unexpected consequences. Assuming under false pretense the identity of a migrant, this corrupt policeman faces a life-changing situation, one in which he experiences the typical spatial dislocation of migrants together with the identity dislocation induced by the new speech he is forced to acquire. As Cristi abandons human speech altogether by learning a whistled language, he suffers a profound internal transformation. When spoken words are no longer connected to his mind, with the whistling taking over his mode of describing reality, Cristi loses his social and moral coherence. The policeman goes rogue and decides to help his erotic companion, Gilda, the wife of a local mafioso, against the clan of Spanish crime syndicate (Figure 3.5).

Arriving on the island of La Gomera, Cristi is taught by the mafia the whistled version of Spanish, called El Silbo. Acquiring this ancient form of language, similar to the "sfyrizo" in Greece, Cristi returns to profound ancestral roots, lost in prehistoric times. These cryptic forms of communication were developed by human beings all over the world, when realizing that articulate sounds can be transformed into musical trills. This is a reversal to a pre-linguistic, pre-modern condition. The whistled speech is one of the most ancient forms of language, its creation explainable for pragmatic reasons. Sheepherding and the existence of humans in mountainous areas

FIGURE 3.5 *Cristi, a corrupt detective, loses his identity and moral compass when trying to learn a new whistled language in* The Whistlers. *Photo credit Vlad Cioplea, courtesy 42 Km Film.*

made communication over larger geographic expanses extremely difficult. Isolated groups of humans developed whistling as language in order to send messages from a mountain top to another. Still present in the Greeks island of Antia, practiced by the Gavião population in Brazil, the Béarnais in the Pyrenees, the Ari in Ethiopia or the inhabitants of Kuskoy in Turkey, these whistled forms of languages are reducing spatial distancing.

As observed by René-Guy Busnel (1976), one of the researchers who worked for many years studying these forms of communication, it is remarkable that different populations are practicing whistled forms of speech by using similar techniques. This "unspoken language" associates physical sounds with whistling, which indicates their common ancestral root. More importantly, it alters one of the essential traits of humanity. When spoken communication is substituted with another form of sonority, closer to birds, this induces a displacement within our profound nature, a distancing (écart) from the basic condition of mankind. The result of this separation in cinema is the alienation of the protagonist and the induced unsettling strangeness for the spectators.

The phenomenon is accentuated in the case of people who are dislocated from their homeland, as the acquisition of a new and foreign language leads to profound changes of identity. A 2002 *Washington Post* story revealed an extremely disquieting phenomenon, typical for mass immigration. As reported in the news story (Schulte 2002) many children who had no native language were unable to communicate properly in any form of human language, thus becoming *alingual*. In these peculiar situations the dominant media used by the children became interpreters of reality. Immigrant children were actually naming "red" as "west," mimicking the characters from a popular program they were watching. Strangely enough, without having words acquired in a natural linguistic environment, children use media induced terms.

In Porumboiu's movie, the efforts of an undercover cop to adapt in a new environment, which is a classic trope of the genre, are amplified by this peculiar form of linguistic acquisition. We are not simply witnessing Cristi learning a device of transmitting secret information, a tool for interaction used by shady characters. We watch the main protagonist entering an *interval*, an interim space redefining his human condition. The Romanian director uses this narrative opportunity for exploring the profound problem of identity loss. This dislocation that produces a transformation of his humanity, altering his natural state of mind, becomes a pretext of exploring the resources of the *alingual* cinema. While, traditionally, movies allow meanings and significations to be transmitted with the help of dialogues and other verbal communication devices, in this non-cinematic intervention a series of questions about the nature of cinema are raised.

While the topic of non-communication represents the explicit component of this story, one based, as always in the Romanian cinema, on a profound moral premise, the existential conflict and the evolution and devolution of Cristi are punctuated by several intervals. Porumboiu explored the technique in almost all his previous productions and it allows *The Whistlers* to investigate another major gap in human communication. Reality, constantly sliced by intervals, either as intermedial spaces (like the abandoned movie sets where the money is hidden) or as intermedial interventions (like classical musing), they indicate the alteration of subjective meanings.

One of the most suggestive modalities of using intertextual gaps is illustrated by the scene in which the undercover detective and the female prosecutor who coordinate his work watch together a John Ford movie. In a movie theater screening *The Searchers* (1956) the two meet as a subterfuge and the influential Western becomes the background facilitating an intermedial and an intra-medial site for film-thinking. When Ethan, the character played by John Wayne, tells reverend Clayton "Looks like you got yourself surrounded," then getting the famous reply: "I can get myself unsurrounded," the film dialogue is extended into the real life of the corrupt Romanian policeman, who himself is trying to avoid a trap. This is more than just a movie-within-movie scene, it functions as a thinking interface. Later the Romanian filmmaker recreates a classical shootout in the backdrop of the abandoned movie set, in a parodic deconstruction of his own technique. Another reference to a classical movie, with metanarrative practicality, is one of the most popular police movies made in Socialist Romania, called *A Police Inspector Calls (Un comisar acuză*, dir. Sergiu Nicolaescu, 1974). An ironic eyewink to the genre he is using as a narrative scaffolding, Porumboiu interpolates a reference to the most famous police commissioner created by the national cinema, the famous inspector Moldovan. The connection is first and foremost ironic, because Moldovan was always portrayed as an incorruptible heroic figure, a true Communist Dirty Harry, which retroactively reflects Cristi as a total opposite. In a self-reflexive movement, the scene displayed on the television set of the hospital is an intratextual self-irony, since the name of the protagonist, Cristi, is a reference to Porumboiu's other genre film, *Police, adjective*. The refractive function is even more relevant, as the injured detective in the movie watches a "real life" detective in another; he is awakening to conscience. Looking at the screen and through it toward us, the viewers, this final gaze takes the thinking *outside* the cinematic.

The same type of narrative intervals are provided by surveillance monitors or mobile phone screens, strategically placed at the most important narrative points. In one of the opening scenes in which Gilda, the wife of the local mafioso, has a love affair with Cristi, their relationship is monitored by overseeing agents through a mirror. Aware that their reality is recorded—a reality displayed for the spectators from multiple perspectives, captured from several points of view—Gilda interacts with the agent, putting on a bodily spectacle. In the interval between the several screens (the cinema screen, the monitor, the mirror), physical reactions are activated and film-thinking is instigated. The spectators, the characters, and protagonists as actors in on-screen acting are simultaneously inside and outside the cinema machine. My interpretation is that they represent the highest form of non-cinematic-thinking.

The act of acquiring the language of birds, which indicates the replacement of human qualities, carries the most important meanings in the film. It is also intertextually referenced with a direct hint to Hitchcock's classic, *The Birds* (1963), since birds are the extreme "other" of humanity. They are non-mammalian creatures "speaking" in a totally different mode; they communicate in a fashion inaccessible to humans. Here we need to use a more intricate intertextual connection to explain the mind frame of the movie. Porumboiu makes a direct reverence to an influential book written by one of the most popular Romanian philosophers, Andrei Pleşu (1994), who argued that the primordial language, one existing before the spoken languages of mankind, was the language of birds. Considering that our existing languages are forms of separation, of division along ethnic or national lines, Pleşu quotes the Quran and Saint Francis of Assisi, suggesting that a return to the original language, used before the Tower of Babel, can bring humanity to a higher level of understanding. Without going into the intricacies of this philosophical text, which basically rediscusses a famous Platonic dialogue, the idea of a language of the birds is extremely important in order to understand Porumboiu's intentions. Even if the Romanian philosopher did not bother to make any reference to the theory expounded by Bertrand Russell in the monumental *Principia Mathematica*, where the British thinker previously elaborated on the "celestial" or "ideal" language, the only one that could solve all our human problems, the conclusions are the same. We become competent speakers of a "native language" in early childhood, and it is through this language that we develop connections with the world around us. However, the speech communities sharing common meanings soon impose on our brains and bodies mental restrictions altering our essence as human beings.

This is precisely what happens with Cristi at the end of his exploits. After the adoption of a language similar to that of the birds and assuming an inhuman form of communication, he is purposefully hit by his surveillance office with a car, which affects his ability to speak like a normal human being. Locked in a hospital, without being able to communicate, Cristi involuntarily and incessantly whistles. The film director masterfully uses this direct and explicit connection, developed throughout the movie, between bird sounds, their natural whistles overlapped with musical elements, and the shrieks of intradiegetic acute sounds. By the denaturalization of verbal speech, induced together with the acquisition of a new identity, the re-articulation of the identity of the main character is naturally occurring.

Here the most important aspect in Porumboiu's explorations of the constraints of human language becomes more explicit when connected with Wittgenstein's observations about language as a game-like activity. This film raises several issues about language distortion, reality alteration, and identity transformation in the lives of all the protagonists. It also deals with the difficulties and barriers, confusions and misunderstandings induced by cinema as a language. This strange phenomenon brings us back to Ludwig Wittgenstein and the "picture theory" of language. In a famous conclusion about language expressed in the *Tractatus Logico-philosophicus* (1922), the Viennese philosopher described our attempts to capture reality through language as indicative of the limits of what we can actually express with words. The already-discussed quote represents the foundation of his philosophical system of thinking, developed as an expansion on the notion of the limits of language (Appelqvist 2020). Wittgenstein's philosophical notes have obvious relevance in cinema, as explained by Szabados and Stojanova. Sense-making in a film is not so much an issue of speech, nor textual explaining. It is not about "telling," as it is a matter of "showing" (Szabados and Stojanova 2011: xiv–xv). Many avant-garde artists have attempted to liberate cinema from the captivity of language, in an effort to explore the capacity of films to communicate exclusively through visual means. This assumption can be elucidated by simplifying the reasoning of the great modern philosopher—if words are pictures of reality, and cinema allows us to create a representation of that reality, then the use of words only reduces our ability to understand that which is already pictured.

As cinema has developed its own modes of visual communication, moviemaking inherited a major linguistic problem from theater and literature. Best illustrated by the practices in hegemonic cinema, where a combination of simplified dialogues and actions resulted in the extraordinary capacity to address large audiences, film speech is today dominated by a particular jargon. Instead of developing into the "universal language" of humanity, as Eisenstein intended in the 1920s, or an "Esperanto for the eyes," as imagined by Vachel Lindsay, the hegemonic cinema has adopted a vernacular form of expression. This shortcoming, analyzed by Miriam Hansen (1991) who overviewed how classical Hollywood cinema took over the world, transformed an instrument of global communication into a provincial language. We are all speaking the vernacular language developed by a particular American version of language. Coupled with a specific narration form, also typical for English literature, these conditions made cinema a localized art. Almost all Hollywood genres can be seen as local responses to the provocations posed by modernity to American society. And, as they are constantly confronted with the language of global Hollywood, national cinemas are also creating their conditional reactions to this language, evolving particular (sometimes provincial) film cultures. Of course, since they are spoken in a formal language and placed in limited cultural contexts, all films are products of vernacularity. And, even if this appears to be a natural occurrence, the linguistic identity of actors or the words spoken in dialogues and other identifiers of nationality perceived as "authentic" remain highly coercive and are inducing predetermined significations (more discussions on these issues in the next chapter).

Thus we must understand *The Whistlers* are more than a simple "crime thriller." The Romanian filmmaker belongs to a group of moviemakers who search for a *substitutive cinematic language* by exploring innovative forms of communication and cinematographic practices. These films, in which at least one or more forms of representation are replaced by other modes of expression, can range from the "moderate" versions—defined as a *paraphrastic cinema*—and the most radical manifestations, in which a total removal of speech is enacted—defined as *alingual cinema*. By *alingual* cinema I do not distinguish the recent re-enactments of silent cinema like *The Artist* (dir. Hazanavicius, 2011) or the refusal of speech through playing with the physical incapacity of the characters, as is the case with the Ukrainian film *The Tribe* (dir. Slaboshpytskiy, 2014). *Alingual* films construct altered states of identity in which the transformations are induced by the changing of the linguistic condition of the protagonists. Clearly a cinema without speech is an almost impossible ideal, but a cinema liberated from the captivity of dialogues and literature, one of the supreme ideals of avant-garde filmmaking, is not impossible. This is an aspiration constantly revisited by newer generations of moviemakers, searching for innovative answers to a century-old problem.

Finally, Porumboiu's movie reminds me of a famous quip by Frank P. Ramsey, who ironically reformulated the famous ending of Wittgenstein's *Tractatus ...* by stating: "What we can't say we can't say, and we can't whistle it either." As Cora Diamond (2011) explained it, Ramsey was pointing to the serious nonsense of philosophy, anticipating the non-philosophical approaches advanced by Laruelle. As Porumboiu is questioning autobiographically the nature of his inner universe, he puts under scrutiny the materiality of cinema, the mechanisms of fiction, the ontology of the celluloid, the reality of television, the abilities of language to communicate, our imagination, while exploring the limitations of cinema. By rethinking his own capacity as a filmmaker, he acts like a non-philosopher.

4

A Magical Mystical Tour into the Romanian Cinematic Mind

The previous chapters addressed the relationship between cinema and philosophy by examining various cinematographic or narrative modes exploring the various "outsides" of the cinematic art. Functioning like incubators of knowledge, they generate a form of *offscreen thinking*. When focusing on examples extracted from recent Romanian films, I intentionally avoided any references to national identity and localized thinking. Limiting the contextualization to the reception of these stories or any mentioning of their local relevance, it allowed a better understanding of the inner functioning of the cinematic mind. Nevertheless, like any form of thinking, cinema has previously established roots in predetermined collective psyche. This remains an essential aspect to be dealt with.

The connections with the national imagination, the influences of the philosophical debates within local culture (in this case the Romanian one), and the links between cinema and the national space/time/state of mind are transparent in all cinematic narratives. Manifested in the social existence of the protagonists, visible in their particular interactions and their reactions to a given context, explicit in the spatial placement or displacement, together with the overall frameworks of significations that cannot be detached from local origins, cinema is always *vernacularized*.

A first major concern must raise questions about the nature of movies in general. Why some stories are perceived negatively in their own national context, and are highly appreciated abroad? How could we explain the low audience rates of these movie, is there an economic or a political reason for a reduced adherence, could it be a result of the collapse of film distribution in post-communist Romania or do we attribute this response to the fact that the general public is not adhering to this stylistics? More abruptly, as some film critics discussed the impact of these productions, do they purposefully present a negative image of our society, thus having a "foreign" agenda?

A short summary of the negative arguments brought up by the detractors of contemporary Romanian cinema indicates that there is a predominant bias. Somehow the presupposition is that the movies created by this new generation of artists are purposefully detrimental and damaging. Viewed from a political standpoint, they seem to be representing "Romanian identity" in a distorted way. As soon as this new group of auteurs appeared after 2000, they have been accused of choosing only "bad" stories, portraying Romania and the Romanians in a negative way. Moreover, as some conservative movie critics (Modorcea 2013) framed the New Wave style, this entire way of making cinema can be described as "a mockery." By pushing everything toward parody and irony, these film directors were apparently creating "anti-Romanian" movies, in turn projecting the image of a "new Romania," a country "full of wankers, of manipulable people," controlled by evil interests. Nevertheless, the hypothesis of an anti-Romanian cabal, revived by Modorcea from older conspiracy theories, can also be identified representative for a national trait. As we will discuss later, the idea that there are hidden interest groups "fooling" a "patient nation," that artists and intellectuals are generating preconceived meanings, remains recurrent in our collective psyche. It discloses a gap in the mind of our society, one which is obviously transposed onscreen.

The assumption is also that somehow such cinematic narratives can have a deeper cognitive impact that they affect political and cultural values. This idea is not perpetuated only by a marginal conspiracy theory group. One of the most important prose writers in contemporary Romanian literature, Nicolae Breban, publicly accused Cristian Mungiu of producing only films about "the misery in Romania" (quoted by Ghioca 2019). This generation of Romanian film directors was constantly accused of intentionally misrepresenting their nation, "exporting" a "miserabilist image," because this form of exotic self-degradation was best received by "Western" viewers, as purported by Breban.

Similar opinions are shared by local politicians and officials, who have been freely and frequently criticizing the recent Romanian productions that are considered to be detrimental. In 2013 a Romanian congressman, Victor Cristea, a Parliamentary representative of the Social-democrat Party (PSD) from Vaslui, openly attacked Călin Peter Netzer's movie *Child's Pose* (*Poziția copilului*, 2013). This MP considered that the content of the production was an explicit "denigration of the Romanian people," demanding the banning of the film as it was "full of obscenities," using "bad language" and was filled with trivial actions (Hotnews 2013). The angered member of the legislative was complaining that such a movie damaged "our image in the world." While politicians and the society overall were making "efforts to educate our children in our schools," moviemakers, he complained, were creating a "derogative" representation of Romanian families and the national educational system. This representative from Vaslui, one of the poorest counties in Romania (and the hometown of Corneliu Porumboiu!), demanded the Parliament to completely stop subsidising this type of cinema, since it provided a "negative example" for the young generations. The feverish debate, giving notoriety to a relatively unknown member of the Romanian Parliament, is not only a maladjusted declaration of an ignorant politician, who believed that there was a conspiracy theory to award prizes only to movies that negatively describe his country. The public discussions and disputes about how these movies depict Romanian culture and society and how they affect the self-image of their fellow countrymen are ongoing. The reception of movies like *Beyond the Hills* or, more recently, the negative reactions against the fictional account of the life at a theological seminary directed by young filmmaker Daniel Sandu, *One Step Behind the Seraphim* (*Un pas în urma serafimilor*, 2017) are indicative. Church vicar Vasile Pârcălabu, also an inhabitant of the famous Vaslui county, described Mungiu's film as a "disgrace" for the Romanian people and the Orthodox Church, claiming that it produced a "bad image" abroad, distorting the traditions and values of this nation (Adevărul 2012). Of course, the vicar conveniently forgot that it was an Orthodox priest who performed the medieval exorcism leading to the death of an innocent young woman.

An important producer and moviemaker of this generation, Tudor Giurgiu, recounted a personal experience, a suggestive event which took place during the Pro Cult festival, organized in Rome, hosted by Accademia di Romania at the end of 2012. The director and the manager of the most important film festival in Romania received an official letter from this public institution, in which he was officially asked to select only those movies which "do not depict a negative image of Romania (drugs, sex, gypsies, alcoholics, trivial language)" (Giurgiu 2012). When described as such, we realize that most of these productions receiving the highest level of international recognition can be understood as negative representations.

We can easily pick and identify a pattern of the "New Wave" storytelling practices, emerging when overlooking their artistic purpose. Some films are describing the failed Romanian medical system (*The Death of Mr. Lăzărescu; Graduation; Thou Shalt Not Kill*); many plots appear to be attacking the Church or questioning the "Christianity" of Romanians (*Beyond the Hills; One Step behind the Seraphim*); some protagonists are either homosexual or incestuous (*Love Sick; Illegitimate*); many are delinquents (*When I Want to Whistle, I Whistle; Loverboy*); some films manipulate history (*The Autobiography of Nicolae Ceaușescu*) or try to revisit it (*I Do Not Care If We Go Down in History as Barbarians*). At a superficial glance, such negative evaluations might even seem appropriate. The most important films of the last two decades disclose an interest of the recent generation of moviemakers for specific types of characters and narrative situations that are negatively charged. Overviewing the themes and topics of the most important productions (see Table 4.1) their main characters exhibit negative emotions and behaviors; they range from severe social anxiety to repressed aggressivity, oscillating between frustration and the incapacity to make clear moral decisions. These problems surface as violent manifestations, often disclosing an inherent instability of the soul, trapped in various states of alienation, fear, and rage that are inducing pain. Their emotional world, together with the social context, can project an interpersonal dynamic dominated by trauma. When we look at the identity of the main protagonists, they are socially disrupted individuals—victims of physical abuse (rape, torture), subjected to moral ambiguity (liars, cheaters), unadapted and marginals, or borderline criminals (abortionists, revenge murderers). Oftentimes the social role of the protagonists is caused by or results with abandonment; children or old people are left behind; emigrating individuals are separated from children, spouses, or lovers; abandoned parents and broken families are trying to cope with estrangement. They go through negative emotional experiences that reverberate as negative types of behaviors, further developed into harmful outcomes, with verbal violence and physical abuse as part of the human interactions. Accidents, awkward social interactions, hostility, and other violent stimuli occupy the center stage of these narratives. This might lead to the conclusion that the movies made after 2000 are building a negative mind-frame, offering justifications to the detractors of this generation of filmmakers.

An extremely insightful explanation is provided by Elsaesser (2019) who noted that such a critical distance is integral to the toolbox of all European movies. While agreeing with the premise presented by the regretted film theorist, who argued that a critical hermeneutics inherited from the Enlightenment project (Elsaesser 2019: 10–11) is still at work, I am expanding on the notion that these movies belong to a post-metaphysical philosophical paradigm. The local resistance to any critical discourses, presuming the existence of an "anti-Romanian" purpose of these films, and their inherent malicious and harmful design, remains indicative of a retrograde component of the Romanian society overall.

On the other hand, there are also the positive and triumphant evaluations, taking into account the beneficial impact this new generation of Romanian filmmakers had by creating one of the major cinematographic schools in Europe. Their widely appreciated productions lead to the international acknowledgement of the Romanian film industry, which is not a small accomplishment. Some even consider that they represent the most profitable national brand (Marcu and Ion 2012), the best "export item" of contemporary Romanian culture. It must be said that, while a contemporary Romanian movie has a medium budget of 500,000–600,000 Euros, when compared to the huge amounts of money spent annually on the so-called "national brand's projects," there could have been made at least fifty films, each able to generate the much more needed global awareness paid advertising can never get. It is relevant that, when the French humorous

TABLE 4.1 List of the most representative movies of the Romanian contemporary cinema: main topics, issues, storylines, and characters.

Movie/director	Type of character(s)	Philosophical issue	Type of emotion	Main plot (traumatic event and moral action)	Social status
Marfa și banii (2001), r. Puiu	Unstable, low reliability	Morally indeterminate	Fear	Illegal transport, moral dilemma	Unemployed, delinquents
Moartea domnului Lăzărescu (2005), r. Puiu	Unstable, powerless	Lack of agency, existential, anxiety, victim of fate (as ananke)	Fear	Sickness, death, physical danger, moral dilemma	Pensioner, marginal
Ryna (2005), r. Zenide	Unstable, powerless	Morally indeterminate, implacable fate (ananke)	Fear, disgust, social embarrassment	Rape, verbal abuse, immoral, moral dilemma	Unemployed
A fost sau n-a fost? (2006), r. Porumboiu	Unstable, low reliability, repressed	Existential anxiety	Social embarrassment, personal and political anxiety	Social awkwardness, alcoholism, moral dilemma	Teachers, pensioners
Hârtia va fi albastră (2006), r. Muntean	Unstable	Lack of agency, implacable fate (ananke)	Fear	Death caused by unethical decision	Soldiers, criminals
4 luni, 3 săptămâni și 2 zile (2007), r. Mungiu	Unstable, powerless	Alienation, moral acedia	Fear	Rape, death, verbal abuse	Students, delinquents
Boogie (2008), r. Muntean	Unstable	Existential anxiety, questioning identity	Social embarrassment, anxiety	Social awkwardness	Unadapted

Movie/director	Type of character(s)	Philosophical issue	Type of emotion	Main plot (traumatic event and moral action)	Social status
Polițist, adjectiv (2009), r. Porumboiu	Unstable, repressed	Questioning identity, morally indeterminate	Social embarrassment	Immoral/moral dilemma	Unadapted, delinquents
Felicia, înainte de toate (2009), r. de Raaf and Rădulescu	Unstable, powerless	Weakness of will (as akrasia)	Unhappiness	Verbal abuse, abandonment	Unadapted, migrants
Cea mai fericită fată din lume (2009), r. Jude	Unstable	Weakness of will (as akrasia)	Unhappiness	Social awkwardness	Unadapted
Aurora (2010), r. Puiu	Violent, unstable, repressed	Alienation, moral acedia	Fear	Social awkwardness, broken family	Unadapted, criminals
Marți, după Crăciun (2010), r. Muntean	Unstable	Moral indecision	Social embarrassment	Social awkwardness, infidelity, verbal violence	Unadapted
Eu când vreau să fluier, fluier (2010), r. Șerban	Violent, repressed, unstable	Morally indeterminate	Unhappiness	Kidnapping, verbal violence	Detainees, delinquents
Loverboy (2011), r. Mitulescu	Unstable, violent	Lack of moral standards (moral acedia)	Fear, social embarrassment	Rape, verbal and physical violence	Unemployed, delinquents

Movie/director	Type of character(s)	Philosophical issue	Type of emotion	Main plot (traumatic event and moral action)	Social status
După dealuri (2012), r. Mungiu	Unstable, repressed, violent	Morally indeterminate	Fear, unhappiness	Death, violence	Unemployed
Toată lumea din familia noastră (2012), r. Jude	Violent, unstable	Identity crisis, personal weakness	Fear, unhappiness	Violence, social awkwardness	Unadapted
Câini (2016), r. Mirică	Violent, abuse	Doubtfulness	Fear, uncertainty	Death, violence	Marginals, delinquents
Poziția copilului (2013), r. Netzer	Unstable, violent	Morally indeterminate	Fear, unhappiness	Death, verbal violence	Unadapted
Când se lasă seara peste București sau metabolism (2013), r. Porumboiu	Unstable, powerless	Doubtfulness, identity crisis	Unhappiness, inadequacy	Social awkwardness	Unadapted
Un etaj mai jos (2015), r. Muntean	Unstable, low reliability	Weakness of will (as *akrasia*)	Fear, social embarrassment	Death	Unadapted
Bacalaureat (2016), r. Mungiu	Unstable, powerless	Doubtfulness	Fear, social embarrassment	Rape	Unadapted
Sieranevada (2016), r. Puiu	Unstable	Uncertainty	Social embarrassment	Death, verbal violence	Unadapted
Touch Me Not (2018), r. Pintilie	Unstable	Doubtfulness, identity crisis	Uncertainty, unhappy	Social awkwardness	Unadapted, sexual disbalance
La Gomera (2019), r. Porumboiu	Unstable, powerless	Moral indecision, moral ambiguity	Fear, social inadequacy	Death by violence	Delinquents

show "Les Guignols d'Info" parodied Cristian Mungiu as a Gypsy beggar at Cannes, trying to get a free movie camera from Steven Spielberg, the joke provoked a huge reaction from the national media, denouncing the improper depiction of the moviemaker and claiming that the national pride was vexed. At the other end of this spectrum, a group of vocal and younger film critics adopted the radical Leftist discourse, and are describing these movies as "self-colonizing" manifestations of the "Western gaze." They also claim that these productions are specially created in order to display a "colonial" representation, presenting the "Eastern" savages in a fashion expected by the West European public.

The ambivalence of these surprising films was also observed by international film researchers, who picked up on this divide and applied paradoxical and sometimes disorienting labels, such as the concept of an "anti-national national" cinema. Trying to explain how it could be possible to have a film exposing the defects of society while portraying it in a realistic fashion, Goss (2015) employed Wayne's taxonomy to describe this specificity. Actually they are fully integrated into the practices of European filmmaking; the contradiction is resulting from cinema production pressures and international reception. Romanian films can be conveniently placed within the category of critical examinations of national myths and contexts, while maintaining their nationally relevant content and relevance. Only when superficially analyzing these productions, by interpreting them as "descriptive narratives," one can confuse their criticism with a mischievous intent. More importantly, and to the topic of this book, the problem remains if these manifestations have a negative function induced externally, or this negation is integral to what was described as the non-cinematic philosophy, part of a non-philosophical function.

Without further detailing the social and political issues, we must consider that these contemporary films are deeply concerned with authenticity, not with self-representation. They are critical without attempting a symbolic manipulation of identity, truly interested only in capturing the profound dimensions of human nature and not representing any "reality of being Romanian." Self-knowledge always represents a difficult intellectual journey; it is a philosophical course which cannot be easily followed. When telling "real stories," these moviemakers are actually refusing the collective fictions of the past. Always situated in the present tense, their approach manages to closely represent a lived experience that is not "against" anything; it is not simply a meditation about the defects of a provincial society. While they are expressions of social realities, they are also recuperating and integrating the real conditions life into meaningful storyworlds by performing a philosophical "cutting off," decoupling the specific reality and searching for universal significations. All the unpleasant things happening to almost every other character in these contemporary Romanian films, which might seem to project a "negative image" in terms of national identity, all the unfavorable depictions of a society which definitely deserves a better portrayal, are linked to deeper layers of thinking. "Bad stories" are more than an option to make cinematic products more marketable on a global network of film distribution.

This observation brings us to a fundamental question, a dilemma that has to do with all cinematic representations. Are the aggression and violence embedded in a particular society mirrored by in the movies, or can films naturally create states of mind, since the medium itself was invented as a form of public attraction. Can the technology, which provokes powerful reactions, also produce profound changes in our state of mind? Can cinema facilitate the formation of a self-image (for individuals or entire communities), or does it function only as a reflection of already-formed identities? Are these movies, which seem to make Romanians "look bad," real depictions of a terrible place, are they "attacking" the most cherished institutions of a nation, thus normally triggering virulent reactions, or are the institutions malfunctioning and do they need an appraisal? Do they destroy the positive image of the "fabulous Romania," are these movies a negative representation of society, or do they provide access to an understanding that goes well beyond such trivial interpretations?

Confronting Our Fear of Looking into the Dark Cinematic Mirror

Cristi Puiu's masterpiece *The Death of Mr. Lăzărescu* (*Moartea domnului Lăzărescu*, 2005), qualified by *The New York Times* and its film critics as among the first twenty-five movies of the twenty-first century, provides us with an appropriate illustration to deal with the complex issues raised before. The opening sequence of this profoundly realistic feature film (Figure 4.1) takes us into the middle of a cinematic situation. We are brought into an already-unfolding situation, with the camera "jumping" from a dark exterior shot, depicting an almost indiscernible block of flats, transitioning abruptly to the apartment of an old man who lives alone. He is feeding his cat, Mirandolina, in a decrepit kitchen and from the very start the entire setting is constructed as a *negation*. Every expectation of the common filmgoer, who is used to receive information from a typical production of the canonic cinema, is subverted. Instead of a glamorous and highly illuminated space, where beautiful movie stars can evolve, we are constrained to watch the comings and goings of one Dante Remus Lăzărescu, a dirty old man, dressed in worn-out clothes, moving around shabby-looking belongings in semi-darkness. The obfuscating half-lights are integral to the stylistics of the Romanian New Wave cinema and, as the aesthetically pleasing images of classical cinema are replaced with the darkened and colorless interiors

FIGURE 4.1 *The opening scene of* The Death of Mr. Lăzărescu *takes us into the decrepit apartment of a solitary old man facing mortality and the nothingness of human existence. Courtesy Mandragora.*

of a real Bucharest apartment, a new form of cinema-thinking is activated. The action-driven narratives are substituted with the banal activities of a fictional character, living alone, surrounded by three cats, carrying absurd conversations on the phone, with almost no interactions with other humans.

The slow-paced dynamics of this first scene, which occupies more than fifty minutes of the movie, is contradicting all the rules of action-driven cinema. Everything about this opening sequence is *non-cinematic*, a complete negation of all the conventions and practices of moviemaking as a form of entertainment. As I will argue in the following, this is only the first level of the *non-philosophical* dimension of this type of cinema. Puncturing our understanding of reality and slicing open gaps into human nature, the storytelling allows the formation of new thoughts and ideas. At the same time, the depiction of Mr. Lăzărescu's exploits confronts the spectators with a dark mirror of Romanian society, a cinematic gesture having profound film-philosophical effects.

By placing the story in a real Bucharest apartment, taking the protagonist to real Romanian hospitals, the narrative becomes a typical "Romanian story" and, simultaneously, is an investigation that negates any local contextualization. Obviously, the tragedy of the protagonist who goes through a nightmarish medical ordeal is a transparent reference to real-life situations—one might even ask why society does not learn from these movies, since reality seems to constantly repeat itself. We must point to the fact that the tragedy of an elderly moribund taken from hospital to hospital, in an endless peregrination of a dead man in a city that has no real contours, is not a negative character invented by the twisted minds of the Romanian New Wave cinema-makers. The drama of Mr. Lăzărescu was first a real event, a true news story about a patient abandoned by the ambulance on a backstreet in Bucharest. On April 23, 1997, the body of a fifty-two-year-old man was discovered half-naked and lifeless on a sidewalk, with the perfusion set still attached to his arm and a pair of striped pajama pants covering one of his legs. The police investigation later identified the man as Constantin Nica and, as the yellow press reported, he was a TB patient transported by an ambulance from one hospital to another. Since he was not hospitalized and had no identity card, he was considered a homeless person; thus, the paramedics had no choice but to abandon him at his last known address. Sensationalist media turned the case into an indictment of the failures in the national medical system; yet, the four different doctors who refused to provide him treatment were never prosecuted. The only condemned person was the nurse from the ambulance, who was sentenced to four years in jail for negligence. Unfortunately, it did not remain a singular situation. In 2008 another man from Reșița died between hospitals, with medics refusing him treatment, then in 2012 a forty-one-year-old man from Tecuci was rejected admission by three hospitals, and he expired in the ambulance.

The direct stimulus of this outside event is explicit. Răzvan Rădulescu, the screenwriter of many other successful recent Romanian films, and Cristi Puiu took this true story and transformed an a-cinematic situation into a profoundly filmic experience. However, the cinematic procedure is not that simple; it does not mean that anybody can create another Palme d'Or winner by taking a shocking event or news story and turn it into a "dark" film. Not all "based on real events" movies are philosophically relevant and even fewer have *non*-philosophical outcomes. One important dimension is the conversion of an *external* event into an *internalized* experience. Immediately after Constantin Nica event, Cristi Puiu began the work on a documentary project at Craiova retirement home, preoccupied with the death of his own elderly father. More importantly, the development of the film must be connected with a personal life event of the director himself, who was hospitalized with Mallory-Weiss syndrome a day after finishing his first movie, *Stuff and Dough* (2001). This gives *The Death of Mr. Lăzărescu* a triple-strand of features. One is the immediate level, the story functions as a *reflective* representation of society, and it is also a form of *reflexive* meditation of the moviemaker.

More to the point of my arguments, this movie creates a *refractive* environment for thinking. By constantly unthinking what we are expecting it to be, the images, the protagonist, and the story become non-philosophical instruments. The constant ambiguity between the outside and the inside, which creates an interpenetration of meanings, allowed several competing explanations in film studies dedicated to Romanian cinema, a field more and more popular among impromptu critics and aspiring academics. The predominant interpretations are quickly following the easily accessible technique of metaphorical deciphering. In the simplest of semiotic readings, providing one quick fix of meanings, we could interpret the striped pajamas worn by Mr. Lăzărescu as connected with the clothing of jailed convicts, then extend on this correlation making it an allegorical reference to Romania as a "carceral society." However, by looking at the gruesome pictures of the real event (Figure 4.2), the terrible truth is that the pajamas worn by the homeless man were closely reproduced by the film director. The true meanings, the non-philosophical dimensions, are not activated by searching for easy solutions.

As indicated by another commonplace reading, which points to the fact that the story must be linked with the fundamental myth dominating the Romanian culture and cultural imagination, an in-depth analysis is relevant

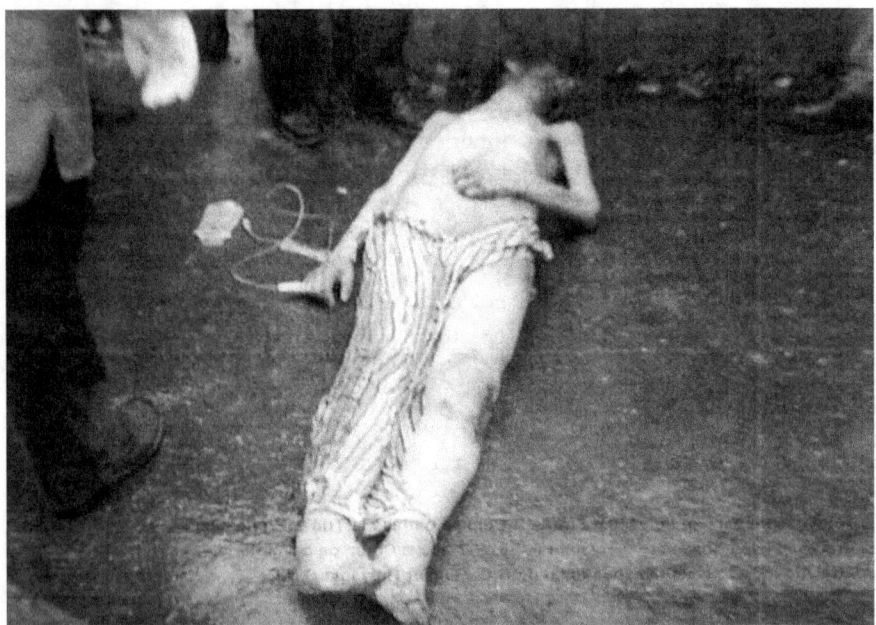

FIGURE 4.2 *News story clipping with the true tragedy of the man abandoned by an ambulance on a sidewalk in Bucharest.*

only when it moves inside the cracks of apparent meanings. This problem will be detailed further; here it would suffice to point to the fact that the name of the ambulance paramedic, Mioara, is a transparent reference to Miorița, a primordial story about the death of a shepherd celebrated as a rite of passage, which is illustrating the acceptance of mortality and a specific vision about human nature. Clearly, when seeing the ambulance paramedic taking Lăzărescu to the several gates of the institutional Infernos, we cannot avoid such connections. The intertextual meanings are explicit and overt. We can perform several other pertinent readings, one that I proposed myself in another study (Pop 2020), since the name Lăzărescu is a hint to Lazarus the resurrected dead man from the Bible, and the recurrent invocations of the name Virgil contain explicit links with Dante's classical poem. Since we will return to the mythological interpretations, for now the key argument remains that, when making accessible such parallelism with the experience of Mr. Lăzărescu, Puiu diverts the attention from the *inside* to the *outside*. When placing the spectators in the middle of everyday life, reaching what Deleuze (1985/1989: 59) described as the "movement of the world," the Romanian filmmaker opens an understanding and knowledge that escape local reality.

Stephen Holden (2006) observed in an early review of the film that this "hospital tale" can take the viewers from all over the world into an easily recognizable "medical hell." Far from being just a "Romanian story," anybody who ever visited an emergency room can relate to this experience. Just as the abortion experience in *4 Months* ... cannot be simply related to a terrible reality from Communist Romania, the tragedy of an old man dying alone is non-relatable to a single context. Assisted by the additional authenticity brought to these fiction films by the handheld camera and the documentary-style approach to reality, together with the genuine mise-en-scènes (the apartment, the ambulance, the hospital are original locations), everything generates a veracious sensation. This is the predominant model, adopted by the majority of directors adhering to the Romanian style of filmmaking. Other recent Romanian filmmakers have tried to emulate this technique, with more or less success, but the aggregated contemporary movies share obvious and easily recognizable patterns, visible both in storytelling practices and in recurrent cinematographic techniques. They have imposed an unmistakable trademark, "the Romanian way" of making movies (Pop 2020) a mode of expression described as the "Romanian style." Today they represent an easily recognizable cinematographic school. Some film critics were quick to describe their inherent "realism" as the common denominator; others were focusing on storytelling practices (described as the "Romanian drama"), or their recurrent subjects or production strategies (when identified as the "New Cinema").

The most difficult problem is not to determine whether or not the overtly assumed stylistics can be understood as purely realist, or if the repetitive narrative techniques are a manifestation of modernist cinema, or an offshoot of the New Wave movements. The labels are unimportant; it does not matter if we describe these movies as coalesced into a "new cinema" or part of the "New Wave" stylistics dominating the cinema in Europe. They certainly generate an unmistakable inflection of the "Romanian state of mind," which raises several issues that cannot be addressed otherwise. When we describe this as a particular form of representing reality, is the "captured" reality a result of cinematic practices or does the social experience grant them to be realistic? Are the moviemaking practices a by-product of transnational influences, or do they overlap with specific circumstances, with cultural, geographic, and philosophical contexts, that have influenced the way in which all Romanian directors made movies?

I argued elsewhere that, when identifying a coherent "Romanian New Wave canon" (Pop 2016), which carries both pan-European characteristics and unique national traits, the stylistic and narratological components in the works of contemporary filmmakers need to be placed in a wider context. My methodological framework for categorizing the cinematic discourses and filmic representations was to use the framework of European moviemaking traditions. By taking into account the paradigmatic transformations made possible by the affiliation of national cinema to the pan-European film industry, to the financing and distributing systems integrating media contents across the European Union, it makes sense to claim that the national is compliant to the transnational.

The National Cinema Hypothesis and the Interzone

The issues of "national heritage" need to be investigated, since the national dimension of these movies influences the meaning-making mechanisms and is simultaneously negated. Whenever one tries to find national identifiers in cinema, this poses several concerns. The most problematic aspect of defining the existence of national cinemas, already widely debated in film theory, is how to account for oxymoronic manifestations such as the "British national cinema" or the heterogeneity of something like the "Quebec National Cinema." Most often the definitions provide a limited understanding, restricted to the external components of moviemaking practices. A simple and mechanical explanation is proposed by Stephen Crofts (1993/2006), who defines all the national cinemas of the world by analogy or difference with Hollywood cinema. The result is the identification of seven distinct categories, basically just another expansion on the Bordwellian model, counterbalancing Hollywood and commercial films with European art cinema. There are several practical factors that could define a national cinema, and they are related to either production or distribution, to the role of the state in financing and to cultural specificity. The entire logic of these evaluations is easily undermined by a central contradiction, made explicit when Crofts claims that "national pride" and the assertion of "national cultural identity" are vital for all art cinemas. We need to take into consideration the numerous situations in which art films are clearly contesting and undermining the "ideals" of national identity, thus functioning as negative manifestations.

Stephen Neale validates the same hypothesis of art cinema competing with the Hollywood film industry and tries to account for the large variety of movies usually described as "art cinema," amongst which the recent Romanian productions invariably end up. The solution is to accept that the "New Waves" are providing a "balance" between the national and international (Neale (1981: 34–5). Such productions, like Cristi Puiu's films discussed here, which obviously carry the "marks of nationality," are participating in the construction and reconstruction of their particular national identities, thus can be relevant for a narrow cultural context. As Neale identifies several traits that make a movie "national" (the national language, the predominance of "auteurist ideologies," together with a particular mode of production and area of circulation), it would appear that our problem is settled. The way in which Romanian movies think and speak is connected to a given set of linguistic and cultural determinants, while maintaining their cross-cultural relevance.

How can we consider contemporary movies to be part of a national "heritage" when their storytelling practices relate so poorly with their publics? To paraphrase Bordwell, why is "the Romanian way of telling stories" perceived by so many as disconnected from their local environment? A corresponding notion, proposed by David Martin-Jones (2006), brings into the debate the issues related to "national narratives," and it could present a solution. The Glasgow University professor advances the presupposition that the "national self-reflection," an evident narrative modality in all these movies, can be associated with larger manifestations, a cultural and political context influencing every European New Wave cinema. Because the construction of national identity has been forcibly changed in Europe after the Second World War, the national traumas, the negative collective experiences, and the transformation of the historical context have created a particular mode of making movies. The predisposition for disrupted narratives, which I defined as *eristetic* storytelling, or the exploration of "nonlinear" storylines, is considered by Martin-Jones as integral to the way in which European cultures dealt with post-war realities. Using the categories proposed by Deleuze, opposing movement-image films to time-image narrations, Martin-Jones follows the central dogmas of "modernist cinema." This reasoning becomes problematic when the film theorist uses Gilles Deleuze to justify the construction of national identity in cinema

(Martin-Jones 2006: 5), especially since the French philosopher was never interested in localized thinking. I find relevant the way in which Martin-Jones reads Christopher Nolan's *Memento* (2000), as a critique of the American cinema linear narration, then assuming that this movie is a re-definition of the "American" national identity. The presupposition that a film like *Memento*, created by a British director, with the main character played by a British-Australian actor, dealing with an amnesiac gangster, and presented in a neo-noir fashion which combines European cinema and an American genre, can be part of a "national identity" is in and of itself highly disputable. Besides the criticism, a relevant aspect of the study carried out by Martin-Jones is worth expanding. By establishing a dialogue between Benedict Anderson's concept of imagined communities and Homhi Bhabha's considerations about narration and nation, together with the Deleuzian terminology related to territorialization and deterritorialization, this methodological model will be useful in the following interpretations.

Another author who suggested replacing the "either/or" dichotomy is Randall Halle (2014: 5). His solution was to propose the existence of a distinct transnational reality, one that is neither narrowly national nor unifyingly European. This needs to be accounted for when dealing with similar productions, by taking into consideration the effects of creating a borderless European Union. This new political reality has a major impact on the collective minds of all Europeans, and the process is also exerting an important influence on the development of the imagined communities of the continent. Through shared media experiences in which the cinematic apparatus (filmmaking and film distribution) plays an important role, contemporary Europe is pushing the national imagination outside the national boundaries (Halle 2014: 13–14). Although Halle completely ignores the Romanian cinema, his conclusion that the European cinema has become a "cinema of interzones" (Halle 2014: 55), made possible by the transformations in film industries and cultivated by financing co-productions, is extremely relevant for understanding the moviemakers discussed here. Such practical explanations must be completed with a discussion about a mental *interzone*, or the "interzone philosophies," specific to the mental space of in-betweenness that characterizes the Romanian nation.

While Halle considers that this space resulted from the accelerated production of distinctions and separations during the European integration, I would argue the contrary that Romania (and many other European countries) was already in an *interzone*. This theory has many supporters in Romanian history and sociology, and, as Lucian Boia, a highly critical historian of the Romanian imaginary, demonstrates systematically, the creation of "Romania" and our contemporary national identity was founded on a "myth of permanent unity" (Boia 2001/2005: 71–2) covering a more profound collective anxiety about a historical disjunction dominating the collective mind.

The Romanian State of In-betweenness: An Imagological Exposition

The Romanians were haunted for centuries by the trauma of their "dismembered" nation. Living for more than a millennium in separate states, this produced several negative consequences, shared with many other ethnic groups who were kept apart under different dominion. In our particular case, there were three major and distinct "Romanian" spaces (Walachia, Moldova, Transylvania), with several others (Bukovina, Dobrogea) gravitating around these separate statal structures. More importantly, the entire Romanian history was driven by the social phantasm of the unaccomplished "Union" and the anguish of territorial dismemberment was reinforced during modern history. After a celebrated Union resulting after the Great War, another important break-up happened during and after the end of the Second World War, with the loss of major parts of the "Greater Romania."

In Central Europe and the Balkans the notion of "national identity" is even more complicated, since often the significant territories of one nation or ethnic group overlap with those of their neighbors. In this part of the world territorial disputes and the forceful occupation of lands have been for centuries malignant sources of cultural offensives, armed conflicts, and, even more tragically, ethnic extermination. Since every nation has its own imagined projection of "national territory," and because such territorial structures are associated with the bloody competition between ethnically distinct groups, almost all forms of territorialization in this part of the world had a tragic and bloody outcome. It may be argued that these constant territorializations and deterritorializations—the use Deleuzian terminology will be explained later—have manifest effects on cinema-thinking.

A historical fact is that contemporary Romania is a product of long processes of territorial indetermination. Unity was sometimes imposed with the help of forceful political and military actions and/or by constant adjustments and revisions. First created as a modern state in 1859, Romania (at that time called the "United Principalities") was composed of dismembered parts of Moldova and Wallachia. Only half of historical Moldova was included in this new state on the map of Europe, with large portions of ethnic Romanians still living in their neighboring empires. Russian empire held on the Eastern part of Moldova, today part of the Republic of Moldova, and in the West the majority of Romanians were part of the Austro-Hungarian empire, their homeland in Transylvania excluded from this political project. Only the south of Bessarabia was briefly included, then exchanged for Dobrogea, a strip of land connecting Walachia with the Black Sea. The major political ideal of the Romanians was to create a "larger Romania," one which could re-integrate the dismembered parts of the imagined national territory had deep effects on the national imaginary. During the First World War Romania was once again broken and parts of it were split, only after the war, due to the unexpected victory of the Triple Entente, of which Romania was a late member, and due to the international policies of Woodrow Wilson, the national borders were redrawn. By 1919 it seemed that the dream of a "Great Romania" was finally accomplished, as the national territory more than doubled. Still, for some nationalists, this was not enough, because the truly "national space" was supposed to reach "from the Dniester to the Tisza," as Mihai Eminescu our "national poet" described it.

This brief historical sketch might seem unrelated to cinema; however, it is a needed parenthesis for understanding and dealing with the imagological component of the Romanian cinematic mind. It provides a methodological structure that allows us to bring together several recurrent manifestations from contemporary film narrations, allowing the contextualized interpretation of positive and negative ethnic or national stereotypes. Such national mythological structures, the political imaginary, and the forms of self-identity are deeply rooted in artistic expressions. I must underline here that, even if the imagological method discusses the stereotyping functions of national imaginaries, my approach is not based on ethno-typical characterizations. The underlying idea is not that nations have characteristics that differentiate them from other ethnic groups, following the infamous "psychology of peoples." There is no converge between the ethnic characterological descriptions and my analytic efforts.

Closer to Benedict Anderson's (1983) conceptualizations of imagined communities, which opened the way to a multitude of studies about the impact of myths and collective representations in the formation of identity, my cinematic imagology approach searches for a framework for understanding how cinema discourses (and their role in the evolution of national imagery) reverberate in film-thinking. The linguistic specificity, manifested in dialogues, the recognizable spatial features, the easily identifiable locations, or the narratives placed in predetermined contexts are all easily available instruments for interpreting movies. Nevertheless, they do not automatically provide clues for the "Romanian cinema-thinking." Larger cognitive structures that are at work have a profound influence on the way in which we think. When studying the components of national mentality it would be important to analyze how cultural productions, of which films are a major component, can relate to the collective representations of the "Self" and of the "Other." The images of national character, the visual representations of self-identity, and the articulation of self-images are even more important now, with Romania being a full member of the European Union, when "Europeanness" has become an influential and disputed component of our cultural sphere. At the crossroads between national, international, transnational, and even post-national issues, cinema plays an important role for untangling such transformations and remains a factor inducing change.

There are several important and systemic imagological investigations, from the textual analysis of major themes, such as alterity and identity (Pageaux 1989), to the "mythocritique" method practiced by Jean-Marc Moura (1994), who founded his imagological approach in the methodologies of comparative literature. Elaborating a repertory of typologies, formulaic images that accumulate as coherent discourses that ultimately contributes to the formation of a collective imaginary (*imaginaire*), in the same fashion that comparative literature describes the usage of literary images in particular national literatures, we can use this framework for interpreting movies. Table 4.1 is intended as a comparative map, including elements from studies discussing the role of national stereotypes or auto-stereotypes (Beller and Leerssen 2007), showing a possible coding of mental images as they are propagated in literature and art as national identities (Laurušaitė 2018). Once again, the purpose is not the same as describing a "national character." Imagology focuses more on analyzing the relationship between the imaginary functions of representations (*imagemes*) and the realities they deal with (*realemes*). When working with "imagemes," ambivalent and binary representations that bring together apparently opposite meanings (for Leerssen these are "Janus faced" structures: "North/South," "central/peripheral" (Leerssen 2000: 277–8)), we are not exposing any national "characteristics." Instead, the imagological interpretation provides us with an insight into the structures of cultural representation and, more importantly, in the thinking processes that conceive particular film contents.

When extending the research instruments of imagological interpretation within the field of cinema research, the analysis can be practiced as a study of representations. Focusing on one or both major typologies—the *auto*-images (or "self-images") and *hetero*-images (or the images of the "Others")—we can reach an understanding inaccessible by direct examination of visual forms or cinematographic techniques. In order to perform such a disciplinary crossover and borrowing from the traditional comparative literature studies, we are conceding that cultural identities are no longer built just by literary discourses. The study of world literature has been replaced by the research of "world cinemas." Badley and Palmer (2006: 11) suggest that dealing with the impact of "global Hollywood" and comparing national production having the American cinema as a reference point is no longer appropriate. There is a global dialogue transcending national borders, as cinema increasingly has become an influential element of the "cultural imagery" of our world today. Films are no longer a way in which national identities are communicated; they constitute a site of experience in which the contact between self-identity and the reception of otherness at a global level provides important insights into how we think. In an era of post-national identities, as Frank Denkler observed in the dictionary entry on cinema in the edited work of Beller and Leerssen (2000: 295–7), movies as mechanisms of generating stereotypes and clichés offer relevant information for cinematic imagological research.

Although we no longer refer to a homogeneous "national self," since movies are created for international audiences, cinema remains also indicative for the self-image of a certain group, transforming localized experiences (events taking place in a specific context) into movements of thought with global relevance.

We need to take into consideration some previous conclusions extracted by imagological interpretations of the way the Romanians "think," illustrated by Dennis Deletant's contribution to the "Romanian chapter" of the volume coordinated by Beller and Leerssen. This British historian, specialized in Romanian studies, comes to the conclusion that the Romanians have carried a "negative image" about themselves throughout history. Linked to stereotypes such as Bram Stoker's projection of an exotic land in which two opposite worlds coexist (Deletant 2007: 225), a major cultural premise identified by many historians, including Western historians studying Romania (Hitchins 2015) keep using. Even before Romania was "Romania" as a modern state, the myth of the "East-West synthesis" provided a marker for the independent kingdoms our ethnic group was divided into. Trapped between the Ottoman influence and dominance, the influence of the West as a source of intellectual inspiration during the bourgeois revolution, and then as part of the Soviet system, Romania had a long history of conflicting identities.

Using this as a central hypothesis, my own assumption in the following is that cinematic imagology interpretations must be based on the presupposition that contemporary Romanian film-thinking was developed in a type of cultural *interval*, manifested as both as a spatial and a temporal *imageme*, that can be only described as *a natural state of in-betweenness*.

Does the Romanian Cinema Think Differently?

This observation leads to a further question: can we identify a specific Romanian *cinematic mind*? If so, did this mode of thinking evolve from the above-mentioned imagological resources, or do we need to consider that the recent films are simply carriers of unrelated ways of thinking? A quick solution to deal with such problems would be further develop the arguments provided by Andrew Higson (1989), who considers that the "national" character of a movie can be easily determined by describing its content (topics, subjects) and by identifying the production standards (locations, distribution). Such practical definitions could lead to the conclusion that, since all the examples discussed here are expressions of a "national" film-making culture, they are also part of the same "cinematic mind." Even when accepting this premise, which is extremely vague, the key problem remains unchanged—do movies make us think about an already-existing reality, do they represent a version of that reality thus changing our thinking or do they have a mind of their own, abstracted from any reality?

I would suggest that one explanation is right in front of us, hidden in plain view, in the titles of all the recent Romanian movies. Looking at the short inventory from Table 4.1 and overt and relevant polysemic function is visible, which could be definitory for the mind-frame of the cinematic case studies analyzed here. If movies have a "mimetic" quality and the human experiences or the urban geographies presented in their film-worlds can provide enough information as to the identity of that particular world, the words used can capture relevant facts. I suggest that these movies disclose a dimension of "Romanianness" not only by their representation of the real world, but how they are engaging the spectators, disclosing a cultural inclination, a specific perception of the world.

Some titles from the canon of contemporary Romanian cinema (Table 4.1) indicate a predilection for meaninglessness which sometimes can reach the most absurd; once more Cristi Puiu is leading the way; movie titles like *Sieranevada* or *Malmkrog* are indecipherable by any measure. Other movies have non-specific identifiers (*Boogie*, *Ryna*), which need supplementary explanations and details. Many word associations and ironic reformulations or sarcastic references put into place to divert our understanding—as I mentioned in the analysis of *The Death of Mr. Lăzărescu* with the announcement of an imminent death which never takes place. Also relevant for our current discussion are the productions that describe a spatial indeterminacy, with locations clearly positioned in an overt in-betweenness (*Beyond the Hills*, *By the Rails*) or choosing uncertain meanings instead of monosemic significations (*Child's Pose*, *Loverboy*) or presenting us with confusing time frames (*12:08 to Bucharest*; *How I Spent the End of the World*).

These intervals of meanings are backed up by a spatial in-betweenness, manifested at the level of individual directorial decisions. Many of these stories take place on the move, with one of the most important tropes being the car. This is augmented by the fact that moviemakers recontextualize the car as a reversed visual trope, with the protagonists framed in over-the-shoulder shots, accentuating their indistinctiveness. Cristi Puiu is a master of such intermediary spaces; *The Death …* illustrates several times how the sensation of in-betweenness can be created in every location (the apartment, the ambulance, the hospital hallways). Ultimately the entire story of the dying old man happens "between" hospitals.

Some film critics (Deaca 2017) observed that the "internal world" of the Romanian cinema-makers, the favorite areas where the action takes place, is indicative of the same predilection for *in-between* spaces. The protagonists evolve in cramped kitchens, packed apartment interiors, and other types of confined quarters. An innovative approach in the national critical discourse is offered by Mircea Deaca, one of the most astute promoters of the cognitive perspectives on the "New Romanian cinema." This film critic elaborated an in-depth analysis of the kitchen as a cognitive space which allows us to understand how the Romanian filmmakers think. These cinematic spaces provide a glimpse of the "conception about reality" (Deaca 2017: 11), since space represents a material form, linked with internal conditioning. In almost all these movies, whenever the characters are sitting at dinner tables, in kitchens or dining rooms, the setting provides an opportunity for the film directors to explore various intervals of thinking. In the empty spaces of these apartments, on the hallways or in the doorways, a special type of non-cinematic thinking occurs. Even when the shooting takes place outside, the preferred spaces are also intermediary contexts, like back alleys, intersections, or other darkened and neutral urban locations.

An important nuance for understanding the logic of these locations for the Romanian contemporary moviemaking is provided by French anthropologist Marc Augé (1992/2008), who observed that modernity has created predefined environments dominated by anonymity (cars, buses, train stations, hotels, or supermarkets) where human beings spend their lives in a spatial indeterminacy and without identity. These *non-places*, considered to be specific to supermodernity (in the original French text "surmodernité"), are a consequence of an overabundant version of modernity, in which time and space are dilated and distorted to an unprecedented level. The predisposition for these *non-places* provides a profound connection to a deeper level of the Romanian culture and mythology, as modernism and modernity only allowing them to resurface. The following section concentrates on explaining these choices from an imagological and mythopoetical perspective.

A Mythopoetic Analysis of the Romanian Mind

Many cultural critics and political commentators have tried to explain the "Romanian mind" by using various forms of psychological deterministic readings. The early studies of Constantin Rădulescu-Motru (1937) provide the best illustration for how the idea of a specific Romanian *mode of thinking* can follow along with a series of ethnic coordinates. The exploration of Romanianness and the ineffable nature of our collective psychology also have a long tradition in psychological studies. From the racially biased studies of Dumitru Drăghicescu (1907) to the more recent cognitivist approaches practiced by Daniel David (2015), there were many attempts to identify <u>the dominant traits of our personal, social, or political behavior.</u> It was Drăghicescu to first stress the role played on the "Romanian psychology" by the apparent historical fact that our ethnic group was positioned in a geographic and political intersection, which he linked with the ethnically relevant term "răspântie," best translatable with turn-off. Such ethnic, linguistic, and psychological juxtapositions dominated ever since the autochthonous evaluations of our specific frame of mind. Another observation made by Drăghicescu (1907: 14–15), that the Romanians are a neo-Latin nation practicing a Christian Orthodox cult, a culture place in-between the Orient and the Occident, existing at the "frontiers of civilizations," was also perpetuated. It is not the place to go into further detail of the various studies which use forms of negative or dichotomic evaluations of the "collective psyche" of this nation. We can go back to the earliest historical and mythological resources available and claim to identify such pervasive dichotomies. As described by one of the most important historians of our literature, George Călinescu, there is an ancestral "sentiment of providence" of the Romanians, structurally inherited by all our cultural productions, which can be linked straight to the Geto-Dacians (Călinescu 1945/2001: 17–18).

Today this is a recurrent cultural stereotype, constantly re-evaluated and recovered in various versions. Such a simplifying approach is followed by the literary critic Sorin Alexandrescu, who coined the concept known as the "Romanian paradox." Considering that our national identity was determined both by a spatial and a temporal paradox, which keep influencing the Romanian culture, politics, and the entire way of thinking, this critic explains how a spatial determination, the "frontier paradox" (Alexandrescu 1998: 12), resulting from the geographic position of the Romanians, can have a major influence on the national psyche. This troubling explanandum is coupled by the Romanian literature professor with a more problematic, temporal paradox. He claims to have detected a predominant predisposition of the Romanians to go "against time" (Alexandrescu 1998: 35). Many others critically evaluate the myths of the Romanian political mind and consider that "Romania is different" (Boia 2012) since they can describe the negative imprints resulting from a millennial existence at the borderlands of Europe. If historically and culturally we can trace the imaginary conditioning of the Romanian collective mind, generated either by the anxiety towards invaders or by the desire to project a glorious past, this ambivalence cannot be properly linked to a single nation or a single ethnic group. Such conclusions would be hard to apply credibly in any interpretation of cinematic contents.

The Difficulties of Defining a Cinematic Nationhood

A foregone conclusion would allow a quick definition of "Romanianess." By precipitately examining only the traits containing illustrations proving the existence of a "national cinema," many film historians have developed their own local version of film theory. When overviewing productions inspired by key historical figures, or representations dealing with historical events, Romanian film industry could appear to have produced a truly national cinema. This accumulates into a "national cinematographic epic" (Saulea 2011), certainly based on a generic predisposition for relating "Romanian" narratives. Yet this is an approach to filmmaking that most likely can be identified in all other cinemas of the world. Movies populated with the greatest and most recognizable historical figures are created in all cultures. The fact that there are several films dealing with topics picked from Romanian history is only an easy choice to define "Romanianism" and "Romanianness" (Colăcel 2018). Overviewing such historical movies, the best outcome is an account of eclectic assemblage of stories, mostly made during state socialism or part of state propaganda. Either by exposing them as fake identity formations, denouncing their role in the political effort to promote nationalism, or by ignoring their importance in the overall cinematic mind, the fact remains that these movies have no cognitive relevance in terms of imagological interpretations. They were created to promote a "nationalistic" view of the world, supported by the political leadership at a given time, not indications for self-representation. To claim that these productions have anything to do with "docudrama" or to suggest that these expensive costume dramas produced by the Communist regime can "make public the inner workings of national history" (Colăcel 2018: 25) are unwarranted inferences.

A better approach to use national cinema as a pathway to describe more profound structures of the national imaginary was practiced by Florentina Andreescu (2013). Overviewing several Romanian productions, this author provides several socio-political explanations coupling Michael Schapiro's (1999) definition of "cinematic nationhood" with a psychoanalytic version of trauma studies. The idea that films can "articulate" dominant political and social discourses is not to be rejected; it allows this interpreter to open a window into the Romanian society and it provides access to levels of collective imagination, otherwise intangible. Focused on the cultural articulation of the projected identity desired by the state (Schapiro 1999: 130–1), Andreescu retroactively reads into some major national myths (like that of Trajan and Dochia or Miorița). The author concludes that Romanians have an excessively passive attitude, even a "masochistic psychic structure" (Andreescu 2013: 49–50), disclosed by the cinematic narratives analyzed. This relevant speculation leads to more problematic conclusions, such as finding here the manifestations of a "colonizing" presence, both during and after communism.

Andreescu is using the national myths as keys to explaining not only how Romanian cinema works, but linking these and other legends (such as Meșterul Manole—Manole Foreman) with an implied "national structure of fantasy" (Andreescu 2013: 55). Besides some relevant findings, by identifying the presumed traits of "the Other" filtered through political interpretations of these meanings (the socialist state, the West), Andreescu only partially recovers the profound imagological mechanisms. For example, by establishing a relationship with the Other as institutional power, the reaction of all Romanians is interpreted as "complacency" and expressions of a presumed "masochistic fantasy," which somehow reappears in cinematic storytelling. Reading into cinematic representations the myths of national identity this author reaches far-fetched conclusions about how such "Romanian fantasy" (Andreescu 2013: 106) pervades movies like *4 Months, 3 Weeks, and 2 Days*.

Such approaches ignore any cognitive dimension of the social experience produced outside the act of watching movies. In Andreescu's interpretation, for instance, the profound "masochistic" dimension of our collective psyche, indicated by the way in which "the Others" are represented as inflictors of pain and sufferance, is identified in the "embodied" experience created by the movies. The social trauma generated by the abortion laws imposed by the Ceaușescu regime that were transposed in Cristian Mungiu's movie did not exist in a cultural vacuum. There are other examples of movies about abortion available for the spectators in Communist Romania. *Picture Postcards with Wild Flowers* (*Ilustrate cu flori de câmp*, dir. Andrei Blaier, 1975) demonstrates that the film directors and the spectators of the time were acutely aware of the ideological meanings contained by movies. It would be a simplistic explanation to pretend that the official thinking was mechanically transmitted, without being processed. The individuals going through those painful experiences, even when watching (or creating) movies, have a knowledge of the screen representations without the information contained by the film-world.

To practice a real "mythopoetics" of Romanian cinema, in the sense used by Kriss Ravetto-Biagioli (2017), would mean to focus only on the process of cinematic mythmaking, since we need to ask whereby movies are transforming ideas into themes, then turning them into narratives, and then convey social meanings, or the other way around. Some recurrent forms of representation that renew "old myths" were not properly contextualized, especially since the main problem with such approaches was that they removed any agency from the moviemakers themselves or they limited the process of creating cinematic meanings to a transfer of political connotations. In fact, as pointed out by Astrid Erll and Ansgar Nünning (2008: 395), sometimes the most influential are the movies that are *not* watched; they have a stronger influence on cultural-historic knowledge by forming ideas *outside* the cinematic experience. While we can certainly deal with movie representations as directly connected with the political mind, they is never the single most significant factor in defining the overall imagination of a community. Another important element we must acknowledge in this context, which raises major methodological issues for a purely imagological approach to cinema-thinking, comes from over-stressing the impact of particular productions and authors. When evaluating cinema productions in the context of their actual viewership, strictly from a statistical point of view, it is highly disputable how influential can be some movies which only have a couple of thousand viewers. As is the case with some of the most remarkable recent productions, which have achieved international notoriety, they are either ignored by the Romanian spectators or used as negative examples. An example is Radu Jude's provocative questioning of recent historical traumas, raising doubts about the role of the Romanian state during the Holocaust, intended by the author as an impulse to make his co-nationals think about the past. The production was largely ignored by the public. An eye-opening film such as *I Do Not Care If We Go Down in History as Barbarians* (*Îmi este indiferent dacă în istorie vom intra ca barbari*, 2018) was viewed by a little more than 9,400 spectators. So, in order to understand their impact on the cognitive mapping or their role in the "thinking in society," these movies can fall under the category of narratives that are re-coding our symbolic understanding of society, but they have to be placed in a broader context.

My main concern is to identify the common elements that could allow us to identify the traits of the "Romanian cinematic mind" without intermixing the problematic dimension of political forms of representation. Here a more difficult line of inquiries should address several other related questions: What is the nature of knowledge provided by the recent Romanian cinematic productions? If these films can provide an insight into the cognitive structures of our society, how can they also provide access to cognitive structures that are representative for larger meanings? Particularly, how can we overview the works of a director like Cristi Puiu, one of the most important contemporary Romanian auteurs, and describe a mindframe existing beyond the local relevance of his masterpieces?

As mentioned before, my own approach is to interrogate the non-philosophical dimension of cinema-thinking, by performing a close analysis of the discursive, narrative, and technical elements of these works and search for indicative elements of their negative dimensions, either those refusing the political, the allegorical, the mythological, and even the cinematographic. The outward components of a movie are important; yet, when searching for the mechanisms of cinema-thinking, especially those not generated only through the cinematic machine, an exploration of other forms of "outside" is necessary.

The Unhappiness of Being (a) Romanian (Film)

Happiness is one of the most important philosophical problems. The ancient Greeks began discussing the coordinates of human existence and our relationship with the gods, destiny, and our life in society by advancing the idea of a "good life." This gravely preoccupied Socrates and was later transformed by a millennium of debates about ethics and morality, becoming the cornerstone of European philosophy. Today we can better quantify the level of happiness using sociological instruments. According to the World Happiness Report, published annually by the United Nations Sustainable Development Solutions Network, the criteria for measuring human wellbeing include economic factors (like the GDP), and several emotional and social factors. According to this report, Romania holds a moderate position at number forty-eight in the global ranking of unhappy nations. It seems that we are happier than other neighbors, at least we feel better than the Greeks (82), the Hungarians (62), or the Bulgarians (97). As a nation, the Romanians score poorly at social generosity and have a disproportionately high political corruption, yet are relatively happy. Then how can we explain the profound unhappiness of so many movie characters, and why is there such a disproportionate number of unfortunate protagonists in our cinema?

We should take into consideration another important factor, which is related to the capacity to feel good about oneself. As indicated by a national survey made in 2012 by the Romanian Institute for Evaluation and Strategy (IRES), Romanians have a very bad self-image. Only 51 percent of Romanians admit they want to live in their own country, and a quarter think they were not born in the right place. Another 2013 poll made by the same Institute discloses the fact that almost 60 percent of the Romanians consider that their country is negatively perceived abroad, especially by other European Union citizens. As many as 42 percent of those interrogated believe Romanians have a "bad" image and 18 percent consider that we have a "really bad" image, with only 38 percent of my fellow countrymen considering that their country was appreciated inside the EU.

As mentioned before, some point to the potential culprit for this negative image of the Romanians and their ancestral nation—the representations provided in cinema. Even though contemporary Romanian cinema has been widely acclaimed by international reviewers and bestowed with innumerable European and global awards, there are people who still believe that the "New Wave" Romanian films are malignant. The worst example is the conservative and popular public speaker, Dan Puric, a former actor turned into social media influencer. This vocal supporter of the purity of the "Romanian soul" publicly accused recent cinema-makers of undermining the traditional values, denouncing their choice for stories purposefully exposing a "pathological debasement," their dealing with abortions or prostitution considered a "menace" to "our spiritual architecture" and the "structure of our souls" (quoted by Tudor 2016).

When asking why the Romanians are unhappy I am echoing Nikos Dimou (2013), who published a book provocatively entitled *On the Unhappiness of Being Greek*," a collection of aphorisms about the philosophical dissatisfaction of our neighbors toward their own country. Even though the ancient Greeks considered that *eudaimonia* (happiness) was the perfect state to which every human being needs to aspire, his collection of maxims and expressions describes a similar predicament of the Greek mentality. Dimou, in a 2012 postscript of the same book, explained that unhappiness derived from a mind divided between past and present, between the Eastern mentality and European aspirations, torn by forces of tradition (mostly coming from the Orthodox Church) and modernity. This is a common "difficult fate," shared by another Orthodox nation, the Romanians.

What else do we lack in order to be happy, to have the "good life" prescribed by the ancient philosophers and many other contemporary spiritual mentors? Classical eudaimonian theories, starting with Socrates and Plato, indicate several pathways to "wellbeing," and three of these are most important—to carry a moral life, to display a virtuous behavior, and to express moderation. When overviewing the most important cinematic productions created by contemporary Romanian film industry (see Table 4.1) the striking observation is that they are replete with unhappy individuals, that almost nobody is anywhere close to such an ideal state of *eudaimonia*. I do not intend to proceed here with elaborating a complete account of these categories, nor to perform a detailed interpretation of every instance in which the protagonists are miserable. Nevertheless, when attempting to understand the excess of painful and bad experiences, we need to find an appropriate vocabulary.

There are at least three sources of suffering which can be identified in these movies, three types of subsequent experiences related to understanding one's own destiny. We can categorize them as follows: *akrasis*, *ananke*, and *accedia*, using the names of ancient mythological figures. The first is the implacable fate, a manifestation of *anánkē*, the Greek goddess of suffering, who was impossible to appease (Lawrence 2013: 38–9). Ananke is necessity in action, a force exerted in our existence by external situations. The best example for this type of suffering induced by the unexpected and unavoidable circumstances of life remains Mr. Lăzărescu, who ends up in the hospital not because of his cancer pains, but because of a stupid accident in the bathroom, happening while waiting for the ambulance with his friend and neighbor inside the apartment. An explanation of ananke is even provided during the discussion between the two neighbors. While standing idly in the doorway, complaining about the fact that Mr. Lăzărescu's daughter abandoned him and left for Canada, they have this moral debate while the old man is mortally injured in the bathroom. As the paramedic arrives, they discover that the old man has fallen in the bathtub, which will ultimately lead to his demise (and not the cancer).

Another type of fatal intervention in Puiu's movies is caused by the alienation of spirit, with the hero a victim of moral and social *acedia*. While the Greek thinkers associated acedia with "the darkness within," in modern times it is the product of a spiritual malaise, manifested as either an emotional burnout or an effect of plethoric existence leading to soul sloppiness. A typical situation of this kind of negligent lack of concern for one's own existence is the story of Viorel, the banal criminal from *Aurora*. At the end of the movie, carrying his inner suffering, barely explicit in words and expressed in awkward interactions, he gets to the police station to confess his atrocious deeds, and he is met with the unfeeling reactions from the policemen mirroring his own slothfulness. Ultimately all the sufferings endured and caused by him are purposeless; the crude reality is that nobody cares about the suffering of other people.

Lastly, there is *akrasis*, or *akrasia*, a form of suffering generated by the desperate attempts to be in control of one's own life, with the final outcome being the discovery that any transformation is impossible. Romanian movies repeatedly activate this mechanism, as most of the protagonists often go blindly and purposefully toward pain and misery. Puiu's version of the "akrastic" hero is Lary, the doctor in *Sieranevada*, who is miserable in his relationships, does nothing to change his life and simply goes about with the current state of affairs, which is provoking him real psychological and physical ailment.

Even if we could find social and economical explanations in the post-communist society and specific to all transition countries, the roots of unhappiness within the Romanian mind-frame are deep, running through our cultural history. An identifiable axiological unhappiness is best described by a book dedicated to the explorations of the "unhappy consciousness." Benjamin Fondane (born in Romania as Beniamin Wechsler) is an important surrealist poet and existentialist philosopher, who wrote several articles about his friend Tristan Tzara and who died at Auschwitz. He tries to elucidate the predisposition of human beings for unhappiness by connecting it with resignation. We are metaphysical beings because we are unhappy, and this is a negative quality producing a state of mind that affects entire cultures. Inspired by the Russian philosopher Lev Shestov, the father of the "philosophy of despair," Fondane (2016) considers that we are "citizens" of a double unhappiness, one social and one metaphysical. Thus unhappiness is a "metaphysical category," brought by Fatum (Fate, linked by Shestov with Anánkē), which provides us with another form of knowledge. This fatalistic view of the world induces a *metaphysical anxiety* caused by the strangeness of life and the Nothingness of existence, in turn generating *existential thoughts*.

The following arguments are going to explore the fatalistic components that form the Romanian cinema-thinking, by proceeding with a close mythological analysis. We must account for this predisposition for unhappiness, which is part of the "national" mind and soul made visible in recent movies, by searching for its resources, that could elucidate why it has such a profound impact. By taking into consideration previous cultural experiences, such cinematic representations might provide the viewers (and the moviemakers) with the ability to satisfy their desire to be liberated from unhappiness through a cathartic effect. On the other hand, such negative experiences onscreen release the minds from the painful sensations induced by external factors and make way for film-thinking.

The Fatalist Hypothesis: Cinema as a Transmitter of Collective Fables and Identities

An early explanation used to decode the Romanian cinema was the observation advanced by Dominique Nasta in the first international overview of the national cinema. Fatalism, claims the film studies professor, is "at the core of the Romanian psyche" (Nasta 2013: 5). This provides important insight and also raises several debatable issues. There are a couple of ancestral stories, like the myths of the shepherd who accepted his anticipated death, or the wife of the monastery builder accepting to be buried alive, which appear to disclose a particular form of pessimistic melancholia that can characterize the "Romanian psyche." Faced with an imminent tragedy and trying to cope with the utter suffering caused by reality, the characters in these stories are constantly reacting with a fatalistic detachment.

Published as an authentic ballad, "Miorița" (The Little Ewe Lamb) remains one of the most important cultural myths in modern Romanian culture. Integrated into literary discourses designed to create a national identity, later evolving in a multitude of forms and representations, this folk song was "discovered" by Vasile Alecsandri, at that time the most important Romanian poet and writer. First edited and published in 1850, the earliest account was noted by Alecu Russo in 1846, and it is relevant that the story came to the attention of a generation of writers and historians that have created the bourgeois Romanian identity. Miorița was ever since a quintessential national myth and, as observed by George Călinescu (1945/2001), it became one of the four foundational myths of Romanian modern culture. According to this literary critic (Călinescu 1945/2001: 41–2) such explanatory narratives, like those illustrating the birth of the Romanian nation (Traian and Dochia), explaining the cosmological place of human beings (Miorița/The Little Ewe Lamb), the accounts of the artistic creation and aesthetic production (Meșterul Manole/Master Manole) or the dynamics of human sexuality (Sburătorul) have archetypal functions.

As it will be explained further along this line of explanations, these are also *macabre* accounts, either describing a cruel death, a form of demonic possession, or condoning criminal acts. In terms of imagological interpretations, they expose multiple levels of stereotyping while disclosing the mechanisms of self-identity. This was usually called the "mioritic attitude," actually a form of *katabasis*, a tendency to accept the fatality of life, which also appears to be manifested in numerous contemporary movies. Such connections allowed many film critics to conclude that an overall fatalistic view of the world can be an indicator for Romanian cinema-thinking. Of course, when quickly looking only for external manifestations and by accepting that a preexisting archetypal characteristic of the national psyche is still at work, the Romanian cinema appears replete with such manifestations.

It would be only too easy to identify situations, narratives, or characters that qualify as "fatalistic." From one of the first fiction films created by the new Socialist industry, *The Mill of Good Luck* (*La moara cu noroc*, 1955), directed by Victor Iliu, an adaptation of a moralizing novel written by Ioan Slavici, where the weak-willed innkeeper navigates between life and death, to its 2015 remake, *Orizont*, directed by Marian Crișan, there seems to be an ongoing preoccupation with the theme and variations of fatality. Some of the most important Romanian productions, which also got international acclaim at their own time, are based on similar explorations of the acceptance of punishment or the implacable death. This is the case with *The Forest of the Hanged* (*Pădurea spânzuraților*, dir. Liviu Ciulei, 1964), or *Reconstruction* (*Reconstituirea*, dir. Lucian Pintilie, 1968), where the marks of resignation appear to be dominant and to indicate a recurrent trait of the "national cinema."

Perhaps the quickest connection with this particular form of fatalism can be established when performing a general overview of movies like *The Death of Mr. Lăzărescu*, where several explicit correspondences can be identified. From the fact that the ambulance nurse is called Mioara (another diminutive of the ewe lamb, Miorița), to the resignation of an old man confronted with imminent death, or the symbolic interpretation of the tragedy of the old pensioner slowly dying as a passage to the underworld during the movie, they all are extremely tempting explanations. The story can be projected as an allegorical representation of the Moldavian shepherd who accepts his destiny, and for some critics, it appears that Dante Remus Lăzărescu is such archetypal figure in contemporary cinema. Gradually giving up his agency and becoming a powerless object, without the possibility to change the implacable ending of his life, Lăzărescu opens up to the mechanisms of an ancestral way of thinking.

Many film critics have accepted wholeheartedly the "mioritic" cultural hypothesis as a good for all interpretation, exporting it over to various cinematic situations. Judith Pieldner (2016) reads into Radu Jude's *Aferim!* (2015) the intention to re-contextualize the "mioritic foothills," a subversion of the presumed idyllic landscape, thus generating a disruption of the mythological representations of the archaic Romanian space (Pieldner 2016: 100). Others who took for granted the "mioritic" formula hastily connect any "resignation" with other social and even political manifestations, as is the case with the thorough study elaborated by Strausz (2017). The Hungarian film critic redefines this archetype by overlapping it with Lefebvre's concept of "hesitation." Basically this re-reading of the "mioritic" elements reverberates with a second-hand interpretation of a formula already proposed by Ambrus Miskolczy, since all the references used by Strausz are indirect quotes to this work, including the discussion about the Mioritic space ("mioritikus tér") as a spatial determination with cultural consequences. This allows the film critic to expand the notion of hesitation and to interpret Romanian contemporary cinema through this poetic practice, manifested as a trope in almost every cinematic discourse, both before and after the Communist regime (Strausz 2017: 32). Once more this pan-ideological function of the overt conflict between the three shepherds in Miorița, with two of them conspiring to kill the most affluent of them, and the victim seemingly displaying resignation as a form of indecision is quickly applied. This, in turn, is transparently linked to the geography of the Romanian landscape, or "Plaiul," which is dominated by constant changes of scenery, from plains to hills and valleys. Influenced by Romanian folklorists and other cultural interpreters, most of them with rural extraction, Strausz is victim to a fallacy of argumentation when discussing about the mioritic determinism. The author himself realizes that a spatial experience connected to rural existence can hardly qualify when describing movies which are almost exclusively taking place in urban contexts. Actually, that particular philosophical space which some believed to be linked to the "mioritic" magical land, is now replaced by another in-betweenness, creating a new imaginary. The hill-valley horizon is now substituted by urban peripheries, the typical post-communist "mahala" and the post-socialist suburban spaces, where the modern and the retrograde coexist, have nothing to do with Miorița.

The reality is that such problematic readings could have been avoided by performing a first-hand documentation. All these issues were previously discussed and clarified by Romanian authors like Ovidiu Papadima or Lucian Blaga, who were also preoccupied during the 1930s and 1940s to identify a "Romanian vision of the world." This was part of a larger debate about the ethnic specificity manifested in cultural forms, mostly due to their fascist fascination, predominant even before the Second World War. Researching Romanian folklore, in a work published initially in 1941, Papadima argued that what seemed to be a form of hesitation (șovăială) was more likely a metaphysical effort to make sense of the absurd, of the nonsensical dimension of existence. Rejecting fatalism, this author identifies an "organic" expression of the harmony between good and evil as a key component of the national spirit. As Lucian Blaga also pointed out in his expanded interpretation of the impact played by Miorița in the Romanian culture, this must be seen as a "sophianic" tale, dealing with spiritual transfiguration and not with physical extermination or the mechanics of existence.

The Miorița story both discovers and explains the real world while hiding meanings in a covert metaphysical structure. These "fables about ourselves" and their movie reversion must always be taken with a grain of salt, as such assessments about storytelling ignore the fact that movies have a cognitive function, in the sense that they organize all our social experiences. As Carroll (1988: 208–9) deciphered the powerless power of movies, even when particular productions can help us better understand the world around us, when we can follow the emotional troubles of the main characters and extract some knowledge, when we ask questions which might even provide answers about life, this Q&A session happening in our minds never solves our real problems. Movies have an influence upon us, but they are not that powerful. This is the sense in which we must understand the *post-metaphysical* function of these productions, as they are not giving us special access into some secret corners of the collective mind; they are not providing mysterious meanings; instead, they perform an *eristetic* refusal of explanations. And this blockage, together with the gaps of understanding, is more thoughtful than we might think.

My question about the role of these narratives is also engaged in a critical dialogue with authors like Christian Salmon (2010) and others, who argue that modern storytelling functions as a collective force, driven by a "new narrative order" that is imposed at a global level by external social forces. Cinema definitely can play an important role in the media visual wars, performing the role of a powerful *dispositif*, capable of transmitting aesthetic, affective, and even conceptual meanings. However, to accept that there is a hidden dimension of cinema allowing spectators to actually "feel" the "cinematic encounter," as argued by Greg Singh (2014) in his post-Jungian explanations, means overlapping feeling and thinking. Even when we are convinced that a story is true, as is the case with the tragedy of *Mr. Lăzărescu*, in and by itself the narration cannot define who we really are, nor can it inculcate ideas about society, humanity, friendship, or solidarity. The speculation that we are the victims of "emotion producing" industries, that ideas can be induced by corporations who are managing the global distribution and consumption of "collective fables" through "storytelling management" (Salmon 2010), lacks any factual support. The presumed "power of Hollywood movies," which are not simply telling us stories, but they are telling us who we are, needs to be put into perspective. Salmon appropriately identifies the role of "emotional capitalism" in coding our experiences and even managing collective identities with the help of a worldwide "fiction economy," in which global companies are transformed into "storytelling organizations." The unanswered question is how television programs, blockbuster movies, or video games can influence our minds or shape our souls through stories? Without insisting too much on this critical view of contemporary media, it is undeniable that story-structures and storyworld building have a huge impact on the cognitive system of the global audience. Stories are important for understanding society, and particular stories can draw our attention to things and ideas we are otherwise unaware of. A powerful visual narration, as is the case with the dying old man from Bucharest, provides a comprehension of the world going beyond the plot or the individual characters involved. This process of organizing narrative information to generate meanings, already explained by narratological cognitivism and cognitive narratology, has to be explored at a deeper level.

The "Miorița Story" and the Presumed Resignation of the Romanians

The meanings of the ballad have generated numerous debates, and the discussions about this quintessential folktale are, in and of themselves, part of the cultural history of Romanian thinking. One of the stereotypical interpretations, which is relevant for the overall effort to decipher the Romanian collective psyche, can be traced back to the nineteenth-century observations of the French historian Jules Michelet, who was the first to translate the ballad for a foreign audience. For Michelet the story displayed the main national trait of the Romanians, that is, their "easy resignation" (quoted by Eliade 1970/1997: 229). As many foreign travelers to Romania have noted, this type of "fatalistic melancholia" shared by the Romanian people was perpetuated culturally, a transparent way of thinking explicit within the Romanian language, filled with untranslatable words expressing multiple "shades of sadness"—like "dor" (longing) and "zbucium" (fidgeting), sometimes as combinations of desire and the troubled nature of the soul. Fermor, who was also impressed by the popular song called "doină," commented on the fact that its rhythms were a mixture of long pauses and a fascinating sense of uselessness (Fermor 2013/2016: 166–8), a definition easily exported to describe recent Romanian films.

Fatalism became a central issue for the Romanian philosophers, and relevantly enough one of the first systematic thinkers of a nation without philosophy for a millenia, Vasile Conta, published an entire work dedicated to the "theory of fatalism." Later transformed into an anti-semitic politician and minister, Conta was claiming that the ideas dominating the nations of the world were determined by their environments. Thus human societies were fatalistically destined to repeat the same "laws," which he describes as "fatal laws" (Conta 1894: 7–8). Although not referring to the particular national characteristics of the Romanians, Conta elaborated a theory of "universal undulation," which is extremely close to the spiritual manifestations later analyzed by Lucian Blaga in his own theory about the mioritic "undulatory space."

During the 1920s and the 1930s, this unique philosopher of Romanian civilization elaborated an innovative theory about the metaphysical condition of his culture, which he called the "undulated infinite." He notoriously linked this to local geography, a typical Romanian space called "Plaiul" (the Land). While this notion is not necessarily describing a material space, as it rather circumscribes an "unconscious horizon," it is predetermined by the fact that the Romanians have indeed lived for millennia in such a "mioritic space" (Blaga 2011: 69), characterized by the continuous "up-and-down." Blaga concluded that this experience has led to the formation of an unconscious manifestation, one that is visible in many artistic articulations. His example is the Romanian popular song called "doină," with its musical manifestation (Blaga 2011: 116) mirroring the collective destiny, also defined by an infinite "climbing and descending" ("suiș și coborâș").

This remains the basis for the theory about a Romanian "stylistic matrix," coherently described in a study dedicated to the mioritic space (*spațiul mioritic*), an archetypal structure making the Romanians different from the Westerners and particularly the Germanic peoples (Blaga 2011: 241). An ethnocentric Blaga, who was more interested in defining the concept of a "cultural soul," further elaborated on the notion of "stylistic matrix" (matricea stilistică), which he believed to be articulated in various forms of discourse (from language, to poetry and music). The best term containing the "Romanian soul" was the poetic use of longing ("dor"), defined by Blaga as "a melancholia, not too heavy, not too soft, of a soul that climbs and descends" (Blaga 2011: 67). As the ultimate expression of the conditions of the national collective psyche, "dorul" was a typical manifestation of "an undulated infinity" (Blaga 2011: 68), also expressed in unique versions of popular songs or national folk dances. Determined by the specific geographic landscapes of Romania (hill-valley/deal-vale), it generated a spiritual matrix of the "Romanian spirit" (duhul românesc), a cosmic rhythm that marked the existence of the "Walachian shepherds," in turn making the Romanian spirituality with a simultaneous movement of anabasis (ascension) and katabasis (descending). It results in a form of migration from fatalism (as katabasis or descent into melancholia), to ascending through an exaggerated optimistic self-confidence.

Perhaps the best illustration of this double indeterminacy is another famous Romanian philosopher, Emil Cioran. Even his destiny seems to be following the anabasis–katabasis trajectory. In the early 1920s and 1930s his writings were centered on the glorification of Romanian vitalism, only to finish his career as the most important representative of fatalism and melancholia in French literature. His ideas revolved around the notion of fatality in history, an ardent topic discussed by the entire camaraderie of his generation. Cioran published as a young man a resounding manifesto calling for the "transfiguration" of the Romanian identity (in a direct reference to the Christic scene). Here he expressed deeper cultural anxieties regarding the great "historical sleep" of the Romanians throughout history. This negative destiny and implicit fatalism, prophesied Cioran, must be replaced by delirium. In order to occupy their rightful position in modern history, the Romanians needed to replace their lack of vitalism and submissive melancholia with imperial revival. This was a discourse that mobilized the fascists at that time, as Cioran talked about a desire to fill the cultural vacuum of Wallachia (neantul valah) and the need to wake the nation from slumber, the combination between nationalist ideology and the religious fervor of death engulfed the nation.

Of course, this historical "lethargy" of the Romanians, the idleness in time, and the lack of involvement came back to haunt Cioran, who could not return to his home country after the Soviet takeover. Like many other fascist sympathizers he stayed in the West as an emigre and managed to integrate with his pessimistic essays in the French culture. His personal journal, published only after his death, shows how he mused about his fatalist melancholia, decrying his own condition as a member of a defeated nation, eternally in bad luck and sadness and darkness (Cioran 1991: 50–2). Deprecating the fact that he was a victim of the "Wallachian male-chance," a destiny that was double foldedly dramatic (Cioran 1991: 65), he draws in the last book written in his native language a self-portrait an embodiment of the "Wallachian spirit" eternally balancing between high and low. Cioran's meditations about his destiny as a human being "born off of nation without luck" (neam fără noroc) allowed him to become the master stylist of the philosophy of disappointment. Melancholia came naturally to Cioran, as he noted later in *Précis de décomposition*, his first collection of essays published in France in 1949 which offered him notoriety. The "bitter venom" (Cioran 1992: 47) generated by the conscience of unhappiness (48) is part of a conscience (already noted in his journal) that comes from a fatalistic movement of the national soul, a result of a collective experience of the Romanians who were "proud to be nothing" throughout history (1991). Sublimated in an extremely elaborated philosophical discourse about decay and degradation, illustrated by his *A Short History of Decay*, the nostalgia of "forever feeling away from a home of your own" (Cioran 1992: 54), and the consequences of historical fatalism, he defines his condition as a result of the "pride of defeat" and "self-pity" (Cioran 1992: 165), very much in the logic of the undulation between up and down, diagnosed by Blaga.

Refuting the Fatalism Dogma

Many authors, however, openly refuted the validity of this pessimistic and depressive dimension of the national psyche that seems to be inherited from Miorița and other archaic tales. In one of the best-documented studies of the phenomenon, Adrian Fochi (1964) used textual analysis to prove that the fatalist theme was in fact induced by later elaborations of the text. These formulaic revisions of the text were not present in the earliest forms of the folk song, initially created as a Christmas carol. Overviewing the genesis of the ballad, from its archaic versions, first appearing in the North of Transylvania, to the published version by Alecsandri collected in Moldova, Fochi concludes that its "feudalist" and submissive dimensions were added later, over-imposed on a Christian motif of sacrifice.

Mircea Eliade, in one of his studies on the history of religions, also uses this interpretation following the archaic theme hypothesis. In fact, Eliade is an exponent of another set of interpretative positions regarding the meanings of this story that can be described as paleo-mythological. It is relevant that one of Eliade's disciples, Ioan Petru Culianu (2006), disclosed the profound fatalism of the historian of religions himself, even if the respected professor kept a low profile after leaving behind his Fascist youth and the related fascination with the cult of death and blood.

As early as 1915 a renowned Romanian folklorist, Theodor Speranția, published his research claiming that Miorița must be linked to the Cabiri cult, a ritualistic incantation used by the ancient Greek and Egyptian mysteries, which was later transferred into popular songs. Theus the murdered shepherd was nothing more than a version of Osiris, killed by his own brother (quoted by Eliade 1972: 230). Other interpreters saw in this narrative a remnant of the Pythagorean wedding hymns, a solar cosmogonic wailing song or even a remainder of the cult of Mithras. Romulus Vulcănescu (1987: 206) presents an exhaustive list of such mythological interpretations, from those connecting the ballad to the presumed Thracian pantheon, to the Hindu myths. These claims, including Eliade's version identifying the ballad with a "pre-Christian cosmology," which is specific for the local peasant versions of religious thinking, are valorizations of an archaic form of spirituality, linked to the beliefs of the Dacians about resurrection and their presumed celebration of death. Ultimately this makes the Moldovan shepherd an allegory of Christ and his sacrificial death, in turn a trope of an agro-pastoral civilization predating Christianity. Very similar to what Blaga defined as a "sophianic worldview," it inherently gives the Romanian mind a superiority that transcends the fatalistic dogma.

With all its mythological, social, and psychological functions, either as a pastoral archaic narrative, as a ritual of initiation, or a worldview of the ancient populations living in a particular geographic area, these opinions can vary from supporting an "optimistic Romanian vision of the world" to the "funerary euphoria" and the desire for death (Bîrlea 1979: 13). Others, such as Dumitru Caracostea, one of the founders of the National Folklore and Literature Institute and a minister during the fascist regime, considered that the story represented a wider expanse of the "Romanian soul" (Caracostea 1927/1969), beyond the actual boundaries of the Romanian state. The two interpretations of the Romanian psyche are irreconcilable. One is inclined toward sadness, dreamy melancholia, and soft resignations, linked to a profound mode of dealing with the absurd metaphysical suffering and the other presumes a Romanian spiritual vitality, a powerful manifestation of a "cosmic nostalgia." Some, like Ovidiu Papadima, argued that Miorița was falsely interpreted (1941/1995: 149–50), due to the fact that the Romantics who discovered the folk song (Russo, Alecsandri) were inclined to present the national spirit in a manner that could make it intelligible for foreign readers. On the contrary, the Romanian folklorist claims, the Romanians shared a "healthy" ethnic and "organic optimism", that our mind-frame was not "resigned, nor fatalistic," but instead "filled with joy" (Papadima 1941/1995: 154). Romanians were endowed with a flexibility which allowed the nation to nevertheless survive during a long history of deceptions and failures. This was for Papacostea an indication of the limited inclination of this nation for metaphysics (22), who, even in its most nostalgic forms of speculation, was extremely stable.

The "mioritic fatalism" interpretations were also contested by two other important Romanian philosophers, Constantin Noica and Mircea Vulcănescu. Both fascist sympathizers (Vulcănescu was condemned for war crimes) explored the "Romanian soul" based on the premise that there was a fundamental difference between "Us" and the "Others" (for him any Westerner), due to a metaphysical predisposition visible in our language. The hypothesis was first advanced by Vulcănescu (1943/1996) in an article published in the right-wing journal *Dreptatea* (December 1932), then expanded in a book dedicated to the "Romanian dimension of existence" (dimensiunea românească a existenței). Based on a primitive form of linguistic determinism, the traits of this "Romanianness" were described in a similar way with what Noica later identified as "the Romanian sentiment of being" (sentimentul românesc al fiinţei). Explaining a series of words that could define the national identity (like "dor"), Noica argued that the Romanian language itself contained the traits of an ontological condition, another mode of "fulfillment," which was not connected to the Western models of certitude (Noica 1996: 58–9). In fact, as documented by Bîrlea (174), the folk songs disclose a deeper link between "dor" and the desolation of the soul, a natural association between longing and wailing (dor-jale). In an effort to prove that the "Romanian spirit" was not fatalistic, that the apparent passivity indicated deeper meanings, Noica coalesces these "modes of being" as coding of a state of mind simultaneously determined and undetermined. As argued by this Romanian disciple of Heidegger, when referring to such metaphysical components, "the intricacies of the Romanian verb" ("iscusirile verbului românesc") are indicative of a superior manifestation of "Being," which is neither stable nor unstable. The main assumption is even more complex, not only that languages are carriers of a "national spirit," but some languages (like the Romanian) reach levels of "philosophical thinking" (Noica 1996: 17). Thus, in order to better understand the national mind, Noica embarks on an in-depth analysis of several words which he believed are manifestations of metaphysical identity placed between openness and closeness. It is relevant for this discussion that almost all his speculations are centered around a type of ambivalence of meanings, with the most relevant terms brought into the discussion being dichotomous couples such as *întru* (inside/outside) (Noica 1996: 31–40; 370–5), followed by *cumpăt* (evaluative thinking) (120–6) *răzoare* (balks) (202–6) or crossroad/răscruce.

The intricate explanations illustrated by the analysis of "întru," a Romanian word which means simultaneously to be "in" (in the interior, inside) and "toward" (the outside, on the move and stationary), that is to be in a search for something which is already found (Noica 1996: 31), are extremely relevant. "Întru" is more than a dialectical reunion generating ambiguous tensions, as it also means to be in, to come from and to be against, to be with and without (371), which further discloses a state of mind that connects the Romanian spirit with its primordial origins (372). Later exemplified by the Romanian philosopher with the concept of "răscruce" (crossroad), it shows what it means to be in a "closed opening," that is to be "întru." Since the term crossroad ("răscruce") has a usage unlike other languages, it can be confusedly identified as an element of indecision or even hesitation, when in fact it is an "opening to multiple possibilities." "Răscruce" is a crossroad which is "a closing that can be opened"; multiple options manifested simultaneously. Noica also explains why the Romanians could have been described as a fatalist, since, when translating expressions such as "it was not meant to be" ("n-a fost să fie"), it could appear to prove a passive predisposition, an attitude of fatalistic acceptance of destiny. In fact the reverse understanding is correct, argues this Heideggerian philosopher, and this kind of reversal is quintessential for the understanding of Romanian "sensibility." He claims that an "ontological becoming" (Noica 1996: 39) is specific for a nation living in the "răzoare," that is determined by a borderless limitation, with an ambivalent nature of opened demarcations, identified as the "becoming into being" (devenirea întru ființă), visible in the "Romanian modulations" of the being.

These arguments continue to be debatable and they remain contested because, as some recent historians have pointed out (Popa 2017: 193), these revisions of the fatalist dogma were clearly elaborated as part of a pro-fascist ideology. As such, the philosophers, writers, and folklorists who have contested the negative dimensions of the passivity myth, often integrated into the nationalist project of that particular political environment, were part of the larger drive for a nationalist revival. On the other hand, Popa's conclusions that the violence against the Romanian Jews and other minorities during the war must be seen as a manifestation of this "liberation" from the mythologies of fatalism (Popa 2017: 194) are also highly disputable. While the ethnocentric vision of the philosophical observations of Vulcănescu, Noica, and Cioran about the "Romanian being" is based on either the interpretations of untranslatable words or problematic redefinitions of self-identity, the fact that our civilization was determined by a specific spatial and political positioning (probably expressed by the word "întru"), between the West and the East, the Orthodox and the Catholic, remains factual.

This long excursion into the genealogical formation of national philosophical thinking is intended as a guide into my following arguments, based on the presupposition that this mode of thinking has representational and narrative functions which can be traced in their expansions into cinematic practices. The imagological framework allows us to place the self-identity mechanisms from myths like Miorița or Master Manole beyond their fatalist connection, or as indicators of cultural predispositions manifested in recent movies. Instead, they show the metaphysical and post-metaphysical potential of these archetypes.

Making Cinema and the Presence of Death

Mircea Eliade further elaborated on these issues and contextualized the mythological functions of "the Magical Sheep" in a comparative study, overviewing larger religious practices, legends, and stories of the peoples in Eastern Europe (1970/1972). He identified the influences of a pre-Indo-European culture, which predated the Geto-Thracian inheritance, providing access to an ancestral vision about death and resurrection. The Chicago University professor of the historian of religions uses this prehistory, which is sometimes explicit in the "dualist" practices of the religions of the Balkans (like Bogomilism), and is also transparent in the previously discussed Romanian legends (Meșterul Manole and Miorița). In his interpretation, the story about the building of Argeș monastery, which originated in Wallachia, the southern part of Romania, shares an important element with the other "foundational" ballad about Miorița.

Meșterul Manole, like Miorița, is, before anything, a narrative about death, centered on apparently morbid plots. A builder who walls off his wife in order to keep the construction from falling, or the shepherd accepting to be killed after debating metaphysical issues with his sheep. Eliade suggests that their common dramatic motif, that of the violent death accepted with serenity, indicates the traces of an archaic ritual (200), conveying the idea of the "beautiful death." Based on the religious accounts about the practices of the Dacians, this particular relationship with death can be seen as a manifestation of a typical metaphysical predisposition. Folklorists like Romulus Vulcănescu support a similar interpretation that these ballads are more relevant from a magic-ritual perspective than they have a cultural-ethnic relevance rooted in prehistory. These stories are mostly about death and the spiritual consequences of dying (Vulcănescu 1987: 206). With Miorița, the soon-to-die shepherd is not only fatalistically accepting his fate, but he is also constructing an imaginary event with cosmogonic functions, enacting a marriage by death, thus transcending the traumatic event.

Contextualized in the history of religions the direct interpretation would be to consider such death as an expression of primitive thinking, by linking these folktales with the myths of the Dacians who were accepting death with joy and laughter, by sacrificing a messenger sent to their god, Zalmoxis (Eliade 1997: 59). This idea, that a pre-Christian cult based on ritualistic death and linked to the "creative dimension" of dying, leads Eliade to the conclusion that many ancient cosmogonic myths are based on the presence of a divine cadaver (448). For Eliade the representation of death in folktales has a cognitive dimension (81); it offers humans a pathway to knowledge into the essence of humanity; just as the folklore is a repository of "facts" and not fictions, these stories can become documents about primordial experiences (180–1). This is why, in his commentaries on Meșterul Manole (399), Eliade claims that the ballad belongs to a "metaphysical realm" (văzduh metafizic), disclosing the archaic mentality that made the narration possible. Myths, legends, and tales are expressions of a way of thinking that produced those particular stories.

While all mythologies and legends include stories about death, with various death myths which are allowing the living to coalesce their ideas about mortality, in terms of cinematic imagology there are innumerable recent Romanian movies driven by a central plot device centered on death and/or the violent consequences leading to an act of killing. In this sense, they are indicative of the Romanian cinematic psyche, as the camera is often used not only to capture life, instead it provides the spectators with a close experience of death. Once again, by overviewing Cristi Puiu's movies we cannot avoid observing that the *funerary representations* are predominant. Ultimately Puiu's mise-en-scènes are *theaters of death*, where the actors perform in a state of mind conditioned by the presence of death and menaced by the specter of the implacable termination of life. This is intrinsic in all major feature films of this remarkable moviemaker—*The Death of Mr. Lăzărescu, Aurora, Sieranevada,* and *Malmkrog* are thematically connected through the centrality of death. Represented either as a process (*Lăzărescu*), as a series of acts of violence, either inducing several deaths (*Aurora*), as a ritual absence of the dead (*Sieranevada*), or a meditation about the end of the world and the death of human kind (*Malmkrog*), they reveal Puiu's fascination for death and the manifestations of dying. These tropes are making his cinema an *ars moriendi*, where the protocols of dying are transposed into thanatological dimensions of moviemaking. As the director acknowledged in several interviews, his stories are explorations based on his personal anxieties about death and dying (Puiu video interview 2016). In these terms, the links with Miorița are no longer psycho-cultural; they provide a thought frame for understanding the cinematic ceremonies and their imagological functions in connection with the experience of nothingness.

Death *outside* the Cinematic

As noted before, the story about the tragical tribulations of Dante Remus Lăzărescu was inspired by real events. It represented Puiu's own reaction to a near-death experience, just as his later movies, like *Sieranevada*, were expressions of his fear regarding his father's demise, a fact acknowledged in various interviews (Puiu 2016; Ciobanu 2017). The director amply discusses his preoccupation with death and the fact that dealing with mortality is always a pathway to meditation. While his personal reactions are not necessarily bearing on the matter at hand, more importantly, when watching any film made by Puiu, the movie theater becomes *a catacomb of cadavers*. The screening room is purposefully transformed into a place where ritualistic displays of mourning and the experiences of dying are re-enacted for the higher purpose of generating film-thinking. Such funerary projections can understandably lead to an imagological connection between the wedding of the dead (*nunta mortului*) performed in folk songs and these transcendental representations transposed on screen. In Romanian folklore, as Vulcănescu (1987: 176–7) indicates, the motif of the heroization of the deceased must be linked with the ancestral practices of "funerary banquets," part of much older forms of "funerary theater." Many other Romanian moviemakers use similar representations of funerary situations, which can be directly linked to the "undulation and death" present in the collective psyche of our ethnic group (Dan Botta quoted by Eliade: 1972: 234). This is a revenant trope since it is capable of projecting into the cognitive experience of the viewers a state of suspended morbidness, together with the attached metaphysical significations linked to the frailty of existence.

The representation of death is not a "Romanian film trademark"; movies all over the world exploit the presence of death and the mortuary nature of representations. Yet, when taking a closer look at *Sieranevada*, the local ritual of the dead-staged onscreen becomes an essential element for revealing the inner mechanics of the post-metaphysical. The story is revolving around a very specific form of commemoration practiced by all Orthodox Christians, a ritual called "parastas" (*parastasis*, or in Greek panikhida). More than a simple memorial service this version of the vigil over the dead is repeated at regular intervals, part of the last rites required by the Church. In *Sieranevada* this event presents the narrative premise—a forty-year-old man goes to the forty-day rememoration of his dead father. Such a transparent plot was superficially identified by many film critics as a "humorous dramedy," superficially noticing the juxtaposition of morbidity and laughter. These are, as I pointed out elsewhere (Pop 2014), key ingredients of the Romanian dark humor; yet, here the story has a different dimension. Built as a series of "in-betweens," with several stories taking place in the same apartment, the movie is also generating a post-cinematic transformation of the space. In a three-bedroom flat the movie camera lingers constantly in the hallways, almost as if the filmmaker is capturing a transparent presence of the soul of the dead man. The storytelling structures, which are also placing the characters in ambiguous developments, are also based on intervals, unexpected and even unexplained interventions, as is the apparition of a junkie from Croatia break any logical connections. More than in the other films in which Cristi Puiu uses the recurrent techniques of transforming a funeral event, or the act of dying and the tragedy of death, into a natural live-action, here we can demonstrate how the non-cinematic dimensions of the filmic device are repurposed as non-philosophical instruments.

Following the observation made by Maurice Merleau-Ponty, that nothing is completely removed from the subjective experience, any ritual of mourning must be understood as an act by which the living are re-embodying the dead. Through a process of re-presenting, the absent or the missing (a lost limb, a departed loved one, the dead) becomes part of the inner motion inside the minds of those still in existence. For the French phenomenologist, the mechanics between the visible and invisible, between the absence and the presence is fundamental (Merleau-Ponty 1968), his entire philosophical argument being that perception, even when it gives us access to the world, at the same time it removes us to the margins of the world, making us invisible.

This dynamic of a non-presence which is meaningful, the absence that obtains a material consistency, is masterfully activated in *Sieranevada*. After the priest performs the traditional incantations and leaves the house, the family enacts a superstitious gesture, which is not part of the approved funerary practices of the Romanian Orthodox Church. The final scene of the movie represents a physical metamorphosis of death, as one of the nephews of the dead man, after reluctantly refusing first, gets dressed in the clothes of the departed and then sits at the table as if the dead person was still there. This is the moment when the non-cinematic and the non-metaphysical are confluent, activating at the highest intensity the non-philosophical meanings. In the fracture of seriousness created by the sarcastic screenwriting of the film director, an intangible meaning appears. The widow of Emil, the dead father, "directs" the entire event as she was a moviemaker—she tells everybody the lines, indicating the precise position and reaction of each member of the family. After this obvious metacinematic reference, Sebi, who entered the living room dressed as the deceased, sits at the table and everybody begins to eat the famous Romanian cabbage rolls with polenta. When banality is fully restored in the presence of tragedy, a non-philosophical disclosure can happen. We have to remember that, whenever everyday life is re-established, this is transformed into a site where the post-metaphysical is activated. Just as the widow tries to explain the source of the ritual, specific to her husband's home county, her attention is diverted by the sickness of the Croatian girl, who, as mentioned before, played no part in the movie. This non-cinematic character drives all the women out the room, and only two men remain at the table, looking at each other. In this filmic emptiness, Lary and Relu, the fatherless brothers, burst into laughter, and their unrelenting chuckle generates a non-philosophical thinking. With Sebi returning, the ending is portraying three men in the typical Rublev iconographic setting, their boisterous and cachinnation explosion of sounds joins the metaphysical and the post-metaphysical, the explicit and the unexplained. This unrecordable achievement of knowledge is made possible only by such punctuations of representation. The final musical accords accompanying the dark screen are not providing any revelations about the deep meanings of life, we are negated access to the metaphysical or the transcendental planes, no catharsis or dramatic disclosure happens.

This is the non-philosophical at work—these movies are not only ritualistic ceremonies, visual re-elaborations of the experience of death, they are also illustrations for the philosophical implications of the state of post-metaphysical in-betweenness (representations of the negative "întru"). The meaninglessness embodied by a character like Mr. Lăzărescu, the non-identity of Viorel, and the cinematic representation of absence with the dead father in *Sieranevada* are different stages of death (the dying, the agent of death, and the absence of the dead), but also contextualized forms of non-presence, absence, and the lack of substance. The old pensioner in Puiu's first feature film, clearly trapped between the worlds, exists only in the space and time of "întru," simultaneously dying and living. This is also the case with the killer in *Aurora* or the deceased parent who is celebrated by his relatives impersonating and accepting his presence. They all are manifestations of the same attitude toward death, but more relevantly, disclosures of an ontological condition of the non-being in moviemaking.

The Philosophising Filmmaker as a Non-philosopher

Cristi Puiu is obviously a moralist with a movie camera, a filmmaker who enjoys philosophizing both onscreen and in a-cinematic contexts. Even though this Romanian filmmaker does not have a corpus of theoretical writings, like the French Nouvelle vague authors, nor does he have a philosophical program, like the Dogme 95 movement, Puiu's public interventions are replete with ideas and meditations. As thoroughly overviewed by the consistent monograph published by Monica Filimon on Cristi Puiu (2017), we can circumscribe the "philosophy of cinema" and the "thinking" of this movie director by referring to a large number of interviews and public statements he made. Filimon (2017: 7–8) maps the vision of this remarkable author and reaches the unavoidable conclusion that his works have a metaphysical dimension, sometimes close to the sacred, filled with "ineffable" meanings, profound examinations of the condition of humanity.

I would argue the contrary that Puiu is a non-philosopher in the strictest Deleuzian sense. In his long and protracted films, with *Malmkrog* offering the utmost example, the philosophical debates are repeated foldings of the same issues. As one problem is folded over the other, the inside becomes the outside and the outside is closing on itself. The nature of the "fold," as explained by the French philosopher (1988) in an intricate manner, is always precarious. In the *non-philosophical* cinema our attention is deceivingly attracted toward the exterior plane of the fold, as are the philosophizing commentaries of the protagonists, which are almost gratuitous and empty. Even if many film critics are ecstatic about the "profound" way in which the characters in the remote villa discuss "heavy" concepts, such as the nature of evil, the presence of the devil in history, and many others, the true meanings are created in the intervals, when the absent servants intervene and the philosophical interactions of their aristocratic patrons are interrupted. By seemingly understanding everything and explaining anything, the film points to the incapacity of explanations. This is the moment when "unthinking" can be activated and the "thoughts" can be discovered.

As indicated in Chapter 1, my understanding of the non-philosophical is based on the observations of François Laruelle, as I diverge from Gregg Lambert's description of the non-philosophical as synonymous with Deleuze non-conceptual (Lambert 2002: 4–5). The American philosopher specialized in Derrida and Deleuze studies makes no reference to Laruelle (not even a bibliographical note) and provides a strictly practical interpretation of the non-philosophical, as a form of "bastard philosophy," one that integrates percepts and affects in the discovery of truth (Lambert 2002: 8). While agreeing with Lambert when he notices that Deleuze was searching for an alternative to traditional metaphysics, based on the need for overcoming the compulsion for transcendence, his overlapping of non-philosophy with the "rivals" of philosophy is too narrow. It must be pointed out that, when Deleuze identified cinema as a new domain where the extraction of concepts was possible, he saw movies as philosophical instruments.

In the case of Cristi Puiu the non-philosophical must be linked with his approach to the moral functions of storytelling. As the director himself admitted, his model for moviemaking was the French cineaste Éric Rohmer, and the cycle of movies entitled *Six Moral Tales* (*Six contes moraux*). The Rohmer–Puiu filiation is explicitly present at the intertextual junction, with Rohmer influenced by Murnau's *Sunrise: A Song of Two Humans* (1927), then Puiu directing a movie entitled *Aurora*, directly inspired by the masterpiece of this German expressionist. There is at least another indirect connection; one of the female characters in Claire's Knee (Le genou de Claire, 1970) is a Romanian woman, named Aurora. Besides this point, the most important connection between the two moviemakers can be extracted from the conclusion presented by Hösle (2016) in his monographic overview of Rohmer's cinema, where he describes the approach of the French director as that of a "non-moralizing moralist." In fact, as Rohmer (1971) acknowledged in an interview with Graham Petrie for the "Film Quarterly" journal, his moral tale had nothing to do with the traditional understanding of morality. He actually describes his stories as "reversed ethical" narrations, constantly filled with ambiguity and amorality.

Following the moralist tradition of French writers like Blaise Pascal or Michel de Montaigne, Rohmer uses his characters as embodiments of philosophical ideas, never making explicit moral judgments about them. As illustrated by Rohmer's best-known film from this series, the third "moral tale" entitled *My Night at Maud's* (*Ma nuit chez Maud*, 1968), there is no condemnation coming from the filmmaker about any of the dilemmas involved. In all the *Contes*, which are usually centered on the decision-making processes of a character placed in a situation of narrative unreliability, there are no outside interventions. This is also one of the most important instruments used by Cristi Puiu, who manages his characters just like Rohmer, by creating ample dialogues as meditations about various topics, like the prolonged debate about communism in *Sierranevada*. Here the Romanian director uses his characters as transparent mouthpieces for controversial ideas. Each time the members of this dysfunctional family get together, they begin arguing about adversarial and contentious issues. Their dialogues range from revisiting the conspiracy theories about the 9/11 attacks, the criminal nature of the communist regime or more frivolous issues such as conjugal infidelity or the spiritual illumination provided by the teachings of Osho. Following Rohmer's example, there is no moral evaluation for any of these opinions; they all remain at the discursive level.

Here cinema acts as a form of *re-thinking*, a non-philosophical machine that allows the philosophizing to become part of the existence of everyday conversations. These dialogues are almost Socratic in their function, since the ancient philosopher used a non-philosophical device. Facing the viewers with the thinking mechanisms of the characters, presented in extremely debatable contexts, the film director acts like a gadfly, persistently elaborating on some of the most annoying aspects of life. *Sieranevada* opens with a bothersome discussion between Lary and his pesky wife—the movie actually begins with a suggestive reference to a similar location with that in *Aurora*, as if the moviemaker was simply continuing the same circular mental rumination, folding references over and over again. After leaving his daughter and wife in the confusion of the crowded Bucharest street, the story resumes with Laura, the doctor's wife quarreling with him for bringing his daughter the wrong dress. For more than fifteen minutes Lary, the main protagonist, remains outside the frame, reacting from time to time in a lowered voice, or appearing in the rear-view mirror of the car, while Laura pounds him with explanations about all the Disney female characters, trying to convince him about the differences between Snow White and Sleeping Beauty, while Lary argues that Walt did not respect the Grimm

Brothers' vision. The non-cinematic device of removing the main character from the center of the visual field is completed by the fascinating interaction between the invisible (Lary) and the visible (Laura), between the trivial and the profound. This becomes the central instrument in the storytelling development, an immediate reminder of the observations made by Deleuze (1980) in his "Leibnitz seminary." The French philosopher points to the fact each time we feel the need to scream, we are not far from the "call of philosophy." In *Sieranevada* the interactions between the various characters clashing about topics like the *Charlie Hebdo* attacks provide the perfect illustrations for this type of pathetic understanding of the philosophical. In the fissures of their thinking, film-thoughts can be created. Whenever we feel like screaming at the screen, yelling at their absurdity, incongruity, or imbecility, whenever the discord and the *eristetic* narration are present, philosophical intuitions are never far behind.

Cinema as a Melancholic Machine

In the theoretical discussions about different filmmaking practices, the predominant conceptual framework is based on the opposition between mainstream or popular cinema and the so-called art cinema. This dichotomy follows Bordwell and Staiger's differentiation between the "Hollywood mode of production," generically identifiable in classical cinema and its counterpart, broadly called "art cinema." The cinema driven by action is directly opposed to European moviemaking, generically described as international art cinema, coalescing all films motivated by the exploration of psychological effects (Bordwell and Staiger 1985: 614). Such a narrow division is similar to the subjectivity–objectivity dichotomy observed by Deleuze (55), who also attributed European cinema traits fundamentally opposing the "American action-image." Later Bordwell (2012) tried to add technical explanations for this opposition between action movies and a type of cinema predisposed to explore the metaphysical dimensions of existence in terms of stylistic devices. The main arguments to understanding how the two different systems work are based on the idea that the use of the long take, which allows the psychologically heavy "temps morts," together with narrative ambiguity and the passivity manifested by the behavior of the characters, are typical "European" forms of expression.

While there are many other nuances when it comes to such simple dialectics between the modes of production and narration, the formula used by the American post-theorist and his stylistic and technical separation became normative in film studies. Many others, like Gibbs and Pye (2017: 18), continued this interpretive tradition and reaffirmed the concept of "oppositional practices," further exploring the divide between a cinema motivated by self-reflection (of modernist descent for Deleuze) and the commercial cinema.

My argument here is that we should expand our understanding of cinema as a "thought machine" beyond the Deleuzian conclusions, who argued that this function is "psycho-mechanic," a "spiritual automaton" (262) that is not determined by technology (280). For the French philosopher the "techniques of the image" are linked to the "metaphysics of the imagination" (58) which puts any technique "at the service of reflection" (187). This is a problematic aspect of cinema, already disputed by Kracauer and Arnheim, and it is relevant for our discussion since it is linked to the notion of cinematic melancholy. As previously acknowledged by Kracauer in his "Introduction" to the *Theory of Film*, there is a distinct melancholy of the photographic camera. The German theorist suggested that this melancholia is an inner predisposition (Kracauer 1960: 17), an indeterminate property of the medium, related in turn to our relationship with reality in this modern society. Contesting this assumption, Arnheim (1963: 295) noted in his criticism of Kracauer that the form in which cinema is reflecting the condition of the modern man, exemplified by the Neorealist movies of Antonioni or De Sica, discloses an unshaped melancholic predisposition, which he calls "melancholy unshaped" because it is not generated by visual forms. Ultimately the question remains if artistic melancholia is induced by the modernist nature of cinema, based on capturing an experience that comes from alienation and estrangement, which in turn makes the melancholic mind a product of modern society recorded by cinema, when in fact melancholia is a mode of cinematic thinking, made possible by the photographic technology itself.

The *intrinsic* understanding of cinema as a thinking-machine must be completed with its *extrinsic* dimension, since the technical dimensions of the cinematic are not simply by-products of an internal state of mind. They result from the setting of the machines of vision we are using. From its very beginning the photographic technologies integrated death as their object, then expanded in the discourses of media representations. There are numerous macabre visual practices, from privately photographing the dead to the public display of corpses (more in Linkman 2011). In the early nineteenth century photography and death became intertwined, as almost everybody had a picture of a dead person in their home, used as either a loving memory of the deceased or commemoration of their existence. As argued by Michele Aaron cinema continued to be a site of proliferating the representations of death, where visualizing death and dying (Aaron 2014: 3–4), as explicit in the obsessive spectacles of death in mainstream cinema (from horror and crime thrillers to productions like the "mondo films"), have put the macabre at the core of this new art.

We need to question the simplistic idea that the ontology of cinema is that of capturing life and reality, when in fact the staggering examples of representations of deaths in movies make them funeral instruments.

As pointed out by Laura Mulvey (2006), who also marks the profound relationship between cinema and death, in practice stillness is cinema's best-kept secret. While creating the illusion of motion, movies are not "moving," they are only very fast successions of stills, of frames that otherwise are "motionless." This has everything to do with the inherent melancholia of the moviemaking machine. Like the other melancholic media (photography, stop-motion animation), the melancholic machines of cinema are producing "thought-images" similar to the dark state of the soul described by Freud in "Mourning and Melancholia" (1917/1957). Expanding on his observations that melancholy was a state of mind that inhibits activity, a pathological stage of passivity, we can identify a *cinema melancholica*, a cinematic mode that is based on the refusal of motion and not by the presence of *homo melancholicus* as a character.

The technical mood of the apparatus functioning as an affect-driven device inducing a melancholic state of mind was described as "slow movie" (Jaffe 2014), "slow cinema" (de Luca 2016), a "cinema of stasis" (Remes 2015), or "organic cinema" (Botz-Bornstein 2017). This mode of expression, which refuses an accelerated time and the fast movement of mass entertainment, provides an aesthetic experience that can be best described in contrastive terms with Hollywood productions. At the extreme end of slow cinema are the experiments that Justin Remes identifies as static filmic experiences, a paradoxical form of "motion pictures without motion" (Remes 2014: 3–4); yet, all movies operate as negative reactions toward the fast-paced style of commercial film industry qualify. They are exploring silence instead of constant noise, slowness instead of excessive dynamism and the overload of action, direct answers to the dominant optimistic, noisy, and superficial narratives. The definitions of slow cinema as a static visual style, dominated by the long take, with austere mise-en-scènes and restrained performances of the actors also allowed the confusion with the so-called global art-house cinema. Of course, such broad definitions can lead to conceptual overlappings, both with Paul Schrader's concept of "transcendental films" (1972) and with Andrew Horton's "cinema of contemplation" (1997).

No wonder that the Romanian moviemakers were often identified as representative for such practices of "international art cinema," mostly due to their predisposition to use long takes, to avoid fast-paced editing and to cultivate a certain narrative ambiguity. Jaffe (2014: 87) uses the works of authors like Cristi Puiu and Cristian Mungiu to illustrate how the predisposition for another type of time-image, which he describes as "wait time," can generate an "aesthetic of slowness." Suggestively enough, many other examples are provided by the movies made by directors from the same region, like Béla Tarr's *Werckmeister harmóniák* (2000) or Aleksandr Sokurov's *Mother and Son* (1997). Another immediate connection is between the filmmakers belonging to the Eastern Orthodox world, like Andrei Tarkovsky, Theo Angelopoulos, and Cristian Mungiu, which allowed Andrew Horton to categorize them as belonging to a melancholic and meditative cinematic mood (Horton 1997: 191).

For Horton the contemplative cinema is opposed to the "fast films" made in Hollywood, with action substituted by meditation (Horton 1997: 10) and a certain "slowness" in editing and rhythm inducing cinematic melancholia. The question, nevertheless, is if we can identify these main distinctive features displayed sometimes by international art cinema, or, as argued by Angelopoulos, this is a type of cinema machine that captures the particular melancholia generated by the tragedies affecting this part of the world, which Horton calls "un-Hollywood" cinema (Horton 1997: 83). For example, what Jaffe identifies as the narrative values of slow motion, an apparent impassive behavior like that of the two young women in *4 Months ...*, is not necessarily a reaction against cinematic stylistics, but rather a result of the historical context in which the movie is taking place. On the other hand, can we attribute the collective passivity of the people in communist Romania, with the apparent resigned attitude of an entire nation faced with the absurdity of the final years of the Ceaușescu dictatorship, to a fatalistic worldview? Is the behavior of Mr. Lăzărescu a manifestation explainable by referring to a national predisposition for accepting humiliation or even as a larger expression of a regional mind-frame in which waiting substitutes action (Horton 1997: 68)?

The Melancholic Long Take and the Thinking Processes of the Romanian Cinema

One solution is to look at the specific effects articulated by cinematic devices, without linking them to external, political or social, processes. When asking if the Romanian cinema has a "mind of its own", we are not trying to understand how moviemakers are using cultural articulations manifested in their representations. Instead, as argued in another work, my hypothesis is that there is a Romanian cinematic syntax (Pop 2014) shared by several directors.

Once more, *The Death of Mr. Lăzărescu* provides ample illustrations for how the cinematographic devices (the observational camera, the long take, or the photographic authenticity) have generated codes that make any movie produced by the contemporary national film industry immediately recognized as a "Romanian film." The most important is the long shot, allowing Puiu to construct a reality in which the camera is a companion of the solitary old man. This approach to shooting the scenes provides an overall atmosphere that is not simply generated by Mr. Lăzărescu's unavoidable tragedy, but also offers a filmic experience that belongs to the melancholic cinema. Clearly the way in which the camera depicts

Mr. Lăzărescu's petty existence in his shady apartment is "realist," carrying an authenticity provided by the "documentarism" of the shot. Yet this depiction of reality is produced by a deeply melancholic camera, presenting the spectator with an unavoidable sensation that what we are seeing is not photographic, but of a funeral nature. While Bazin linked the photographic camera with its ability to induce the sensation of reality, we must observe that in Puiu's movie the predominant metaphysical relationship is with the representation of death not of life. For Bazin, when the motion picture camera is used to capture reality continuously, it automatically induces an "ontological identity between the object and its photographic image" (Bazin 1972: 98). The notion that there is an "ontogenetic realism," which generates an "aesthetic of reality" achieved through cinematographic devices, together with his idea that an "authentic reality" can be achieved as the camera restores reality for the viewer, is flawed. Using the movies of Orson Welles as an example, the French critic believed that the language of cinema evolves toward increased levels of "reality." Bazin thus introduced the erroneous notion that the refusal of montage and the realist shots transmitting "the continuum of reality" (Bazin 1967: 37) were part of a cinematic revolution placing movies "in the service of realism" (38). Coupling the deep-focus style of photography with the sequence-shots, since he was fascinated by the Italian Neorealists like Visconti, who used them to create masterful spatiotemporal continuities, the correlation between the truthfulness cinema and the technical creation of the "longue durée" is not compulsory.

These explanations leave intact the question asked at the beginning of this study. Is cinema simply recording the behavior of human beings (ethical or political) or the moral practices are external to our condition and, by consequence, morality and thinking can be induced by cinematic tools? Jean-Luc Godard (1959: 62) advances a provocative answer when stating that a traveling-shot was a moral question (le travelling est affaire de morale). By attributing tracking shots with the power of morality, the Swiss director discussing with Rohmer, Rivette, and other French film critics and moviemakers observes that the type of cinema practiced by modern filmmakers like Jean Renoir, who practiced the long take, is based on the much older relationship between *ethics and aesthetics*. In opposition with Bazin's absolute notion of "*plan-séquence*," based on the presumptive "realistic" nature of the eye of the camera, where the continuous shot uninterrupted by any cut (découpage) is automatically inducing realism, the fact of the matter is that this technique can be used in any type of cinema. As indicated by several metaphysical and contemplative films, the long take is a philosophical tool that is not conditioned by the reality of a story. A moviemaker can use the sequence-shot to make metaphysical statements; and the reverse is also true, even without the slow-paced shots or the long takes, a film is able to generate the same effect.

In *The Death of Mr. Lăzărescu*, after a short opening establishing shot with the exterior of the block, the first half of the movie is stitched together from several sequence-shots that are not continuous. As the events take place inside a dimly lit apartment, where Dante Lăzărescu feeds his cats and tries to call an ambulance, his reality is deceivingly discontinuous. The camera follows the old man as he is talking with the animals only for a couple of minutes, then fixates repetitively on his conversations with the emergency phone operator. These episodes are then juxtaposed with expanded silences and altogether they coalesce into less than fifteen minutes of solitude, powerlessness, and despair. Seven more minutes spent with the sickly pensioner on the hallway outside his apartment, now trying to get help from his neighbors, then thirteen more minutes in the development of the story are used until the ambulance arrives. Mioara, the nurse in charge of that night's emergencies, takes about seventeen minutes of the filmic time to finally decide to take Lăzărescu away. Thus what appears to be a sequence of almost an hour are in fact fragmented minutes (fifty-three minutes into the story) with the dying old man never leaving his block of flats, yet constantly moving back and forth. The entire scene, which might seem to be extremely long and tedious, is unlike what the French critic appreciated in Orson Welles, the masterful continuity in the opening of Touch of Evil (1958). As noted by Jaffe, in the work of Cristi Puiu or Cristian Mungiu the duration of the shot itself is not necessarily typical for the logic of "slow cinema." Nevertheless, even when movie editing is fast-paced, or the logic of the long take is not activated, the overall sensation remains intact.

Why did the Romanian directors, starting with Cristi Puiu, decide to choose these devices? Why the long take and the mobile camera are often the preferred instruments of these moviemakers? Is it a "strategy of hesitation," made possible by the "hesitant camera," as Strausz labeled the Romanian cinema when trying to identify the various cinematographic dimensions of uncertainty? Can the hand-held camera techniques be considered expressions of instability, an oscillation of the visuality which makes these images manifestations of a "hesitant" historical and space-temporal determinacy? The Hungarian film critic suggests that the dominant modality of contemporary Romanian moviemakers expresses their state of vacillation, where the mobile camera embodies the estrangement of modernism. Another misreading is the implicit confusion with the "art house tradition" (Strausz 2017: 240).

An obvious result of these techniques is made visible when we compare them with the seemingly endless shots developed by Aleksandr Sokurov in *Russian Ark* (2002) or the manipulation of the long take in *Birdman* (2014), both were digitally edited and enhanced. The purpose of melancholic cinema is to convey an overall atmosphere, not to explore any capacities of the device. A melancholic long take does not need to be mechanically efficient, and the evaluation of the temporality of the shot is not adding anything to the impact. In stark opposition to the "total realism" theories, claiming that somehow the contemporary Romanian cinema is reproducing reality, by using the obsolete idea advanced by Bazin, the camera has no ontological power to enact reality. The camera is an instrument of metaphysical experience; it is never "real," nor "a document." Striving for authenticity is part of the director's mind, as it becomes obvious in Cristi Puiu's works, where subjectivity is purposefully assumed in order to accentuate a transcendental understanding.

Like the death of Dante Remus Lăzărescu, which never happens in the movie, the purpose is to be in the presence of death, not to show death. And more importantly, cinema works with affects that are not time constricted, as the characters we watch on screen are or will be dead when we encounter them. When witnessing Ioan Fiscuteanu, the actor playing the dying Lăzărescu, we cannot avoid the melancholic realization that he died of cancer in 2007, only two years after his character's ordeal took place. The images with him on screen are forever those of a dead man playing a dying man and, just like Dante Lăzărescu who initially protests initially against the abuse of the ambulance driver or the attitude of the doctors, then gradually becomes resigned and accepts his fate, the sensation of the movie is that of absolute in-betweenness.

Dis-located Characters, Deterritorialized Cinema, Extra-moral Filmmaking

The majority of the protagonists in Cristi Puiu's movies have a dis-centered existence. The stories are either young men and women on the road (*Stuff and Dough*), a dying man never finding his peace and constantly on the move (*The Death of Mr. Lăzărescu*), a killer wandering about without having a place of his own (*Aurora*), and this constant movement between places induces a mental state projecting their in-betweenness. Best illustrated by Mr. Lăzărescu, who goes up and down, from feeling secure to utter insecurity, from having hope and dignity to total humiliation, the "emotional undulation," which accentuates the melancholia of the viewers, is not instability, nor an anxiety specific to modernity. This spatial in-betweenness is aggravated by the lack of identity. None of the characters have a real narrative background, and we know almost nothing about their past or future (as is the case with the dying old man). The spectators are often presented with *intervals of existence*.

We must couple these observations with the theories of "cinematic geography" and the idea that spatial structures influence our brains, following Lakoff (1987) and his observations about the correlation between our mindsets and our kinaesthetic experiences. In cognitive theory the assumption is that the spatial codes are manifested in cinematic codes. In conventional cinema the visual identity of the space where the narrative takes place is extremely important; movies like New York or San Francisco provide the viewers with a cognitive map allowing spatial contextualization and orientation. In reality identity does not have to be determined by external elements. A movie can take place in a specific "Romanian" location, and it can even cast "Romanian" actors, without being "Romanian." The best example is Maren Ade's highly rated film, *Toni Erdmann* (2016). Shot on location in Bucharest and in Moldova, distributing well-known Romanian actors, and displaying many cinematographic elements specific to Romanian moviemaking, all these elements qualify this production as an exceptional Romanian film.

Cristi Puiu explicitly challenges the validity of the thesis advanced by the national cinema theories. There are no signs to point the spectators toward a specific geography. Although almost all his stories are taking place in Bucharest—as the film director announced years ago, he intended to create a cycle of movies entitled "Six stories from the outskirts of Bucharest," a clear reverence to Rohmer—the capital city of Romania is completely deterritorialized. It is not a miserable city as depicted by the post-communist filmmakers. With the space emptied of any urban identity, his no-identity protagonists can devolve and degrade—obviously as a negation of the classical heroes who grow and have a progressive development. Even when using a-filmic reality, as is the apartment from *Sieranevada*, where an actual space was used and the man of the house just recently died at the time of shooting, this identification has no documentary value; it can be any building in almost any city of the world.

In fact, like many other contemporary Romanian filmmakers, the storytelling is located in geographic in-betweenness, where the "national" character is no longer defined by a local specificity, even when taking place in apparently pre-determined national contexts—as in Mungiu's *Beyond the Hills*, which is located in an Orthodox monastery in Eastern Romania. The storytelling is not determined by spatiality, actually the Bucharest of Mr. Lăzărescu *or* that of Viorel from *Aurora* are *no-memory-places*, or in the terminology used by Augé they are "non-lieux de mémoire." The absence of recognizable symbols and of elements connecting them with a "national identity" makes possible the construction of a "non-place."

This propensity is taken to the extreme in *Malmkrog* (2020), where Cristi Puiu creates an absolute "non-place," an interstice where people have "no-place," the unadulterated geography where the *non*-philosophical can be released. Malmkrog, the German name of the remote village in Transylvania, named inconsequentially Mălâncrav, where the director actually shot this slow movie divided artificially in six chapters, one of each character (Nikolai, Madeleine, Olga, Ingrida, Edouard, and István). The implication of constructing this setting is best explained by the notions advanced by

Guattari and Deleuze in *A Thousand Plateaus* (1987), when attempting to produce a new theory of signs. In order to better understand the terminology, which is developed in a series of intricate interpretative techniques, albeit providing insights into the representation mechanisms of all arts, we can turn to a simpler explanation, useful in defining the formation of spatial identity. As explained in Ronald Bogue (1999: 94), in a seminal essay about the relationship between art and territory, all artistic productions operate in a way best compared with the territorial activities of animals. All species, and in this particular example dogs, can insert meaning into their living spaces (through scent and other physical displays), then prohibiting other animals from reconfiguring that meaning. Such an ethological explanation helps us understand better how territorial determinacy and indeterminacy work when dealing with cinema as a cultural sign. This animal characteristic is expanded by Guattari and Deleuze (1987: 355) to the social and political activities of humans. Any space or environment—a region, a country, and even the cosmos—can be coded (or territorialized), reinvested with other meanings (re-territorialized), or decoded (deterritorialized) (Figure 4.3).

When the "terrain" of representations is deterritorialized, as it is the case with the three hours and twenty minutes prolonged discussions, sometimes monologues without reference or interlocutors about faith, wars, morality, justice, or the Bible, the decoding ceases to have any conjunctions or meanings. Within this non-story, with no background and nothing to determine identities, the group of aristocrats who philosophize with the words of Russian theologian Vladimir Solovyov are transformed into an

FIGURE 4.3 Malmkrog *is a non-place where a deterritorialized reality creates the empty backdrop for philosophizing about the nature of humanity.*

indistinct non-cinematic mechanism. As the content of their dialogues is completely deterritorialized, the encounter transported from the Alps in the Apafi villa in Transylvania—which has no relations whatsoever with the characters created by the Russian mystical philosopher to convey his theories about the imminent coming of the Antichrist—these "territory" of the conversations about "War, Progress and the End of World" become pointless. With the plot-less and point-less the non-philosophical can recharge and manifest in re-territorialized meanings.

In the conclusions of a memorable work, Deleuze (1968/1994: 288) discusses the nature of "Ideas" and indicates two major "powers" that were constantly invoked throughout this book. Through disguise and decentering Ideas are in fact manifested as "erewhons"; they have no *inside* and no *outside*. Then, in a footnote of this explanation, Deleuze (333) details what he means by this function, as he was referring to the ability to be a "no-where" which is rearranged as a "now-here." In his disguised "costume drama," Puiu exercises the same capacity. By hiding his own cinematographic instruments, to all intents and purposes abandoning the qualities that certified him as one of the most important film directors of his time, he created an absolute non-place, an ideal context for non-relations, which define his six protagonists. In this no-where (understood as "non-lieu") the filmmaker is able to instantiate the "now-here" of film-thoughts.

Some haphazard critics questioned Puiu's choice for Solovyov, for being an outdated moral philosopher. This good friend of Dostoevsky, deeply involved in the intellectual circles of pre-war Sankt Petersburg, is neither the most important Russian thinker, nor the text a fundamental philosophical reading. The choice for this particular story, with allegorical characters like The General, the Politician, The Lady, or Mr. Z exploring the roots of moral evil in modern society, is purposefully counter-intuitive. Obviously this kind of philosophizing delivers a contradictory result than his previous works.

More relevant for our discussion is that *Malmkrog* raises concerns about several film-philosophy assumptions, many of which we already addressed, and allows a reformulating of our initial set of categories. Is this film "*doing* philosophy," is it "about" philosophical ideas or does it confirm the thesis that "films *are* philosophy"? We must consider that the films discussed until now are actually moving beyond the strong moral reasoning which seems to characterize the Romanian contemporary films. Of course, anybody watching the story of the two young women raped in *4 Months* ... will naturally think about the nature of good and evil, of right and wrong decisions; any spectator exposed to the tragedy of Mr. Lăzărescu is going to think about the existence of suffering, the unhappiness of life and be filled with a sort of pessimism and fatalism. Nevertheless, as I tried to argue in each case study interpretation, the moral scenarios and the thought experiments presented have another component than what meets the eye. While the traditional ethical explanations in film theory (Saxton 2010) are in favor of the *intrinsic* approach, considering morality a part of the cinematic form, where every *mise-en-scène* becomes a moralizing opportunity, these movies have an *extra*-ethical dimension. The expected moral lesson is undermined and, when joined with the breaking of cinematographic rules and the activation of the non-cinematic, the film ends without any foreclosure. The *non*-moralism of the *non*-cinematic is illustrated by Cristi Puiu at the end of *Aurora*, when his alter-ego character turns himself to the Police. The moralist moviemaker takes a turn toward the dark humor and the absurd; the atrocious banality of evil works like a nooshock. Instead of the strong reactions to the atrocious crimes, which the protagonist calmly describes at the precinct, he is faced with a non-reaction. Everybody around him is preoccupied with trivialities and nobody is shocked or revolted by the heinous acts. The man who just confessed that he killed four people in cold blood is left alone in the room, while the policemen go for a coffee and discuss derisory matters. The lack of reactions or involvement on behalf of the policemen, similar to the detachment of the doctors in the story about the old man trapped in the intervals of the medical system, is a denial of what makes a movie to "be philosophical."

We can use the criteria enounced by Daniel Shaw (2006) to identify a philosophical film and illustrate how all these circumstances are denied in post-metaphysical cinema. After watching the drama of the protagonist, the already-existing philosophical "questions and concerns" are not resolved or further extended. The preexisting philosophical theories do not provide a better understanding of life and no mirroring of philosophical theories is put into place. Ultimately, as it will be argued in the Epilogue, a rear-view mirroring is activated. To the categories proposed by Shaw, the "truly philosophical" films and the "philosophically interesting films," we must add the displaced and deterritorialized philosophical cinema. Films *are* philosophical and can *do* philosophy even if they are non-philosophical.

The significance and importance of *non-place* explored with the protagonist in *Aurora* disclose how the displacement functions. Even if we know that the events are located in a geographical Bucharest, without getting any forms of orientation and almost constantly placed in "no-wheres" (such as railways or parking lots), the criminal father becomes himself a non-person. As he wanders around (relevantly enough Cristi Puiu plays the main character), the expected outcome is a potential revelation about his reality. Instead, all the needless ambulations create an imaginary territory, a space which has only the appearance of having determined coordinates; yet, it only projects an uncertain reality. In *Aurora*, the rides and walks of the protagonist describe an illegible spatial identity, expanded on the identity of Viorel, the criminal anti-hero. Moving back and forth between train lines and indistinct roads, going from one apartment to another, from his undetermined workplace to an indeterminate store, he leads an existence trapped in a transitional geography.

From the very beginning of the movie, when we first encounter this murderous husband in a daily routine at his obscure workplace, we are presented with his chaotic movements from one point to another. He is constantly changing direction, seemingly confused and disoriented and this unusual behavior continues for the entire duration of the movie. He goes to various places; he gets into indeterminate situations and he behaves in ways that the viewers cannot explain or connect with the help of any logical devices. It is precisely because the identity and motivations are inexplicable, in the gaps and lack of continuity, in the movements in and out of narrative intervals, the unthinkable can be thought. A relevant incident disclosing how the interval functions is the bathroom accident scene. When his upper floor neighbors flood his apartment we are misled and the unexpected outcome of this encounter is extremely relevant. In the representational interstice created here, we are provided with insights into the mind of this stifled character. True meanings are created between the explicit level of the story and the suggested. The abusive father and mother of the young child who, when playing with toys in the bathroom, created an accident, are having a conversation in which Viorel becomes a silent witness. The interaction is not what it appears to be since the protagonist himself, who has a large collection of model cars and playthings, is a participant in this apparently useless incident. The narrative interval becomes a projection of the absent past, part of the story of Viorel as a boy, that we are never told and never disclosed.

This strange character from *Aurora* is deterritorialized, both physically and mentally; he has no codes attached to his physical identity and the subjective existence he leads is emptied and meaningless. While looking like a grown man, he behaves like a child, always window watching, changing his direction, not having any coherent behavior. Once again, this might be easily confused with a modernist "uncertainty" or "hesitation," when in fact he shows no faltering, he displays no remorse, he commits the murders without any doubt and in a long-time premeditated fashion. These mood swings and changes of trajectory make Viorel an *abnormal flâneur*, an abject stroller who turns the bourgeois territory of his town into a de-territorialized geography. As a pointless and itinerant figure, he wanders around unmapping the space, and, unlike the classical heroes who are always in a central position on-screen, he evolves in the offscreen.

Ultimately the non-place creates a non-identity, transforming Viorel into a para-protagonist (as a para-being, a non-person). Even if Viorel is not socially marginal, in a strictly economic sense, the way in which he experiences life and human relationships is always at the periphery. Viorel exists in a no-space, dwelling in a negative space, with the apartment under repairs accentuating his solitude, in turn amplified by his relational emptiness. The film director reinforces this sensation with the help of cinematographic coding and decoding (as repetitive territorializations and deterritorializations). The protagonist is framed in doorways or between buildings, trapped between walls and furniture, which accentuate the fact that his existence is in a permanent in-between. This criminal father is often separated from his own world, through de-framing (décadrage), as various objects block the full access of the viewers into his space we are constantly left guessing what is going on not only in the cinematic space, but, while coerced to make cognitive efforts and understand what is going on, we enter the mind of a murderer. Deaca (2013) interprets the de-framing operated by the cinematographer as a device inducing as a form of visual violence. I agree with his definition of the "scalpel-like" camera which is acting like a surgical instrument, but I claim that its function is to slice open the intervals of thinking. As I explained in the discussion about *4 Months ...*, the offscreen is used as a dimension film-thinking by negation. When Viorel perpetrates his crimes we are never given access to the actual acts. The first crime appears to be committed against an unknown couple. Then, as he kills his mother-in-law, the atrocious gesture remains in the unshown, with the camera only gradually moving toward the trajectory of the actions. Removed from actions, the cinematic is pushed toward the thinking (Figure 4.4).

Aurora not only represents the absolute experience of the *in-between*, which causes the viewers to enter in a form of *liminal thinking*, but it

FIGURE 4.4 *Viorel, the murderous husband from* Aurora, *is trapped in a mental in-betweenness. Courtesy Mandragora.*

also brings about a cerebral limbo where, together with the protagonist, situated as in a state of continuous liminality, the film begins to think. The movie proves once more that cinema is able to produce negative knowledge, with the help of the *sub-framing* devices, commonly used by painters to emphasize elements that are not inside the visual field. Repurposed by Puiu, who himself was trained as a painter, the exclusion of elements from the visual is never gratuitous or coerced. The pro-filmic space, that is, the locations, objects, and other elements intentionally introduced in front of the camera, is negated and discharged of significations. In the majority of film productions, and certainly in classical cinema, the moviemakers use the "power of their brain" in order to build a coherent visual universe where the story can develop. In *Aurora,* Puiu transfers the thought processes from the center toward the margins. With everything decentered and de-coded, this absence of traits and characteristics facilitates an over-coding that takes shape in the subjective understanding of the spectators.

While in the classical forms of storytelling the apparition of the subject *inside* the visual field is based on explicitness and descriptivism, aiming directly to create knowledge and understanding, Puiu practices a dislocation of his protagonist. Together with the de-dramatization of the story and the deterritorialization of the cinematographic instruments, he creates a type of film-thinking otherwise unavailable. As we observed in all the other Romanian films discussed here, the *insterstice* between the visible and invisible, the external and the internal are the predilect conditions for transcending the limits of cinematic comprehension. In this state of suspension, the creation of interim moments in time and space, the construction of liminality, the series of interrupted movements, actions that lead to a certain point, then abruptly changing direction, film-thoughts are activated.

Epilogue: Rear-view Glances into the Post-metaphysical Cinema

To understand how the movies discussed here can be used as illustrations for a post-metaphysical cinema a final theoretical metaphor is required. I am fully aware that "post-metaphysical" is a perilous notion, and to justify that a new condition exists in a cinema concerned with the nature of being, while simultaneously displacing the attention, could have been better served by the notion of *non*-metaphysical. Although better suited in the series *non*-cinematic, or *non*-philosophical, the term is already filled with pejorative connotations. The *non*-metaphysical is associated already in film theory with the lack of depth, most often used in disparaging characterizations of conventional cinema.

If the mirror is a favored trope in the metaphysical cinema, exemplified by Tarkovsky's homonymous film, the rear-view mirror is the privileged way in which post-metaphysical cinema discloses its own thought processes. Unlike the typical "metaphysical condition" reflected by so-called art films, which provide the central illustrations and arguments for the film *as* philosophy paradigm, the *post*-metaphysical condition places us in front of screens that are functioning like rear-view mirrors. As indicated in earlier parts of this book, this visual trope is recurrent in contemporary Romanian movies. Thus, a post-metaphysical cinema is not simply reflective of society, as it does not provide a reflexive stance on the moral self of the characters or a self-reflection of the filmmaker as contemplations of the human condition. In order to understand how the post-metaphysical functions we must perform a final lateral rear-view observation on cinema as a medium, using Marshall McLuhan's toolbox of prophetic media concepts (more in Theall 1971). All technologically intermediated mental experiences made possible with the extra-cinematic tools presented in this book are *in-versions* of the dominant modes of expression. To expand on the metaphor, the only way in which we can see the head of the Medusa without being transformed into a block of stone, without freezing our minds in retarded thinking, is to look from outside within, to glance behind an opaque reflection or to take a quick look in a mirror allowing a retro vision.

Cinema as a post-philosophical and post-metaphysical machine is a negation of the traditional definitions about the metaphysical which are perpetuating a particular confusion in understanding the inner works of cinema, an understanding we can attribute to Umberto Eco (1976: 607). In the explanations about the tripartite system of articulations in cinematographic images the Italian semiologist included a third dimension, one to account for Pasolini's mode of making movies. Thus, whenever a moviemaker takes a leap from the concrete codes of cinematic language, dislocating the first two articulations, and especially the first one which is directly connected with reality, a transcendental knowledge or a spiritual disclosure takes place. Paisley Livingston (2009), the strongest proponent of the philosophical relevance of films, albeit disguised as a "moderate" devotee, takes generous examples from Ingmar Bergman's movies to fuel a set of arguments repeated undigested by many film studies. A level of meanings that are not "thought about," an understanding that is not rational or intellectual, remains unaccounted for. This leads to the conclusion supported by Livingston (200) who argues that, although films "do not have thoughts," filmmakers can use the cinematic to "express philosophical ideas of genuine complexity and significance." The respectable philosophy professor cannot see the dialectical error because the two definitions of the metaphysical in cinema—a transcendental dimension, which connects us with the mysterious and indefinable, and the ability of each and every film to make us think about something more than the visible—are not incompatible. In fact, as Deleuze (1985/1989: 210–11) explained this double determination, cinema is capable of two "movements," one made possible by the projection of images and the second through the projection of cerebral processes.

Last but not least, there is an even larger and more inclusive view, supported by Stanley Cavell (1971), who considers that movies are not simply popular forms of entertainment, claiming that all films have a metaphysical dimension, being able to carry significations beyond the technical aspects of the cinematic production. Terence Malick's productions and other mainstream films that have a poetic quality are considered to be naturally inclined to raise philosophical questions, often combined with the depiction of problematic situations and existential challenges. Bergman is always invoked whenever film critics claim that "physical films" can produce "metaphysical questions" (Cardullo 2012: 211), elevating cinema to a level beyond the representations of the real, a "spiritual style" or a "contemplative attitude" (Horton 1997), a philosophical potential characterized by a special "mode of looking" conveying more than direct and explicit meanings. Horton argues that, unlike in the attempt of icons to transcend the material—as understood by the Byzantine tradition, where the depiction of the saints or of God himself allowed direct access to the "spiritual" level—contemplative cinema has a metaphysical capacity connecting us with the unseen. Cinematic images have a metaphysical property to open up an enigmatic dimension.

The cinema examples discussed represented my own initial search for a metaphysical dimension to cinema, starting with the arguments Deleuze has thoroughly explored; how can cinematographic motion and temporality generate a knowledge that is unavailable in other arts and visual media such as painting or photography? My investigation led to the conclusion that movies can work both as forms of popular philosophy and as *non-*philosophical instruments. Contemporary moviemaking practices developed specialized tools, created particularly for our post-post-modern times, a moment in the evolution of humanity in which segregated groups of humans can meditate collectively and individually about their condition.

Another problematic concept I used to disclose this propensity toward the post-metaphysical is the non-cinematic. To clarify the nature of these changes, we must return one final time to François Laruelle (2011), who provided a more detailed explanation when defining "non-photography." In a similar fashion, the non-cinematic must not be described as a negation of the photographic camera, since the essence of the cinematographic image is not undermined by those elements which do not appear to be in accordance with its ontological values. As Laruelle indicates, immanence and transcendence are not separated; in fact they are brought together in the post-metaphysical. The various practices of negating the ontology of the apparatus (the non-cinematic) and the ability of the storytelling to remove the meanings from the field of vision, which normally can orient the spectator, the absence of clues from the depicted reality, and the symbolic emptiness are achieved the same end.

Just as in the rear-view mirror of a moving car, when we look at the images on-the-screen we are only seeing the past, never the present; thus, any representation which appears to be "in the now" is always of something else, of what it used to be. By consequence, to be "in the knowing" of the cinematic does not require presence in the time and space of cinema; thinking is not happening only in the experience of seeing film images. Thoughts are also contained in the immaterial dimension of our experience with that reality, one that is outside the physical while still inside the perceptual field. In a movie where there are no more objects represented onscreen, where the perceived images are confusing and opaque, the "old" definitions of metaphysics as the understanding of "being" are no longer applicable. Neither can the poetic nor can the allegorical explanations justify the "nowhere" of these experiences. The post-metaphysical provides access to a knowledge that is absent while in the present, not as Kantian metaphysics suggested to an understanding of the otherwise unavailable. It is not an attempt to know what lies beyond our capacity of knowing about ourselves.

Following Agamben (1998), who identified the "crisis of metaphysics" in our societies satiated with visual representations, we also have to observe and account for the fact that many filmmakers, not just the Romanian artists discussed here, are raising questions otherwise impossible to formulate with traditional instruments of the cinematic. The post-metaphysical is made possible by the non-cinematic, which is not a denial of cinematography or a rejection of the true nature of the cinematographic. Non-cinema is not a negative reaction to the incapacity of moviemaking to be more "profound." The *extra*-medial is only an alternative pathway to push the limits of moviemaking as an exploration of the limits of film-thoughts. These film directors who qualify as "post-metaphysicians," by contradicting the conventions of the cinematic grammar and its rhetorical devices, remain connected with everyday life and are not moving beyond that particular reality represented. The post-metaphysical thus is not a search for mystical ideas, nor an exercise in projecting events and meanings onto another plane, inaccessible to the immediately perceivable.

In traditional film theory the thing that blocked realist cinema from being metaphysical was the constant presence of the immediate, of life as a manifestation of the real. The same is true with the philosophical inquiries based on transcendental thinking. As Bergson (1934/2012) indicates, metaphysics was born with the first debates about the relativity of our knowledge about reality. The initial metaphysical inquiries were an effort of moving away from appearances; thus, for a long time the metaphysical attempts of ancient and pre-modern philosophers were conditioned by detachment from life, which must be dismissed as a purely intellectual effort. Bergson suggests instead that intuition, previously discredited by scientist approaches, is the faculty that can provide the transpositional ability to discover the true knowledge of the mind.

The post-metaphysical paradigm is a provisory explanatory model, an attempt to overcome the definitions of cinema as a metaphysical mechanism separating the material (the bodies of actors, the reality of the locations) from the subjective (the spiritual and affective impact). The post-metaphysical is not a critique of traditional metaphysics. My post-metaphysical concept derives from a criticism raised by Badiou (2000: 16) against Deleuze and his efforts to illustrate philosophical concepts with the help of film examples. No matter how remarkable, the concepts that appear to be "extracted" from cinema (like the notions of movement and time) are always connected with the *intrinsic* functions of the cinematic machine.

So, by denouncing the "philosophical requisitioning" of cinema practiced by Gilles Deleuze, inclining the scales in favor of concepts and distinctions, I decided to pursue with Badiou the indistinctions and impurities, where the non-philosophical understanding resides. Cinema can be non-philosophical because it is a non-art, as Badiou (2013: 141) convincingly argues. It is precisely because cinema has an impure technological component, which is imbued in its forms and artistic expressions; it can create new thoughts.

In this bastardry of cinema we can proceed with the reassessment of the philosophical. Movies naturally integrate philosophical ideas because cinema creates a special condition where "films can think"; however, this "cinematic thinking" is nothing more than a phantom of an idea or the passing of an idea, a manifestation of the total impurity of film-ideas (Badiou: 238). As Mullarkey (2009) suggests, the essence of cinema is that it has no essence, which provides a type of non-metaphysical knowledge.

Another conceptual stereotype we must reject is the commonplace premise advanced by some authors who link the metaphysical capacity particularly with the "Continental" tradition of philosophy as self-reflexive instrument. Implicitly this makes almost all European art films naturally inclined toward the metaphysical, as James Phillips (2008) interprets the "New Cinemas." Manifested in their intrinsic "longueur" (2–3) and the apparent "boredom," which is explicit in the Romanian recent cinema, the claim that productions have an ontological determination, an essence of moviemaking which provides access to "the transcendental structures of experience" (Phillips 2008: 8), is unfounded. Following this logic, all the New Cinemas of Europe (from the Italian Neorealists to the French Nouvelle Vague) share an inherent "proximity" with European philosophy, which is translatable in their cinematic output. The "philosophical" dimension is inherent also in the Romanian New Wave movies like *The Death of Mr. Lăzărescu* or *4 Months, 3 Weeks and 2 Days*, which are "philosophical" only because they belong to the European metaphysical agenda. Their profound humanism or their deep truthfulness, the stories that allow the spectators to have access to experience that transcends the immediate reality, would be enough to qualify them as metaphysical.

The paradigm shift brought by the post-metaphysical and the non-philosophical in cinema is not about the exploration of philosophical dialogues that "transcend" action, or the interpretation of images that open to a realm unavailable to immediate perception, nor an account of the various media involved in contemporary moviemaking practices. By post-metaphysical I understand the research of the non-transparent intervals, the opaque in-betweenness manifested in settings, storytelling, or character development. Cinema is non-philosophical not *inside* the cinematic resources; instead, it takes shape through the operations of intermedial interactions. As explained before, my use of intermediality expands to all forms of questioning the ontology of the cinematic medium, from the total absence of any cinematography, as in Porumboiu's movies, to the intertextual references to Disney in Cristi Puiu's dialogues. While commonly the *inter* in *intermediality* is understood as that relationship between media, here the *inter* refers to the *in-betweenness* created by the different mediums reunited in a particular film. Moving beyond Raymond Bellour (2012) and his seminal study about the in-betweenness of images, which narrows the discussion to the relationship between photography, video, and films, abandoning the notion of philosophical intermedialities proposed by

Deleuze and Guattari (1987/1994), I am alternatively proposing the post-metaphysical suspension.

The post-metaphysical does not mean a new "anti-metaphysics," just as the non-philosophical is not a negation or a rejection of philosophy. The post-metaphysical, together with the non-cinematic, is manifested *only* in the presence of metaphysic questioning and through cinematographic techniques. When a non-philosophical component of a movie is activated, one does not have to be a filmosopher or a philosopher to understand the thoughts and Ideas. While not abandoning the Aristotelian understanding of metaphysics as the foundation of all thinking, the post-metaphysical provides a *negative understanding*, taking place when we are *forbidden* to see. The concern is not so much about *what* is philosophy or *how* cinema images think. In the examples extracted from recent Romanian cinema, I question *where* the philosophical is located. Film-thinking happens *outside* the frames, not in the *onscreen* exchanges of ideas, activated by characters, situations, or storyworlds. Film-thoughts are hidden in the philosophical interval, in the fracture between the immediately visible and the absent, the cinematographic and the non-cinematic.

BIBLIOGRAPHY

Aaron, Michele. *Death and the Moving Image: Ideology, Iconography and I.* Edinburgh: Edinburgh University Press, 2014.

Ádám, Gyorgy ed. *Visceral Perception. Understanding Internal Cognition.* New York: Springer, 1998.

Adevărul, "Cristian Mungiu, criticat de Biserica din Vaslui: Filmul său este o rușine". September 25, 2012. Available online adevarul.ro/locale/vaslui/cristian-mungiu-criticat-biserica-vaslui-filmul-rusine-video-1_50aee7a37c42d5a663a19482/index.html.

Adorno, Theodor W. "Transparencies on Film." In *The Culture Industry: Selected Essays on Mass Culture.* Edited by J. M. Bernstein, 154–61. New York: Routledge, 1991.

Adorno, Theodor W. *Aesthetic Theory.* London: Bloomsbury Academic, 2013.

Agamben, Giorgio. *Homo Sacer.* Translated by Daniel Heller-Roazen. Stanford: Stanford University Press, 1998.

Alexandrescu, Sorin. *Paradoxul român.* Colecția Recuperări. București: Univers, 1998.

Allen, Richard and Murray Smith. "Introduction. Film Theory and Philosophy." In *Film Theory and Philosophy.* Edited by Richard Allen and Murray Smith, 1–35. Oxford: Clarendon Press, 1997.

Andersen, Nathan. *Film, Philosophy, and Reality: Ancient Greece to Godard.* New York: Routledge. 2019.

Andersen, Nathan. *Shadow Philosophy: Plato's Cave and Cinema,* New York: Routledge. 2014.

Anderson, Benedict. *Imagined Communities: Reflections on the Origin and Spread of Nationalism.* London: Verso, 1983.

Andreescu Florentina C. *From Capitalism to Communism: Nation and State in Romanian Cultural Production.* New York: Palgrave Macmillan, 2013.

Andreescu Florentina C. and Sean P. Quinn. "Women, Language, and Sacrifice." In *Genre and the (Post-)Communist Woman: Analyzing Transformations of the Central and Eastern European Female Ideal.* Edited by Florentina Andreescu and Michael J. Shapiro, 11–29. Oxon: Routledge, 2016.

Andrew, Dudley. "Andre Bazin: Dark Passage into the Mystery of Being." In *Thinking in the Dark: Cinema, Theory, Practice.* Edited by Murray Pomerance and R. Barton Palmer, 136–49. New Brunswick: Rutgers University Press, 2016.

Appelqvist, Hanne. "Introduction." In *Wittgenstein and the Limits of Language.* Edited by Hanne Appleqvist, 1–23. London: Routledge, 2020.

Arnheim, Rudolf. *Film as Art.* Berkeley: University of California Press, 1957.

Arnheim, Rudolf. "Melancholy Unshaped." *The Journal of Aesthetics and Art Criticism* 21, no. 3 (1963). DOI: 10.2307/427438.

Astruc, Alexandre. "The Birth of the New Avant-garde: The Caméra-stylo," first published as "Du Stylo à la caméra et de la caméra au stylo." *L'Écran française*, 30 March (1948). Available online http://www.newwavefilm.com/about/camera-stylo-astruc.shtml.

Augé, Marc. *Non-places: Introduction to an Anthropology of Supermodernity*. London: Verso, 2008, first French ed., *Non-lieux. Introduction à une anthropologie de la surmodernité*, Paris: Le Seuil, 1992.

Aumont, Jacques, Alain Bergala, Michel Marie, and Marc Vernet. *L'Esthetique du film*. Paris: Nathan, 1983.

Badley, Linda and R. Barton Palmer. "Introduction." In *Traditions in World Cinema*. Edited by Linda Badley, R. Barton Palmer, and Steven Jay Schneider, 1–14. New Brunswick: Rutgers University Press, 2006.

Badiou, Alain. *Cinema*. Translated by Susan Spitzer. Cambridge: Polity Press, 2013.

Badiou, Alain. *Deleuze: The Clamor of Being*. Minneapolis: University of Minnesota Press, 2000.

Badiou, Alain. *Handbook of Inaesthetics*. Meridian. Stanford: Stanford University Press, 2004.

Baracco, Alberto. *Hermeneutics of the Film World: A Ricœurian Method for Film Interpretation*. Cham: Palgrave Macmillan, 2017.

Barattoni, Luca. *Italian Post-Neorealist Cinema*. Edinburgh: Edinburgh University Press, 2012.

Barrow, Sarah. "4 luni, 2 săptămâni şi 2 zile/4 Months, 3 Weeks and 2 Days." In *The Routledge Encyclopedia of Films*. Edited by Sabine Haenni, Sarah Barrow and John White, 1–2. New York: Routledge, 2015.

Barthes, Roland. *Empire of Signs*. Translated by Richard Howard. New York: Hill and Wang, 1983.

Barthes, Roland. *Mythologies*. New York: Hill and Wang, 1972, first ed. Paris: Editions du Seuil, 1957.

Baudry, Jean-Louis. "Le dispositif. Approches métapsychologiques de l'impression de réalité." *Communications* 23 (1975): 56–72, English version "The Apparatus: Metapsychological Approaches to the Impression of Reality in Cinema." *Film Theory and Criticism*. Edited by Leo Braudy and Marshall Cohen. Oxford: Oxford University Press, 2009.

Bazin, André. *What Is Cinema?* Essays selected and translated by Hugh Gray, foreword by Jean Renoir, vol. 1. Berkeley: University of California Press, 1967.

Bazin, André. *What is Cinema? Volume II*. Essays selected and translated by Hugh Gray. Berkeley: University of California Press, 1972.

BBC Culture. "The 21st Century's 100 Greatest Films." Available online https://www.bbc.com/culture/article/20160819-the-21st-centurys-100-greatest-films.

Beller, Manfred and Joep Leerssen, eds. *Imagology: The Cultural Construction and Literary Representation of National Characters. A Critical Survey*. Amsterdam: Rodopi, 2007.

Bellour, Raymond. *Raymond Bellour: Between-The-Images*. Documents, 6. Zurich: JRP/Ringier, 2012.

Ben Shaul, Nitzan S. *Cinema of Choice: Optional Thinking and Narrative Movies*. New York: Berghahn Books, 2012.
Bergman, Paul and Michael Asimow. *Reel Justice: The Courtroom Goes to the Movies*. Kansas City, MO: Andrews McMeel Publishing, 2006.
Bergson, Henri. *The Creative Mind: An Introduction to Metaphysics*. Translated by Mabelle L. Andison. Mineola, NY: Dover Publications, 2007, first French ed., *La Pensée et le mouvant: Essais et conférences*. Paris: F. Alcan, 1934. Available https://fr.wikisource.org/wiki/La_Pens%C3%A9e_et_le_mouvant.
Bergson, Henri. *L'évolution créatrice*. Paris: Alcan, 1907; English translation Arthur Mitchell, *Creative Evolution*. New York: Henri Holt and Company, 1911.
Bergson, Henri. "Life and Consciousness." In *Mind-Energy: Lectures and Essays*. Translated by Wildon H. Carr, 1–28. Westport: Greewood Press, 1975.
Bergson, Henri. *Matière et mémoire. Essai sur la relation du corps à l'esprit*. Paris: Les Presses universitaires de France, 1939, first ed., 1896. Available online http://classiques.uqac.ca/classiques/bergson_henri/matiere_et_memoire/matiere_et_memoire.html.
Bernard, Sheila Curran and Kenn Rabin. *Archival Storytelling: A Filmmaker's Guide to Finding, Using, and Licensing Third-party Visuals and Music*. New York: Macmillan, 2009.
Bilenko, Natalia and Valkyrie Savage. "Using Image Processing to Improve Reconstruction of Movies from Brain Activity". Available online https://vimeo.com/169779284, 2016.
Bîrlea, Ovidiu. *Poetică folclorică*. București: Univers, 1979.
Blaga, Lucian. *Trilogia culturii*. Orizont și stil, Spațiul mioritic, Geneza metaforei și sensul culturii. Bucuresti: Humanitas, 2011.
Blassnigg, Martha. "Clairvoyance, Cinema, and Consciousness." In *Screen Consciousness: Cinema, Mind and World*. Edited by Robert Pepperell and Michael Punt, 105–22. Consciousness, Literature & the Arts, 4. Amsterdam: Rodopi, 2006.
Bogdan, Cătălin. "Prin desișuri." *Revista 22*, June 21, 2016. Available online http://revista22.ro/70254405/prin-desiuri.html.
Bogue, Ronald. "Art and Territory." In *A Deleuzian Century?* Edited by Ian Buchanan, 85–102. Durham: Duke University Press, 1999.
Bogue, Ronald. *Deleuze on Cinema*. Deleuze and the Arts, 1. New York: Routledge, 2003.
Boia, Lucian. *De ce este România altfel*. București: Humanitas, 2012.
Boia, Lucian. *History and Myth in Romanian Consciousness*. Budapest: Central European University Press, 2001.
Boia, Lucian. *Romania: Borderland of Europe*. Topographics. London: Reaktion Books, 2001, Romanian edition, *România, țară de frontieră a Europei*. 2nd ed. București: Humanitas, 2005.
Bonitzer, Pascal. *Decadrages: Peinture et cinema*. Paris: Cahiers du Cinema/Editions de l'Etoile, 1985, first published as "Décadrages." *Cahiers du cinéma*, Nr. 284 (1978).
Bordwell, David. "The Classical Hollywood Style: 1917–60." In *The Classical Hollywood Cinema: Film Style and Mode of Production to 1960*. Edited by David Bordwell, Janet Staiger and Kristin Thompson, 1–87. New York: Columbia University Press, 1985.

Bordwell, David and Janet Staiger. "Since 1960: the persistence of a mode of film practice." In *The Classical Hollywood Cinema: Film Style and Mode of Production to 1960*. Edited by David Bordwell, Janet Staiger, and Kristin Thompson, 367–77. New York: Columbia University Press, 1985.

Bordwell, David. *Planet Hong Kong: Popular Cinema and the Art of Entertainment*. Cambridge: Harvard University Press, 2000.

Bordwell, David. *The Way Hollywood Tells It. Story and Style in Modern Movies*. Berkeley: University of California Press, 2006.

Bordwell, David. "The Art Cinema as a Mode of Film Practice." In *Poetics of Cinema*, 151–69. New York: Routledge, 2012.

Botz-Bornstein, Thorsten. *Organic Cinema: Film, Architecture, and the Work of Béla Tarr*. New York: Berghahn, 2017.

Bowman, Paul. *Rancière And Film*. Critical Connections. Edinburgh: Edinburgh University Press, 2013.

Brace, Patricia and Robert Arp, eds. *The Philosophy of J.J. Abrams*. The Philosophy of Popular Culture. Lexington: University Press of Kentucky, 2014.

Bradshaw, Peter. "Cannes 2012: Beyond the Hills—Review." *The Guardian*, May 20, 2012. Available online https://www.theguardian.com/film/2012/may/20/beyond-the-hills-film-review.

Bradshaw, Peter. "Graduation Review—A Five-star Study of Grubby Bureaucratic Compromise." *The Guardian*, May 19, 2016. Available online https://www.theguardian.com/film/2016/may/19/graduation-review-cristian-mungiu-romania-cannes-2016.

Brown, Tom. *Breaking the Fourth Wall Direct Address in the Cinema*. Edinburgh: Edinburgh University Press, 2012.

Brown, William. *Supercinema. Film-Philosophy for the Digital Age*. New York: Berghahn Books, 2013.

Brown, William. *Non-Cinema?: Global Digital Film-making and the Multitude*. New York: Bloomsbury, 2018.

Buckland, Warren. "Introduction: Puzzle Plots." In *Puzzle Films: Complex Storytelling in Contemporary Cinema*. Edited by Warren Buckland, 1–12. Oxford: Wiley-Blackwell, 2009.

Burch, Noël. *Theory of Film Practice*. Translated by Helen Lane. Princeton: Princeton University Press, 1981, first French ed., *Praxis du cinéma*. Paris: Editions Gallimard, 1969.

Burgin, Victor. *The Remembered Film*. London: Reaktion, 2004.

Burnett, Ron. *How Images Think*. Cambridge: MIT Press, 2004.

Busnel René Guy and Classe André. *Whistled Languages*. Communication and Cybernetics, 13. Berlin: Springer-Verlag, 1976.

Cabañas, Kaira M. *Off-screen Cinema. Isidore Isou and the Lettrist Avant-Garde*. Chicago, IL: University of Chicago Press, 2015.

Colebrook, Claire. *Deleuze: A Guide for the Perplexed*. London: Continuum, 2006.

Cameron, Oliver G. *Visceral Sensory Neuroscience: Interoception*. Oxford: Oxford University Press, 2002.

Cardullo, Bert. *European Directors and their Films: Essays on Cinema*. Lanham: Scarecrow Press, 2012.

Carroll, Noël. *Mystifying Movies: Fads & Fallacies in Contemporary Film Theory*. New York: Columbia University Press, 1988.

Carroll, Noël. *The Philosophy of Horror: Or, Paradoxes of the Heart*. New York: Routledge, 1990.
Carroll, Noël. *Theorizing the Moving Image*. Cambridge: Cambridge University Press, 1996.
Carroll, Noël. "Philosophizing through the Moving Image: The Case of Serene Velocity." *Journal of Aesthetics and Art Criticism* 64, no. 1, Special Issue: Thinking through Cinema: Film as Philosophy, Winter (2006a): 173–85.
Carroll, Noël. "Introduction to Part VIII." In *Philosophy of Film and Motion Pictures: An Anthology*. Edited by Noël Carroll and Jinhee Choi, 323–34. Malden: Blackwell Publishing, 2006b.
Carroll, Noël. *The Philosophy of Motion Pictures*. Malden, MA: Blackwell Publishing, 2008.
Carroll, Noël. "Philosophical Insight, Emotion, and Popular Fiction." In *Narrative, Emotion, and Insight*. Edited by Noël Carroll and John Gibson, 45–68. University Park, PA: Penn State University Press, 2011.
Carroll, Noël. *Minerva's Night Out: Philosophy, Pop Culture, and Moving Pictures*. Malden, MA: Wiley-Blackwell, 2013.
Carroll, Noël. "Movie-Made Philosophy." In *Film as Philosophy*. Edited by Bernd Herzogenrath, 265–85. Minneapolis: University of Minnesota Press, 2017.
Carroll, Noël, Laura T. Di Summa, and Shawn Loht, eds. *The Palgrave Handbook of the Philosophy of Film and Motion Pictures*. Cham: Palgrave Macmillan, 2019.
Caracostea, Dumitru. *Poezia tradițională română*, vol. I. București: Editura pentru literatură, first published in 1927.
Cavell, Stanley. *The World Viewed. Reflections on the Ontology of Film*. Cambridge: Harvard University Press, 1971.
Călinescu, George. *Istoria literaturii române: compendiu (The History of Romanian Literature)*. București: Litera Internațional, 2001, first edition 1945.
ChèzeThierry. "Baccalauréat: Mungiu ausculte brillamment la société roumaine." *L'Express*, May 19, 2016. Available online http://www.lexpress.fr/culture/cinema/baccalaureat-mungiu-ausculte-brillamment-la-societe-roumaine_1793472.html.
Chion, Michel. *Audio-vision: Sound on Screen*. New York: Columbia University Press, 1994.
Ciobanu, Alina. Interview. *Mediafax*, July 2, 2017. Available online https://www.hotnews.ro/stiri-film-21850348-interviu-regizorul-cristi-puiu-despre-filme-copilaria-balta-alba-menta-ciocolata-macanache.htm.
Cioran, Emil. *Îndreptar pătimaș*. București: Humanitas, 1991.
Cioran, Emil. *Tratat de descompunere*. București: Humanitas, 1992, first French ed., 1949.
Cohen-Séat, Gilbert. *Essai sur les principes d'une philosophie du cinéma, Tome I. Introduction générale: notions fondamentales et vocabulaire de filmologie*. Paris: Presses universitaires de France, 1946.
Colăcel, Onoriu. *The Romanian Cinema of Nationalism: Historical Films as Propaganda and Spectacle*. Jefferson, MO: McFarland, 2018.
Colman, Felicity. "Introduction: What Is Film-philosophy?" In *Film, Theory and Philosophy: The Key Thinkers*. Edited by Felicity Colman, 1–19. Montreal, Quebec: McGill-Queens University Press, 2009.

Conta, Vasile. *Teoria fatalismului (The Theory of Fatalism)*. Editura Librăriei Școalelor, 1894, first French ed., 1877. Available online https://commons.wikimedia.org/wiki/File:Vasile_Conta_-_Teoria_fatalismului.pdf.
Cox, Damian and Michael Levine. *Thinking through Film: Doing Philosophy, Watching Movies*. Chichester: Wiley-Blackwell, 2012.
Crocker, Stephen. *Bergson and the Metaphysics of Media*. New York: Palgrave Macmillan, 2013.
Crofts, Stephen. "Concepts of National Cinema." In *Theorising National Cinema*. Edited by Valentina Vitali and Paul Willemen, 44–60. London: British Film Institute, 2006.
Culianu, Ioan Petru. *Fantasmele nihilismului: secretul doctorului Eliade (The Phantasms of Nihilism: The Secret of Doctor Eliade)*. Iasi: Polirom, 2006.
D'Aloia, Adriano and Ruggero Eugeni. "Neurofilmology: An Introduction." *Cinéma & Cie* 14, no. 22–23 (2014): 9–26.
Dargis, Manohla. "Friend Indeed Who Doesn't Judge or Flinch." *The New York Times*, January 25, 2008. Available online https://www.nytimes.com/2008/01/25/movies/25mont.html.
Davies, David. "Can Philosophical Thought Experiments Be 'Screened'?" In *Thought Experiments in Science, Philosophy, and the Arts*. Edited by Frappier Mélanie, Letitia Meynell, and James Robert Brown, 223–38. New York: Routledge, 2012.
David, Daniel. *Psihologia poporului român: profilul psihologic al românilor într-o monografie cognitiv-experimentală*. Iași: Polirom, 2015.
Deaca, Mircea Valeriu. *Cinematograful postfilmic. Note și lecturi despre filmul contemporan*. Timișoara: Brumar, 2013.
Deaca, Mircea-Valeriu. *Investigații în analiza cognitivă de film*. Timișoara: Brumar, 2015.
Deaca, Mircea. *O bucătărie ca în filme. Scenotopul bucătăriei în Noul Cinema Românesc*. Cluj-Napoca: Editura Mega, 2017.
Deamer, David. *Deleuze's Cinema Books: Three Introductions to the Taxonomy of Images*. Edinburgh: Edinburgh University Press, 2016.
Deletant, Denis. "Romanians." In *Imagology: The Cultural Construction and Literary Representation of National Characters. A Critical Survey*. Edited by Manfred Beller and Joep Leerssen, 223–5. Amsterdam: Rodopi, 2007.
Deleuze, Gilles. *Cinema 1: The Movement Image*. Minneapolis: University of Minnesota Press, 1986, French edition *L'image-Mouvement. Cinéma, 1*. Paris: Éditions de Minuit, 1983.
Deleuze, Gilles. *Cinema 2: The Time-image*. Translated by Hugh Tomlinson and Robert Galeta. Minneapolis: University of Minnesota Press, 1989; French ed., *Cinéma II, L'image-temps*. Paris: Éditions de Minuit, 1985.
Deleuze, Gilles. "The Deleuze Seminars. Leibniz: Philosophy and the Creation of Concepts," April 15, 1980. Available online https://deleuze.cla.purdue.edu/index.php/seminars/leibniz-philosophy-and-creation-concepts/lecture-01.
Deleuze, Gilles and Claire Parnet. *Dialogues*. Paris: Flammarion, 1996.
Deleuze, Gilles. *Difference and Repetition*. Translated by Paul Patton. New York: Columbia University Press, 1994, first French ed., *Différence et Répétition*. Paris: PUF, 1968.

Deleuze, Gilles. *The Fold: Leibniz and the Baroque*, first French ed. *Le pli: Leibniz et le baroque*. Paris: Éditions de Minuit, 1988.
Deleuze, Gilles. "Le cerveau c'est l'ecran. Entretien avec Gilles Deleuze."*Cahiers du Cinéma* 380 (February 1986): 24–32, reprinted as "The Brain Is the Screen: An Interview with Gilles Deleuze" in *The Brain is the Screen, Deleuze and the Philosophy of Cinema*. Edited by Gregory Flaxman. Minneapolis: University of Minnesota Press, 2000.
Deleuze, Gilles. *Pourparlers*. Paris: Éditions de Minuit, 1990.
Deleuze, Gilles and Félix Guattari. *Qu'est-ce que la philosophie?* Paris: Éditions de Minuit, 1991; English ed., *What Is Philosophy?* New York: Columbia University Press, 1994.
Deleuze, Gilles and Félix Guattari. *A Thousand Plateaus: Capitalism and Schizophrenia*. Minneapolis: University of Minnesota Press, 1987.
Derrida, Jacques. *The Truth in Painting*. Chicago, IL: University of Chicago Press, 1987.
Diamond, Cora. "We Can't Whistle It Either: Legend and Reality." *European Journal of Philosophy* 19, no. 3 (2011). Doi: 10.1111/j.1468-0378.2010.00398.x.
Dimou, Nikos. *On the Unhappiness of Being Greek*. Ropley: Zero Books, 2013.
Drăghicescu, Dumitru. *Din psihologia poporului român*. Librăria Leon Alcalay. București: Librăria Leon Alcalay, 1907.
Ebert, Roger. "The Price of An Abortion." RogerEbert.com, February 7, 2008. Available online https://www.rogerebert.com/reviews/4-months-3-weeks-and-2-days-2008.
Eco, Umberto."Articulations of the Cinematic Code." In *Movies and Methods: An Anthology, Volume 1*. Edited by Bill Nichols, 590–607. Berkeley: University of California Press, 1976.
Eig, Jonathan. "A Beautiful Mind(fuck): Hollywood Structures of Identity." *Jump Cut: A Review of Contemporary Media* 46 (2003). Available online http://www.ejumpcut.org/archive/jc46.2003/eig.mindfilms/index.html.
Eisenstein, Sergei. "Beyond the Shot." 1949. In *Film Form: Essays in Film Theory*. Edited and translated by Jay Leyda, 28–44. A Harvest Book. San Diego, CA: Harcourt, Brace, Jovanovich, 1977.
Eisenstein, Sergei. "Montage." 1937. In *Selected Works, vol. 2, Towards a Theory of Montage*. Edited by Michael Glenny and Richard Taylor, 11–58. London: British Film Institute, 1991.
Eisenstein, Sergei. "Notes for a Film of 'Capital'." Translated by Maciej Sliwowski, Jay Leyda, and Annette Michelson. *October* 2 (Summer 1976): 3–26.
Eisenstein, Sergei. "The Problem of the Materialist Approach to Form." 1925. In *Selected Works, Volume 1, Writing 1922–34*. Edited by Richard Taylor, 59–64. London: BFI Publishing, 1988.
Eliade, Mircea. "The Magical Sheep." In *Zamolxis, the Vanishing God: Comparative Studies in the Religions and Folklore of Dacia and Eastern Europe*. Translated by W.R. Trask. Chicago, IL: Chicago University Press, 1972, Romanian ed., *De la Zalmoxis la Genghis-Han. Studii comparative despre religiile și folclorul Daciei și Europei Orientale*, 1997, first French ed., *De Zalmoxis à Genghis-Khan: Études Comparatives Sur Les Religions Et Le Folklore De La Dacie Et De L'europe Orientale*. Bibliothèque Historique. Paris: Payot, 1970.

Eliade, Mircea. *Drumul spre centru (The Road towards the Center)*. București: Humanitas, 1991.

Elleström, Lars. *Media Borders, Multimodality and Intermediality*. London: Palgrave Macmillan, 2010.

Elsaesser, Thomas. *Weimar Cinema and After: Germany's Historical Imaginary*. London: Routledge, 2000.

Elsaesser, Thomas. *European Cinema: Face to Face with Hollywood*. Amsterdam: Amsterdam University Press, 2005.

Elsaesser, Thomas. "The Mind-Game Film." In *Puzzle Films: Complex Storytelling in Contemporary Cinema*. Edited by Warren Buckland, 13–14. Oxford: Wiley-Blackwell, 2009.

Elsaesser, Thomas. *European Cinema and Continental Philosophy. Film as Thought Experiment*. New York: Bloomsbury Academic, 2019.

Epstein, Jean. *Bonjour Cinéma: Le cinématographe vu de l'Etna et autres ecrits*. Écrits Complets. Vol II, 1920–8. Montreuil: Les Éditions de l'Oeil, 2019, first ed., *Bonjour Cinema*. Éditions De La Sirène, 1921.

Epstein, Jean. *Critical Essays and New Translations*. Edited by Sarah Keller and Jason N. Paul. Film Theory in Media History. Amsterdam: Amsterdam University Press, 2014.

Epstein, Jean. *L'Intelligence d'une machine*. Éditions Jacques Melot, 1946. Available online http://classiques.uqac.ca/classiques/epstein_jean/intelligence_machine/intelligence_une_machine.pdf.

Epstein, Jean. *L'Intelligence d'une machine*. 4. ed. Classiques Du Cinéma. Paris: Éditions Jacques Melot, 1946. Available http://classiques.uqac.ca/classiques/epstein_jean/ intelligence_machine/intelligence_une_machine.pdf.

Epstein, Jean. *Le cinéma du diable*. Jacques Melot, 1947. Available online http://classiques.uqac.ca/classiques/epstein_jean/cinema_du_diable/cinema_du_diable.html.

Erll, Astrid and Ansgar Nünning. *Cultural Memory Studies: An International and Interdisciplinary Handbook*. Media and Cultural Memory; Medien Und Kulturelle Erinnerung, 8. Berlin: Walter De Gruyter, 2008.

Fahle, Oliver. "Das Außen." In *Essays zur Film-Philosophie*. Edited by Lorenz Engell, Oliver Fahle, Vinzenz Hediger, and Christiane Voss, 117–67. Schriften Des Internationalen Kollegs Für Kulturtechnikforschung Und Medienphilosophie, Bd. 24. Paderborn: Fink, 2015.

Falzon, Christopher. *Philosophy Goes to the Movies. An Introduction to Philosophy*. London: Routledge, 2002.

Felperin, Leslie. "The Whistlers ('La Gomera') Film Review." *Hollywood Reporter*, May 18, 2019. Available https://www.hollywoodreporter.com/review/whistlers-review-1211959.

Fermor, Patrick Leigh. *Drum întrerupt: de la Porțile de Fier până la Muntele Athos*. Translated by Mariana Piroteala, Humanitas, 2016, first ed., *The Broken Road: Travels from Bulgaria to Mount Athos*, 2013.

Ferraris, Maurizio and Enrico Terrone. *Cinema and Ontology*. Milan: Mimesis International, 2019.

Filimon, Monica. *Cristi Puiu*. Contemporary Film Directors. Urbana: University of Illinois Press, 2017.

Fondane, Benjamin. *Existential Monday: Philosophical Essays*. Edited by Bruce Baugh and Andrew Rubens. New York: New York Review Books, 2016.

Flaxman, Gregory, ed. *The Brain Is the Screen, Deleuze and the Philosophy of Cinema*. Minneapolis: University of Minnesota Press, 2000.

Flaxman, Gregory. *Gilles Deleuze and the Fabulation of Philosophy*. Minneapolis: University of Minnesota Press, 2012.

Flaxman, Gregory. "Sci-Phi: Gilles Deleuze and the Future of Philosophy." In *Deleuze, Guattari and the Production of the New*. Edited by Simon O'Sullivan and Stephen Zepke, 11–21. New York: Continuum International Publishing Group, 2008.

Flusser, Vilém. *Für eine Philosophie der Fotografie*. Edition Flusser, 2018, English version, *Towards a Philosophy of Photography*. London: Reaktion, 2000.

Fochi, Adrian. *Miorița. Tipologie, circulație, geneză, texte*. Bucuresti: Editura Academiei R.P. R., 1964.

Ford, Hamish. *Post-War Modernist Cinema and Philosophy: Confronting Negativity and Time*. Basingstoke: Palgrave Macmillan, 2012. https://doi.org/10.1057/9781137283528.

Frampton, Daniel. *Filmosophy*. London: Columbia University Press, 2006.

Frampton, Daniel. "Notes on Filmosophy: A Reply to Reviews." *New Review of Film and Television Studies* 6, no. 3 (2008): 365–74.

Frankfurt, Harry G. *On Bullshit*. Princeton: Princeton University Press, 2005.

Freud, Sigmund. "Mourning and Melancholia." In *Collected Papers vol. IV*. Translated by Joan Riviere, 152–70. London: Hogarth Press, 1957, first published in 1917.

Friedberg, Anne. *The Virtual Window: From Alberti to Microsoft*. Cambridge: MIT Press, 2006.

Fumerton, Richard A and Diane Jeske. *Introducing Philosophy through Film: Key Texts, Discussion, and Film Selections*. Chichester: Wiley-Blackwell, 2010.

Furman, Orit, Nimrod Dorfman, Uri Hasson, Lila Davachi, and Yadin Dudai. "They Saw a Movie: Long-term Memory for an Extended Audiovisual Narrative." *Learning & Memory* 14, no. 6 (2007): 457–67.

Furze, Robert. *The Visceral Screen: Between the Cinemas of John Cassavetes and David Cronenberg*. Bristol: Intellect, 2015.

Gallese, Vittorio and Michele Guerra. *The Empathic Screen: Cinema and Neuroscience*. Oxford: Oxford University Press, 2020; Italian ed., *Lo Schermo Empatico: Cinema E Neuroscienze*. Scienza E Idee, 263. Milan: Cortina, 2015.

Gaut, Berys Nigel. *A Philosophy of Cinematic Art*. Cambridge: Cambridge University Press, 2010.

Gauthier, Guy. *Vingt leçons sur l'image et le sens*. Paris: Edilig, 1982.

Gavaler, Chris and Nathaniel Jason Goldberg. *Superhero Thought Experiments: Comic Book Philosophy*. Iowa City: University of Iowa Press, 2019.

Ghioca, Florin. "Breban, despre Patapievici." *Adevărul*, May 5, 2015. Available online https://adevarul.ro/cultura/arte/breban-despre-patapievici--i-s-a-parut-e-fel-guru-culturii-injurat-haimana-ordinara-istoria-acestui-popor-1_5548c90bcfbe376e35df8e4d/index.html.

Gibbs, John and Douglas Pye. "Introduction 1: The Long Take—Critical Approaches." In *The Long Take: Critical Approaches*. Edited by John Gibbs and Douglas Pye, 1–26. London: Palgrave Macmillan, 2017.

Gilmore, Richard. *Doing Philosophy at the Movies*. Albany: State University of New York, 2005.

Gilmore, Richard. *Searching for Wisdom In Movies: From the Book of Job to Sublime Conversations*. Cham: Springer International Publishing, 2017.

Giurgiu, Tudor. "Filmele si imaginea Romaniei." *Hotnews*, October 30, 2012. Available online https://www.hotnews.ro/stiri-cultura-13515991-filmele-imaginea-romaniei.htm.

Godard, Jean-Luc. "Hiroshima notre amour." *Cahiers du cinema*, 97, July 1959, reprinted in *Cahiers Du Cinéma, the 1950s: Neo-Realism, Hollywood, New Wave*. Edited by Jim Hillier. Harvard Film Studies. Cambridge: Harvard University Press, 1985.

Goodenough, Jerry. "Introduction: A Philosopher Goes to Cinema." In *Film as Philosophy: Essays in Cinema after Wittgenstein and Cavell*. Edited by Rupert J. Read and Jerry Goodenough. New York: Palgrave Macmillan, 2005.

Goss, Brian Michael. "*Four Months, Three Weeks and Two Days* (2007) and *Beyond the Hills* (2012): Romanian auteur Cristian Mungiu and the Paradoxes of 'Anti-national National Cinema'." *Journal of European Popular Culture* 6, no. 1 (2015): 44–5.

Gracia, Jorge J. E. *Mel Gibson's Passion and Philosophy: The Cross, the Questions, the Controversy*. Popular Culture and Philosophy, Vol. 10. Chicago: Open Court, 2004.

Greene, Richard and K. Silem Mohammad. *Quentin Tarantino and Philosophy: How to Philosophize with a Pair of Pliers and a Blowtorch*. Popular Culture and Philosophy, Vol. 29. Chicago, IL: Open Court, 2007.

Groys, Boris. *An Introduction to Antiphilosophy*. Translated by David Fernbach. London: Verso, 2012.

Gulino, Paul. *Screenwriting: The Sequence Approach. The Hidden Structure of Successful Screenplays*. New York: Continuum, 2004.

Habermas, Jürgen. *Postmetaphysical Thinking: Between Metaphysics and the Critique of Reason*. Cambridge: Polity Press, 1992.

Halle, Randall. *The Europeanization of Cinema: Interzones and Imaginative Communities*. Urbana: University of Illinois Press, 2014.

Hanley, Richard, ed. *South Park and Philosophy: Bigger, Longer, and More Penetrating*. Popular Culture and Philosophy, Vol. 26. Chicago, IL: Open Court, 2007.

Hansen, Miriam. *Babel and Babylon: Spectatorship in American Silent Film*. Cambridge, MA: Harvard University Press, 1991.

Hasson, Uri, Ohad Landesman, Barbara Knappmeyer, Ignacio Vallines, Nava Rubin, and David J. Heeger. "Neurocinematics: The Neuroscience of Film." *Projections* 2, no. 1 (2008): 1–26. https://doi.org/10.3167/proj.2008.020102.

Heath, Stephen. "Jaws, Ideology and Film Theory." In *Movies and Methods: Vol. 2: An Anthology*. Edited by Bill Nichols, 509–14. Berkeley: University of California Press, 1985.

Herzogenrath, Bernd. "Travels in Intermedia[lity]: An Introduction." In *Travels in Intermedia[lity]: ReBlurring the Boundaries*. Edited by Bernd Herzogenrath, 1–14. Interfaces: Studies in Visual Culture. Hanover: Dartmouth College Press, 2012.

Higson, Andrew. "The Concept of National Cinema." *Screen* 30, no. 4 (1989): 36–47.

Hitchins, Keith. *Scurtă istorie a României*. Iași: Polirom 2015

Holden, Stephen, "The Death of Mr. Lazarescu Tells a Modern Hospital Tale." *The New York Times*, April 26, 2006. Available online https://www.nytimes.com/2006/04/26/movies/the-death-of-mr-lazarescu-tells-a-modern-hospital-tale.html.

Horkheimer, Max and Theodor W. Adorno. *Dialectic of Enlightenment: Philosophical Fragments*. Edited by Gunzelin Schmid Noerr and translated by Edmund Jephcott. Stanford University Press, 2002, first ed., 1947.

Horton, Andrew. *The Films of Theo Angelopoulos: A Cinema of Contemplation*. Princeton Modern Greek Studies. Princeton, NJ: Princeton University Press, 1997.

Hösle, Vittorio. *Eric Rohmer: Filmmaker and Philosopher*. Philosophical Filmmakers. New York: Bloomsbury Academic, 2016.

Hotnews. September 24, 2013. Available online https://www.hotnews.ro/stiri-cultura-15642245-pozitia-copilului-cel-mai-succes-film-romanesc-din-ultimii-ani-criticat-deputat-psd-tribuna-parlamentului-noi-venim-mai-dam-artistului-bani-denigreze-faca-inculti-injure-invatamantul-romanesc.htm.

Hunt, Lester. "Motion Pictures as a Philosophical Resource." In *Philosophy of Film and Motion Pictures: An Anthology*. Edited by Noël Carroll and Jinhee Choi, 397–405. Malden, MA: Blackwell Publishing, 2006.

IRES. "Mândria și disperarea de a fi români" [The Pride and Disperation of Being Romanian], 2012. Available online https://ires.ro/articol/212/mandria-si-disperarea-de-a-fi-rom-n.

Irwin, William. "Computers, Caves, and Oracles: Neo and Socrates". In *The Matrix and Philosophy: Welcome to the Desert of the Real*. Edited by William Irwin. Chicago: Open Court Publishing, 2002.

Jaffe, Ira. *Slow Movies: Countering the Cinema of Action*. New York: Columbia University Press, 2014.

Jameson, Fredric. *Signatures of the Visible*. New York: Routledge, 1992.

Jihoon, Kim. *Between Film, Video, and the Digital: Hybrid Moving Images in the Post-media Age*. New York: Bloomsbury, 2016.

Kahn, Paul W. *Finding Ourselves at the Movies: Philosophy for a New Generation*. New York: Columbia University Press, 2013.

Kawin, Bruce F. *Mindscreen: Bergman, Godard, and First-Person Film*. Princeton, NJ: Princeton University Press, 1978.

Keating, Patrick. *The Dynamic Frame: Camera Movement in Classical Hollywood*. New York: Columbia University Press, 2019.

Keesey, Douglas. *Catherine Breillat*. Manchester: Manchester University Press, 2015.

Kennick, William E. "The Ineffable." In *The Encyclopedia of Philosophy*. Edited by P. Edwards. New York: Macmillan, 1967.

Kovács, András Bálint. "Andrey Tarkovsky." In *The Routledge Companion to Philosophy and Film*. Edited by Paisley Livingston and Carl Plantinga, 581–90. New York: Routledge, 2009.

Kovács, András Bálint. *Screening Modernism: European Art Cinema, 1950–1980*. Cinema and Modernity. Chicago, IL: University of Chicago Press, 2007.

Kowalski, Dean A., ed. *Steven Spielberg and Philosophy: We're Gonna Need a Bigger Book*. The Philosophy of Popular Culture. Lexington: The University Press of Kentucky, 2008.

Kracauer, Siegfried. *From Caligari to Hitler: A Psychological History of the German Film*. Princeton, NJ: Princeton University Press, 1966.
Kracauer, Siegfried. *The Mass Ornament: Weimar Essays*. Translated by Thomas Y. Levin. Cambridge, MA: Harvard University Press, 1995.
Kracauer, Siegfried. *Theory of Film: The Redemption of Physical Reality*. New York: Oxford University Press, 1960.
Kuhn, Annette. "What to do with Cinema Memory?." In *Explorations in New Cinema History: Approaches and Case Studies*. Edited by Maltby, Richard, Biltereyst Daniël, and Philippe Meers, 85–98. Malden, MA: Wiley-Blackwell, 2011.
Lakoff, George and Mark Johnson. *Metaphors We Live By*. Chicago, IL: University of Chicago Press, 1980.
Lakoff, George and Mark Johnson. *Philosophy in The Flesh: The Embodied Mind and Its Challenge To Western Thought*. New York: Basic Books, 1999.
Lakoff, George. *Women, Fire, and Dangerous Things: What Categories Reveal about the Mind*. Chicago: University of Chicago Press, 1987.
Lambert, Gregg. *Non-philosophy of Gilles Deleuze*. London: The Athlone Press, 2002.
Laruelle, François. *The Concept of Non-Photography*. Translated by Robin Mackay. Falmouth: Urbanomic, 2011.
Laruelle, François. *Philosophy and Non-philosophy*. Minneapolis, MN: Univocal Publishing, 2013, first French ed., *Philosophie et non-philosophie*. Brussels: Pierre Mardaga, 1989.
Laruelle, François. *Principles of Non-philosophy*. New York: Bloomsbury, 2013, first ed., *Principes de la non-philosophie*. Paris: Presses Universitaires de France, 1996.
Laurušaitė, Laura. "Imagology as Image Geology." In *Imagology Profiles: The Dynamics of National Imagery in Literature*. Edited by Laura Laurušaitė, 8–27. Newcastle upon Tyne: Cambridge Scholars Publishers, 2018.
Lawrence, Stuart. *Moral Awareness in Greek Tragedy*. Oxford: Oxford University Press, 2013.
Leerssen, Joep. "The Rhetoric of National Character: A Programmatic Survey." *Poetics Today* 21, no. 2 (2000): 267–92.
Linkman, Audrey. *Photography and Death*. Exposures. London: Reaktion Books, 2011.
Litch, Mary M. and Amy Karofsky. *Philosophy through Film*. New York: Routledge, 2002.
Livingston, Paisley. *Art and Intention: A Philosophical Study*. Oxford: Clarendon Press, 2005.
Livingston, Paisley. "The Bold Thesis Retried." In *Philosophy and Film: Bridging Divides*. Edited by Christina Rawls, Diana Neiva, and Steven Gouveia, 81–91. New York: Routledge, 2019.
Livingston, Paisley. *Cinema, Philosophy, Bergman: On Film as Philosophy*. Oxford: Oxford University Press, 2009.
Livingston, Paisley and Carl Plantinga, eds. *The Routledge Companion to Philosophy and Film*. New York: Routledge, 2009.
Livingston, Paisley. "Theses on Cinema as Philosophy." *Journal of Aesthetics and Art Criticism* 64, no. 1 (2006): 11–18.

De Luca, Tiago. *Slow Cinema*. Edinburgh: Edinburgh University Press, 2016.
Lyotard, Jean-François. "L'acinéma." *Revue d'esthétique* 26, no. 2–4 (1973): 357–69; republished in *Des dispositifs pulsionnels*. Paris: Union Générale d'Éditions, 1973.
Lyotard, Jean-François. "Notes on the Critical Function of the Work of Art." In *Driftworks*. Edited by R. McKeon, 69–83. Columbia: Columbia University Press, 1984.
Maoilearca, John Ó. "When the Twain Shall Meet: On the Divide between Analytic and Continental Film Philosophy." In *The Palgrave Handbook of the Philosophy of Film and Motion Pictures*. Edited by Carroll Noël, Laura T. Di Summa, and Shawn Loht, 259–83. Cham, Switzerland: Palgrave Macmillan, 2019.
Marrati, Paola. *Gilles Deleuze: Cinema and Philosophy*. Parallax. Baltimore, MD: The Johns Hopkins University Press, 2008.
Marcu, Diana and Raluca Ion. "Noul val din filmul românesc, primul brand valabil de țară. Puiu, Mitulescu, Porumboiu și Mustață povestesc pentru Gândul despre ofensiva cinematografiei românești." *Gândul*, March 23, 2012. Available online http://www.gandul.info/stiri/noul-val-din-filmul-romanesc-primul-brand-valabil-de-tara-puiu-mitulescu-porumboiu-si-mustata-povestesc-pentru-gandul-despre-ofensiva-cinematografiei-romanesti-5585051.
Martin-Jones, David. *Deleuze, Cinema and National Identity:* Narrative Time in National Contexts. Edinburgh: Edinburgh University Press, 2006.
McClelland, Richard T. and Brian B. Clayton, eds. *The Philosophy of Clint Eastwood*. Lexington, KY: The University Press of Kentucky, 2014.
McClelland, Thomas. "The Philosophy of Film and Film as Philosophy." *Cinema: Journal of Philosophy and the Moving Image* 2 (2011): 11–35. Available online http://cjpmi.ifilnova.pt/2-mcclelland.
McGinn, Colin. *Mindfucking: A Critique of Mental Manipulation*. Stocksfield: Acumen Publishing, 2008.
McGinn, Colin. *Mindsight: Image, Dream, Meaning*. Cambridge: Harvard University Press, 2004.
Merleau-Ponty, Maurice. "The Film and the New Psychology." In *Sense and Non-Sense*. Translated by Hubert L Dreyfus and Patricia Allen Dreyfus. Northwestern University Studies in Phenomenology & Existential Philosophy, 48–59. Evanston: Northwestern University Press, 1964.
Merleau-Ponty, Maurice. *The Visible and the Invisible: Followed by Working Notes*. Edited by Claude Lefort and translated by Alphonso Lingis. Northwestern University Studies in Phenomenology & Existential Philosophy. Evanston: Northwestern University Press, 1968.
Metz, Christian. *Film Language: A Semiotics of the Cinema*. New York: Oxford University Press, 1974.
Michelson, Annette. "Reading Eisenstein Reading *Capital*." *October* 2, Summer (1976): 26–38.
Modorcea, Grid. "Grid Modorcea despre încremenirea în proiect: 'Sunt o babă comunistă.'" *Ziaristi online*, September 3, 2013. Available online http://www.ziaristionline.ro/2013/09/02/grid-modorcea-despre-incremenirea-in-proiect-sunt-o-baba-comunista/.
Moura, Jean-Marc. "Imagologie littéraire et mythocritique: rencontres et divergences de deux recherches comparatistes." In *Mythes et littérature*. Edited by Pierre Brunel, 129–41. Paris: PUF, 1994.

Mulhall, Stephen. *On Film*. London: Routledge, 2002.
Mulhall, Stephen. "In Space No-one Can Hear You Scream: Aknowledging the Human Voice in the Alien Universe." In *Film as Philosophy: Essays in Cinema after Wittgenstein and Cavell*. Edited by Rupert J. Read and Jerry Goodenough, 57–71. New York: Palgrave Macmillan, 2005.
Mullarkey, John. "Film as Philosophy. A Mission Impossible." In *European Film Theory*. Edited by Temenuga Trifonova, 65–79. Afi Film Readers. New York: Routledge, 2009b.
Mullarkey, John. "Films Cannot Philosophise (and Neither Can Philosophy): Introduction to a Non-Philosophy of Cinema." In *New Takes in Film-Philosophy*. Edited by Havi Carel and Greg Tuck, 86–100. Palgrave Macmillan, 2011.
Mullarkey, John. *Refractions of Reality: Philosophy and the Moving Image*. Basingstoke: Palgrave Macmillan, 2009.
Mulvey, Laura. *Death 24x a Second: Stillness and the Moving Image*. London: Reaktion Books, 2006.
Mungiu-Pippidi, Alina. "Lovitura de pedeapsă." In romaniacurata.ro, June 7, 2016. Available online http://www.romaniacurata.ro/lovitura-de-pedeapsa/.
Nannicelli, Ted. *A Philosophy of the Screenplay*. Routledge Studies in Contemporary Philosophy. New York: Routledge, 2013.
Nasta, Dominique. *Contemporary Romanian Cinema: The History of an Unexpected Miracle*. New York: Columbia University Press, 2013.
Neale, Stephen. "Art Cinema as Institution." *Screen* 22, no. 1 (1981): 11–40.
Neidich, Warren. *Blow-up: Photography, Cinema, and the Brain*. New York: D.A.P./Distributed Art, 2003.
Neupert, Richard John. *The End: Narration and Closure in the Cinema*. Contemporary Film and Television Series. Detroit: Wayne State University Press, 1995.
Nishimoto, Shinji, An T. Vu, Thomas Naselaris, Yuval Benjamini, Bin Yu, and Jack L. Gallant. "Supplemental Information Reconstructing Visual Experiences from Brain Activity Evoked by Natural Movies." *Current Biology* 21, no. 19 (2011): 1641–6. https://doi.org/10.1016/j.cub.2011.08.031.
Noica, Constantin. "Cel ce stă pe răzoare." *Cuvânt împreună despre rostirea românească (A Word Together About the Romanian Language)*. București: Humanitas, 1996.
Nöth, Winfried. "Semiotic foundations of iconicity in language and literature." In *The Motivated Sign: Iconicity in Language and Literature 2*. Edited by Olga Fischer and Max Nänny, 17–28. Amsterdam: John Benjamins Publishing Company, 2001.
Pageaux, Daniel-Henri. "De l'imagerie culturelle a l'imaginaire." In *Précis de littérature comparée*. Edited by Pierre Brunel and Yves Chevrel, 133–61. Paris: Presses universitaires de France, 1989.
Pamerleau, William C. *Existentialist Cinema*. New York: Palgrave Macmillan, 2009.
Papadima, Ovidiu. *O viziune românească asupra lumii (A Romanian Vision of the World)*. București: Saeculum, 1995, first ed., 1941.
Peretz, Eyal. *The Off-screen: An Investigation of the Cinematic Frame*. Stanford: Stanford University Press, 2017.

Perkins, Claire. *American Smart Cinema*. Edinburgh: Edinburgh University Press, 2012.
Phillips, James. "Introduction: What Can Cinema Do?" In *Cinematic Thinking: Philosophical Approaches to the New Cinema*. Edited by James Phillips, 1–9. Stanford: Stanford University Press, 2008.
Pieldner, Judith. "History, Cultural Memory and Intermediality in Radu Jude's Aferim!." *Acta Universitatis Sapientiae*, Film and Media Studies, 13 (2016): 89–105. DOI: 10.1515/ausfm-2016-0016.
Pippin, Robert B. *Filmed Thought: Cinema as Reflective Form*. Chicago, IL: The University of Chicago Press, 2020.
Pleşu, Andrei. *Limba păsărilor (The language of birds)*. Bucureşti: Humanitas, 1994.
Pop, Doru. "The Latest European New Wave: Cinematic Realism and Everyday Aesthetics in Romanian Cinema." In *European Cinema in the Twenty-first Century: Discourses, Directions and Genres*. Edited by Ingrid Lewis and Laura Canning, 149–66. Cham: Palgrave Macmillan, 2020.
Pop, Doru. "Making and Breaking the New Wave Canon in Romanian Cinema." In *Cultural Studies Approaches in the Study of Eastern European Cinema: Spaces, Bodies, Memories*. Edited by Andrea Virginás, 268–88. Newcastle-upon-Tyne: Cambridge Scholars Publishing, 2016.
Pop, Doru. *Romanian New Wave Cinema: An Introduction*. Jefferson, MO: McFarland, 2014.
Popa, Ion. *The Romanian Orthodox Church and the Holocaust*. Bloomington: Indiana University Press, 2017.
Popescu, Cristian Tudor. "Corupţie cu delicateţuri." *Republica.ro*, May 22, 2016. Available online https://republica.ro/coruptie-cu-delicateturi.
Porumboiu, Corneliu. "Ancheta domnului Porumboiu", interview by Lavinia Gliga. *DoR* 16, 2014. Available online http://www.decatorevista.ro/porumboiu-dor16/.
Porumboiu, Corneliu. Press conference. *Mediafax*, September 18, 2013. Available online http://www.mediafax.ro/cultura-media/corneliu-porumboiu-despre-metabolism-am-realizat-filmul-cu-un-soi-de-nostalgie-pentru-pelicula-11353000.
Puiu, Cristi. "Dacă afli după moarte că Dumnezeu există?" Video interview, *Adevarul*, August 29, 2016. Available online https://adevarul.ro/cultura/arte/cristi-puiu-dacaafli-moarte-dumnezeu-existai-1_57c485b45ab6550cb833e6e2/index.html.
Puiu, Cristi. Interview. *Evenimentul zilei*, March 4, 2007. Available online https://evz.ro/cristi-puiu-si-frica-de-moarte-432782.html?v=347635&page=1.
Rancière, Jacques. *The Aesthetic Unconscious*. Cambridge: Polity Press, 2009.
Rancière, Jacques. *Film Fables*. Talking Images Series. London: Berg Publishers, 2006.
Rancière, Jacques. *Intervals of Cinema*. Translated by John Howe. London: Verso, 2014, first French edition *Les Écarts du cinéma*. Paris: La Fabrique, 2011.
Rancière, Jacques. *The Politics of Aesthetics. The Distribution of the Sensible*. Edited and translated by Gabriel Rockhill. New York: Bloomsbury Academic, 2013.
Ravetto-Biagioli, Kriss. *Mythopoetic Cinema: On the Ruins of European Identity*. New York: Columbia University Press, 2017.

Rădulescu-Motru, Constantin. *Psihologia poporului român*. Edited by Alexandru Boboc. Paideia, 1999, first ed., 1937.
Remes, Justin. *Motion(Less) Pictures: The Cinema of Stasis*. Film and Culture. New York: Columbia University Press, 2015.
Richardson, Michael. *Surrealism and Cinema*. Oxford: Berg, 2006.
Rivette, Jacques. "De l'Abjection." *Cahiers du Cinéma* 120, June (1961): 54–5.
Rodowick, David Norman. "Introduction: What Does Time Express?" In *Afterimages of Gilles Deleuze's Film Philosophy*. Edited by D. N. Rodowick, xiii–xxv. Minneapolis: University of Minnesota Press, 2010.
Rohmer, Eric. "Eric Rohmer: An Interview." *Film Quarterly* 24, no. 4 (Summer 1971): 34–41, republished in *Eric Rohmer: Interviews*, 10–11. Edited by Fiona Handyside. University Press of Mississippi, 2013.
Roquemore, Joseph H. *History Goes to the Movies: A Viewer's Guide to the Best (and Some of the Worst) Historical Films Ever Made*. First ed. New York: Main Street Books/Doubleday, 1999.
Rowlands, Mark. *The Philosopher at the End of the Universe: Philosophy Explained through Science Fiction Films*. London: Ebury Publishing, 2012.
Rowlands, Mark. *Sci-phi: Philosophy from Socrates to Schwarzenegger*. New York: Thomas Dunne Books/St. Martin's Griffin, 2005.
Russell, Bruce. "Replies to Carroll and Wartenberg." *Film and Philosophy* 12 (2008): 35–40.
Salmon, Christian. *Storytelling: Bewitching the Modern Mind*. London: Verso, 2010.
Sandqvist, Tom. *Dada East: The Romanians of Cabaret Voltaire*. Cambridge: MIT Press, 2006.
Saulea, Elena. *Epopeea națională cinematografică*. București: Biblioteca Bucureștilor, 2011.
Saxton, Libby. "Tracking Shots Are a Question of Morality: Ethics, Aesthetics, Documentary." In *Film and Ethics: Foreclosed Encounters*. Edited by Lisa Downing and Libby Saxton, 22–35. London: Routledge, 2010.
Schmerheim, Philipp. *Skepticism Films: Knowing and Doubting the World in Contemporary Cinema*. New York: Bloomsbury Academic, 2017.
Schrader, Paul. *Transcendental Style in Film: Ozu, Bresson, Dreyer*. Oakland: University of California Press, 1972.
Schulte, Brigid. "Trapped between 2 Languages." *The Washington Post*, June 9, 2002. Available online https://www.washingtonpost.com/archive/politics/2002/06/09/trapped-between-2-languages/a0af2b45-1ead483b-94c9-5bfc45d1eb87.
Schwarze, Kelly. *A Filmmaking Mindset: The New Path of Today's Filmmaker*. Indie Film Factory, 2020.
Scruton, Roger. "Photography and Representation." In *Philosophy of Film and Motion Pictures: An Anthology*. Edited by Noël Carroll and Jinhee Choi, 138–66. Malden, MA: Blackwell Publishing, 2006, first published in *Critical Inquiry*, Vol. 7, No. 3, Spring 1981, pp. 577–603.
Séguin, Louis. *L'espace du cinéma: hors-champ, hors d'œuvre, hors-jeu*. Toulouse: Editions Ombres, 1999.
Sellier, Geneviève. *Masculine Singular: French New Wave Cinema*. Durham: Duke University Press, 2008.

Shamir, Tal S. *Cinematic Philosophy*. New York: Palgrave Macmillan, 2016.
Shapiro, Michael J. *Cinematic Political Thought: Narrating Race, Nation, and Gender*. New York: New York University Press, 1999.
Shaw, Daniel. "On Being Philosophical and Being John Malkovich." *Journal of Aesthetics and Art Criticism* 64, no. 1 (2006): 111–18.
Shaw, Daniel. *Film and Philosophy: Taking Movies Seriously*. Short Cuts Series, 41. London: Wallflower, 2008.
Shaw, Daniel. *Movies with Meaning: Existentialism through Film*. London: Bloomsbury Academic, 2017.
Shimamura Arthur P., ed. *Psychocinematics: Exploring Cognition at the Movies*. Oxford: Oxford University Press, 2013.
Singh, Gregory Matthew. *Feeling Film: Affect and Authenticity in Popular Cinema*. London: Routledge, 2014.
Sinnerbrink, Robert. "Filmosophy/Film as Philosophy." In *The Palgrave Handbook of the Philosophy of Film and Motion Pictures*. Edited by Noël Carroll, Laura Teresa Di Summa-Knoop, and Shawn Loht, 513–40. Cham: Palgrave Macmillan, 2019.
Smith, Greg M. *Film Structure and the Emotion System*. Cambridge: Cambridge University Press, 2003.
Smith, William G. *Plato and Popcorn: A Philosopher's Guide to 75 Thought-Provoking Movies*. Jefferson, MO: McFarland, 2004.
Smuts, Aaron. "Film as Philosophy: In Defense of a Bold Thesis." *Journal of Aesthetics and Art Criticism* 67, no. 4 (2009): 409–20.
Souriau, Étienne. *L'Univers filmique*. Coll. Bibliothèque d'esthétique. Paris: Flammarion, 1953.
Stewart, Garrett. *Framed Time: Toward a Postfilmic Cinema*. Cinema and Modernity Series. Chicago, IL: University Of Chicago Press, 2007.
Stiegler, Bernard. *Technics and Time 3: Cinematic Time and the Question of Malaise*. Translated by Stephen Barker. Stanford, CA: Stanford University Press, 2011.
Stoehr, Kevin. "By Cinematic Means Alone: The Russell-Wartenburg-Carroll Debate." *Film and Philosophy* 15 (2011): 111–26.
Strausz, László. *Hesitant Histories on the Romanian Screen*. London: Palgrave Macmillan, 2017.
Szabados Béla and Christina Stojanova, eds. *Wittgenstein at the Movies: Cinematic Investigations*. Lanham: Lexington Books, 2011.
Teays, Wanda. *Seeing the Light: Exploring Ethics through Movies*. Malden, MA: Wiley-Blackwell, 2012.
Theall, Donald F. *The Medium Is the Rear View Mirror, Understanding McLuhan*. Montreal: McGill-Queen's University Press, 1971.
Thomas-Fogiel, Isabelle. *The Death of Philosophy: Reference and Self-reference in Contemporary Thought*. New York: Columbia University Press, 2011. https://doi.org/10.7312/thom14778.
Thompson, Kristin. *Storytelling in the New Hollywood: Understanding Classical Narrative Technique*. Cambridge: Harvard University Press, 1999.
Totok, William. "Trivialitatea vandabila." Radio France International Romania, February 11, 2014. Available online http://www.rfi.ro/cultur-61970-trivialitatea-vandabil.
Turvey, Malcolm. *Doubting Vision: Film and the Revelationist Tradition*. Oxford: Oxford University Press, 2008.

Turvey, Malcom. *The Filming of Modern Life: European Avant-garde Film of the 1920s*. Cambridge: The MIT Press, 2013.
Tzara, Tristan. "Lecture on Dada." 1922. Available online http://100yearsofdada.blogspot.com/2014/06/public-lecture-on-dada-tristan-tzara.html.
Tzara, Tristan. "Sept Manifestes Dada." In *Œuvres Completes I, 1912–1924*. Edited by H. Béhar, 353–90. Paris: Flammarion, 1975.
Vanoye, Françis. *Reçit écrit, reçit filmique*. Cinéma et récit, 1. Paris: Éditions Nathan, 1989.
Vaughan, Hunter. *Where Film Meets Philosophy: Godard, Resnais, and Experiments in Cinematic Thinking*. New York: Columbia University Press, 2013.
Vulcănescu, Mircea. *Dimensiunea românească a existenței*. Edited by Marin Diaconu. Bucuresti: Editura Fundației culturale Române, 1996, first edition 1943.
Vulcănescu, Romulus. *Mitologie română*. Bucuresti: Editura Academiei Române, 1987.
Walton, Kendall. "Transparent Pictures: On the Nature of Photographic Realism." In *Photography and Philosophy: Essays on the Pencil of Nature*. Edited by Scott Walden, 14–49. Malden, MA: Blackwell Publishing, 2008.
Wartenberg, Thomas. "Film as Philosophy. The Pro Position." *Current Controversies in Philosophy of Film*. Edited by Katherine Thomson-Jones, 165–80. New York: Routledge, Taylor & Francis Group, 2016.
Wartenberg, Thomas E. "On the Possibility of Cinematic Philosophy." In *New Takes in Film-philosophy*. Edited by Carel Havi and Greg Tuck, 9–24. Basingstoke: Palgrave Macmillan, 2011.
Wartenberg, Thomas, "Philosophy of Film." *The Stanford Encyclopedia of Philosophy* (Winter 2015 Edtion). Edited by Edward N. Zalta, https://plato.stanford.edu/archives/win2015/entries/film/.
Wartenberg, Thomas E. *Thinking on Screen: Film as Philosophy*. London: Routledge, 2007.
Weissberg, Jay. "Locarno Film Review: 'When Evening Falls on Bucharest or Metabolism,'", *Variety*, August 13, 2013. Available online http://variety.com/2013/film/global/when-evening-falls-on-bucharest-or-metabolism-review-locarno-film-festival-1200577482/.
Willis, Holly. *Fast Forward: The Future(s) of the Cinematic Arts*. New York: Columbia University Press, 2016.
Willis, Holly. *New Digital Cinema: Reinventing the Moving Image*. London: Wallflower Press, 2005.
Wittgenstein, Ludwig. Tractatus Logico-Philosophicus. Translated by Paul Kegan. New York: Harcourt Brace & Company, 1922.
Yacavone, David. *Film Worlds: A Philosophical Aesthetics of Cinema*. New York: Columbia University Press, 2015.
Yanal, Robert J. *Hitchcock as Philosopher*. Jefferson, MO: McFarland, 2005.
Zacks, Jeffrey M. *Flicker: Your Brain on Movies*. Oxford: Oxford University Press, 2015.
Žižek, Slavoj. "Éléments d'autocritique (ou comment j'ai raté la séance d'*Avatar*)," interview with Stéphane Delorme and Jean-Philippe Tessé. In *Cahiers du Cinéma*, 655, April 2010.

INDEX

4 Months, 3 Weeks and 2 Days (film) 83–5, 87, 89, 92–3, 96, 101, 102, 105, 107, 109, 112, 113, 114, 119, 120, 122, 124, 138, 150, 187, 199, 224, 230, 233, 239

absence 58, 88, 97, 103, 110, 113, 119, 124, 155, 156, 160, 163, 165, 175, 177, 227, 229, 230, 240
absurd 113, 122, 141, 184, 195, 206, 221, 231
a-cinema, a-cinematic 20–1, 141, 163, 185, 218
Adorno 17–8, 49, 50, 115
ambiguity 54, 74, 94, 112, 117
  and cinema of ambiguity 109, 119, 133, 157, 221, 223
  moral ambiguity 167, 178, 220
Anderson, Benedict 190, 192
Angelopoulos, Theo 223–4
anti-philosophical 48, 57, 59, 61, 72, 132
Antonioni 11, 17, 53, 60, 74, 116
Avant-garde 11, 20, 21, 51, 54, 57, 59, 69, 116, 117, 118, 136–42, 172, 173

Badiou, Alain 60, 81, 91, 121, 238–9
Barthes, Roland 135, 159, 163, 165
Bazin, André 19, 57, 64, 89, 92, 225, 227
Bergman, Ingmar 15, 49, 55, 236
Bergson, Henri 59, 74, 75–9, 238
Blaga, Lucian 206, 208, 209, 211
Bonitzer, Pascal 53, 89
Bordwell, David 13, 53, 55, 109, 116, 120, 138, 163, 164, 188, 189, 221

Buñuel, Luis 97, 137
Burch, Noël 90, 148, 150

Cardullo, Bert 87, 236
Carroll, Noël 28, 39, 47, 50, 54, 62, 72, 116–17, 140, 207
cave, myth of the 7, 46, 130–2
Cavell, Stanley 23, 45, 55, 66, 236
cinema-thinking 17, 19, 86, 88, 107, 121, 136, 184, 191, 192, 199–200, 203, 205
cine-philosophy 5, 8, 43–4, 46
Cohen-Séat, Gilbert 8–9, 91

Dadaism 57, 60, 139–43
dark humor 86, 127, 135, 157, 216, 231
Death of Mr. Lăzărescu, The (film) 86, 89, 101, 119, 177, 183–6, 195, 202, 205, 207, 215, 216, 218, 224–7
décadrage 54, 89, 233
de-dramatization 134, 153–6, 234
de-framing 109, 150, 233
Deleuze, Gilles 6, 10, 20, 30, 35–7, 52, 54, 69–78, 88, 116–17, 187–8, 219, 221, 229–30, 236–8
Derrida, Jacques 56, 148, 150–1, 219
Descartes, René 7, 46, 66, 67
deterritorialized 190–1, 227–8, 229–34
dialectic, also dialectical 8, 42, 64, 68, 77, 107, 148, 213, 221, 236
Duchamp, Marcel 60, 140, 141, 143, 157

Eisenstein, Sergei 4, 65–6, 149, 172
Eliade, Mircea 208, 211, 214–15, 216
Elsaesser, Thomas 23, 39, 44, 56, 133, 178

INDEX

Epstein, Jean 30, 40, 54, 57–60, 68
extra-cinematic 4, 7, 17–19, 21, 24, 43, 48, 72, 87, 89, 91, 93, 118, 123, 132, 145, 150–2, 154, 235
extramedial, also extramediality 148, 151–2

Falzon, Christopher 4, 28
fatalism, also fatalistic 203–5, 208–14, 224, 230
filmosophy 1, 8, 60, 67–9, 81
   also filmosopher 5–6, 204
   also filmosophical 54, 68–69
film-philosophy 1, 8–9, 13, 22, 27, 30, 33, 36, 38, 43, 46, 47, 54–5, 73, 80, 129, 132, 230
film-thinking 22, 32, 37, 42, 43, 51, 54, 55, 61, 64, 67–9, 77, 95, 112, 128, 133, 143, 170, 171, 192, 194, 204, 216, 233, 234, 240
Flaxman, Gregory 46, 71, 74
Frampton, Daniel 8, 31, 40, 54, 60, 67–9

gap also gaps 61, 75, 77, 81, 85–6, 106, 108, 117, 121–2, 124, 132, 155, 156, 160, 170, 176, 184, 207, 232
Goddard, Jean-Luc 15, 51, 53, 55, 62, 74, 77, 87, 117, 132, 154, 158, 163, 225
Graduation (film) 89, 102–9, 111–12, 114–15, 119, 123–4, 177
Groys, Boris 60–1

Habermas, Jürgen 80
hesitation 121, 134, 206, 226, 232

imagological 191–6, 199, 204, 214–16
in-betweenness 22, 108, 147, 190–5, 206, 218, 227–8, 239
intermedial also intermediality 130, 144, 146, 148, 151, 152, 162, 170, 239
interstice 53, 76, 78, 81, 86, 87, 88, 146, 228, 232
interval 35, 74–9, 81, 85–6, 88, 106–11, 118, 120–3, 125, 144, 146, 148, 150, 159, 160, 167, 170, 194–6, 217, 219, 227, 231–3, 239–40

Jameson, Fredric 42

Kovács, András Bálint 22, 54
Kracauer, Siegfried 42–3, 222

Lakoff, George 13–14, 227
Laruelle, François 37, 72–3, 173, 219, 237
Livingston, Paisley 6, 28, 30, 35, 38, 57, 236
Lyotard, Jean-François 19–21, 90

melancholia 204, 209–11, 221–4, 227
Merleau-Ponty, Maurice 16, 167, 217
metacinematic 81, 116, 143, 150, 158, 159, 217
metaphysical 5, 7, 8, 16, 21, 22, 24, 32, 37, 41, 48, 53, 56, 63, 79, 80, 81, 91, 203, 206, 208, 211, 212, 214, 215, 216, 218, 221, 225, 227, 235–40
Metz, Christian 8, 163
Minimalist also minimalism 50, 54, 87, 96, 130, 154, 155, 161
modernist 35, 63, 65, 66, 67, 68, 88, 101, 102, 121, 128, 145, 170, 200, 201, 234
morality 8, 14, 102, 201, 220, 225, 229, 231
   also moralist 218, 220, 231
Mullarkey, John 30, 31, 49, 55, 73, 88, 239
Mungiu, Cristian 83, 86–9, 93, 95–119, 135, 150, 176, 177, 182, 199, 223, 228
mythological 100, 187, 192, 197, 200, 202, 203, 205, 211, 214

non-cinematic 4, 18–19, 24, 25, 39, 48, 72–3, 83, 86, 87, 91–5, 104, 108–11, 113–16, 121, 123, 124, 125, 128, 134, 137–9, 141, 144, 146, 148, 151, 155, 161–3, 165–7, 169, 171, 182, 196, 217,

221, 230, 231, 235, 237–8, 240
non-philosophical 34, 37, 39, 61, 71, 72–73, 88, 92, 122, 131, 132, 134, 173, 182, 184, 185–86, 200, 217–20, 228, 230, 231, 235, 237, 238–40
nooshock 77, 81, 86, 231

offscreen 14, 15, 16, 17, 81, 89–93, 107, 108, 145, 150–2, 162, 164, 175, 176, 232, 233
onscreen 2, 6, 8, 9–12, 13, 14, 15, 16, 19, 20, 21, 81, 90, 91, 95, 128, 130, 131, 138, 143, 144, 145, 148, 149, 151, 152, 163, 164, 165, 166, 176, 204, 216, 218, 237, 240

Peretz, Eyal 90–1
Plato also Platonic 2, 4, 7, 38, 46, 66, 80, 109, 129–32, 133, 171, 202
Porumboiu, Corneliu 18, 22, 23, 24, 39, 51, 89, 105, 127–36, 139, 143–8, 150–73, 177, 239
post-cinema 92–4
    also post-cinematic 110, 137, 216
post-metaphysical 24, 34, 37, 78–81, 122, 178, 207, 214, 216, 217, 218, 231, 235–40

Puiu, Cristi 86, 89, 119, 129, 135, 138, 183–9, 195, 200, 203, 215–34, 239

Rancière, Jacques 56–7, 60–1, 77, 85, 94–5, 108, 112
Ray, Man 17, 140–2, 145
Resnais, Alain 21, 70, 74, 118

Scruton, Roger 48–9
    also Carroll-Scrutton debate 72
Strausz, László 121, 205–6, 226
surrealist 17, 117, 140–1, 203

Tarr, Béla 68, 142, 223
A Thousand Plateaus 229, 240
tragedy 85, 87–8, 96, 101, 106, 111, 134, 185, 187, 204–5, 207, 217, 224, 230
Tzara, Tristan 139–42, 203

unthinkable 86, 91, 96, 105, 232

visceral 16, 24, 127, 134, 135, 158–9
    also visceral cinema 162–7

Wartenberg, Thomas 1, 2, 5, 28, 30, 35, 38–9, 43, 47
Wittgenstein, Ludwig 85, 113, 172, 173

Žižek, Slavoj 3, 42

www.ingramcontent.com/pod-product-compliance
Lightning Source LLC
Chambersburg PA
CBHW062124300426
44115CB00012BA/1801